DIANA OF THE CROSSWAYS

DIANA OF THE CROSSWAYS

. . . A NOVEL . . .
BY GEORGE MEREDITH

WESTMINSTER
ARCHIBALD CONSTABLE & CO Ltd
2 WHITEHALL GARDENS 1902

BUTLER & TANNER,
THE SELWOOD PRINTING WORKS,
FROME, AND LONDON.

INSCRIBED

TO

FREDERICK POLLOCK

CONTENTS

A lady of high distinction for wit and beauty, the daughter of an illustrious Irish House, came under the shadow of a calumny.

It has latterly been examined and exposed as baseless. The story of " Diana of the Crossways " is to be read as fiction.

DIANA OF THE CROSSWAYS

CHAPTER I

OF DIARIES AND DIARISTS TOUCHING THE HEROINE

AMONG the Diaries beginning with the second quarter of our century, there is frequent mention of a lady then becoming famous for her beauty and her wit: "an unusual combination," in the deliberate syllables of one of the writers, who is, however, not disposed to personal irony when speaking of her. It is otherwise in his case: and a general fling at the sex we may deem pardonable, for doing as little harm to womankind as the stone of an urchin cast upon the bosom of mother Earth; though men must look some day to have it returned to them, which is a certainty; — and indeed full surely will our idle-handed youngster too, in his riper season, be heard complaining of a strange assault of wanton missiles, coming on him he knows not whence; for we are all of us distinctly marked to get back what we give, even from the thing named inanimate nature.

The "LEAVES FROM THE DIARY OF HENRY WILMERS" are studded with examples of the dinner-table wit of the time, not always worth quotation twice; for smart remarks have their measured distances, many requiring to be à brûle pourpoint, or within throw of the pistol, to make it hit; in other words, the majority of them are addressed directly to our muscular system, and they have no effect when we stand beyond the range. On the contrary, they reflect sombrely on the springs of hilarity in the generation preceding us; — with due reserve of credit, of course,

1

to an animal vivaciousness that seems to have wanted so small an incitement. Our old yeomanry farmers returning to their beds over ferny commons under bright moonlight from a neighbour's harvest-home, eased their bubbling breasts with a ready roar not unakin to it. Still the promptness to laugh is an excellent progenitorial foundation for the wit to come in a people; and undoubtedly the diarial record of an imputed piece of wit is witness to the spouting of laughter. This should comfort us while we skim the sparkling passages of the "Leaves." When a nation has acknowledged that it is as yet but in the fisti-cuff stage of the art of condensing our purest sense to golden sentences, a readier appreciation will be extended to the gift: which is to strike not the dazzled eyes, the unanticipating nose, the ribs, the sides, and stun us, twirl us, hoodwink, mystify, tickle and twitch, by dexterities of lingual sparring and shuffling, but to strike roots in the mind, the Hesperides of good things.

We shall then set a price on the "unusual combination." A witty woman is a treasure; a witty Beauty is a power. Has she actual beauty, actual wit? — not simply a tidal material beauty that passes current any pretty flippancy or staggering pretentiousness? Grant the combination, she will appear a veritable queen of her period, fit for homage; at least meriting a disposition to believe the best of her, in the teeth of foul rumour; because the well of true wit is truth itself, the gathering of the precious drops of right reason, wisdom's lightning; and no soul possessing and dispensing it can justly be a target for the world, however well armed the world confronting her. Our temporary world, that Old Credulity and stone-hurling urchin in one, supposes it possible for a woman to be mentally active up to the point of spiritual clarity and also fleshly vile; a guide to life and a biter at the fruits of death; both open mind and hypocrite. It has not yet been taught to appreciate a quality certifying to sound citizenship as authoritatively as acres of land in fee simple, or coffers of bonds, shares and stocks, and a more imperishable guarantee. The multitude of evil reports which it takes for proof, are marshalled against her without question of the nature of the victim, her temptress beauty being a sufficiently presumptive delinquent. It does not pretend to know the whole, or naked body of the facts; it knows enough for its fumy dubiousness; and excepting the sentimental of men, a rocket-headed horde, ever at the heels of fair faces for ignition, and up starring away at a hint of tearfulness; — excepting further by chance a solid champion man, or some generous woman capable of faith in the pelted solitary of her sex, our temporary world blows direct East on her shivering person. The scandal is warrant for that; the circumstances of the scandal emphasize the warrant. And how clever she is! Cleverness is an attribute of the selecter missionary lieutenants of Satan. We pray to be defended from her cleverness: she flashes bits of speech that catch men in their unguarded corner. The wary stuff their ears, the stolid bid her best sayings rebound on her reputation. Nevertheless the world, as Christian, remembers its professions, and a portion of it joins the burly in morals by extending to her a rough old charitable mercifulness; better than sentimental ointment, but the heaviest blow she has to bear, to a character swimming for life.

That the lady in question was much quoted, the Diaries and Memoirs testify. Hearsay as well as hearing was at work to produce the abundance; and it was a novelty in England, where (in company) the men are the pointed talkers, and the women conversationally fair Circassians. They are, or they know that they should be; it comes to the same. Happily our civilization has not prescribed the veil to them. The mutes have here and there a sketch or label attached to their names: they are "strikingly handsome;" they are "very good-looking;" occasionally they are noted as "extremely entertaining:" in what manner, is inquired by a curious posterity, that in so many matters is left unendingly to jump the empty and gaping figure of interrogation over its own full stop. Great ladies must they be, at the web of politics, for us to hear them cited discoursing. Henry Wilmers is not content to quote the beautiful Mrs. Warwick, he attempts a portrait. Mrs. Warwick is "quite Grecian." She might "pose for a statue." He presents her in carpenter's lines, with a dab of school-box colours, effective to those whom the Keepsake fashion can stir. She has a straight nose, red lips, raven hair, black eyes, rich complexion, a remarkably fine bust, and she walks well, and has an agreeable voice; likewise "delicate extremities." The writer was created for popularity, had he chosen to bring his art into our literary market.

Perry Wilkinson is not so elaborate: he describes her in his "Recollections" as a splendid brune, eclipsing all the blondes coming near her: and "what is more, the beautiful creature can talk." He wondered, for she was young, new to society. Subsequently he is rather ashamed of his wonderment, and accounts for it by "not having known she was Irish." She "turns out to be Dan Merion's daughter."

We may assume that he would have heard if she had any whiff of a brogue. Her sounding of the letter R a trifle scrupulously is noticed by Lady Pennon: "And last, not least, the lovely Mrs. Warwick, twenty minutes behind the dinner-hour, and *r-r-really* fearing she was late." After alluding to the soft influence of her beauty and ingenuousness on the vexed hostess, the kindly old marchioness adds, that it was no wonder she was late, "for just before starting from home she had broken loose from her husband for good, and she entered the room absolutely houseless!" She was not the less "astonishingly brilliant." Her observations were often "so unexpectedly droll I laughed till I cried." Lady Pennon became in consequence one of the stanch supporters of Mrs. Warwick.

Others were not so easily won. Perry Wilkinson holds a balance when it goes beyond a question of her wit and beauty. Henry Wilmers puts the case aside, and takes her as he finds her. His cousin, the clever and cynical Dorset Wilmers, whose method of conveying his opinions without stating them was famous, repeats on two occasions when her name appears in his pages, "handsome, lively, witty;" and the stressed repetition of calculated brevity while a fiery scandal was abroad concerning the lady, implies weighty substance — the reservation of a constable's truncheon, that could legally have knocked her character down to the pavement. We have not to ask what he judged. But Dorset Wilmers was a political opponent of the eminent Peer who yields the second name to the scandal, and politics in his day flushed the conceptions of men. His short references to "that Warwick-Dannisburgh affair" are not verbally malicious. He gets wind of the terms of Lord Dannisburgh's will and testament, noting them without comment. The oddness of the instrument in one respect may have served his turn; we have no grounds for thinking him malignant. The death of his enemy closes his allusions to Mrs. Warwick. He was growing ancient, and gout narrowed the circle he whirled in. Had he known this "handsome, lively, witty" apparition as a woman having political and social views of her own, he would not, one fancies, have been so stingless. Our England exposes a sorry figure in his Reminiscences. He struck heavily, round and about him, wherever he moved; he had by nature a tarnishing eye that cast discolouration. His unadorned harsh substantive statements, excluding the adjectives, give his Memoirs the appearance of a body of facts, attractive to the historic Muse, which has learnt to esteem those brawny sturdy giants marching club on shoulder, independent of henchman, in preference to your panoplied knights with their puffy squires, once her favourites, and wind-filling to her columns, ultimately found indigestible.

His exhibition of his enemy Lord Dannisburgh is of the class of noble portraits we see swinging over inn-portals, grossly unlike in likeness. The possibility of the man's doing or saying this and that adumbrates the improbability: he had something of the character capable of it, too much good sense for the performance. We would think so, and still the shadow is round our thoughts. Lord Dannisburgh was a man of ministerial tact, official ability, Pagan morality; an excellent general manager, if no genius in statecraft. But he was careless of social opinion, unbuttoned, and a laugher. We know that he could be chivalrous toward women, notwithstanding the perplexities he brought on them, and this the Dorset-Diary does not show.

His chronicle is less mischievous as regards Mrs. Warwick than the paragraphs of Perry Wilkinson, a gossip presenting an image of perpetual chatter, like the waxen-faced street advertizements of light and easy dentistry. He has no belief, no disbelief; names the pro-party and the con;

recites the case, and discreetly, over-discreetly; and pictures the trial, tells the list of witnesses, records the verdict: *so* the case went, and some thought one thing, some another thing: only it is reported for positive that a miniature of the incriminated lady was cleverly smuggled over to the jury, and juries sitting upon these cases, ever since their bedazzlement by Phryne, as you know. . . . And then he relates an anecdote of the husband, said to have been not a bad fellow before he married his Diana; — and the naming of the Goddess reminds him that the second person in the indictment is now everywhere called ' The elderly shepherd;' — but immediately after the bridal bells this husband became sour and insupportable; and either she had the trick of putting him publicly in the wrong, or he lost all shame in playing the churlish domestic tyrant. The instances are incredible of a gentleman.   Perry Wilkinson gives us two or three; one on the authority of a personal friend who witnessed the scene; at the Warwick whist-table, where the fair Diana would let loose her silvery laugh in the intervals.   She was hardly out of her teens, and should have been dancing instead of fastened to a table.   A difference of fifteen years in the ages of the wedded pair accounts poorly for the husband's conduct, however solemn a business the game of whist.   We read that he burst out at last, with bitter mimicry, "yang — yang — yang ! " and killed the bright laugh, shot it dead. She had outraged the decorum of the square-table only while the cards were making.   Perhaps her too-dead ensuing silence, as of one striving to bring back the throbs to a slain bird in her bosom, allowed the gap between the wedded pair to be visible, for it was dated back to prophecy as soon as the trumpet proclaimed it.

But a multiplication of similar instances, which can serve no other purpose than that of an apology, is a miserable vindication of innocence.   The more we have of them the darker the inference.   In delicate situations the chatterer is noxious.   Mrs. Warwick had numerous apologists.   Those trusting to her perfect rectitude were rarer. The liberty she allowed herself in speech and action must have been trying to her defenders in a land like ours; for here, and able to throw its shadow on our giddy upper-circle, the rigour of the game of life, relaxed though it may sometimes appear, would satisfy the staidest whist-player. She did not wish it the reverse, even when claiming a space for laughter: "the breath of her soul," as she called it, and as it may be felt in the early youth of a lively nature. She, especially, with her multitude of quick perceptions and imaginative avenues, her rapid summaries, her sense of the comic, demanded this aërial freedom.

We have it from Perry Wilkinson that the union of the divergent couple was likened to another union always in a Court of Law. There was a distinction; most analogies will furnish one; and here we see England and Ireland changing their parts, until later, after the breach, when the Englishman and Irishwoman resumed a certain resemblance to the yoked Islands.

Henry Wilmers, I have said, deals exclusively with the wit and charm of the woman. He treats the scandal as we might do in like manner if her story had not to be told. But these are not reporting columns; very little of it shall trouble them. The position is faced, and that is all. The position is one of the battles incident to women, their hardest. It asks for more than justice from men, for generosity, our civilization not being yet of the purest. That cry of hounds at her disrobing by Law is instinctive. She runs, and they give tongue; she is a creature of the chase. Let her escape unmangled, it will pass in the record that she did once publicly run, and some old dogs will persist in thinking her cunninger than the virtuous, which never put themselves in such positions, but ply the distaff at home. Never should reputation of woman trail a scent! How true! and true also that the women of wax-work never do; and that the women of happy marriages do not; nor the women of holy nunneries; nor the women lucky in their arts. It is a test of the civilized to see and hear, and add no yapping to the spectacle.

Thousands have reflected on a Diarist's power to cancel our Burial Service. Not alone the cleric's good work is upset by him, but the sexton's as well. He howks the graves, and transforms the quiet worms, busy on a single poor peaceable body, into winged serpents that disorder

sky and earth with a deadly flight of zig-zags, like military rockets, among the living. And if these are given to
cry too much, to have their tender sentiments considered,
it cannot be said that History requires the flaying of them.
A gouty Diarist, a sheer gossip Diarist, may thus, in the
bequest of a trail of reminiscences, explode our temples
(for our very temples have powder in store), our treasuries,
our homesteads, alive with dynamitic stuff; nay, disconcert our inherited veneration, dislocate the intimate con-
nexion between the tugged flaxen forelock and a title.

No similar blame is incurred by Henry Wilmers. No
blame whatever, one would say, if he had been less copious,
or not so subservient, in recording the lady's utterances;
for though the wit of a woman may be terse, quite spontaneous, as this lady's assuredly was here and there, she
is apt to spin it out of a museful mind, at her toilette, or
by the lonely fire, and sometimes it is imitative; admirers
should beware of holding it up to the withering glare of
print: she herself, quoting an obscure maxim-monger, says
of these lapidary sentences, that they have merely "*the
value of chalk-eggs, which lure the thinker to sit,*" and tempt
the vacuous to strain for the like, one might add; besides
flattering the world to imagine itself richer than it is in
eggs that are golden. Henry Wilmers notes a multitude
of them. "The talk fell upon our being creatures of habit,
and how far it was good: She said: — It is there that we
see ourselves crutched between love grown old and indifference ageing to love." Critic ears not present at the
conversation catch an echo of maxims and aphorisms over-
channel, notwithstanding a feminine thrill in the irony of
"ageing to love." The quotation ranks rather among the
testimonies to her charm.

She is fresher when speaking of the war of the sexes.
For one sentence out of many, though we find it to be but
the clever literary clothing of a common accusation: —
"*Men may have rounded Seraglio Point: they have not yet
doubled Cape Turk.*"

It is war, and on the male side, Ottoman war: her
experience reduced her to think so positively. Her main
personal experience was in the social class which is prim-
itively venatorial still, canine under its polish.

She held a brief for her beloved Ireland. She closes a discussion upon Irish agitation by saying rather neatly: "*You have taught them it is English as well as common human nature to feel an interest in the dog that has bitten you.*"

The dog periodically puts on madness to win attention; we gather then that England, in an angry tremour, tries him with water-gruel to prove him sane.

Of the Irish priest (and she was not of his retinue), when he was deemed a revolutionary, Henry Wilmers notes her saying: "Be in tune with him; he is in the key-note for harmony. He is shepherd, doctor, nurse, comforter, anecdotist and fun-maker to his poor flock; and you wonder they see the burning gateway of their heaven in him? Conciliate the priest."

It has been partly done, done late, when the poor flock have found their doctoring and shepherding at other hands: their "bulb-food and fiddle," that she petitioned for, to keep them from a complete shaving off their patch of bog and scrub soil, without any perception of the tremendous trans-atlantic magnification of the fiddle, and the splitting discord of its latest inspiriting jig.

And she will not have the consequences of the "weariful old Irish duel between Honour and Hunger judged by bread and butter juries."

She had need to be beautiful to be tolerable in days when Englishmen stood more openly for the strong arm to maintain the Union. Her troop of enemies was of her summoning.

Ordinarily her topics were of wider range, and those of a woman who mixed hearing with reading, and observation with her musings. She has no doleful ejaculatory notes, of the kind peculiar to women at war, containing one-third of speculative substance to two of sentimental —a feminine plea for comprehension and a squire; and it was probably the reason (as there is no reason to suppose an emotional cause) why she exercised her evident sway over the mind of so plain and straightforward an Englishman as Henry Wilmers. She told him that she read rapidly, "a great deal at one gulp," and thought in flashes —a way with the makers of phrases. She wrote, she confessed, laboriously. The desire to prune, compress, over-charge, was a torment to the nervous woman writing under a sharp necessity for payment. Her songs were shot off on the impulsion; prose was the heavy task. "To be pointedly rational," she said, "is a greater difficulty for me than a fine delirium." She did not talk as if it would have been so, he remarks. One is not astonished at her appearing an "actress" to the flat-minded. But the basis of her woman's nature was pointed flame. In the fulness of her history we perceive nothing histrionic. Capricious or enthusiastic in her youth, she never trifled with feeling; and if she did so with some showy phrases and occasionally proffered commonplaces in gilt, as she was much excited to do, her moods of reflection were direct, always large and honest, universal as well as feminine.

Her saying that "A woman in the pillory restores the original bark of brotherhood to mankind," is no more than a cry of personal anguish. She has golden apples in her apron. She says of life: "*When I fail to cherish it in every fibre the fires within are waning,*" and that drives like rain to the roots. She says of the world, generously, if with tapering idea: "From the point of vision of the angels, this ugly monster, only half out of slime, must appear our one constant hero."

It can be read maliciously, but abstain.

She says of Romance: "*The young who avoid that region escape the title of Fool at the cost of a celestial crown.*" Of Poetry: "*Those that have souls meet their fellows there.*"

But she would have us away with sentimentalism. Sentimental people, in her phrase, "*fiddle harmonics on the strings of sensualism,*" to the delight of a world gaping for marvels of musical execution rather than for music. For our world is all but a sensational world at present, in maternal travail of a soberer, a braver, a brighter-eyed. Her reflections are thus to be interpreted, it seems to me. She says, "The vices of the world's nobler half in this day are feminine." We have to guard against "half-conceptions of wisdom, hysterical goodness, an impatient charity" — against the elementary state of the altruistic virtues, distinguishable as the sickness and writhings of our egoism to cast its first slough. Idea is there. The funny part of it is our finding it in books of fiction composed for payment. Manifestly this lady did not "chameleon" her pen from the colour of her audience: she was not of the uniformed rank and file marching to drum and fife as gallant interpreters of popular appetite, and going or gone to soundlessness and the icy shades.

Touches inward are not absent: "To have the sense of the eternal in life is a short flight for the soul. To have had it, is the soul's vitality."

And also: "Palliation of a sin is the hunted creature's refuge and final temptation. Our battle is ever between spirit and flesh. Spirit must brand the flesh, that it may live."

You are entreated to repress alarm. She was by preference light-handed; and her saying of oratory, that "*It is always the more impressive for the spice of temper which renders it untrustworthy*," is light enough.

On Politics she is rhetorical and swings: she wrote to spur a junior politician: "It is the first business of men, the school to mediocrity, to the covetously ambitious a sty, to the dullard his amphitheatre, arms of Titans to the desperately enterprising, Olympus to the genius."

What a woman thinks of women, is the test of her nature. She saw their existing posture clearly, yet believed, as men disincline to do, that they grow. She says that "In their judgements upon women men are females, voices of the present (sexual) dilemma." They desire to have " a still woman, who can make a constant society of her pins and needles." They create by stoppage a volcano, and are amazed at its eruptiveness. "We live alone, and do not much feel it till we are visited." Love is presumeably the visitor. Of the greater loneliness of women, she says: "It is due to the prescribed circumscription of their minds, of which they become aware in agitation. Were the walls about them beaten down, they would understand that solitariness is a common human fate and the one chance of growth, like space for timber." As to the sensations of women after the beating down of the walls, she owns that the multitude of the timorous would yearn in shivering affright for the old prison-nest, according to the sage prognostic of men; but the flying of a valiant few

would form a vanguard. And we are informed that the
beginning of a motive life with women must be in the
head, equally with men (by no means a truism when she
wrote). Also that "men do not so much fear to lose the
hearts of thoughtful women as their strict attention to
their graces." The present market is what men are for
preserving: an observation of still reverberating force.
Generally in her character of the feminine combatant there
is a turn of phrase, like a dimple near the lips, showing
her knowledge that she was uttering but a tart measure of
the truth. She had always too much lambent humour to
be the dupe of the passion wherewith, as she says, "we
lash ourselves into the persuasive speech distinguishing
us from the animals."

The instances of her drollery are rather hinted by the
Diarists for the benefit of those who had met her and could
inhale the atmosphere at a word. Drolleries, humours,
reputed witticisms, are like odours of roast meats, past
with the picking of the joint. Idea is the only vital
breath. They have it rarely, or it eludes the chronicler.
To say of the great erratic and forsaken Lady A$_{****}$, after
she had accepted the consolations of Bacchus, that her
name was properly signified in asterisks; "as she was now
nightly an Ariadne in heaven through her God," sounds to
us a roundabout, with wit somewhere and fun nowhere.
Sitting at the roast we might have thought differently.
Perry Wilkinson is not happier in citing her reply to his
compliment on the reviewers' unanimous eulogy of her
humour and pathos: — the "merry clown and poor panta-
loon demanded of us in every work of fiction," she says,
lamenting the writer's compulsion to go on producing them
for applause until it is extremest age that knocks their
knees. We are informed by Lady Pennon of "the most
amusing description of the first impressions of a pretty
English simpleton in Paris;" and here is an opportunity
for ludicrous contrast of the French and English styles of
pushing flatteries — "piping to the charmed animal," as
Mrs. Warwick terms it in another place: but Lady Pennon
was acquainted with the silly woman of the piece, and
found her amusement in the "wonderful truth" of that
representation.

Diarists of amusing passages are under an obligation to paint us a realistic revival of the time, or we miss the relish. The odour of the roast, and more, a slice of it is required, unless the humorous thing be preternaturally spirited to walk the earth as one immortal among a number less numerous than the mythic Gods. "He gives good dinners," a candid old critic said, when asked how it was that he could praise a certain poet. In an island of chills and fogs, cœlum crebris imbribus ac nebulis fœdum, the comic and other perceptions are dependent on the stirring of the gastric juices. And such a revival by any of us would be impolitic, were it a possible attempt, before our systems shall have been fortified by philosophy. Then may it be allowed to the Diarist simply to relate, and we can copy from him.

Then, ah! then, moreover, will the novelist's Art, now neither blushless infant nor executive man, have attained its majority. We can then be veraciously historical, honestly transcriptive. Rose-pink and dirty drab will alike have passed away. Philosophy is the foe of both, and their silly cancelling contest, perpetually renewed in a shuffle of extremes, as it always is where a phantasm falseness reigns, will no longer baffle the contemplation of natural flesh, smother no longer the soul issuing out of our incessant strife. Philosophy bids us to see that we are not so pretty as rose-pink, not so repulsive as dirty drab; and that instead of everlastingly shifting those barren aspects, the sight of ourselves is wholesome, bearable, fructifying, finally a delight. Do but perceive that we are coming to philosophy, the stride toward it will be a giant's — a century a day. And imagine the celestial refreshment of having a pure decency in the place of sham; real flesh; a soul born active, wind-beaten, but ascending. Honourable will fiction then appear; honourable, a fount of life, an aid to life, quick with our blood. Why, when you behold it you love it — and you will not encourage it? — or only when presented by dead hands? Worse than that alternative dirty drab, your recurring rose-pink is rebuked by hideous revelations of the filthy foul; for nature will force her way, and if you try to stifle her by drowning, she comes up, not the fairest part of her upper-

most! Peruse your Realists — really your castigators for
not having yet embraced Philosophy. As she grows in
the flesh when discreetly tended, nature is unimpeachable,
flower-like, yet not too decoratively a flower; you must
have her with the stem, the thorns, the roots, and the fat
bedding of roses. In this fashion she grew, says historical fiction; thus does she flourish now, would say the
modern transcript, reading the inner as well as exhibiting
the outer.

And how may you know that you have reached to Philosophy? You touch her skirts when you share her hatred
of the sham decent, her derision of sentimentalism. You
are one with her when — but I would not have you a thousand years older! Get to her, if in no other way, by the
sentimental route: — that very winding path, which again
and again brings you round to the point of original impetus,
where you have to be unwound for another whirl; your
point of original impetus being the grossly material, not
at all the spiritual. It is most true that sentimentalism
springs from the former, merely and badly aping the latter;
— fine flower, or pinnacle flame-spire, of sensualism that
it is, could it do other? — and accompanying the former it
traverses tracts of desert, here and there couching in a
garden, catching with one hand at fruits, with another at
colours; imagining a secret ahead, and goaded by an appetite, sustained by sheer gratifications. Fiddle in harmonics as it may, it will have these gratifications at all
costs. Should none be discoverable, at once you are at
the Cave of Despair, beneath the funereal orb of Glaucoma,
in the thick midst of poniarded, slit-throat, rope-dependent
figures, placarded across the bosom Disillusioned, Infidel,
Agnostic, Miserrimus. That is the sentimental route to
advancement. Spirituality does not light it; evanescent
dreams are its oil-lamps, often with wick askant in the
socket.

A thousand years! You may count full many a thousand by this route before you are one with divine Philosophy. Whereas a single flight of brains will reach and
embrace her; give you the savour of Truth, the right use
of the senses, Reality's infinite sweetness; for these things
are in philosophy; and the fiction which is the summary

of actual Life, the within and without of us, is, prose or
verse, plodding or soaring, philosophy's elect handmaiden.
To such an end let us bend our aim to work, knowing that
every form of labour, even this flimsiest, as you esteem it,
should minister to growth. If in any branch of us we fail
in growth, there is, you are aware, an unfailing aboriginal
democratic old monster that waits to pull us down; certainly the branch, possibly the tree; and for the welfare
of Life we fall. You are acutely conscious of yonder old
monster when he is mouthing at you in politics. Be wary
of him in the heart; especially be wary of the disrelish of
brainstuff. You must feed on something. Matter that is
not nourishing to brains can help to constitute nothing but
the bodies which are pitched on rubbish heaps. Brainstuff
is not lean stuff; the brainstuff of fiction is internal history, and to suppose it dull is the profoundest of errors;
how deep, you will understand when I tell you that it is
the very football of the holiday-afternoon imps below.
They kick it for pastime; they are intelligences perverted.
The comic of it, the adventurous, the tragic, they make
devilish, to kindle their Ogygian hilarity. But sharply
comic, adventurous, instructively tragic, it is in the interwinding with human affairs, to give a flavour of the modern
day reviving that of our Poet, between whom and us yawn
Time's most hollow jaws. Surely we owe a little to Time,
to cheer his progress; a little to posterity, and to our
country. Dozens of writers will be in at yonder yawning breach, if only perusers will rally to the philosophic
standard. They are sick of the woodeny puppetry they
dispense, as on a race-course to the roaring frivolous.
Well, if not dozens, half-dozens; gallant pens are alive;
one can speak of them in the plural. I venture to say that
they would be satisfied with a dozen for audience, for a
commencement. They would perish of inanition, unfed,
unapplauded, amenable to the laws perchance for an assault
on their last remaining pair of ears or heels, to hold them
fast. But the example is the thing; sacrifices must be
expected. The example might, one hopes, create a taste.
A great modern writer, of clearest eye and head, now departed, capable in activity of presenting thoughtful women,
thinking men, groaned over his puppetry, that he dared

not animate them, flesh though they were, with the fires of positive brainstuff. He could have done it, and he is of the departed! Had he dared, he would (for he was Titan enough) have raised the Art in dignity on a level with History, to an interest surpassing the narrative of public deeds as vividly as man's heart and brain in their union excel his plain lines of action to eruption. The everlasting pantomime, suggested by Mrs. Warwick in her exclamation to Perry Wilkinson, is derided, not unrighteously, by our graver seniors. They name this Art the pasture of idiots, a method for idiotizing the entire population which has taken to reading; and which soon discovers that it can write likewise, *that* sort of stuff at least. The forecast may be hazarded, that if we do not speedily embrace Philosophy in fiction, the Art is doomed to extinction, under the shining multitude of its professors. They are fast capping the candle. Instead, therefore, of objurgating the timid intrusions of Philosophy, invoke her presence, I pray you. History without her is the skeleton map of events: Fiction a picture of figures modelled on no skeleton-anatomy. But each, with Philosophy in aid, blooms, and is humanly shapely. To demand of us truth to nature, excluding Philosophy, is really to bid a pumpkin caper. As much as legs are wanted for the dance, Philosophy is required to make our human nature credible and acceptable. Fiction implores you to heave a bigger breast and take her in with this heavenly preservative helpmate, her inspiration and her essence. You have to teach your imagination of the feminine image you have set up to bend your civilized knees to, that it must temper its fastidiousness, shun the grossness of the overdainty. Or, to speak in the philosophic tongue, you must turn on *yourself*, resolutely track and seize that burrower, and scrub and cleanse him; by which process, during the course of it, you will arrive at the conception of the right heroical woman for *you* to worship: and if you prove to be of some spiritual stature, you may reach to an ideal of the heroical feminine type for the worship of mankind, an image as yet in poetic outline only, on our upper skies.

"So well do we know ourselves, that we one and all determine to know a purer," says the heroine of my columns. Philosophy in fiction tells, among various other matters, of the perils of this intimate acquaintance with a flattering familiar in the "purer" — a person who more than ceases to be of use to us after his ideal shall have led up men from their flint and arrowhead caverns to inter-communicative daylight. For when the fictitious creature has performed that service of helping to civilize the world, it becomes the most dangerous of delusions, causing first the individual to despise the mass, and then to join the mass in crushing the individual. Wherewith let us to our story, the froth being out of the bottle.

CHAPTER II

AN IRISH BALL

In the Assembly Rooms of the capital city of the Sister Island there was a public Ball, to celebrate the return to Erin of a British hero of Irish blood, after his victorious Indian campaign; a mighty struggle splendidly ended; and truly could it be said that all Erin danced to meet him; but this was the pick of the dancing, past dispute the pick of the supping. Outside those halls the supping was done in Lazarus fashion, mainly through an excessive straining of the organs of hearing and vision, which imparted the readiness for more, declared by physicians to be the state inducing to sound digestion. Some one spied the figure of the hero at a window and was fed; some only to hear the tale chewed the cud of it; some told of having seen him mount the steps; and sure it was that at an hour of the night, no matter when, and never mind a drop or two of cloud, he would come down them again, and have an Irish cheer to freshen his pillow. For 'tis Ireland gives England her soldiers, her generals too. Farther away, over field and bogland, the whiskies did their excellent ancient service of watering the dry and drying the damp, to the toast of "Lord Larrian, God bless him! he's an honour

to the old country!" and a bit of a sigh to follow, hints of
a story, and loud laughter, a drink, a deeper sigh, settling
into conversation upon the brave Lord Larrian's deeds,
and an Irish regiment he favoured — had no taste for the
enemy without the backing of his "boys." Not he. Why,
he'd never march to battle and they not handy; because
when he struck he struck hard, he said. And he has a
wound on the right hip and two fingers off his left hand;
has bled for England, to show her what Irishmen are when
they're well treated.

The fine old warrior standing at the upper end of the
long saloon, tall, straight, grey-haired, martial in his
aspect and decorations, was worthy to be the flag-pole for
enthusiasm. His large grey eyes lightened from time to
time as he ranged them over the floating couples, and
dropped a word of inquiry to his aide, Captain Sir Lukin
Dunstane, a good model of a cavalry officer, though somewhat a giant, equally happy with his chief in passing the
troops of animated ladies under review. He named as
many as were known to him. Reviewing women exquisitely attired for inspection, all variously and charmingly
smiling, is a relief after the monotonous regiments of men.
Ireland had done her best to present the hero of her blood
an agreeable change; and he too expressed a patriotic
satisfaction on hearing that the faces most admired by
him were of the native isle. He looked upon one that
came whirling up to him on a young officer's arm and
swept off into the crowd of tops, for a considerable while
before he put his customary question. She was returning
on the spin when he said, —

"Who is she?"

Sir Lukin did not know. "She's a new bird; she
nodded to my wife; I'll ask."

He manœuvred a few steps cleverly to where his wife
reposed. The information he gathered for the behoof of
his chief was, that the handsome creature answered to the
name of Miss Merion; Irish; aged somewhere between
eighteen and nineteen; a dear friend of his wife's, and he
ought to have remembered her; but she was a child when
he saw her last.

"Dan Merion died, I remember, about the day of my

sailing for India," said the General. "She may be his daughter."

The bright cynosure rounded up to him in the web of the waltz, with her dark eyes for Lady Dunstane, and vanished again among the twisting columns.

He made his way, handsomely bumped by an apologetic pair, to Lady Dunstane, beside whom a seat was vacated for him; and he trusted she had not over-fatigued herself.

"Confess," she replied; "you are perishing to know more than Lukin has been able to tell you. Let me hear that you admire her: it pleases me; and you shall hear what will please you as much, I promise you, General."

"I do. Who would n't?" said he frankly.

"She crossed the Channel expressly to dance here to-night at the public Ball in honour of you."

"Where she appears, the first person falls to second rank, and accepts it humbly."

"That is grandly spoken."

"She makes everything in the room dust round a blazing jewel."

"She makes a poet of a soldier. Well, that you may understand how pleased I am, she is my dearest friend, though she is younger than I, as may be seen; she is the only friend I have. I nursed her when she was an infant; my father and Mr. Dan Merion were chums. We were parted by my marriage and the voyage to India. We have not yet exchanged a syllable: she was snapped up, of course, the moment she entered the room. I knew she would be a taking girl: how lovely, I did not guess. You are right, she extinguishes the others. She used to be the sprightliest of living creatures, and to judge by her letters, that has not faded. She 's in the market, General."

Lord Larrian nodded to everything he heard, concluding with a mock doleful shake of the head. "My poorest subaltern!" he sighed, in the theatrical but cordially melancholy style of green age viewing Cytherea's market.

His poorest subaltern was richer than he in the wherewithal to bid for such prizes.

"What is her name in addition to Merion?"

"Diana Antonia Merion. Tony to me, Diana to the world."

" She lives over there ? "

" In England, or anywhere ; wherever she is taken in. She will live, I hope, chiefly with me."

"And honest Irish ? "

" Oh, she 's Irish."

" Ah ! " the General was Irish to the heels that night.

Before further could be said the fair object of the dialogue came darting on a trip of little runs, both hands out, all her face one tender sparkle of a smile ; and her cry proved the quality of her blood : " Emmy ! Emmy ! my heart ! "

" My dear Tony ! I should not have come but for the hope of seeing you here."

Lord Larrian rose and received a hurried acknowledgment of his courtesy from the usurper of his place.

" Emmy ! we might kiss and hug ; we 're in Ireland. I burn to ! But you 're not still ill, dear ? Say no ! That Indian fever must have gone. You do look a dash pale, my own ; you 're tired."

" One dance has tired me. Why were you so late ? "

" To give the others a chance ? To produce a greater impression by suspense ? No and no. I wrote you I was with the Pettigrews. We caught the coach, we caught the boat, we were only two hours late for the Ball ; so we did wonders. And good Mrs. Pettigrew is pining somewhere to complete her adornment. I was in the crush, spying for Emmy, when Mr. Mayor informed me it was the duty of every Irishwoman to dance her toes off, if she 'd be known for what she is. And twirl ! a man had me by the waist, and I dying to find you."

" Who was the man ? "

" Not to save these limbs from the lighted stake could I tell you ! "

" You are to perform a ceremonious bow to Lord Larrian."

" Chatter first ! a little ! "

The plea for chatter was disregarded. It was visible that the hero of the night hung listening and in expectation. He and the Beauty were named to one another, and they chatted through a quadrille. Sir Lukin introduced a fellow Harrovian of old days, Mr. Thomas Redworth, to his wife.

" Our weather-prophet, meteorologist," he remarked, to set them going ; " you remember, in India, my pointing to you his name in a newspaper-letter on the subject. He was generally safe for the cricketing days."

Lady Dunstane kindly appeared to call it to mind, and she led upon the theme — queried at times by an abrupt "Eh?" and "I beg pardon," for manifestly his gaze and one of his ears, if not the pair, were given to the young lady discoursing with Lord Larrian. Beauty is rare; luckily is it rare, or, judging from its effect on men, and the very stoutest of them, our world would be internally a more distracted planet than we see, to the perversion of business, courtesy, rights of property, and the rest. She perceived an incipient victim, of the hundreds she anticipated, and she very tolerantly talked on: "The weather and women have some resemblance they say. Is it true that he who reads the one can read the other?"

Lord Larrian here burst into a brave old laugh, exclaiming, "Oh! good!"

Mr. Redworth knitted his thick brows. "I beg pardon? Ah! women! Weather and women? No; the one point more variable in women makes all the difference."

"Can you tell me what the General laughed at?"

The honest Englishman entered the trap with promptitude. "She said: — who is she, may I ask you?"

Lady Dunstane mentioned her name.

Daughter of the famous Dan Merion? The young lady merited examination for her father's sake. But when reminded of her laughter-moving speech, Mr. Redworth bungled it; he owned he spoilt it, and candidly stated his inability to see the fun. "She said, St. George's Channel in a gale ought to be called St. Patrick's — something — I missed some point. That quadrille-tune, the Pastourelle, or something . . ."

"She had experience of the Channel last night," Lady Dunstane pursued, and they both, while in seeming converse, caught snatches from their neighbours, during a pause of the dance.

The sparkling Diana said to Lord Larrian, "You really decline to make any of us proud women by dancing to-night?"

The General answered: "I might do it on two stilts; I can't on one." He touched his veteran leg.

"But surely," said she, "there's always an inspiration coming to it from its partner in motion, if one of them takes the step."

He signified a woeful negative. "My dear young lady, you say dark things to grey hairs!"

She rejoined: "If we were over in England, and you fixed on me the stigma of saying dark things, I should never speak without being thought obscure."

"It's because you flash too brightly for them."

"I think it is rather the reminiscence of the tooth that once received a stone when it expected candy."

Again the General laughed; he looked pleased and warmed. "Yes, that's their way, that's their way!" and he repeated her words to himself, diminishing their importance as he stamped them on his memory, but so heartily admiring the lovely speaker, that he considered her wit an honour to the old country, and told her so. Irish prevailed up to boiling-point.

Lady Dunstane, not less gratified, glanced up at Mr. Redworth, whose brows bore the knot of perplexity over a strong stare. He, too, stamped the words on his memory, to see subsequently whether they had a vestige of meaning. Terrifically precocious, he thought her. Lady Dunstane, in her quick sympathy with her friend, read the adverse mind in his face. And her reading of the mind was right, wrong altogether her deduction of the corresponding sentiment.

Music was resumed to confuse the hearing of the eavesdroppers.

They beheld a quaint spectacle: a gentleman, obviously an Englishman, approached, with the evident intention of reminding the Beauty of the night of her engagement to him, and claiming her, as it were, in the lion's jaws. He advanced a foot, withdrew it, advanced, withdrew; eager for his prize, not over enterprising; in awe of the illustrious General she entertained — presumeably quite unaware of the pretender's presence; whereupon a voice was heard: "Oh! if it was minuetting you meant before the lady, I'd never have disputed your right to perform, sir." For it seemed that there were two claimants in the field, an Irishman and an Englishman; and the former, having a livelier sense of the situation, hung aloof in waiting for

her eye; the latter directed himself to strike bluntly at
his prey; and he continued minuetting, now rapidly blinking, flushed, angry, conscious of awkwardness and a tangle
incapable of extrication.   He began to blink horribly under
the raillery of his rival.   The General observed him, but
as an object remote and minute, a fly or gnat.   The face
of the brilliant Diana was entirely devoted to him she
amused.

Lady Dunstane had the faint lines of a decorous laugh
on her lips, as she said: "How odd it is that our men
show to such disadvantage in a Ball-room. I have seen
them in danger, and there they shine first of any, and one
is proud of them.   They should always be facing the elements or in action."   She glanced at the minuet, which
had become a petrified figure, still palpitating, bent forward, an interrogative reminder.

Mr. Redworth reserved his assent to the proclamation of
any English disadvantage.   A whiff of Celtic hostility in
the atmosphere put him on his mettle.   "Wherever the
man is tried," he said.

"My lady!" the Irish gentleman bowed to Lady Dunstane.   "I had the honour . . . Sullivan Smith . . . at the
castle . . ."

She responded to the salute, and Mr. Sullivan Smith
proceeded to tell her, half in speech, half in dots most
luminous, of a civil contention between the English gentleman and himself, as to the possession of the loveliest of
partners for this particular ensuing dance, and that they
had simultaneously made a rush from the Lower Courts,
namely, their cards, to the Upper, being the lady; and
Mr. Sullivan Smith partly founded his preferable claim on
her Irish descent, and on his acquaintance with her eminent
defunct father — one of the ever-radiating stars of his
quenchless country.

Lady Dunstane sympathized with him for his not intruding his claim when the young lady stood pre-engaged, as
well as in humorous appreciation of his imaginative logic.

"There will be dancing enough after supper," she said.

"If I could score one dance with her, I'd go home
supperless and feasted," said he.   "And that's not saying
much among the hordes of hungry troopers tip-toe for the

signal to the buffet. See, my lady, the gentleman, as we
call him ; there he is working his gamut perpetually up to da
capo. Oh ! but it 's a sheep trying to be wolf ; he 's sheep-
eyed and he 's wolf-fanged, pathetic and larcenous ! Oh,
now ! who 'd believe it ! — the man has dared . . . I 'd as
soon think of committing sacrilege in a cathedral ! ' "

The man was actually, to quote his indignant rival,
" breaching the fortress," and pointing out to Diana Merion
" her name on his dirty scrap of paper " : a shocking sight
when the lady's recollection was the sole point to be aimed
at, and the only umpire. " As if all of us could n't have
written that, and had n't done it ! " Mr. Sullivan Smith
groaned disgusted. He hated bad manners, particularly in
cases involving ladies ; and the bad manners of a Saxon
fired his antagonism to the race ; individual members of
which he boasted of forgiving and embracing, honouring.
So the man blackened the race for him, and the race was
excused in the man. But his hatred of bad manners was
vehement, and would have extended to a fellow-country-
man. His own were of the antecedent century, therefore
venerable.

Diana turned from her pursuer with a comic woeful lifting of the brows at her friend. Lady Dunstane motioned
her fan, and Diana came, bending head.

" Are you bound in honour ? "

" I don't think I am. And I do want to go on talking
with the General. He is so delightful and modest — my
dream of a true soldier ! — telling me of his last big battle,
bit by bit, to my fishing."

" Put off this person for a square dance down the list,
and take out Mr. Redworth — Miss Diana Merion, Mr.
Redworth : he will bring you back to the General, who
must not totally absorb you, or he will forfeit his
popularity."

Diana instantly struck a treaty with the pertinacious
advocate of his claims, to whom, on his relinquishing her,
Mr. Sullivan Smith remarked : " Oh ! sir, the law of it,
where a lady 's concerned ! You 're one for evictions, I
should guess, and the anti-human process. It 's that letter
of the law that stands between you and me and mine and
yours. But you 've got your congee, and my blessing
on ye ! "

"It was a positive engagement," said the enemy.

Mr. Sullivan Smith derided him. "And a pretty partner you've pickled for yourself when she keeps her positive engagement!"

He besought Lady Dunstane to console him with a turn. She pleaded weariness. He proposed to sit beside her and divert her. She smiled, but warned him that she was English in every vein. He interjected: "Irish men and English women! though it's putting the cart before the horse — the copper pennies where the gold guineas should be. So here's the gentleman who takes the oyster, like the lawyer of the fable. English is he? But we read, the last shall be first. And English women and Irish men make the finest coupling in the universe."

"Well, you must submit to see an Irish woman led out by an English man," said Lady Dunstane, at the same time informing the obedient Diana, then bestowing her hand on Mr. Redworth to please her friend, that he was a schoolfellow of her husband's.

"Favour can't help coming by rotation, except in very extraordinary circumstances, and he was ahead of me with you, and takes my due, and 't would be hard on me if I were n't thoroughly indemnified." Mr. Sullivan Smith bowed. "You gave them just the start over the frozen minute for conversation; they were total strangers, and he does n't appear a bad sort of fellow for a temporary mate, though he's not perfectly sure of his legs. And that we'll excuse to any man leading out such a fresh young beauty of a Bright Eyes — like the stars of a winter's night in the frosty season over Columkill, or where you will, so that's in Ireland, to be sure of the likeness to her."

"Her mother was half English."

"Of course she was. And what was my observation about the coupling? Dan Merion would make her Irish all over. And she has a vein of Spanish blood in her; for he had; and she's got the colour. — But you spoke of their coupling — or I did. Oh, a man can hold his own with an English roly-poly mate: he's not stifled. But a woman has n't his power of resistance to dead weight. She's volatile, she's frivolous, a rattler and gabbler — have n't I heard what they say of Irish girls over there? She marries,

and it's the end of her sparkling. She must choose at
home for a perfect harmonious partner."

Lady Dunstane expressed her opinion that her couple
danced excellently together.

"It'd be a bitter thing to see, if the fellow could n't dance,
after leading her out!" sighed Mr. Sullivan Smith. "I
heard of her over there. They call her the Black Pearl,
and the Irish Lily — because she's dark. They rack their
poor brains to get the laugh of us."

"And I listen to you," said Lady Dunstane.

"Ah! if all England, half, a quarter, the smallest piece
of the land were like you, my lady, I'd be loyal to the
finger-nails. Now, is she engaged ? — when I get a word
with her ? "

"She is nineteen, or nearly, and she ought to have five
good years of freedom, I think."

"And five good years of serfdom I'd serve to win her!"

A look at him under the eyelids assured Lady Dunstane
that there would be small chance for Mr. Sullivan Smith,
after a life of bondage, if she knew her Diana, in spite of
his tongue, his tact, his lively features and breadth of
shoulders.

Up he sprang. Diana was on Mr. Redworth's arm.
"No refreshments," she said; and "this is my refreshment," taking the seat of Mr. Sullivan Smith, who
ejaculated, —

"I must go and have that gentleman's name." He
wanted a foe.

"You know you are ready to coquette with the General
at any moment, Tony," said her friend.

"Yes, with the General! "

"He is a noble old man."

"Superb. And don't say ' old man.' With his uniform
and his height and his grey head, he is like a glorious
October day just before the brown leaves fall."

Diana hummed a little of the air of Planxty Kelly, the
favourite of her childhood, as Lady Dunstane well remembered, and they smiled together at the scenes and times it
recalled.

"Do you still write verses, Tony? "

"I could about him. At one part of the fight he thought

he would be beaten. He was overmatched in artillery, and it was a cavalry charge he thundered on them, riding across the field to give the word of command to the couple of regiments, riddled to threads, that gained the day. That is life — when we dare death to live! I wonder at men, who are *men*, being anything but soldiers! I told you, madre, my own Emmy, I forgave you for marrying, because it was a soldier."

"Perhaps a soldier is to be the happy man. But you have not told me a word of yourself. What has been done with the old Crossways?"

"The house, you know, is mine. And it's all I have: ten acres and the house, furnished, and let for less than two hundred a year. Oh! how I long to evict the tenants! They can't have my feeling for the place where I was born. They're people of tolerably good connections. middling wealthy, I suppose, of the name of Warwick, and, as far as I can understand, they stick there to be near the Sussex Downs, for a nephew, who likes to ride on them. I've a half engagement, barely legible, to visit them on an indefinite day, and can't bear the idea of strangers masters in the old house. I must be driven there for shelter, for a roof, some month. And I could make a pilgrimage in rain or snow just to doat on the outside of it. That's your Tony."

"She's my darling."

"I hear myself speak! But your voice or mine, madre, it's one soul. Be sure I am giving up the ghost when I cease to be one soul with you, dear and dearest! No secrets, never a shadow of a deception, or else I shall feel I am not fit to live. Was I a bad correspondent when you were in India?"

"Pretty well. Copious letters when you did write."

"I was shy. I knew I should be writing to Emmy and *another*, and only when I came to the flow could I forget him. He is very finely built; and I dare say he has a head. I read of his deeds in India and quivered. But he was just a bit in the way. Men are the barriers to perfect naturalness, at least, with girls, I think. You wrote to me in the same tone as ever, and at first I had a struggle to reply. And I, who have such pride in being always myself!"

Two staring semi-circles had formed, one to front the
Hero, the other the Beauty. These half moons impercepti-
bly dissolved to replenish, and became a fixed obstruction.

"Yes, they look," Diana made answer to Lady Dunstane's
comment on the curious impertinence. She was getting
used to it, and her friend had a gratification in seeing how
little this affected her perfect naturalness.

"You are often in the world — dinners, dances?" she
said.

"People are kind."

"Any proposals?"

"Nibbles."

"Quite heart-free?"

"Absolutely."

Diana's unshadowed bright face defied all menace of an
eclipse.

The block of sturdy gazers began to melt. The General
had dispersed his group of satellites by a movement with
the Mayoress on his arm, construed as the signal for procession to the supper-table.

CHAPTER III

THE INTERIOR OF MR. REDWORTH AND THE EXTERIOR
OF MR. SULLIVAN SMITH

"It may be as well to take Mr. Redworth's arm; you will
escape the crush for you," said Lady Dunstane to Diana.
"I don't sup. Yes! go! You must eat, and he is handiest to conduct you."

Diana thought of her chaperon and the lateness of the
hour. She murmured, to soften her conscience, "Poor
Mrs. Pettigrew!"

And once more Mr. Redworth, outwardly imperturbable,
was in the maëlstrom of a happiness resembling tempest.
He talked, and knew not what he uttered. To give this
matchless girl the best to eat and drink was his business,
and he performed it. Oddly, for a man who had no loaded

design, marshalling the troops in his active and capacious cranium, he fell upon calculations of his income, present and prospective, while she sat at the table and he stood behind her. Others were wrangling for places, chairs, plates, glasses, game-pie, champagne: she had them; the lady under his charge to a certainty would have them; so far good; and he had seven hundred pounds per annum — seven hundred and fifty, in a favourable aspect, at a stretch. . . .

"Yes, the pleasantest thing to me after working all day is an opera of Carini's," he said, in full accord with her taste, "and Tellio for tenor, certainly."

— A fair enough sum for a bachelor: four hundred personal income, and a prospect of higher dividends to increase it; three hundred odd from his office, and no immediate prospects of an increase there; no one died there, no elderly martyr for the advancement of his juniors could be persuaded to die; they were too tough to think of retiring. Say, seven hundred and fifty. . . . eight hundred, if the commerce of the country fortified the Bank his property was embarked in; or eight-fifty: or nine, ten. . . .

"I could call him my poet also," Mr. Redworth agreed with her taste in poets. "His letters are among the best ever written — or ever published: the raciest English I know. Frank, straight out: capital descriptions. The best English letter-writers are as good as the French — You don't think so? — in their way, of course. I dare say we don't sufficiently cultivate the art. We require the supple tongue a closer intercourse of society gives."

— Eight or ten hundred. Comfortable enough for a man in chambers. To dream of entering as a householder on that sum, in these days, would be stark nonsense: and a man two removes from a baronetcy has no right to set his reckoning on deaths: — if he does, he becomes a sort of meditative assassin. But what were the Fates about when they planted a man of the ability of Tom Redworth in a Government office! Clearly they intended him to remain a bachelor for life. And they sent him over to Ireland on inspection duty for a month to have sight of an Irish Beauty. . . .

"Think war the finest subject for poets?" he exclaimed.
"Flatly no: I don't think it.   I think exactly the reverse.
It brings out the noblest traits in human character?   I
won't own that even.   It brings out some: but under
excitement, when you have not always the real man. —
Pray don't sneer at domestic life.   Well, there was a suspicion of disdain. — Yes, I can respect the hero, military
or civil; with this distinction, that the military hero aims
at personal reward — "
    "He braves wounds and death," interposed Diana.
    "Whereas the civilian hero — "
    "Pardon me, let me deny that the soldier-hero aims at a
personal reward," she again interposed.
    "He gets it."
    "If he is not beaten."
    "And then he is no longer a hero."
    "He is to me."
She had a woman's inveterate admiration of the profession of arms.   Mr. Redworth endeavoured to render practicable an opening in her mind to reason.   He admitted
the grandeur of the poetry of Homer.   We are a few cen-
turies in advance of Homer.   We do not slay damsels for
a sacrifice to propitiate celestial wrath; nor do we revel in
details of slaughter.   He reasoned with her; he repeated
stories known to him of civilian heroes, and won her assent
to the heroical title for their deeds, but it was languid, or
not so bright as the deeds deserved — or as the young lady
could look; and he insisted on the civilian hero, impelled
by some unconscious motive to make her see the thing he
thought, also the thing he was — his plain mind and matter-
of-fact nature.   Possibly she caught a glimpse of that.
After a turn of fencing, in which he was impressed by
the vibration of her tones when speaking of military
heroes, she quitted the table, saying: "An argument between one at supper and another handing plates, is rather
unequal if eloquence is needed.   As Pat said to the constable when his hands were tied, you beat me with the
fists, but my spirit is towering and kicks freely."
    — Eight hundred? a thousand a year, two thousand, are
as nothing in the calculation of a householder who means
that the mistress of the house shall have the choicest of

the fruits and flowers of the Four Quarters; and Thomas
Redworth had vowed at his first outlook on the world of
women, that never should one of the sisterhood coming
under his charge complain of not having them in profu-
sion. Consequently he was a settled bachelor. In the
character of disengaged and unaspiring philosophical bachelor, he reviewed the revelations of her character betrayed
by the beautiful virgin devoted to the sanguine coat. The
thrill of her voice in speaking of soldier-heroes shot him
to the yonder side of a gulf. Not knowing why, for he
had no scheme, desperate or other, in his head, the least
affrighted of men was frightened by her tastes, and by her
aplomb, her inoffensiveness in freedom of manner and self-
sufficiency — sign of purest breeding: and by her easy,
peerless vivacity, her proofs of descent from the blood of
Dan Merion — a wildish blood. The candour of the look
of her eyes in speaking, her power of looking forthright at
men, and looking the thing she spoke, and the play of her
voluble lips, the significant repose of her lips in silence,
her weighing of the words he uttered, for a moment before
the prompt apposite reply, down to her simple quotation
of Pat, alarmed him; he did not ask himself why. His
manly self was not intruded on his cogitations. A mere
eight hundred or thousand per annum had no place in that
midst. He beheld her quietly selecting the position of
dignity to suit her: an eminent military man, or statesman, or wealthy nobleman: she had but to choose. A
war would offer her the decorated soldier she wanted. A
war! Such are women of this kind! The thought revolted
him, and pricked his appetite for supper. He did service
by Mrs. Pettigrew, to which lady Miss Merion, as she
said, promoted him, at the table, and then began to refresh
in person, standing.

"Malkin! that's the fellow's name;" he heard close at
his ear.

Mr. Sullivan Smith had drained a champagne-glass,
bottle in hand, and was priming the successor to it. He
cocked his eye at Mr. Redworth's quick stare. "Malkin!
And now we'll see whether the interior of him is grey, or
black, or tabby, or tortoise-shell, or any other colour of
the Malkin breed."

He explained to Mr. Redworth that he had summoned
Mr. Malkin to answer to him as a gentleman for calling
Miss Merion a jilt. "The man, sir, said in my hearing,
she jilted him, and that's to call the lady a jilt. There's
not a point of difference, not a shade. I overheard him.
I happened by the blessing of Providence to be by when
he named her publicly jilt. And it's enough that she's a
lady to have me for her champion. The same if she had
been an Esquimaux squaw. I'll never live to hear a lady
insulted."

"You don't mean to say you're the donkey to provoke a
duel!" Mr. Redworth burst out gruffly, through turkey
and stuffing.

"And an Irish lady, the young Beauty of Erin!" Mr.
Sullivan Smith was flowing on. He became frigid, he
politely bowed: "Two, sir, if you have n't the grace to
withdraw the offensive term before it cools and can't be
obliterated."

"Fiddle! and go to the deuce!" Mr. Redworth cried.

"Would a soft slap o' the cheek persuade you, sir?"

"Try it outside, and don't bother me with nonsense of
that sort at my supper. If I'm struck, I strike back. I
keep my pistols for bandits and law-breakers. Here," said
Mr. Redworth, better inspired as to the way of treating an
ultra of the isle; "touch glasses: you're a gentleman, and
won't disturb good company. By-and-by."

The pleasing prospect of by-and-by renewed in Mr.
Sullivan Smith his composure. They touched the foaming
glasses: upon which, in a friendly manner, Mr. Sullivan
Smith proposed that they should go outside as soon as Mr.
Redworth had finished supper — *quite* finished supper: for
the reason that the term "donkey" affixed to him was like
a minster cap of schooldays, ringing bells on his topknot,
and also that it stuck in his gizzard.

Mr. Redworth declared the term to be simply hypothet-
ical. "*If* you fight, you're a donkey for doing it. But
you won't fight."

"But I will fight."

"He won't fight."

"Then for the honour of your country you must. But
I'd rather have him first, for I have n't drunk with him,

and it should be a case of necessity to put a bullet or a couple of inches of steel through the man you 've drunk with. And what 's in your favour, she danced with ye. She seemed to take to ye, and the man she has the smallest sugar-melting for is sacred if he 's not sweet to me. *If he retracts!*"

"Hypothetically, No."

"But supposititiously?"

"Certainly."

"Then we grasp hands on it. It 's Malkin or nothing!" said Mr. Sullivan Smith, swinging his heel moodily to wander in search of the foe. How one sane man could name another a donkey for fighting to clear an innocent young lady's reputation, passed his rational conception.

Sir Lukin hastened to Mr. Redworth to have a talk over old schooldays and fellows.

"I 'll tell you what," said the civilian, "there are Irishmen and Irishmen. I 've met cool heads and long heads among them, and you and I knew Jack Derry, who was good at most things. But the burlesque Irishman can't be caricatured. Nature strained herself in a fit of absurdity to produce him, and all that Art can do is to copy."

This was his prelude to an account of Mr. Sullivan Smith, whom, as a specimen, he rejoiced to have met.

"There 's a chance of mischief," said Sir Lukin. "I know nothing of the man he calls Malkin. I 'll inquire presently."

He talked of his prospects, and of the women. Fair ones, in his opinion, besides Miss Merion were parading; he sketched two or three of his partners with a broad brush of epithets.

"It won't do for Miss Merion's name to be mixed up in a duel," said Redworth.

"Not if she 's to make her fortune in England," said Sir Lukin. "It 's probably all smoke."

The remark had hardly escaped him when a wreath of metaphorical smoke, and fire, and no mean report, startled the company of supping gentlemen. At the pitch of his voice, Mr. Sullivan Smith denounced Mr. Malkin in presence for a cur masquerading as a cat.

"And that is not the scoundrel's prime offence. For

2

what d' ye think? He trumps up an engagement to dance
with a beautiful lady, and because she can't remember,
binds her to an oath for a dance to come, and then, holding her prisoner to 'm, he sulks, the dirty dog-cat goes
and sulks, and he won't dance and won't do anything but
screech up in corners that he's jilted. He said the word.
Dozens of gentlemen heard the word. And I demand an
apology of Misterr Malkin — *or* . . *!* And none of your
guerrier nodding and bravado, Misterr Malkin, at me, if
you please. The case is for settlement between gentlemen."

The harassed gentleman of the name of Malkin, driven
to extremity by the worrying, stood in braced preparation
for the English attitude of defence. His tormentor drew
closer to him.

"Mind, I give you warning, if you lay a finger on me
I'll knock you down," said he.

Most joyfully Mr. Sullivan Smith uttered a low melodious cry. "For a specimen of manners, in an assembly
of ladies and gentlemen . . . I ask ye!" he addressed the
ring about him, to put his adversary entirely in the wrong
before provoking the act of war. And then, as one intending gently to remonstrate, he was on the point of stretching out his finger to the shoulder of Mr. Malkin, when
Redworth seized his arm, saying: "I'm your man: me
first: you're due to me."

Mr. Sullivan Smith beheld the vanishing of his foe in a
cloud of faces. Now was he wroth on patently reasonable
grounds. He threatened Saxondom. Man up, man down,
he challenged the race of short-legged, thickset, wooden-
pated curmudgeons: and let it be pugilism if their white
livers shivered at the notion of powder and ball. Redworth, in the struggle to haul him away, received a blow
from him. "And you've got it! you would have it!"
roared the Celt.

"Excuse yourself to the company for a misdirected
effort," Redworth said; and he observed generally: "No
Irish gentleman strikes a blow in good company."

"But that's true as Writ! And I offer excuses — if
you'll come along with me and a couple of friends. The
thing has been done before by torchlight — and neatly."

"Come along, and come alone," said Redworth.

A way was cleared for them. Sir Lukin hurried up to Redworth, who had no doubt of his ability to manage Mr. Sullivan Smith.

He managed that fine-hearted but purely sensational fellow so well that Lady Dunstane and Diana, after hearing in some anxiety of the hubbub below, beheld them entering the long saloon amicably, with the nods and looks of gentlemen quietly accordant.

A little later, Lady Dunstane questioned Redworth, and he smoothed her apprehensions, delivering himself, much to her comfort, thus: "In no case would any lady's name have been raised. The whole affair was nonsensical. He's a capital fellow of a kind, capable of behaving like a man of the world and a gentleman. Only he has, or thinks he has, like lots of his countrymen, a raw wound — something that itches to be grazed. Champagne on that ! . . . Irishmen, as far as I have seen of them, are, like horses, bundles of nerves; and you must manage them, as you do with all nervous creatures, with firmness, but good temper. You must never get into a fury of the nerves yourself with them. Spur and whip they don't want; they'll be off with you in a jiffy if you try it. They want the bridle-rein. That seems to me the secret of Irish character. We English are not bad horsemen. It's a wonder we blunder so in our management of such a people."

"I wish you were in a position to put your method to the proof," said she.

He shrugged. "There's little chance of it!"

To reward him for his practical discretion, she contrived that Diana should give him a final dance; and the beautiful girl smiled quickly responsive to his appeal. He was, moreover, sensible in her look and speech that he had advanced in her consideration to be no longer the mere spinning stick, a young lady's partner. By which he humbly understood that her friend approved him. A gentle delirium enfolded his brain. A householder's life is often begun on eight hundred a year: on less: on much less: — sometimes on nothing but resolution to make a fitting income, carving out a fortune. Eight hundred may

stand as a superior basis. That sum is a distinct point of
vantage. If it does not mean a carriage and Parisian mil-
linery and a station for one of the stars of society, it means
at any rate security; and then, the heart of the man being
strong and sound . . .

"Yes," he replied to her, "I like my experience of Ireland and the Irish; and better than I thought I should.
St. George's Channel ought to be crossed oftener by both
of us."

"I'm always glad of the signal," said Diana.

He had implied the people of the two islands. He
allowed her interpretation to remain personal, for the sake
of a creeping deliciousness that it carried through his
blood.

"Shall you soon be returning to England?" he ventured
to ask.

"I am Lady Dunstane's guest for some months."

"Then you will. Sir Lukin has an estate in Surrey.
He talks of quitting the Service."

"I can't believe it!"

His thrilled blood was chilled. She entertained a sentiment amounting to adoration for the profession of arms!

Gallantly had the veteran General and Hero held on into
the night, that the festivity might not be dashed by his
departure; perhaps, to a certain degree, to prolong his
enjoyment of a flattering scene. At last Sir Lukin had
the word from him, and came to his wife. Diana slipped
across the floor to her accommodating chaperon, whom, for
the sake of another five minutes with her beloved Emma,
she very agreeably persuaded to walk in the train of Lord
Larrian, and forth they trooped down a pathway of nodding heads and curtsies, resembling oak and birch-trees
under a tempered gale, even to the shedding of leaves, for
here a turban was picked up by Sir Lukin, there a jewelled
ear-ring by the self-constituted attendant, Mr. Thomas
Redworth. At the portico rang a wakening cheer, really
worth hearing. The rain it rained, and hats were form-
less, as in the first conception of the edifice, backs were
damp, boots liquidly musical, the pipe of consolation
smoked with difficulty, with much pulling at the stem,
but the cheer arose magnificently, and multiplied itself,

touching at the same moment the heavens and Diana's heart — at least, drawing them together; for she felt exalted, enraptured, as proud of her countrymen as of their hero.

"That's the natural shamrock, after the artificial!" she heard Mr. Redworth say, behind her.

She turned and sent one of her brilliant glances flying over him, in gratitude for a timely word well said. And she never forgot the remark, nor he the look.

CHAPTER IV

CONTAINING HINTS OF DIANA'S EXPERIENCES AND OF WHAT THEY LED TO

A FORTNIGHT after this memorable Ball the principal actors of both sexes had crossed the Channel back to England, and old Ireland was left to her rains from above and her undrained bogs below; her physical and her mental vapours; her ailments and her bog-bred doctors; as to whom the governing country trusted they would be silent or discourse humorously.

The residence of Sir Lukin Dunstane, in the county of Surrey, inherited by him during his recent term of Indian services, was on the hills, where a day of Italian sky, or better, a day of our breezy South-west, washed from the showery night, gives distantly a tower to view, and a murky web, not without colour: the ever-flying banner of the metropolis, the smoke of the city's chimneys, if you prefer plain language. At a first inspection of the house, Lady Dunstane did not like it, and it was advertized to be let, and the auctioneer proclaimed it in his dialect. Her taste was delicate; she had the sensitiveness of an invalid: twice she read the stalking advertizement of the attractions of Copsley, and hearing Diana call it "the plush of speech," she shuddered; she decided that a place where her husband's family had lived ought not to stand forth meretriciously spangled and daubed, like a show-booth at

a fair, for a bait; though the grandiloquent man of adver-
tizing letters assured Sir Lukin that a public agape for
the big and gaudy mouthful is in no milder way to be
caught; as it is apparently the case. She withdrew the
trumpeting placard. Retract we likewise "banner of the
metropolis." That plush of speech haunts all efforts to
swell and illuminate citizen prose to a princely poetic.

Yet Lady Dunstane herself could name the bank of
smoke, when looking North-eastward from her summer-
house, the flag of London: and she was a person of the
critical mind, well able to distinguish between the simple
metaphor and the superobese. A year of habitation induced her to conceal her dislike of the place in love: cat's
love, she owned. Here, she confessed to Diana, she would
wish to live to her end. It seemed remote, where an
invigorating upper air gave new bloom to her cheeks; but
she kept one secret from her friend.

Copsley was an estate of nearly twelve hundred acres,
extending across the ridge of the hills to the slopes North
and South. Seven counties rolled their backs under this
commanding height, and it would have tasked a pigeon to
fly within an hour the stretch of country visible at the
Copsley windows. Sunrise to right, sunset leftward, the
borders of the grounds held both flaming horizons. So
much of the heavens and of earth is rarely granted to a
dwelling. The drawback was the structure, which had no
charm, scarce a face. "It is written that I should live in
barracks," Lady Dunstane said. The colour of it taught
white to impose a sense of gloom. Her cat's love of the
familiar inside corners was never able to embrace the outer
walls. Her sensitiveness, too, was racked by the presentation of so pitiably ugly a figure to the landscape. She
likened it to a coarse-featured country wench, whose clean-
ing and decorating of her countenance makes complexion
grin and ruggedness yawn. Dirty, dilapidated, hung with
weeds and parasites, it would have been more tolerable.
She tried the effect of various creepers, and they were as
a staring paint. What it was like then, she had no heart
to say.

One may, however, fall on a pleasureable resignation in
accepting great indemnities, as Diana bade her believe,

when the first disgust began to ebb. "A good hundred over there would think it a Paradise for an asylum:" she signified London. Her friend bore such reminders meekly. They were readers of books of all sorts, political, philosophical, economical, romantic; and they mixed the diverse readings in thought, after the fashion of the ardently youthful. Romance affected politics, transformed economy, irradiated philosophy. They discussed the knotty question, Why things were not *done*, the things being confessedly to do; and they cut the knot. Men, men calling themselves statesmen, declined to perform that operation, because, forsooth, other men objected to have it performed on them. And common humanity declared it to be for the common weal! If so, then it is clearly indicated as a course of action: we shut our eyes against logic and the vaunted laws of economy. They are the knot we cut; or would cut, had we the sword. Diana did it to the tune of Garryowen or Planxty Kelly. O for a despot! The cry was for a beneficent despot, naturally: a large-minded benevolent despot. In short, a despot to obey their bidding. Thoughtful young people who think through the heart soon come to this conclusion. The heart is the beneficent despot they would be. He cures those miseries; he creates the novel harmony. He sees all difficulties through his own sanguine hues. He is the musical poet of the problem, demanding merely to have it solved that he may sing: clear proof of the necessity for solving it immediately.

Thus far in their pursuit of methods for the government of a nation, to make it happy, Diana was leader. Her fine ardour and resonance, and more than the convincing ring of her voice, the girl's impassioned rapidity in rushing through any perceptible avenue of the labyrinth, or beating down obstacles to form one, and coming swiftly to *some* solution, constituted her the chief of the pair of democratic rebels in questions that clamoured for instant solution. By dint of reading solid writers, using the brains they possessed, it was revealed to them gradually that their particular impatience came perhaps of the most earnest desire to get to a comfortable termination of the inquiry: — the heart aching for mankind sought a nest for itself. At this point Lady Dunstane took the lead. Diana had to be tugged to follow. She could not accept a "perhaps" that cast dubiousness on her disinterested championship. She protested a perfect certainty of the single aim of her heart outward. But she reflected. She discovered that her friend had gone ahead of her.

The discovery was reached, and even acknowledged, before she could persuade herself to swallow the repulsive truth. O self! self! self! are we eternally masking in a domino that reveals your hideous old face when we could be most positive we had escaped you? Eternally! the desolating answer knelled. Nevertheless the poor, the starving, the overtaxed in labour, *they* have a right to the cry of Now! now! They have; and if a cry could conduct us to the secret of aiding, healing, feeding, elevating them, we might swell the cry. As it is, we must lay it on our wits patiently to track and find the secret; and meantime do what the individual with his poor pittance can. A miserable contribution! sighed the girl. Old Self was perceived in the sigh. She was haunted.

After all, one must live one's life. Placing her on a lower pedestal in her self-esteem, the philosophy of youth revived her; and if the abatement of her personal pride was dispiriting, she began to see an advantage in getting inward eyes.

"It's infinitely better I should know it, Emmy — I'm a reptile! Pleasure here, pleasure there, I'm always thinking of pleasure. I shall give up thinking and take to drifting. Neither of us can do more than open purses; and mine's lean. If the old Crossways had no tenant, it would be a purse all mouth. And charity is haunted, like everything we do. Only I say with my whole strength — yes, I am sure, in spite of the men professing that they are practical, the rich will not move without a goad. I have and hold — you shall hunger and covet, until you are strong enough to force my hand: — that's the speech of the wealthy. And they are Christians. In name. Well, I thank heaven I'm at war with myself."

"You always manage to strike out a sentence worth remembering, Tony," said Lady Dunstane. "At war with ourselves, means the best happiness we can have."

It suited her, frail as her health was, and her wisdom

striving to the spiritual of happiness. War with herself was far from happiness in the bosom of Diana. She wanted external life, action, fields for energies, to vary the struggle. It fretted and rendered her ill at ease. In her solitary rides with Sir Lukin through a long winter season, she appalled that excellent but conventionally-minded gentleman by starting, nay supporting, theories next to profane in the consideration of a land-owner. She spoke of Reform : of the Repeal of the Corn Laws as the simple beginning of the grants due to the people. She had her ideas, of course, from that fellow Redworth, an occasional visitor at Copsley; and a man might be a donkey and think what he pleased, since he had a vocabulary to back his opinions. A woman, Sir Lukin held, was by nature a mute in politics. Of the thing called a Radical woman, he could not believe that she was less than monstrous : "with a nose," he said ; and doubtless, horse teeth, hatchet jaws, slatternly in the gown, slipshod, awful. As for a girl, an unmarried, handsome girl, admittedly beautiful, her interjections, echoing a man, were ridiculous, and not a little annoying now and then, for she could be piercingly sarcastic. Her vocabulary in irony was a quiverful. He admired her and liked her immensely ; complaining only of her turn for unfeminine topics. He pardoned her on the score of the petty difference rankling between them in reference to his abandonment of his Profession, for here she was patriotically wrong-headed. Everybody knew that he had sold out in order to look after his estates of Copsley and Dunena, secondly : and in the first place, to nurse and be a companion to his wife. He had left her but four times in five months; he had spent just three weeks of that time away from her in London. No one could doubt of his having kept his pledge, although his wife occupied herself with books and notions and subjects foreign to his taste — his understanding, too, he owned. And Redworth had approved of his retirement, had a contempt for soldiering. "Quite as great as yours for civilians, I can tell you," Sir Lukin said, dashing out of politics to the vexatious personal subject. Her unexpressed disdain was ruffling.

"Mr. Redworth recommends work : he respects the working soldier," said Diana.

Sir Lukin exclaimed that he had been a working soldier; he was ready to serve if his country wanted him. He directed her to anathematize Peace, instead of scorning a fellow for doing the duties next about him: and the mention of Peace fetched him at a bound back to politics. He quoted a distinguished Tory orator, to the effect, that any lengthened term of peace bred maggots in the heads of the people.

"Mr. Redworth spoke of it: he translated something from Aristophanes for a retort," said Diana.

"Well, we're friends, eh?" Sir Lukin put forth a hand.

She looked at him surprised at the unnecessary call for a show of friendship; she touched his hand with two tips of her fingers, remarking, "I should think so, indeed."

He deemed it prudent to hint to his wife that Diana Merion appeared to be meditating upon Mr. Redworth.

"That is a serious misfortune, if true," said Lady Dunstane. She thought so for two reasons: Mr. Redworth generally disagreed in opinion with Diana, and contradicted her so flatly as to produce the impression of his not even sharing the popular admiration of her beauty; and, further, she hoped for Diana to make a splendid marriage. The nibbles threatened to be snaps and bites. There had been a proposal, in an epistle, a quaint effusion, from a gentleman avowing that he had seen her and had *not* danced with her on the night of the Irish ball. He was rejected, but Diana groaned over the task of replying to the unfortunate applicant, so as not to wound him. "Shall I have to do this often, I wonder?" she said.

"Unless you capitulate," said her friend.

Diana's exclamation: "May I be heart-free for another ten years!" encouraged Lady Dunstane to suppose her husband quite mistaken.

In the Spring Diana went on a first pilgrimage to her old home, The Crossways, and was kindly entertained by the uncle and aunt of a treasured nephew, Mr. Augustus Warwick. She rode with him on the Downs. A visit of a week humanized her view of the intruders. She wrote almost tenderly of her host and hostess to Lady Dunstane: they had but "the one fault of spoiling their nephew."

Him she described as a "gentlemanly official," a picture of
him. His age was thirty-four. He seemed "fond of her
scenery." Then her pen swept over the Downs like a flying horse. Lady Dunstane thought no more of the gentlemanly official. He was a barrister who did not practise:
in nothing the man for Diana. Letters came from the
house of the Pettigrews in Kent; from London; from Halford Manor in Hertfordshire; from Lockton Grange in
Lincolnshire: after which they ceased to be the thrice
weekly; and reading the latest of them, Lady Dunstane
imagined a flustered quill. The letter succeeding the
omission contained no excuse, and it was brief. There
was a strange interjection, as to the wearifulness of constantly wandering, like a leaf off the tree. Diana spoke
of looking for a return of the dear winter days at Copsley.
That was her station. Either she must have had some disturbing experience, or Copsley was dear for a Redworth
reason thought the anxious peruser; musing, dreaming,
putting together divers shreds of correspondence and test-
ing them with her intimate knowledge of Diana's character,
Lady Dunstane conceived that the unprotected beautiful
girl had suffered a persecution, it might be an insult. She
spelt over the names of the guests at the houses. Lord
Wroxeter was of evil report: Captain Rampan, a Turf
captain, had the like notoriety. And it is impossible in a
great house for the hostess to spread her ægis to cover
every dame and damsel present. She has to depend on the
women being discreet, the men civilized.

"How brutal men can be!" was one of Diana's inci-
dental remarks, in a subsequent letter, relating simply to
masculine habits. In those days the famous ancestral plea
of "the passion for his charmer" had not been altogether
socially quashed down among the provinces, where the
bottle maintained a sort of sway, and the beauty which
inflamed the sons of men was held to be in coy expectation
of violent effects upon their boiling blood. There were,
one hears that there still are, remnants of the pristine
male, who, if resisted in their suing, conclude that they are
scorned, and it infuriates them: some also whose "passion
for the charmer" is an instinct to pull down the standard
of the sex, by a bully imposition of sheer physical ascen-

dency, whenever they see it flying with an air of gallant
independence : and some who dedicate their lives to a study
of the arts of the Lord of Reptiles, until they have worked
the crisis for a display of him in person.   Assault or siege,
they have achieved their triumphs; they have dominated
a frailer system of nerves, and a young woman without
father, or brother, or husband, to defend her, is cryingly a
weak one, therefore inviting to such an order of heroes.
Lady Dunstane was quick-witted and had a talkative husband ; she knew a little of the upper social world of her
time.   She was heartily glad to have Diana by her side
again.

Not a word of any serious experience was uttered.   Only
on one occasion while they conversed, something being
mentioned of her tolerance, a flush of swarthy crimson shot
over Diana, and she frowned, with the outcry, "Oh! I
have discovered that I can be a tigress!"

Her friend pressed her hand, saying, "The cause a good
one!"

"Women have to fight."

Diana said no more.   There had been a bad experience
of her isolated position in the world.

Lady Dunstane now indulged a partial hope that Mr.
Redworth might see in this unprotected beautiful girl a
person worthy of his esteem.   He had his opportunities,
and evidently he liked her.   She appeared to take more
cordially to him.   She valued the sterling nature of the
man.   But they were a hopeless couple, they were so
friendly.   Both ladies noticed in him an abstractedness of
look, often when conversing, as of a man in calculation;
they put it down to an ambitious mind.   Yet Diana said
then, and said always, that it was he who had first taught
her the art of observing.   On the whole, the brilliant marriage seemed a fairer prospect for her; how reasonable to
anticipate, Lady Dunstane often thought when admiring
the advance of Diana's beauty in queenliness, for never did
woman carry her head more grandly, more thrillingly make
her presence felt; and if only she had been an actress
showing herself nightly on a London stage, she would before now have met the superb appreciation, melancholy to
reflect upon!

Diana regained her happy composure at Copsley. She had, as she imagined, no ambition. The dulness of the place conveyed a charm to a nature recovering from disturbance to its clear smooth flow. Air, light, books, and her friend, these good things she had; they were all she wanted. She rode, she walked, with Sir Lukin or Mr. Redworth, for companion; or with Saturday and Sunday guests, Lord Larrian, her declared admirer, among them. "Twenty years younger!" he said to her, shrugging, with a merry smile drawn a little at the corners to sober sourness; and she vowed to her friend that she would not have had the heart to refuse him. "Though," said she, "speaking generally, I cannot tell you what a foreign animal a husband would appear in my kingdom." Her experience had wakened a sexual aversion, of some slight kind, enough to make her feminine pride stipulate for perfect independence, that she might have the calm out of which imagination spreads wing. Imagination had become her broader life, and on such an earth, under such skies, a husband who is not the fountain of it, certainly is a foreign animal: he is a discordant note. He contracts the ethereal world, deadens radiancy. He is gross fact, a leash, a muzzle, harness, a hood, whatever is detestable to the free limbs and senses. It amused Lady Dunstane to hear Diana say, one evening when their conversation fell by hazard on her future, that the idea of a convent was more welcome to her than the most splendid marriage. "For," she added, "as I am sure I shall never know anything of this love they rattle about and rave about, I shall do well to keep to my good single path; and I have a warning within me that a step out of it will be a wrong one — for me, dearest!"

She wished her view of the yoke to be considered purely personal, drawn from no examples and comparisons. The excellent Sir Lukin was passing a great deal of his time in London. His wife had not a word of blame for him; he was a respectful husband, and attentive when present; but so uncertain, owing to the sudden pressure of engagements, that Diana, bound on a second visit to The Crossways, doubted whether she would be able to quit her friend, whose condition did not allow of her being left solitary at Copsley. He came nevertheless a day before Diana's

appointed departure on her round of visits. She was
pleased with him, and let him see it, for the encouragement
of a husband in the observance of his duties. One of the
horses had fallen lame, so they went out for a walk, at
Lady Dunstane's request. It was a delicious afternoon of
Spring, with the full red disk of sun dropping behind the
brown beech-twigs. She remembered long afterward the
sweet simpleness of her feelings as she took in the scent of
wild flowers along the lanes and entered the woods — jaws
of another monstrous and blackening experience. He fell
into the sentimental vein, and a man coming from that
heated London life to these glorified woods, might be excused for doing so, though it sounded to her just a little
ludicrous in him. She played tolerantly second to it; she
quoted a snatch of poetry, and his whole face was bent to
her, with the petition that she would repeat the verse.
Much struck was this giant ex-dragoon. Ah! how fine!
grand! He would rather hear that than any opera: it was
diviner! "Yes, the best poetry is," she assented. "On
your lips," he said. She laughed. "I am not a particularly melodious reciter." He vowed he could listen to her
eternally, eternally. His face, on a screw of the neck and
shoulders, was now perpetually three-quarters fronting.
Ah! she was going to leave.— "Yes, and you will find my
return quite early enough," said Diana, stepping a trifle
more briskly. His fist was raised on the length of the
arm, as if in invocation. "Not in the whole of London is
there a woman worthy to fasten your shoe-buckles! My
oath on it! I look; I can't spy one." Such was his
flattering eloquence.

She told him not to think it necessary to pay her compliments. "And here, of all places!" They were in the
heart of the woods. She found her hand seized — her waist.
Even then, so impossible is it to conceive the unimaginable
even when the apparition of it smites us, she expected some
protesting absurdity, or that he had seen something in
her path.— What did she hear? And from her friend's
husband!

If stricken idiotic, he was a gentleman; the tigress she
had detected in her composition did not require to be called
forth; half-a-dozen words, direct, sharp as fangs and teeth,

with the eyes burning over them, sufficed for the work of defence. — "The man who swore loyalty to Emma!" Her reproachful repulsion of eyes was unmistakable, withering; as masterful as a superior force on his muscles. — What thing had he been taking her for? — She asked it within: and he of himself, in a reflective gasp. Those eyes of hers appeared as in a cloud, with the wrath above: she had the look of a Goddess in anger. He stammered, pleaded across her flying shoulder — Oh! horrible, loathsome, pitiable to hear! . . . "A momentary aberration . . . her beauty . . . he deserved to be shot! . . . could not help admiring . . . quite lost his head . . . on his honour! never again!"

Once in the roadway, and Copsley visible, she checked her arrowy pace for breath, and almost commiserated the dejected wretch in her thankfulness to him for silence. Nothing exonerated him, but at least he had the grace not to beg secresy. That would have been an intolerable whine of a poltroon, adding to her humiliation. He abstained; he stood at her mercy without appealing.

She was not the woman to take poor vengeance. But, oh! she was profoundly humiliated, shamed through and through. The question, was I guilty of any lightness — anything to bring this on me? would not be laid. And how she pitied her friend! This house, her heart's home, was now a wreck to her: nay, worse, a hostile citadel. The burden of the task of meeting Emma with an open face, crushed her like very guilt. Yet she succeeded. After an hour in her bedchamber she managed to lock up her heart and summon the sprite of acting to her tongue and features: which ready attendant on the suffering female host performed his liveliest throughout the evening, to Emma's amusement, and to the culprit ex-dragoon's astonishment; in whom, to tell the truth of him, her sparkle and fun kindled the sense of his being less criminal than he had supposed, with a dim vision of himself as the real proven donkey for not having been a harmless dash more so. But, to be just as well as penetrating, this was only the effect of her personal charm on his nature. So it spurred him a moment, when it struck this doleful man that to have secured one kiss of those fresh and witty sparkling lips he would endure forfeits, pangs, anything

save the hanging of his culprit's head before his Emma.
Reflection washed him clean. Secresy is not a medical
restorative, by no means a good thing for the baffled
amorously-adventurous cavalier, unless the lady's character
shall have been firmly established in or over his hazy
wagging noddle. Reflection informed him that the honourable, generous, proud girl spared him for the sake of the
house she loved. After a night of tossing, he rose right
heartily repentant. He showed it in the best manner, not
dramatically. On her accepting his offer to drive her down
to the valley to meet the coach, a genuine illumination
of pure gratitude made a better man of him, both to look
at and in feeling. She did not hesitate to consent; and
he had half expected a refusal. She talked on the way
quite as usual, cheerfully, if not altogether so spiritedly.
A flash of her matchless wit now and then reduced him to
that abject state of man beside the fair person he has
treated high cavalierly, which one craves permission to
describe as pulp. He was utterly beaten.

The sight of Redworth on the valley road was a relief
to them both. He had slept in one of the houses of the
valley, and spoke of having had the intention to mount
to Copsley. Sir Lukin proposed to drive him back. He
glanced at Diana, still with that calculating abstract air
of his; and he was rallied. He confessed to being absorbed
in railways, the new lines of railways projected to thread
the land and fast mapping it.

"You've not embarked money in them?" said Sir
Lukin.

The answer was: "I have; all I possess." And Redworth
for a sharp instant set his eyes on Diana, indifferent to
Sir Lukin's bellow of stupefaction at such gambling on the
part of a prudent fellow.

He asked her where she was to be met, where written to,
during the Summer, in case of his wishing to send her
news.

She replied: "Copsley will be the surest. I am always
in communication with Lady Dunstane." She coloured
deeply. The recollection of the change of her feeling for
Copsley suffused her maiden mind.

The strange blush prompted an impulse in Redworth

to speak to her at once of his venture in railways. But what would she understand of them, as connected with the mighty stake he was playing for? He delayed. The coach came at a trot of the horses, admired by Sir Lukin, round a corner. She entered it, her maid followed, the door banged, the horses trotted. She was off.

Her destiny of the Crossways tied a knot, barred a gate, and pointed to a new direction of the road on that fine spring morning, when beech-buds were near the burst, cowslips yellowed the meadow-flats, and skylarks quivered upward.

For many long years Redworth had in his memory, for a comment on procrastination and excessive scrupulousness in his calculating faculty, the blue back of a coach.

He declined the vacated place beside Sir Lukin, promising to come and spend a couple of days at Copsley in a fortnight — Saturday week. He wanted, he said, to have a talk with Lady Dunstane. Evidently he had railways on the brain, and Sir Lukin warned his wife to be guarded against the speculative mania, and advise the man, if she could.

CHAPTER V

CONCERNING THE SCRUPULOUS GENTLEMAN WHO CAME
TOO LATE

ON the Saturday of his appointment Redworth arrived at Copsley, with a shade deeper of the calculating look under his thick brows, habitual to him latterly. He found Lady Dunstane at her desk, pen in hand, the paper untouched; and there was an appearance of trouble about her somewhat resembling his own, as he would have observed, had he been open-minded enough to notice anything, except that she was writing a letter. He begged her to continue it; he proposed to read a book till she was at leisure.

"I have to write, and scarcely know how," said she, clearing her face to make the guest at home, and taking a chair by the fire, "I would rather chat for half an hour."

She spoke of the weather, frosty, but tonic; bad for the last days of hunting, good for the farmer and the country, let us hope.

Redworth nodded assent. It might be surmised that he was brooding over those railways, in which he had embarked his fortune. Ah! those railways! She was not long coming to the wailful exclamation upon them, both to express her personal sorrow at the disfigurement of our dear England, and lead to a little, modest offering of a woman's counsel to the rash adventurer; for thus could she serviceably put aside her perplexity awhile. Those railways! When would there be peace in the land? Where one single nook of shelter and escape from them! And the English, blunt as their senses are to noise and hubbub, would be revelling in hisses, shrieks, puffings and screeches, so that travelling would become an intolerable affliction. "I speak rather as an invalid," she admitted; "I conjure up all sorts of horrors, the whistle in the night beneath one's windows, and the smoke of trains defacing the landscape; hideous accidents too. They will be wholesale and past help. Imagine a collision! I have borne many changes with equanimity, I pretend to a certain degree of philosophy, but this mania for cutting up the land does really cause me to pity those who are to follow us. They will not see the England we have seen. It will be patched and scored, disfigured . . . a sort of barbarous Maori visage — England in a New Zealand mask. You may call it the sentimental view. In this case, I am decidedly sentimental: I love my country. I do love quiet, rural England. Well, and I love beauty, I love simplicity. All that will be destroyed by the refuse of the towns flooding the land — barring accidents, as Lukin says. There seems nothing else to save us."

Redworth acquiesced. "Nothing."

"And you do not regret it?" he was asked.

"Not a bit. We have already exchanged opinions on the subject. Simplicity must go, and the townsman meet his equal in the countryman. As for beauty, I would sacrifice that to circulate gumption. A bushelful of non-sense is talked pro and con: it always is at an innovation. What we are now doing, is to take a longer and a quicker stride, that is all."

"And establishing a new field for the speculator."

"Yes, and I am one, and this is the matter I wanted to discuss with you, Lady Dunstane," said Redworth, bending forward, the whole man devoted to the point of business.

She declared she was complimented; she felt the compliment, and trusted her advice might be useful, faintly remarking that she had a woman's head: and "not less" was implied as much as "not more," in order to give strength to her prospective opposition.

All his money, she heard, was down on the railway table. He might within a year have a tolerable fortune: and, of course, he *might* be ruined. He did not expect it; still he fronted the risks. "And now," said he, "I come to you for counsel. I am not held among my acquaintances to be a marrying man, as it's called."

He paused. Lady Dunstane thought it an occasion to praise him for his considerateness.

"You involve no one but yourself, you mean?" Her eyes shed approval. "Still the day may come. . . . I say only that it may: and the wish to marry is a rosy colouring . . . equal to a flying chariot in conducting us across difficulties and obstructions to the deed. And then one may have to regret a previous rashness."

These practical men are sometimes obtuse: she dwelt on that vision of the future.

He listened, and resumed: "My view of marriage is, that no man should ask a woman to be his wife unless he is well able to support her in the comforts, not to say luxuries, she is accustomed to." His gaze had wandered to the desk; it fixed there. "That is Miss Merion's writing," he said.

"The letter?" said Lady Dunstane, and she stretched out her hand to press down a leaf of it. "Yes; it is from her."

"Is she quite well?"

"I suppose she is. She does not speak of her health."

He looked pertinaciously in the direction of the letter, and it was not rightly mannered. That letter, of all others, was covert and sacred to the friend. It contained the weightiest of secrets.

"I have not written to her," said Redworth.

He was astonishing: "To whom? To Diana? You

could very well have done so, only I fancy she knows
nothing, has never given a thought to railway stocks and
shares; she has a loathing for speculation."

"And speculators too, I dare say."

"It is extremely probable." Lady Dunstane spoke with
an emphasis, for the man liked Diana, and would be moved
by the idea of forfeiting her esteem.

"She might blame me if I did anything dishonourable."

"She certainly would."

"She will have no cause."

Lady Dunstane began to look, as at a cloud charged with
remote explosions: and still for the moment she was un-
suspecting. But it was a flitting moment. When he went
on, and very singularly droning to her ear: "The more a
man loves a woman, the more he should be positive, before
asking her, that she will not have to consent to a loss of
position, and I would rather lose her than fail to give her
all — not be sure, as far as a man can be sure, of giving
her all I think she's worthy of:" then the cloud shot a
lightning flash, and the doors of her understanding swung
wide to the entry of a great wonderment. A shock of pain
succeeded it. Her sympathy was roused so acutely that
she slipped over the reflective rebuke she would have addressed to her silly delusion concerning his purpose in
speaking of his affairs to a woman. Though he did not
mention Diana by name, Diana was clearly the person. And
why had he delayed to speak to her? — Because of this
venture of his money to make him a fortune, for the assurance of her future comfort! Here was the best of men for
the girl, not displeasing to her; a good, strong, trustworthy
man, pleasant to hear and to see, only erring in being a trifle
too scrupulous in love: and a fortnight back she would have
imagined he had no chance; and now she knew that the
chance was excellent in those days, with this revelation in
Diana's letter, which said that all chance was over.

"The courtship of a woman," he droned away, "is in my
mind not fair to her until a man has to the full enough
to sanction his asking her to marry him. And if he throws
all he possesses on a stake . . . to win her — give her what
she has a right to claim, he ought. . . . Only at present
the prospect seems good . . . He ought of course to wait.

Well, the value of the stock I hold has doubled, and it increases. I am a careful watcher of the market. I have friends — brokers and railway Directors. I can rely on them."

"Pray," interposed Lady Dunstane, "specify — I am rather in a mist — the exact point upon which you do me the honour to consult me." She ridiculed herself for having imagined that such a man would come to consult her upon a point of business.

"It is," he replied, "this: whether, as affairs now stand with me — I have an income from my office, and personal property . . . say between thirteen and fourteen hundred a year to start with — whether you think me justified in asking a lady to share my lot?"

"Why not? But will you name the lady?"

"Then I may write at once? In your judgement . . . Yes, the lady. I have not named her. I had no right. Besides, the general question first, in fairness to the petitioner. You might reasonably stipulate for more for a friend. She could make a match, as you have said . . ." he muttered of "brilliant," and "the highest;" and his humbleness of the honest man enamoured touched Lady Dunstane. She saw him now as the man of strength that she would have selected from a thousand suitors to guide her dear friend.

She caught at a straw: "Tell me, it is not Diana?"

"Diana Merion!"

As soon as he had said it he perceived pity, and he drew himself tight for the stroke. "She's in love with some one?"

"She is engaged."

He bore it well. He was a big-chested fellow, and that excruciating twist within of the revolution of the wheels of the brain snapping their course to grind the contrary to that of the heart, was revealed in one short lift and gasp, a compression of the tremendous change he underwent.

"Why did you not speak before?" said Lady Dunstane. Her words were tremulous.

"I should have had no justification."

"You might have won her!" She could have wept; her sympathy and her self-condolence under disappointment at Diana's conduct joined to swell the feminine flood.

The poor fellow's quick breathing and blinking reminded her of cruelty in a retrospect. She generalized, to ease her spirit of regret, by hinting it without hurting: "Women really are not puppets. They are not so excessively luxurious. It is good for young women in the early days of marriage to rough it a little." She found herself droning, as he had done.

He had ears for nothing but the fact.

"Then I am too late!"

"I have heard it to-day."

"She is engaged! Positively?"

Lady Dunstane glanced backward at the letter on her desk. She had to answer the strangest of letters that had ever come to her, and it was from her dear Tony, the baldest intimation of the weightiest piece of intelligence which a woman can communicate to her heart's friend. The task of answering it was now doubled. "I fear so, I fancy so," she said, and she longed to cast eye over the letter again, to see if there might possibly be a loophole behind the lines.

"Then I must make my mind up to it," said Redworth. "I think I'll take a walk."

She smiled kindly. "It will be our secret."

"I thank you with all my heart, Lady Dunstane."

He was not a weaver of phrases in distress. His blunt reserve was eloquent of it to her, and she liked him the better; could have thanked him too for leaving her promptly.

When she was alone she took in the contents of the letter at a hasty glimpse. It was of one paragraph, and fired its shot like a cannon with the muzzle at her breast: —

"My own Emmy, — I have been asked in marriage by Mr. Warwick, and have accepted him. Signify your approval, for I have decided that it is the wisest thing a waif can do. We are to live at The Crossways for four months of the year, so I shall have Dada in his best days and all my youngest dreams, my sunrise and morning dew, surrounding me; my old home for my new one. I write

in haste, to you first, burning to hear from you. Send
your blessing to yours in life and death, through all
transformations,

"Tony."

That was all. Not a word of the lover about to be decorated with the title of husband. No confession of love,
nor a single supplicating word to her friend, in excuse
for the abrupt decision to so grave a step. Her previous
description of him, as a "gentlemanly official" in his
appearance, conjured him up most distastefully. True,
she might have made a more lamentable choice; — a silly
lordling, or a hero of scandals; but if a gentlemanly official
was of stabler mould, he failed to harmonize quite so well
with the idea of a creature like Tony. Perhaps Mr. Redworth also failed in something. Where was the man fitly
to mate her! Mr. Redworth, however, was manly and
trustworthy, of the finest Saxon type in build and in character. He had great qualities, and his excess of scrupulousness was most pitiable.

She read: "The wisest thing a waif can do." It bore a
sound of desperation. Avowedly Tony had accepted him
without being in love. Or was she masking the passion?
No: had it been a case of love, she would have written
very differently to her friend.

Lady Dunstane controlled the pricking of the wound
inflicted by Diana's novel exercise in laconics where the
fullest flow was due to tenderness, and despatched felici-
tations upon the text of the initial line: "Wonders are
always happening." She wrote to hide vexation beneath
surprise; naturally betraying it. "I must hope and pray
that you have not been precipitate." Her curiosity to
inspect the happiest of men, the most genuine part of her
letter, was expressed coldly. When she had finished the
composition she perused it, and did not recognize herself
in her language, though she had been so guarded to cover
the wound her Tony dealt their friendship — in some degree
injuring their sex. For it might now, after such an
example, verily seem that women are incapable of a trans-
lucent perfect confidence: — their impulses, caprices, des-
perations, tricks of concealment, trip a heart-whole

friendship. Well, to-morrow, if not to-day, the tripping may be expected! Lady Dunstane resigned herself sadly to a lowered view of her Tony's character. This was her unconscious act of reprisal. Her brilliant beloved Tony, dazzling but in beauty and the gifted mind, stood as one essentially with the common order of women. She wished to be settled, Mr. Warwick proposed, and for the sake of living at The Crossways she accepted him — she, the lofty scorner of loveless marriages! who had said — how many times! that nothing save love excused it! She degraded their mutual high standard of womankind. Diana was in eclipse, full three parts. The bulk of the gentlemanly official she had chosen obscured her. But I have written very carefully, thought Lady Dunstane, dropping her answer into the post-bag. She had, indeed, been so careful, that to cloak her feelings, she had written as another person. Women with otiose husbands have a task to preserve friendship.

Redworth carried his burden through the frosty air at a pace to melt icicles in Greenland. He walked unthinkingly, right ahead, to the red West, as he discovered when pausing to consult his watch. Time was left to return at the same pace and dress for dinner; he swung round and picked up remembrances of sensations he had strewn by the way. She knew these woods; he was walking in her footprints; she was engaged to be married. Yes, his principle, never to ask a woman to marry him, never to court her, without bank-book assurance of his ability to support her in cordial comfort, was right. He maintained it, and owned himself a donkey for having stuck to it. Between him and his excellent principle there was war, without the slightest division. Warned of the danger of losing her, he would have done the same again, confessing himself donkey for his pains. The principle was right, because it was due to the woman. His rigid adherence to the principle set him belabouring his donkey-ribs, as the proper due to himself. For he might have had a chance, all through two Winters. The opportunities had been numberless. Here, in this beech wood; near that thorn-bush; on the juniper slope; from the corner of chalk and sand in junction, to the corner of clay and chalk; all the length of the wooded ridge he had reminders of her presence and his priceless chances: and still the standard of his conduct said No, while his heart bled.

He felt that a chance had been. More sagacious than Lady Dunstane, from his not nursing a wound, he divined in the abruptness of Diana's resolution to accept a suitor, a sober reason, and a fitting one, for the wish that she might be settled. And had he spoken! — If he had spoken to her, she might have given her hand to him, to a dishonourable brute! A blissful brute. But a worse than donkey. Yes, his principle was right, and he lashed with it, and prodded with it, drove himself out into the sour wilds where bachelordom crops noxious weeds without a hallowing luminary, and clung to it, bruised and bleeding though he was.

The gentleness of Lady Dunstane soothed him during the term of a visit that was rather like purgatory sweetened by angelical tears. He was glad to go, wretched in having gone. She diverted the incessant conflict between his insubordinate self and his castigating, but avowedly sovereign, principle. Away from her, he was the victim of a flagellation so dire that it almost drove him to revolt against the lord he served, and somehow the many memories at Copsley kept him away. Sir Lukin, when speaking of Diana's "engagement to that fellow Warwick," exalted her with an extraordinary enthusiasm, exceedingly hard for the silly beast who had lost her to bear. For the present the place dearest to Redworth of all places on earth was unendurable.

Meanwhile the value of railway investments rose in the market, fast as asparagus-heads for cutting: a circumstance that added stings to reflection. Had he been only a little bolder, a little less the fanatical devotee of his rule of masculine honour, less the slave to the letter of success. . . . But why reflect at all? Here was a goodly income approaching, perhaps a seat in Parliament; a station for the airing of his opinions — and a social status for the wife now denied to him. The wife was denied to him; he could conceive of no other. The tyrant-ridden, reticent, tenacious creature had thoroughly wedded her in mind; her view of things had a throne beside his own, even in their differences. He perceived, agreeing or disagreeing, the motions of her brain, as he did with none other of women; and this it is which stamps character on her, divides her from them, upraises and enspheres. He declined to live with any other of the sex.

Before he could hear of the sort of man Mr. Warwick was — a perpetual object of his quest — the bridal bells had rung, and Diana Antonia Merion lost her maiden name. She became the Mrs. Warwick of our footballing world.

Why she married, she never told. Possibly, in amazement at herself subsequently, she forgot the specific reason. That which weighs heavily in youth, and commits us to desperate action, will be a trifle under older eyes to blunter senses, a more enlightened understanding. Her friend Emma probed for the reason vainly. It was partly revealed to Redworth, by guess-work and a putting together of pieces, yet quite luminously, as it were by touch of tentacle-feelers — one evening that he passed with Sir Lukin Dunstane, when the lachrymose ex-dragoon and son of Idlesse, had rather more than dined.

CHAPTER VI

THE COUPLE

Six months a married woman, Diana came to Copsley to introduce her husband. They had run over Italy: "the Italian Peninsula," she quoted him in a letter to Lady Dunstane: and were furnishing their London house. Her first letters from Italy appeared to have a little bloom of sentiment. Augustus was mentioned as liking this and that in the land of beauty. He patronized Art, and it was a pleasure to hear him speak upon pictures and sculptures; he knew a great deal about them. "He is an authority." Her humour soon began to play round the fortunate man, who did not seem, to the reader's mind, to bear so well a sentimental clothing. His pride was in being very English

on the Continent, and Diana's instances of his lofty appre-
ciations of the garden of Art and Nature, and statuesque
walk through it, would have been more amusing if her
friend could have harmonized her idea of the couple. A
description of "a bit of a wrangle between us" at Lucca,
where an Italian post-master on a journey of inspection,
claimed a share of their carriage and audaciously attempted
entry, was laughable, but jarred. Would she some day
lose her relish for ridicule, and see him at a distance?
He was generous, Diana said: she saw fine qualities in
him. It might be that he was lavish on his bridal tour.
She said he was unselfish, kind, affable with his equals;
he was cordial to the acquaintances he met. Perhaps his
worst fault was an affected superciliousness before the
foreigner, not uncommon in those days. "You are to
know, dear Emmy, that we English are the aristocracy of
Europeans." Lady Dunstane inclined to think we were;
nevertheless, in the mouth of a "gentlemanly official" the
frigid arrogance added a stroke of caricature to his deportment. On the other hand, the reports of him gleaned by
Sir Lukin sounded favourable. He was not taken to be
preternaturally stiff, nor bright, but a goodish sort of fellow; good horseman, good shot, good character. In short,
the average Englishman, excelling as a cavalier, a slayer,
and an orderly subject. That was a somewhat elevated
standard to the patriotic Emma. Only she would never
have stipulated for an average to espouse Diana. Would
he understand her, and value the best in her? Another
and unanswered question was, how could she have conde-
scended to wed with an average? There was transparently
some secret not confided to her friend.

He appeared. Lady Dunstane's first impression of him
recurred on his departure. Her unanswered question
drummed at her ears, though she remembered that Tony's
art in leading him out had moderated her rigidly judicial
summary of the union during a greater part of the visit.
But his requiring to be led out, was against him. Considering the subjects, his talk was passable. The subjects
treated of politics, pictures, Continental travel, our manu-
factures, our wealth and the reasons for it — excellent
reasons well-weighed. He was handsome, as men go;

rather tall, not too stout, precise in the modern fashion of
his dress, and the pair of whiskers encasing a colourless
depression up to a long, thin, straight nose, and closed
lips indicating an aperture. The contraction of his mouth
expressed an intelligence in the attitude of the firmly
negative. The lips opened to smile, the teeth were faultless: an effect was produced, if a cold one — the colder for
the unparticipating northern eyes; eyes of that half cloud
and blue, which make a kind of hueless grey, and are
chiefly striking in an authoritative stare. Without con-
tradicting, for he was exactly polite, his look signified a
person conscious of being born to command: in fine, an
aristocrat among the "aristocracy of Europeans." His
differences of opinion were prefaced by a "Pardon me,"
and pausing smile of the teeth; then a succinctly worded
sentence or two, a perfect settlement of the dispute. He
disliked argumentation. He said so, and Diana remarked
it of him, speaking as a wife who merely noted a characteristic. Inside his boundary, he had neat phrases, opinions
in packets. Beyond it, apparently the world was void of
any particular interest. Sir Lukin, whose boundary would
have shown a narrower limitation had it been defined,
stood no chance with him. Tory versus Whig, he tried
a wrestle, and was thrown. They agreed on the topic of
Wine. Mr. Warwick had a fine taste in wine. Their
after-dinner sittings were devoted to this and the allitera-
tive cognate theme, equally dear to the gallant ex-dragoon,
from which it resulted that Lady Dunstane received sat-
isfactory information in a man's judgement of him.
"Warwick is a clever fellow, and a thorough man of the
world, I can tell you, Emmy." Sir Lukin further observed
that he was a gentlemanly fellow. "A gentlemanly official!" Diana's primary dash of portraiture stuck to him,
so true it was! As for her, she seemed to have forgotten
it. Not only did she strive to show him to advantage by
leading him out; she played second to him, subserviently,
fondly; she quite submerged herself, content to be dull if
he might shine; and her talk of her husband in her friend's
blue-chamber boudoir of the golden stars, where they had
discussed the world and taken counsel in her maiden days,
implied admiration of his merits. He rode superbly: he

knew Law: he was prepared for any position: he could speak really eloquently; she had heard him at a local meeting. And he loved the old Crossways almost as much as she did. "He has promised me he will never ask me to sell it," she said, with a simpleness that could hardly have been acted.

When she was gone, Lady Dunstane thought she had worn a mask, in the natural manner of women trying to make the best of their choice; and she excused her poor Tony for the artful presentation of him at her own cost. But she could not excuse her for having married the man. Her first and her final impression likened him to a house locked up and empty: — a London house conventionally furnished and decorated by the upholsterer, and empty of inhabitants. How a brilliant and beautiful girl could have committed this rashness, was the perplexing riddle: the knottier because the man was idle: and Diana had ambition; she despised and dreaded idleness in men. — Empty of inhabitants even to the ghost! Both human and spiritual were wanting. The mind contemplating him became reflectively stagnant.

I must not be unjust! Lady Dunstane hastened to exclaim, at a whisper that he had at least proved his appreciation of Tony; whom he preferred to call Diana, as she gladly remembered: and the two were bound together for a moment warmly by her recollection of her beloved Tony's touching little petition: "You will invite us again?" and then there had flashed in Tony's dear dark eyes the look of their old love drowning. They were not to be thought of separately. She admitted that the introduction to a woman of her friend's husband is crucially trying to him: he may well show worse than he is. Yet his appreciation of Tony in espousing her, was rather marred by Sir Lukin's report of him as a desperate admirer of beautiful woman. It might be for her beauty only, not for her spiritual qualities! At present he did not seem aware of their existence. But, to be entirely just, she had hardly exhibited them or a sign of them during the first interview: and sitting with his hostess alone, he had seized the occasion to say, that he was the happiest of men. He said it with the nearest approach to fervour she had noticed. Perhaps the very

fact of his not producing a highly favourable impression,
should be set to plead on his behalf. Such as he was, he
was himself, no simulator. She longed for Mr. Redworth's
report of him.

Her compassion for Redworth's feelings when beholding the woman he loved another man's wife, did not soften
the urgency of her injunction that he should go speedily,
and see as much of them as he could. "Because," she
gave her reason, "I wish Diana to know she has not lost a
single friend through her marriage, and is only one the
richer."

Redworth buckled himself to the task. He belonged to
the class of his countrymen who have a dungeon-vault for
feelings that should not be suffered to cry abroad, and into
this oubliette he cast them, letting them feed as they
might, or perish. It was his heart down below, and in no
voluntary musings did he listen to it, to sustain the thing.
Grimly lord of himself, he stood emotionless before the
world. Some worthy fellows resemble him, and they are
called deep-hearted. He was dungeon-deep. The prisoner
underneath might clamour and leap; none heard him or
knew of him; nor did he ever view the day. Diana's
frank: "Ah, Mr. Redworth, how glad I am to see you!"
was met by the calmest formalism of the wish for her
happiness. He became a guest at her London house, and
his report of the domesticity there, and notably of the
lord of the house, pleased Lady Dunstane more than her
husband's. He saw the kind of man accurately, as far as
men are to be seen on the surface; and she could say
assentingly, without anxiety: "Yes, yes," to his remarks
upon Mr. Warwick, indicative of a man of capable head in
worldly affairs, commonplace beside his wife. The noble
gentleman for Diana was yet unborn, they tacitly agreed.
Meantime one must not put a mortal husband to the fiery
ordeal of his wife's deserts, they agreed likewise. "You
may be sure she is a constant friend," Lady Dunstane said
for his comfort; and she reminded herself subsequently of
a shade of disappointment at his imperturbable rejoinder:
"I could calculate on it." For though not at all desiring
to witness the sentimental fit, she wished to see that he
held an image of Diana: — surely a woman to kindle poets

and heroes, the princes of the race; and it was a curious
perversity that the two men she had moved were merely
excellent, emotionless, ordinary men, with heads for business. Elsewhere, out of England, Diana would have been
a woman for a place in song, exalted to the skies. Here
she had the destiny to inflame Mr. Redworth and Mr.
Warwick, two railway Directors, bent upon scoring the
country to the likeness of a child's lines of hop-scotch in
a gravel-yard.

As with all invalids, the pleasure of living backward
was haunted by the tortures it evoked, and two years later
she recalled this outcry against the Fates. She would
then have prayed for Diana to inflame none but such men
as those two. The original error was, of course, that rash
and most inexplicable marriage, a step never alluded to by
the driven victim of it. Lady Dunstane heard rumours of
dissensions. Diana did not mention them. She spoke
of her husband as unlucky in railway ventures, and of a
household necessity for money, nothing further. One day
she wrote of a Government appointment her husband had
received, ending the letter: "So there is the end of our
troubles." Her friend rejoiced, and afterward looking
back at her satisfaction, saw the dire beginning of them.

Lord Dannisburgh's name, as one of the admirers of
Mrs. Warwick, was dropped once or twice by Sir Lukin.
He had dined with the Warwicks, and met the eminent
member of the Cabinet at their table. There is no harm
in admiration, especially on the part of one of a crowd
observing a star. No harm can be imputed when the
husband of a beautiful woman accepts an appointment from
the potent Minister admiring her. So Lady Dunstane
thought, for she was sure of Diana to her inmost soul.
But she soon perceived in Sir Lukin that the old Dog-
world was preparing to yelp on a scent. He of his nature
belonged to the hunting pack, and with a cordial feeling
for the quarry, he was quite with his world in expecting
to see her run, and readiness to join the chase. No great
scandal had occurred for several months. The world was
in want of it; and he, too, with a very cordial feeling for
the quarry, piously hoping she would escape, already had
his nose to ground, collecting testimony in the track of

her. He said little to his wife, but his world was getting so noisy that he could not help half pursing his lips, as with the soft whistle of an innuendo at the heels of it. Redworth was in America, engaged in carving up that hemisphere. She had no source of information but her husband's chance gossip; and London was death to her; and Diana, writing faithfully twice a week, kept silence as to Lord Dannisburgh, except in naming him among her guests. She wrote this, which might have a secret personal signification: "We women are the verbs passive of the alliance, we have to learn, and if we take to activity, with the best intentions, we conjugate a frightful disturbance. We are to run on lines, like the steam-trains, or we come to no station, dash to fragments. I have the misfortune to know I was born an active. I take my chance."

Once she coupled the names of Lord Larrian and Lord Dannisburgh, remarking that she had a fatal attraction for antiques.

The death of her husband's uncle and illness of his aunt withdrew her to The Crossways, where she remained nursing for several months, reading diligently, as her letters showed, and watching the approaches of the destroyer. She wrote like her former self, subdued by meditation in the presence of that inevitable. The world ceased barking. Lady Dunstane could suppose Mr. Warwick to have now a reconciling experience of his wife's noble qualities. He probably did value them more. He spoke of her to Sir Lukin in London with commendation. "She is an attentive nurse." He inherited a considerable increase of income when he and his wife were the sole tenants of The Crossways, but disliking the house, for reasons hard to explain by a man previously professing to share her attachment to it, he wished to sell or let the place, and his wife would do neither. She proposed to continue living in their small London house rather than be cut off from The Crossways, which, he said, was ludicrous: people should live up to their position; and he sneered at the place, and slightly wounded her, for she was open to a wound when the cold fire of a renewed attempt at warmth between them was crackling and showing bits of flame, after she had given proof of her power to serve. Service to himself and his relatives affected him. He deferred to her craze for The Crossways, and they lived in a larger London house, "up to their position," which means ever a trifle beyond it, and gave choice dinner-parties to the most eminent. His jealousy slumbered. Having ideas of a seat in Parliament at this period, and preferment superior to the post he held, Mr. Warwick deemed it sagacious to court the potent patron Lord Dannisburgh could be; and his wife had his interests at heart, the fork-tongued world said. The cry revived. Stories of Lord D. and Mrs. W. whipped the hot pursuit. The moral repute of the great Whig lord and the beauty of the lady composed inflammable material.

"Are you altogether cautious?" Lady Dunstane wrote to Diana; and her friend sent a copious reply: "You have the fullest right to ask your Tony anything, and I will answer as at the Judgement bar. You allude to Lord Dannisburgh. He is near what Dada's age would have been, and is, I think I can affirm, next to my dead father and my Emmy, my dearest friend. I love him. I could say it in the streets without shame; and you do not imagine me shameless. Whatever his character in his younger days, he can be honestly a woman's friend, believe me. I see straight to his heart; he has no disguise; and unless I am to suppose that marriage is the end of me, I must keep him among my treasures. I see him almost daily; it is not possible to think I can be deceived; and as long as he does me the honour to esteem my poor portion of brains by coming to me for what he is good enough to call my counsel, I shall let the world wag its tongue. Between ourselves, I trust to be doing some good. I know I am of use in various ways. No doubt there is a danger of a woman's head being turned, when she reflects that a powerful Minister governing a kingdom has not considered her too insignificant to advise him; and I am sensible of it. I am, I assure you, dearest, on my guard against it. That would not attach me to him, as his homely friendliness does. He is the most amiable, cheerful, *benignant* of men; he has no feeling of an enemy, though naturally his enemies are numerous and venomous. He is full of observation and humour. How he would amuse you! In many respects accord with you. And I should not have a spark of jealousy. Some day I shall beg permission to bring him to Copsley. At present, during the Session, he is too busy, as you know. Me — his 'crystal spring of wisdom' — he can favour with no more than an hour in the afternoon, or a few minutes at night. Or I get a pencilled note from the benches of the House, with an anecdote, or news of a Division. I am sure to be enlivened.

"So I have written to you fully, simply, frankly. Have perfect faith in your Tony, who would, she vows to heaven, die rather than disturb it and her heart's beloved."

The letter terminated with one of Lord Dannisburgh's anecdotes, exciting to merriment in the season of its freshness; — and a postscript of information: "Augustus expects a mission — about a month; uncertain whether I accompany him."

Mr. Warwick departed on his mission. Diana remained in London. Lady Dunstane wrote entreating her to pass the month — her favourite time of the violet yielding to the cowslip — at Copsley. The invitation could not be accepted, but the next day Diana sent word that she had a surprise for the following Sunday, and would bring a friend to lunch, if Sir Lukin would meet them at the corner of the road in the valley leading up to the heights, at a stated hour.

Lady Dunstane gave the listless baronet his directions, observing: "It's odd, she never will come alone since her marriage."

"Queer," said he of the serenest absence of conscience; and that there must be something not entirely right going on, he strongly inclined to think.

CHAPTER VII

THE CRISIS

It was a confirmed suspicion when he beheld Lord Dannisburgh on the box of a four-in-hand, and the peerless Diana beside him, cockaded lackeys in plain livery and the lady's maid to the rear. But Lord Dannisburgh's visit was a compliment, and the freak of his driving down under the beams of Aurora on a sober Sunday morning capital fun; so with a gaiety that was kept alive for the invalid Emma to partake of it, they rattled away to the heights, and climbed them, and Diana rushed to the arms of her friend, whispering and cooing for pardon if she startled her, guilty of a little whiff of blarney : — Lord Dannisburgh wanted so much to be introduced to her, and she so much wanted her to know him, and she hoped to be graciously excused for thus bringing them together, "that she might be chorus to them!" Chorus was a pretty fiction on the part of the thrilling and topping voice. She was the very radiant Diana of her earliest opening day, both in look and speech, a queenly comrade, and a spirit leaping and shining like a mountain water. She did not seduce, she ravished. The judgement was taken captive and flowed with her. As to the prank of the visit, Emma heartily enjoyed it and hugged it for a holiday of her own, and doting on the beautiful, dark-eyed, fresh creature, who bore the name of the divine Huntress, she thought her a true Dian in stature, step, and attributes, the genius of laughter ` superadded. None else on earth so sweetly laughed, none so spontaneously, victoriously provoked the healthful openness. Her delicious chatter, and her museful sparkle in listening, equally quickened every sense of life. Adorable as she was to her friend Emma at all times, she that day struck a new fountain in memory. And it was pleasant to see the great lord's admiration of this wonder. One could firmly believe in their friendship, and his winning ideas from the abounding bubbling well. A recurrent smile beamed on his face when hearing and observing her. Certain dishes provided at the table were Diana's favourites, and he relished them, asking for a second help, and remarking that her taste was good in that as in all things. They lunched, eating like boys. They walked over the grounds of Copsley, and into the lanes and across the meadows of the cowslip, rattling, chatting, enlivening the frosty air, happy as children biting to the juices of ripe apples off the tree. But Tony was the tree, the dispenser of the rosy gifts. She had a moment of reflection, only a moment, and Emma felt the pause as

though a cloud had shadowed them and a spirit had been
shut away. Both spoke of their happiness at the kiss of
parting. That melancholy note at the top of the wave to
human hearts conscious of its enforced decline was repeated
by them, and Diana's eyelids blinked to dismiss a tear.

"You have no troubles?" Emma said.

"Only the pain of the good-bye to my beloved," said
Diana. "I have never been happier — never shall be!
Now you know him you think with me? I knew you
would. You have seen him as he always is — except when
he is armed for battle. He is the kindest of souls. And
soul I say. He is the one man among men who gives me
notions of a soul in men."

The eulogy was exalted. Lady Dunstane made a little
mouth for Oh, in correction of the transcendental touch,
though she remembered their foregone conversations upon
men — strange beings that they are! — and understood
Diana's meaning.

"Really! really! honour!" Diana emphasized her ex-
travagant praise, to print it fast. "Hear him speak of
Ireland."

"Would he not speak of Ireland in a tone to catch
the Irishwoman?"

"He is past thoughts of catching, dearest. At that age
men are pools of fish, or what you will: they are not
anglers. Next year, if you invite us, we will come again."

"But you will come to stay in the Winter?"

"Certainly. But I am speaking of one of my holidays."

They kissed fervently. The lady mounted: the grey and
portly lord followed her; Sir Lukin flourished his whip,
and Emma was left to brood over her friend's last words:
"One of my holidays." Not a hint to the detriment of her
husband had passed. The stray beam balefully illuminating her marriage slipped from her involuntarily. Sir
Lukin was troublesome with his ejaculations that evening,
and kept speculating on the time of the arrival of the
four-in-hand in London; upon which he thought a great
deal depended. They had driven out of town early, and
if they drove back late they would not be seen, as all the
cacklers were sure then to be dressing for dinner, and he
would not pass the Clubs. "I couldn't not suggest it,"

he said. "But Dannisburgh's an old hand. But they say he snaps his fingers at tattle, and laughs. Well, it does n't matter for *him*, perhaps, but a game of two. . . . Oh! it 'll be all right. They can't reach London before dusk. And the cat's away."

"It 's more than ever incomprehensible to me how she could have married that man," said his wife.

"I 've long since given it up," said he.

Diana wrote her thanks for the delightful welcome, telling of her drive home to smoke and solitude, with a new host of romantic sensations to keep her company. She wrote thrice in the week, and the same addition of one to the ordinary number next week. Then for three weeks not a line. Sir Lukin brought news from London that Warwick had returned, nothing to explain the silence. A letter addressed to The Crossways was likewise unnoticed. The supposition that they must be visiting on a round, appeared rational; but many weeks elapsed, until Sir Lukin received a printed sheet in the superscription of a former military comrade, who had marked a paragraph. It was one of those journals, now barely credible, dedicated to the putrid of the upper circle, wherein initials raised sewer-lamps, and Asmodeus lifted a roof, leering hideously. Thousands detested it, and fattened their crops on it. Domesticated beasts of superior habits to the common will indulge themselves with a luxurious roll in carrion, for a revival of their original instincts. Society was largely a purchaser. The ghastly thing was dreaded as a scourge, hailed as a refreshment, nourished as a parasite. It professed undaunted honesty, and operated in the fashion of the worms bred of decay. Success was its boasted justification. The animal world, when not rigorously watched, will always crown with success the machine supplying its appetites. The old dog-world took signal from it. The one-legged devil-god waved his wooden hoof, and the creatures in view, the hunt was uproarious. Why should we seem better than we are ? — down with hypocrisy, cried the censor morum, spicing the lamentable derelictions of this and that great person, male and female. The plea of corruption of blood in the world, to excuse the public chafing of a grievous itch, is not less old than sin; and

it offers a merry day of frisky truant running to the
animal made unashamed by another and another stripped,
branded, and stretched flat. Sir Lukin read of Mr. and
Mrs. W. and a distinguished Peer of the realm. The
paragraph was brief; it had a flavour. Promise of more
to come, pricked curiosity. He read it enraged, feeling
for his wife; and again indignant, feeling for Diana. His
third reading found him out: he felt for both, but as a
member of the whispering world, much behind the scenes,
he had a longing for the promised insinuations, just to
know what they could say, or dared say. The paper was
not shown to Lady Dunstane. A run to London put him
in the tide of the broken dam of gossip. The names were
openly spoken and swept from mouth to mouth of the
scandalmongers, gathering matter as they flew. He
knocked at Diana's door, where he was informed that the
mistress of the house was absent. More than official
gravity accompanied the announcement. Her address was
unknown. Sir Lukin thought it now time to tell his
wife. He began with a hesitating circumlocution, in order
to prepare her mind for bad news. She divined immediately that it concerned Diana, and forcing him to speak
to the point, she had the story jerked out to her in a
sentence. It stopped her heart.

The chill of death was tasted in that wavering ascent from
oblivion to recollection. Why had not Diana come to her,
she asked herself, and asked her husband; who, as usual,
was absolutely unable to say. Under compulsory squeezing,
he would have answered, that she did not come because she
could not fib so easily to her bosom friend: and this he
thought, notwithstanding his personal experience of Diana's
generosity. But he had other personal experiences of her
sex, and her sex plucked at the bright star and drowned it.

The happy day of Lord Dannisburgh's visit settled in
Emma's belief as the cause of Mr. Warwick's unpardonable
suspicions and cruelty. Arguing from her own sensations
of a day that had been like the return of sweet health to her
frame, she could see nothing but the loveliest freakish innocence in Diana's conduct, and she recalled her looks, her
words, every fleeting gesture, even to the ingenuousness of
the noble statesman's admiration of her, for the confusion

of her unmanly and unworthy husband. And Emma was
nevertheless a thoughtful person; only her heart was at the
head of her thoughts, and led the file, whose reasoning was
accurate on erratic tracks. All night her heart went at
fever pace. She brought the repentant husband to his knees,
and then doubted, strongly doubted, whether she would,
whether in consideration for her friend she could, intercede
with Diana to forgive him. In the morning she slept
heavily. Sir Lukin had gone to London early for further
tidings. She awoke about midday, and found a letter on
her pillow. It was Diana's. Then while her fingers eagerly
tore it open, her heart, the champion rider over-night, sank.
It needed support of facts, and feared them: not in distrust
of that dear persecuted soul, but because the very bravest of
hearts is of its nature a shivering defender, sensitive in the
presence of any hostile array, much craving for material
support, until the mind and spirit displace it, depute it to
second them instead of leading.

She read by a dull November fog-light a mixture of the
dreadful and the comforting, and dwelt upon the latter in
abandonment, hugged it, though conscious of evil and the
little that there was to veritably console.

The close of the letter struck the blow. After bluntly
stating that Mr. Warwick had served her with a process, and
that he had no case without suborning witnesses, Diana said:
" But I leave the case, and him, to the world. Ireland, or
else America, it is a guiltless kind of suicide to bury myself
abroad. He has my letters. They are such as I can own to
you, and ask you to kiss me — and kiss me when you have
heard all the evidence, all that I can add to it, kiss me.
You know me too well to think I would ask you to kiss
criminal lips. But I cannot face the world. In the dock,
yes. Not where I am expected to smile and sparkle, on
pain of incurring suspicion if I show a sign of oppression.
I cannot do that. I see myself wearing a false grin — your
Tony! No, I do well to go. This is my resolution; and in
consequence, my beloved! my only truly loved on earth! I
do not come to you, to grieve you, as I surely should. Nor
would it soothe me, dearest. This will be to you the best of
reasons. It could not soothe me to see myself giving pain
to Emma. I am like a pestilence, and let me swing away to

the desert, for there I do no harm. I know I am right. I
have questioned myself — it is not cowardice. I do not
quail. I abhor the part of actress. I should do it well —
too well; destroy my soul in the performance. Is a good
name before such a world as this worth that sacrifice? A
convent and self-quenching; — cloisters would seem to me
like holy dew. But that would be sleep, and I feel the
powers of life. Never have I felt them so mightily. If it
were not for being called on to act and mew, I would stay,
fight, meet a bayonet-hedge of charges and rebut them.
I have my natural weapons and my cause. It must be confessed that I have also more knowledge of men and the
secret contempt — it must be — the best of them entertain
for us. Oh! and we confirm it if we trust them. But they
have been at a wicked school.

"I will write. From whatever place, you shall have
letters, and constant. I write no more now. In my present
mood I find no alternative between rageing and drivelling.
I am henceforth dead to the world. Never dead to Emma
till my breath is gone — poor flame! I blow at a bed-room
candle, by which I write in a brown fog, and behold what I
am — though not even serving to write such a tangled
scrawl as this. I am of no mortal service. In two days I
shall be out of England. Within a week you shall hear
where. I long for your heart on mine, your dear eyes.
You have faith in me, and I fly from you! — I must be mad.
Yet I feel calmly reasonable. I know that this is the thing
to do. Some years hence a grey woman may return, to hear
of a butterfly Diana, that had her day and disappeared.
Better than a mewing and courtseying simulacrum of the
woman — I drivel again. Adieu. I suppose I am not liable
to capture and imprisonment until the day when my name
is cited to appear. I have left London. This letter and I
quit the scene by different routes — I would they were one.
My beloved! I have an ache — I think I am wronging you.
I am not mistress of myself, and do as something within
me, wiser than I, dictates. — You will write kindly. Write
your whole heart. It is not compassion I want, I want you.
I can bear stripes from you. Let me hear Emma's voice
— the true voice. This running away merits your re-

proaches. It will look like — I have more to confess : the *tigress* in me wishes it were! I should then have a reckless passion to fold me about, and the glory — infernal, if you name it so, and so it would be — of suffering for and *with* some one else. As it is, I am utterly solitary, sustained neither from above nor below, except within myself, and that is all fire and smoke, like their new engines. — I kiss this miserable sheet of paper. — Yes, I judge that I have run off a line — and what a line! — which hardly shows a trace for breathing things to follow until they feel the transgression in wreck. How immensely nature seems to prefer men to women! — But this paper is happier than the writer.

" Your Tony."

That was the end. Emma kissed it in tears. They had often talked of the possibility of a classic friendship between women, the alliance of a mutual devotedness men choose to doubt of. She caught herself accusing Tony of the lapse from friendship. Hither should the true friend have flown unerringly.

The blunt ending of the letter likewise dealt a wound. She reperused it, perused and meditated. The flight of Mrs. Warwick! She heard that cry — fatal! But she had no means of putting a hand on her. — "Your Tony." The coldness might be set down to exhaustion : it might, yet her not coming to her friend for counsel and love was a positive weight in the indifferent scale. She read the letter backwards, and by snatches here and there; many perusals and hours passed before the scattered creature exhibited in its pages came to her out of the flying threads of the web as her living Tony, whom she loved and prized, and was ready to defend against the world. By that time the fog had lifted; she saw the sky on the borders of milky cloudfolds. Her invalid's chill sensitiveness conceived a sympathy in the baring heavens, and lying on her sofa in the drawing-room she gained strength of meditative vision, weak though she was to help, through ceasing to brood on her wound and herself. She cast herself into her dear Tony's feelings; and thus it came, that she imagined Tony would visit The Crossways, where she kept souvenirs of her father, his cane, and his writing-desk, and a precious miniature of him hanging above it, before leaving England for ever. The fancy sprang to certainty; every speculation confirmed it. Had Sir Lukin been at home she would have despatched him to The Crossways at once. The West wind blew, and gave her a view of the Downs beyond the weald from her southern window. She thought it even possible to drive there and reach the place, on the chance of her vivid suggestion, some time after nightfall; but a walk across the room to try her forces was too convincing of her inability. She walked with an ebony silver-mounted stick, a present from Mr. Redworth. She was leaning on it when the card of Thomas Redworth was handed to her.

CHAPTER VIII

IN WHICH IS EXHIBITED HOW A PRACTICAL MAN AND A DIVINING WOMAN LEARN TO RESPECT ONE ANOTHER

"You see, you are my crutch," Lady Dunstane said to him, raising the stick in reminder of the present.

He offered his arm and hurriedly informed her, to dispose of dull personal matter, that he had just landed. She looked at the clock. "Lukin is in town. You know the song: 'Alas, I scarce can go or creep While *Lukin* is away.' I do not doubt you have succeeded in your business over there. Ah! Now I suppose you have confidence in your success. I should have predicted it, had you come to me." She stood, either musing or in weakness, and said abruptly: "Will you object to lunching at One o'clock?"

"The sooner the better," said Redworth. She had sighed: her voice betrayed some agitation, strange in so serenely-minded a person.

His partial acquaintance with the Herculean Sir Lukin's reputation in town inspired a fear of his being about to receive admission to the distressful confidences of the wife, and he asked if Mrs. Warwick was well. The answer sounded ominous, with its accompaniment of evident pain: "I think her health is good."

Had they quarrelled? He said he had not heard a word of Mrs. Warwick for several months.

"I heard from her this morning," said Lady Dunstane, and motioned him to a chair beside the sofa, where she half reclined, closing her eyes. The sight of tears on the eyelashes frightened him. She roused herself to look at the clock. "Providence or accident, you are here," she said. "I could not have prayed for the coming of a truer man. Mrs. Warwick is in great danger. . . . You know our love. She is the best of me, heart and soul. Her husband has chosen to act on vile suspicions — baseless, I could hold my hand in the fire and swear. She has enemies, or the jealous fury is on the man — I know little of him. He has commenced an action against her. He will rue it. But she . . . you understand this of women at least; — they are not cowards in all things! — but the horror of facing a public scandal: — my poor girl writes of the hatefulness of having to act the complacent — put on her accustomed self! She would have to go about, a mark for the talkers, and behave as if nothing were in the air — full of darts! Oh, that general whisper! — it makes a coup de massue — a gale to sink the bravest vessel: — and a woman must preserve her smoothest front: chat, smile — or else! — Well, she shrinks from it. I should too. She is leaving the country."

"Wrong!" cried Redworth.

"Wrong indeed. She writes, that in two days she will be out of it. Judge her as I do, though you are a man, I pray. You have seen the hunted hare. It is our education — we have something of the hare in us when the hounds are full cry. Our bravest, our best, have an impulse to run. 'By this, poor Wat far off upon a hill.' Shakespeare would have the divine comprehension. I have thought all round it and come back to him. She is one of Shakespeare's women: another character, but one of his own: — another Hermione! I dream of him — seeing her with that eye of steady flame. The bravest and best of us at bay in the world need an eye like his, to read deep and not be baffled by inconsistencies."

Insensibly Redworth blinked. His consciousness of an exalted compassion for the lady was heated by these flights

of advocacy to feel that he was almost seated beside the
sovereign poet thus eulogized, and he was of a modest
nature.

"But you are practical," pursued Lady Dunstane, observing signs that she took for impatience. "You are
thinking of what can be done. If Lukin were here I
would send him to The Crossways without a moment's
delay, on the chance, the mere chance:— it shines to me!
If I were only a little stronger! I fear I might break
down, and it would be unfair to my husband. He has
trouble enough with my premature infirmities already. I
am certain she will go to The Crossways. Tony is one of
the women who burn to give last kisses to things they
love. And she has her little treasures hoarded there.
She was born there. Her father died there. She is three
parts Irish — superstitious in affection. I know her so
well. At this moment I *see* her there. If not, she has
grown unlike herself."

"Have you a stout horse in the stables?" Redworth
asked.

"You remember the mare Bertha; you have ridden her."

"The mare would do, and better than a dozen horses."
He consulted his watch. "Let me mount Bertha, I engage
to deliver a letter at The Crossways to-night."

Lady Dunstane half inclined to act hesitation in accepting the aid she sought, but said: "Will you find your way?"

He spoke of three hours of daylight and a moon to rise.
"She has often pointed out to me from your ridges where
The Crossways lies, about three miles from the Downs,
near a village named Storling, on the road to Brasted.
The house has a small plantation of firs behind it, and a
bit of river — rare for Sussex — to the right. An old
straggling red brick house at Crossways, a stone's throw
from a fingerpost on a square of green: roads to Brasted,
London, Wickford, Riddlehurst. I shall find it. Write
what you have to say, my lady, and confide it to me. She
shall have it to-night, if she's where you suppose. I'll
go, with your permission, and take a look at the mare.
Sussex roads are heavy in this damp weather, and the frost
coming on won't improve them for a tired beast. We
haven't our rails laid down there yet."

"You make me admit some virtues in the practical," said Lady Dunstane; and had the poor fellow vollied forth a tale of the everlastingness of his passion for Diana, it would have touched her far less than his exact memory of Diana's description of her loved birthplace.

She wrote:

"I trust my messenger to tell you how I hang on you. I see my ship making for the rocks. You break your Emma's heart. It will be *the second* wrong step. I shall not survive it. The threat has made me incapable of rushing to you, as I might have had strength to do yesterday. I am shattered, and I wait panting for Mr. Redworth's return *with you*. He has called, by accident, as we say. Trust to him. If ever heaven was active to avert a fatal mischance it is to-day. You will not stand against my supplication. It is my life I cry for. I have no more time. He starts. He leaves me to pray — like the mother seeing her child on the edge of the cliff. Come. This is your breast, my Tony! And your soul warns you it is *right* to come. Do rightly. Scorn other counsel — the coward's. Come with our friend — the one man known to me who can be a friend of women.

"Your EMMA."

Redworth was in the room. "The mare'll do it well," he said. "She has had her feed, and in five minutes will be saddled at the door."

"But you must eat, dear friend," said the hostess.

"I'll munch at a packet of sandwiches on the way. There seems a chance, and the time for lunching may miss it."

"You understand . . . ?"

"Everything, I fancy."

"If she is there!"

"One break in the run will turn her back."

The sensitive invalid felt a blow in his following up the simile of the hunted hare for her friend, but it had a promise of hopefulness. And this was all that could be done by earthly agents, under direction of spiritual, as her imagination encouraged her to believe.

She saw him start, after fortifying him with a tumbler of choice Bordeaux, thinking how Tony would have said she was like a lady arming her knight for battle. On the back of the mare he passed her window, after lifting his hat, and he thumped at his breast-pocket, to show her where the letter housed safely. The packet of provision bulged on his hip, absurdly and blessedly to her sight, not unlike the man, in his combination of robust serviceable qualities, as she reflected during the later hours, until the sun fell on smouldering November woods, and sensations of the frost he foretold bade her remember that he had gone forth riding like a huntsman. His great-coat lay on a chair in the hall, and his travelling-bag was beside it. He had carried it up from the valley, expecting hospitality, and she had sent him forth half naked to weather a frosty November night! She called in the groom, whose derision of a great-coat for any gentleman upon Bertha, meaning work for the mare, appeased her remorsefulness. Brisby, the groom, reckoned how long the mare would take to do the distance to Storling, with a rider like Mr. Redworth on her back. By seven, Brisby calculated, Mr. Redworth would be knocking at the door of the Three Ravens Inn, at Storling, when the mare would have a decent grooming, and Mr. Redworth was not the gentleman to let her be fed out of his eye. More than that, Brisby had some acquaintance with the people of the inn. He begged to inform her ladyship that he was half a Sussex man, though not exactly born in the county; his parents had removed to Sussex after the great event; and the Downs were his first field of horse-exercise, and no place in the world was like them, fair weather or foul, Summer or Winter, and snow ten feet deep in the gullies. The grandest air in England, he had heard say.

His mistress kept him to the discourse, for the comfort of hearing hard bald matter-of-fact; and she was amused and rebuked by his assumption that she must be entertaining an anxiety about master's favourite mare. But, ah! that Diana had delayed in choosing a mate; had avoided her disastrous union with perhaps a more imposing man, to see the true beauty of masculine character in Mr. Redworth, as he showed himself to-day. How could he have doubted succeeding? One grain more of faith in his energy, and Diana might have been mated to the right husband for her — an open-minded clear-faced English gentleman. Her speculative ethereal mind clung to bald matter-of-fact to-day. She would have vowed that it was the sole potentially heroical. Even Brisby partook of the reflected rays, and he was very benevolently considered by her. She dismissed him only when his recounting of the stages of Bertha's journey began to fatigue her and deaden the medical efficacy of him and his like. Stretched on the sofa, she watched the early sinking sun in South-western cloud, and the changes from saffron to intensest crimson, the crown of a November evening, and one of frost. Redworth struck on a southward line from chalk-ridge to sand, where he had a pleasant footing in familiar country, under beeches that browned the ways, along beside a meadow-brook fed by the heights, through pines and across deep sand-ruts to full view of weald and Downs. Diana had been with him here in her maiden days. The coloured back of a coach put an end to that dream. He lightened his pocket, surveying the land as he munched. A favourable land for rails: and she had looked over it: and he was now becoming a wealthy man: and she was a married woman straining the leash. His errand would not bear examination, it seemed such a desperate long shot. He shut his inner vision on it, and pricked forward. When the burning sunset shot waves above the juniper and yews behind him, he was far on the weald, trotting down an interminable road. That the people opposing railways were not people of business, was his reflection, and it returned persistently: for practical men, even the most devoted among them, will think for themselves; their army, which is the rational, calls them to its banners, in opposition to the sentimental; and Redworth joined it in the abstract, summoning the horrible state of the roads to testify against an enemy wanting almost in common humaneness. A slip of his excellent stepper in one of the half-frozen pits of the highway was the principal cause of his confusion of logic; she was half on her knees. Beyond the market town the roads were so bad that he quitted them, and with the indifference of an engineer, struck a

line of his own South-eastward over fields and ditches,
favoured by a round horizon moon on his left. So for a
couple of hours he went ahead over rolling fallow land to
the meadow-flats and a pale shining of freshets; then hit
on a lane skirting the water, and reached an amphibious
village; five miles from Storling, he was informed, and a
clear traverse of lanes, not to be mistaken, "if he kept a
sharp eye open."   The sharpness of his eyes was divided
between the sword-belt of the starry Hunter and the shifting lanes that zig-zagged his course below.   The Downs
were softly illumined; still it amazed him to think of a
woman like Diana Warwick having an attachment to this
district, so hard of yield, mucky, featureless, fit but for
the rails she sided with her friend in detesting.   Reasonable women, too! The moon stood high on her march as
he entered Storling.   He led his good beast to the stables
of The Three Ravens, thanking her and caressing her.
The ostler conjectured from the look of the mare that he
had been out with the hounds and lost his way.   It
appeared to Redworth singularly, that near the ending of
a wild goose chase, his plight was pretty well described
by the fellow.   However, he had to knock at the door of
The Crossways now, in the silent night time, a certainly
empty house, to his fancy.   He fed on a snack of cold meat
and tea, standing, and set forth, clearly directed, "if he
kept a sharp eye open."   Hitherto he had proved his capacity, and he rather smiled at the repetition of the formula
to him, of all men.   A turning to the right was taken, one
to the left, and through the churchyard, out of the gate,
round to the right, and on.   By this route, after an hour,
he found himself passing beneath the bare chestnuts of the
churchyard wall of Storling, and the sparkle of the edges
of the dead chestnut-leaves at his feet reminded him of
the very ideas he had entertained when treading them.
The loss of an hour strung him to pursue the chase in
earnest, and he had a beating of the heart as he thought
that it might be serious.   He recollected thinking it so at
Copsley.   The long ride, and nightfall, with nothing in
view, had obscured his mind to the possible behind the
thick obstruction of the probable; again the possible waved
its marsh-light.   To help in saving her from a fatal step,

supposing a dozen combinations of the conditional mood, became his fixed object, since here he was — of that there was no doubt; and he was not here to play the fool, though the errand were foolish. He entered the churchyard, crossed the shadow of the tower, and hastened along the path, fancying he beheld a couple of figures vanishing before him. He shouted; he hoped to obtain directions from these natives: the moon was bright, the gravestones legible; but no answer came back, and the place appeared to belong entirely to the dead. "I've frightened them," he thought. They left a queerish sensation in his frame. A ride down to Sussex to see ghosts would be an odd experience; but an undigested dinner of tea is the very grandmother of ghosts; and he accused it of confusing him, sight and mind. Out of the gate, now for the turning to the right, and on. He turned. He must have previously turned wrongly somewhere — and where? A light in a cottage invited him to apply for the needed directions. The door was opened by a woman, who had never heard tell of The Crossways, nor had her husband, nor any of the children crowding round them. A voice within ejaculated: "Crassways!" and soon upon the grating of a chair, an old man, whom the woman named her lodger, by way of introduction, presented himself with his hat on, saying: "I knows the spot they calls Crassways," and he led. Redworth understood the intention that a job was to be made of it, and submitting, said: "To the right, I think." He was bidden to come along, if he wanted "they Crassways," and from the right they turned to the left, and further sharp round, and on to a turn, where the old man, otherwise incommunicative, said: "There, down thik theer road, and a post in the middle."

"I want a house, not a post!" roared Redworth, spying a bare space.

The old man despatched a finger travelling to his nob. "Naw, there's ne'er a house. But that's crassways for four roads, if it's crassways you wants."

They journeyed backward. They were in such a maze of lanes that the old man was master, and Redworth vowed to be rid of him at the first cottage. This, however, they were long in reaching, and the old man was promptly through the garden-gate, hailing the people and securing information, before Redworth could well hear. He smiled at the dogged astuteness of a dense-headed old creature determined to establish a claim to his fee. They struck a lane sharp to the left.

"You 're Sussex?" Redworth asked him, and was answered: "Naw; the Sheers."

Emerging from deliberation, the old man said: "Ah 'm a Hampshireman."

"A capital county!"

"Heigh!" The old man heaved his chest. "Once!"

"Why, what has happened to it?"

"Once it were a capital county, I say. Hah! you asks me what have happened to it. You take and go and look at it now. And down heer 'll be no better soon, I tells 'em. When ah was a boy, old Hampshire was a proud country, wi' the old coaches and the old squires, and Harvest Homes, and Christmas merryings. — Cutting up the land! There 's no pride in livin' theer, nor anywhere, as I sees, now."

"You mean the railways."

"It 's the Devil come up and abroad ower all England!" exclaimed the melancholy ancient patriot.

A little cheering was tried on him, but vainly. He saw with unerring distinctness the triumph of the Foul Potentate, nay his personal appearance "in they theer puffin' engines." The country which had produced Andrew Hedger, as he stated his name to be, would never show the same old cricketing commons it did when he was a boy. Old England, he declared, was done for.

When Redworth applied to his watch under the brilliant moonbeams, he discovered that he had been listening to this natural outcry of a decaying and shunted class full three-quarters of an hour, and The Crossways was not in sight. He remonstrated. The old man plodded along. "We must do as we 're directed," he said.

Further walking brought them to a turn. Any turn seemed hopeful. Another turn offered the welcome sight of a blazing doorway on a rise of ground off the road. Approaching it, the old man requested him to "bide a bit," and stalked the ascent at long strides. A vigorous old fellow. Redworth waited below, observing how he joined the group at the lighted door, and, as it was apparent, put his question of the whereabout of The Crossways. Finally, in extreme impatience, he walked up to the group of spectators. They were all, and Andrew Hedger among them, the most entranced and profoundly reverent, observing the dissection of a pig.

Unable to awaken his hearing, Redworth jogged his arm, and the shake was ineffective until it grew in force.

"I've no time to lose; have they told you the way?"

Andrew Hedger yielded his arm. He slowly withdrew his intent fond gaze from the fair outstretched white carcase, and with drooping eyelids, he said: "Ah could eat hog a solid hower!"

He had forgotten to ask the way, intoxicated by the aspect of the pig; and when he did ask it, he was hard of understanding, given wholly to his last glimpses.

Redworth got the directions. He would have dismissed Mr. Andrew Hedger, but there was no doing so. "I'll show ye on to the Crossways *House*," the latter said, implying that he had already earned something by showing him the Crossways post.

"Hog's my feed," said Andrew Hedger. The gastric springs of eloquence moved him to discourse, and he unburdened himself between succulent pauses. "They've killed him early. He's fat; and he might ha' been fatter. But he's fat. They've got their Christmas ready, that they have. Lord! you should see the chitterlings, and the sausages hung up to and along the beams. That's a crown for any dwellin'! They runs 'em round the top of the room — it's like a May-day wreath in old times. Home-fed hog! They've a treat in store, they have. And snap your fingers at the world for many a long day. And the hams! They cure their own hams at that house. Old style! That's what I say of a hog. He's good from end to end, and beats a Christian hollow. Everybody knows it and owns it."

Redworth was getting tired. In sympathy with current conversation, he said a word for the railways: they would certainly make the flesh of swine cheaper, bring a heap of hams into the market. But Andrew Hedger remarked

with contempt that he had not much opinion of foreign
hams: nobody knew what they fed on. Hog, he said,
would feed on anything, where there was no choice —
they had wonderful stomachs for food. Only, when they
had a choice, they left the worst for last, and home-fed
filled them with stuff to make good meat and fat — "what
we calls prime bacon." As it is not right to damp a native
enthusiasm, Redworth let him dilate on his theme, and
mused on his boast to eat hog a *solid hour*, which roused
some distant classic recollection: — an odd jumble.

They crossed the wooden bridge of a flooded stream.

"Now ye have it," said the hog-worshipper; "that may
be the house, I reckon."

A dark mass of building, with the moon behind it,
shining in spires through a mound of firs, met Redworth's
gaze. The windows all were blind, no smoke rose from
the chimneys. He noted the dusky square of green, and
the finger-post signalling the centre of the four roads.
Andrew Hedger repeated that it was the Crossways house,
ne'er a doubt. Redworth paid him his expected fee, whereupon Andrew, shouldering off, wished him a hearty good
night, and forthwith departed at high pedestrian pace,
manifestly to have a concluding look at the beloved
anatomy.

There stood the house. Absolutely empty! thought
Redworth. The sound of the gate-bell he rang was like
an echo to him. The gate was unlocked. He felt a return
of his queer churchyard sensation when walking up the
garden-path, in the shadow of the house. Here she was
born: here her father died: and this was the station of
her dreams, as a girl at school near London and in Paris.
Her heart was here. He looked at the windows facing
the Downs with dead eyes. The vivid idea of her was a
phantom presence, and cold, assuring him that the bodily
Diana was absent. Had Lady Dunstane guessed rightly,
he might perhaps have been of service!

Anticipating the blank silence, he rang the house-bell.
It seemed to set wagging a weariful tongue in a corpse.
The bell did its duty to the last note, and one thin revival
stroke, for a finish, as in days when it responded livingly
to the guest. He pulled, and had the reply, just the

same, with the faint terminal touch, resembling exactly a "There!" at the close of a voluble delivery in the negative. Absolutely empty. He pulled and pulled. The bell wagged, wagged. This had been a house of a witty host, a merry girl, junketting guests; a house of hilarious thunders, lightnings of fun and fancy. Death never seemed more voiceful than in that wagging of the bell.

For conscience' sake, as became a trusty emissary, he walked round to the back of the house, to verify the total emptiness. His apprehensive despondency had said that it was absolutely empty, but upon consideration he supposed the house must have some guardian: likely enough, an old gardener and his wife, lost in deafness doubleshotted by sleep! There was no sign of them. The night air waxed sensibly crisper. He thumped the back-doors. Blank hollowness retorted on the blow. He banged and kicked. The violent altercation with wood and wall lasted several minutes, ending as it had begun. Flesh may worry, but is sure to be worsted in such an argument.

"Well, my dear lady!" — Redworth addressed Lady Dunstane aloud, while driving his hands into his pockets for warmth — "we've done what we could. The next best thing is to go to bed and see what morning brings us."

The temptation to glance at the wild divinings of dreamy-witted women from the point of view of the practical man, was aided by the intense frigidity of the atmosphere in leading him to criticize a sex not much used to the exercise of brains. "And they hate railways!" He associated them, in the matter of intelligence, with Andrew Hedger and Company. They sank to the level of the temperature in his esteem — as regarded their intellects. He approved their warmth of heart. The nipping of the victim's toes and finger-tips testified powerfully to that.

Round to the front of the house at a trot, he stood in moonlight. Then, for involuntarily he now did everything running, with a dash up the steps he seized the sullen pendant bell-handle, and worked it pumpwise, till he perceived a smaller bell-knob beside the door, at which he worked piston-wise. Pump and piston, the hurly-burly and the tinkler created an alarm to scare cat and mouse and Cardinal spider, all that run or weave in desolate houses, with the good result of a certain degree of heat to his frame. He ceased, panting. No stir within, nor light. That white stare of windows at the moon was undisturbed.

The Downs were like a wavy robe of shadowy grey silk. No wonder that she had loved to look on them!

And it was no wonder that Andrew Hedger enjoyed prime bacon. Bacon frizzling, fat rashers of real home-fed on the fire — none of your foreign — suggested a genial refreshment and resistance to antagonistic elements. Nor was it, granting health, granting a sharp night — the temperature at least fifteen below zero — an excessive boast for a man to say he could go on eating for a solid hour.

These were notions darting through a half nourished gentleman nipped in the frame by a severely frosty night. Truly a most beautiful night! She would have delighted to see it here. The Downs were like floating islands, like fairy-laden vapours; solid, as Andrew Hedger's hour of eating; visionary, as too often his desire!

Redworth muttered to himself, after taking the picture of the house and surrounding country from the sward, that he thought it about the sharpest night he had ever encountered in England. He was cold, hungry, dispirited, and astoundingly stricken with an incapacity to separate any of his thoughts from old Andrew Hedger. Nature was at her pranks upon him.

He left the garden briskly, as to the legs, and reluctantly. He would have liked to know whether Diana had recently visited the house, or was expected. It could be learnt in the morning; but his mission was urgent and he on the wings of it. He was vexed and saddened.

Scarcely had he closed the garden-gate when the noise of an opening window arrested him, and he called. The answer was in a feminine voice, youngish, not disagreeable, though not Diana's.

He heard none of the words, but rejoined in a bawl: "Mrs. Warwick! — Mr. Redworth!"

That was loud enough for the deaf or the dead.

The window closed. He went to the door and waited. It swung wide to him; and, O marvel of a woman's divination of a woman! there stood Diana.

CHAPTER IX

SHOWS HOW A POSITION OF DELICACY FOR A LADY AND
    GENTLEMAN WAS MET IN SIMPLE FASHION WITHOUT
    HURT TO EITHER

REDWORTH'S impulse was to laugh for very gladness of
heart, as he proffered excuses for his tremendous alarums:
and in doing so, the worthy gentleman imagined he must
have persisted in clamouring for admission because he
suspected, that if at home, she would require a violent
summons to betray herself. It was necessary to him to
follow his abashed sagacity up to the mark of his happy
animation.

"Had I known it was you!" said Diana, bidding him
enter the passage. She wore a black silk mantilla and
was warmly covered.

She called to her maid Danvers, whom Redworth remembered: a firm woman of about forty, wrapped, like her
mistress, in head-covering, cloak, scarf, and shawl. Telling her to scour the kitchen for firewood, Diana led into
a sitting-room. "I need not ask — you have come from
Lady Dunstane," she said. "Is she well?"

"She is deeply anxious."

"You are cold. Empty houses are colder than out of
doors. You shall soon have a fire."

She begged him to be seated.

The small glow of candle-light made her dark rich
colouring orange in shadow.

"House and grounds are open to a tenant," she resumed.
"I say good-bye to them to-morrow morning. The old
couple who are in charge sleep in the village to-night. I
did not want them here. You have quitted the Government service, I think?"

"A year or so since."

"When did you return from America?"

"Two days back."

"And paid your visit to Copsley immediately?"

"As early as I could."

"That was true friendliness.   You have a letter for me?"
"I have."

He put his hand to his pocket for the letter.

"Presently," she said.   She divined the contents, and
nursed her resolution to withstand them.   Danvers had
brought firewood and coal.   Orders were given to her, and
in spite of the opposition of the maid and intervention of
the gentleman, Diana knelt at the grate, observing: "Allow
me to do this.   I can lay and light a fire."

He was obliged to look on: she was a woman who spoke
her meaning.   She knelt, handling paper, firewood and
matches, like a housemaid.   Danvers proceeded on her
mission, and Redworth eyed Diana in the first fire-glow.
He could have imagined a Madonna on an old black Spanish
canvas.

The act of service was beautiful in gracefulness, and
her simplicity in doing the work touched it spiritually.
He thought, as she knelt there, that never had he seen
how lovely and how charged with mystery her features
were; the dark large eyes full on the brows; the proud
line of a straight nose in right measure to the bow of the
lips; reposeful red lips, shut, and their curve of the slum-
ber-smile at the corners.   Her forehead was broad; the
chin of a sufficient firmness to sustain that noble square;
the brows marked by a soft thick brush to the temples;
her black hair plainly drawn along her head to the knot,
revealed by the mantilla fallen on her neck.

Elegant in plainness, the classic poet would have said
of her hair and dress.   She was of the women whose wits
are quick in everything they do.   That which was proper
to her position, complexion, and the hour, surely marked
her appearance.   Unaccountably this night, the fair fleshly
presence over-weighted her intellectual distinction, to an
observer bent on vindicating her innocence.   Or rather, he
saw the hidden in the visible.

Owner of such a woman, and to lose her!   Redworth
pitied the husband.

The crackling flames reddened her whole person.   Gazing, he remembered Lady Dunstane saying of her once,
that in anger she had the nostrils of a war horse.   The
nostrils now were faintly alive under some sensitive im-

pression of her musings. The olive cheeks, pale as she
stood in the doorway, were flushed by the fire-beams,
though no longer with their swarthy central rose, tropic
flower of a pure and abounding blood, as it had seemed.
She was now beset by battle. His pity for her, and his
eager championship, overwhelmed the spirit of compassion
for the foolish wretched husband. Dolt, the man must be,
Redworth thought; and he asked inwardly, Did the miserable tyrant suppose of a woman like this, that she would
be content to shine as a candle in a grated lanthorn? The
generosity of men speculating upon other men's possessions is known. Yet the man who loves a woman has
to the full the husband's jealousy of her good name. And
a lover, that without the claims of the alliance, can be
wounded on her behalf, is less distracted in his homage
by the personal luminary, to which man's manufacture of
balm and incense is mainly drawn when his love is
wounded. That contemplation of her incomparable beauty,
with the multitude of his ideas fluttering round it, did
somewhat shake the personal luminary in Redworth. He
was conscious of pangs. The question bit him: How far
had she been indiscreet or wilful? and the bite of it was
a keen acid to his nerves. A woman doubted by her husband, is always, and even to her champions in the first
hours of the noxious rumour, until they have solidified in
confidence through service, a creature of the wilds, marked
for our ancient running. Nay, more than a cynical world,
these latter will be sensible of it. The doubt casts her
forth, the general yelp drags her down; she runs like the
prey of the forest under spotting branches; clear if we
can think so, but it has to be thought in devotedness: her
character is abroad. Redworth bore a strong resemblance
to his fellowmen, except for his power of faith in this
woman. Nevertheless it required the superbness of her
beauty and the contrasting charm of her humble posture
of kneeling by the fire, to set him on his right track of
mind. He knew and was sure of her. He dispersed the
unhallowed fry in attendance upon any stirring of the reptile part of us, to look at her with the eyes of a friend.
And if . . . ! — a little mouse of a thought scampered out
of one of the chambers of his head and darted along the

passages, fetching a sweat to his brows.   Well, whatsoever
the fact, his heart was hers!   He hoped he could be charitable to women.

She rose from her knees and said: "Now, please, give
me the letter."

He was entreated to excuse her for consigning him to
firelight when she left the room.

Danvers brought in a dismal tallow candle, remarking
that her mistress had not expected visitors: her mistress
had nothing but tea and bread and butter to offer him.
Danvers uttered no complaint of her sufferings; happy in
being the picture of them.

"I'm not hungry," said he.

A plate of Andrew Hedger's own would not have tempted
him.   The foolish frizzle of bacon sang in his ears as he
walked from end to end of the room; an illusion of his
fancy pricked by a frost-edged appetite.   But the anticipated contest with Diana checked and numbed the craving.

Was Warwick a man to proceed to extremities on a mad
suspicion? — What kind of proof had he?

Redworth summoned the portrait of Mr. Warwick before him, and beheld a sweeping of close eyes in cloud,
a long upper lip in cloud; the rest of him was all cloud.
As usual with these conjurations of a face, the index of
the nature conceived by him displayed itself, and no more;
but he took it for the whole physiognomy, and pronounced
of the husband thus delineated, that those close eyes of
the long upper lip would both suspect and proceed madly.

He was invited by Danvers to enter the dining-room.

There Diana joined him.

"The best of a dinner on bread and butter is, that one
is ready for supper soon after it," she said, swimming to
the tea-tray.   "You have dined?"

"At the inn," he replied.

"The Three Ravens!   When my father's guests from
London flooded The Crossways, The Three Ravens provided the overflow with beds.   On nights like this I have
got up and scraped the frost from my window-panes to see
them step into the old fly, singing some song of his.   The
inn had a good reputation for hospitality in those days.   I
hope they treated you well?"

"Excellently," said Redworth, taking an enormous mouthful, while his heart sank to see that she who smiled to encourage his eating had been weeping. But she also consumed her bread and butter.

"That poor maid of mine is an instance of a woman able to do things against the grain," she said. "Danvers is a foster-child of luxury. She loves it; great houses, plentiful meals, and the crowd of twinkling footmen's calves. Yet you see her here in a desolate house, consenting to cold, and I know not what, terrors of ghosts! poor soul. I have some mysterious attraction for her. She would not let me come alone. I should have had to hire some old Storling grannam, or retain the tattling keepers of the house. She loves her native country too, and disdains the foreigner. My tea you may trust."

Redworth had not a doubt of it. He was becoming a tea-taster. The merit of warmth pertained to the beverage. "I think you get your tea from Scoppin's, in the City," he said.

That was the warehouse for Mrs. Warwick's tea. They conversed of Teas; the black, the green, the mixtures; each thinking of the attack to come, and the defence. Meantime, the cut bread and butter having flown, Redworth attacked the loaf. He apologized.

"Oh! pay me a practical compliment," Diana said, and looked really happy at his unfeigned relish of her simple fare.

She had given him one opportunity in speaking of her maid's love of native country. But it came too early.

"They say that bread and butter is fattening," he remarked.

"You preserve the mean," said she.

He admitted that his health was good. For some little time, to his vexation at the absurdity, she kept him talking of himself. So flowing was she, and so sweet the motion of her mouth in utterance, that he followed her lead, and he said odd things and corrected them. He had to describe his ride to her.

"Yes! the view of the Downs from Dewhurst," she exclaimed. "Or any point along the ridge. Emma and I once drove there in Summer, with clotted cream from her dairy, and we bought fresh-plucked wortleberries, and stewed them in a hollow of the furzes, and ate them with ground biscuits and the clotted cream iced, and thought it a luncheon for seraphs. Then you dropped to the road round under the sand-heights — and meditated railways!"

"Just a notion or two."

"You have been very successful in America?"

"Successful; perhaps; we exclude extremes in our calculations of the still problematical."

"I am sure," said she, "you always have faith in your calculations."

Her innocent archness dealt him a stab sharper than any he had known since the day of his hearing of her engagement. He muttered of his calculations being human; he was as much of a fool as other men — more!

"Oh! no," said she.

"Positively."

"I cannot think it."

"I know it."

"Mr. Redworth, you will never persuade me to believe it."

He knocked a rising groan on the head, and rejoined: "I hope I may not have to say so to-night."

Diana felt the edge of the dart. "And meditating railways, you scored our poor land of herds and flocks; and night fell, and the moon sprang up, and on you came. It was clever of you to find your way by the moonbeams."

"That's about the one thing I seem fit for!"

"But what delusion is this, in the mind of a man succeeding in everything he does!" cried Diana, curious despite her wariness. "Is there to be the revelation of a hairshirt ultimately? — a Journal of Confessions? You succeeded in everything you aimed at, and broke your heart over one chance miss?"

"My heart is not of the stuff to break," he said, and laughed off her fortuitous thrust straight into it. "Another cup, yes. I came . . ."

"By night," said she, "and cleverly found your way, and dined at The Three Ravens, and walked to The Crossways, and met no ghosts."

"On the contrary — or at least I saw a couple."

"Tell me of them; we breed them here. We sell them periodically to the newspapers."

"Well, I started them in their natal locality. I saw them, going down the churchyard, and bellowed after them with all my lungs. I wanted directions to The Crossways; I had missed my way at some turning. In an instant they were vapour."

Diana smiled. "It was indeed a voice to startle delicate apparitions! So do roar Hyrcanean tigers, Pyramus and Thisbe-slaying lions! One of your ghosts carried a loaf of bread, and dropped it in fright; one carried a pound of fresh butter for home consumption. They were in the churchyard for one in passing to kneel at her father's grave and kiss his tombstone."

She bowed her head, forgetful of her guard.

The pause presented an opening. Redworth left his chair and walked to the mantelpiece. It was easier to him to speak, not facing her.

"You have read Lady Dunstane's letter," he began.

She nodded. "I have."

"Can you resist her appeal to you?"

"I must."

"She is not in a condition to bear it well. You will pardon me, Mrs. Warwick . . ."

"Fully! Fully!"

"I venture to offer merely practical advice. You have thought of it all, but have not felt it. In these cases, the one thing to do is to make a stand. Lady Dunstane has a clear head. She sees what has to be endured by you. Consider: she appeals to me to bring you her letter. Would she have chosen me, or any man, for her messenger, if it had not appeared to her a matter of life and death? — You count me among your friends."

"One of the truest."

"Here are two, then, and your own good sense. For I do not believe it to be a question of courage."

"He has commenced. Let him carry it out," said Diana.

Her desperation could have added the cry — And give me freedom! That was the secret in her heart. She had struck on the hope for the detested yoke to be broken at any cost.

"I decline to meet his charges. I despise them. If my friends have faith in me — and they may! — I want nothing more."

"Well, I won't talk commonplaces about the world," said Redworth. "We can none of us afford to have it against us. Consider a moment: to your friends you are the Diana Merion they knew, and they will not suffer an injury to your good name without a struggle. But if you fly? You leave the dearest you have to the whole brunt of it."

"They will, if they love me."

"They will. But think of the shock to her. Lady Dunstane reads you . . ."

"Not quite. No, not if she even wishes me to stay!" said Diana.

He was too intent on his pleading to perceive a signification.

"She reads you as clearly in the dark as if you were present with her."

"Oh! why am I not ten years older!" Diana cried, and tried to face round to him, and stopped paralyzed. "Ten years older, I could discuss my situation, as an old woman of the world, and use my wits to defend myself."

"And then you would not dream of flight before it!"

"No, she does not read me: no! She saw that I might come to The Crossways. She — no one but myself can see the wisdom of my holding aloof, in contempt of this baseness."

"And of allowing her to sink under that which your presence would arrest. Her strength will not support it."

"Emma! Oh, cruel!" Diana sprang up to give play to her limbs. She dropped on another chair. "Go I must, I cannot turn back. She saw my old attachment to this place. It was not difficult to guess . . . Who but I can see the wisest course for me!"

"It comes to this, that the blow aimed at you in your absence will strike her, and mortally," said Redworth.

"Then I say it is terrible to have a friend," said Diana, with her bosom heaving.

"Friendship, I fancy, means one heart between two."

His unstressed observation hit a bell in her head, and set

it reverberating. She and Emma had spoken, written, the very words. She drew forth her Emma's letter from under her left breast, and read some half-blinded lines.

Redworth immediately prepared to leave her to her feelings — trustier guides than her judgement in this crisis.

"Adieu, for the night, Mrs. Warwick," he said, and was guilty of eulogizing the judgement he thought erratic for the moment. "Night is a calm adviser. Let me presume to come again in the morning. I dare not go back without you."

She looked up. As they faced together each saw that the other had passed through a furnace, scorching enough to him, though hers was the delicacy exposed. The reflection had its weight with her during the night.

"Danvers is getting ready a bed for you; she is airing linen," Diana said. But the bed was declined, and the hospitality was not pressed. The offer of it seemed to him significant of an unwary cordiality and thoughtlessness of tattlers that might account possibly for many things — supposing a fool or madman, or malignants, to interpret them.

"Then, good night," said she.

They joined hands. He exacted no promise that she would be present in the morning to receive him; and it was a consolation to her desire for freedom, until she reflected on the perfect confidence it implied, and felt as a quivering butterfly impalpably pinned.

CHAPTER X

THE CONFLICT OF THE NIGHT

HER brain was a steam-wheel throughout the night; everything that could be thought of was tossed, nothing grasped.

The unfriendliness of the friends who sought to retain her recurred. For look — to fly could not be interpreted as a flight. It was but a stepping aside, a disdain of defend-

ing herself, and a wrapping herself in her dignity. Women
would be with her. She called on the noblest of them to
justify the course she chose, and they did, in an almost
audible murmur.

And O the rich reward. A black archway-gate swung
open to the glittering fields of freedom.

Emma was not of the chorus. Emma meditated as an
invalid. How often had Emma bewailed to her that the
most grievous burden of her malady was her fatal tendency
to brood sickly upon human complications! She could not
see the blessedness of the prospect of freedom to a woman
abominably yoked. What if a miserable woman were
dragged through mire to reach it! Married, the mire was
her portion, whatever she might do. That man — but pass
him!

And that other — the dear, the kind, careless, high-
hearted old friend. He could honestly protest his guiltless-
ness, and would smilingly leave the case to go its ways. Of
this she was sure, that her decision and her pleasure would
be his. They were tied to the stake. She had already
tasted some of the mortal agony. Did it matter whether
the flames consumed her?

Reflecting on the interview with Redworth, though she
had performed her part in it placidly, her skin burned. It
was the beginning of tortures if she stayed in England.

By staying to defend herself she forfeited her attitude of
dignity and lost all chance of her reward. And name the
sort of world it is, dear friends, for which we are to sacrifice
our one hope of freedom, that we may preserve our fair
fame in it!

Diana cried aloud, "My freedom!" feeling as a butterfly
flown out of a box to stretches of sunny earth beneath
spacious heavens. Her bitter marriage, joyless in all its
chapters, indefensible where the man was right as well as
where insensately wrong, had been imprisonment. She
excused him down to his last madness, if only the bonds
were broken. Here, too, in this very house of her happiness with her father, she had bound herself to the man :
voluntarily, quite inexplicably. Voluntarily, as we say.
But there must be a spell upon us at times. Upon young
women there certainly is.

The wild brain of Diana, armed by her later enlightenment as to the laws of life and nature, dashed in revolt at the laws of the world when she thought of the forces, natural and social, urging young women to marry and be bound to the end.

It should be a spotless world which is thus ruthless.

But were the world impeccable it would behave more generously.

The world is ruthless, dear friends, because the world is hypocrite! The world cannot afford to be magnanimous, or even just.

Her dissensions with her husband, their differences of opinion, and puny wranglings, hoistings of two standards, reconciliations for the sake of decency, breaches of the truce, and his detested meanness, the man behind the mask; and glimpses of herself too, the half-known, half-suspected, developing creature claiming to be Diana, and unlike her dreamed Diana, deformed by marriage, irritable, acerb, rebellious, constantly justifiable against him, but not in her own mind, and therefore accusing him of the double crime of provoking her and perverting her — these were the troops defiling through her head while she did battle with the hypocrite world.

One painful sting was caused by the feeling that she could have loved — whom? An ideal. Had he, the imagined but unvisioned, been her yoke-fellow, would she now lie raising caged-beast cries in execration of the yoke? She would not now be seeing herself as hare, serpent, tigress! The hypothesis was reviewed in negatives: she had barely a sense of softness, just a single little heave of the bosom, quivering upward and leadenly sinking, when she glanced at a married Diana heartily mated. The regrets of the youthful for a life sailing away under medical sentence of death in the sad eyes of relatives resemble it. She could have loved. Good-bye to that!

A woman's brutallest tussle with the world was upon her. She was in the arena of the savage claws, flung there by the man who of all others should have protected her from them. And what had she done to deserve it? She listened to the advocate pleading her case; she primed him to admit the charges, to say the worst, in contempt of legal

4

prudence, and thereby expose her transparent honesty. The very things awakening a mad suspicion proved her innocence. But was she this utterly simple person? Oh, no! She was the Diana of the pride in her power of fencing with evil — by no means of the order of those ninny young women who realize the popular conception of the purely innocent. She had fenced and kept her guard. Of this it was her angry glory to have the knowledge. But she had been compelled to fence. Such are men in the world of facts, that when a woman steps out of her domestic tangle to assert, because it is a tangle, her rights to partial independence, they sight her for their prey, or at least they complacently suppose her accessible. Wretched at home, a woman ought to bury herself in her wretchedness, else may she be assured that not the cleverest, wariest guard will cover her character.

Against the husband her cause was triumphant. Against herself she decided not to plead it, for this reason, that the preceding Court, which was the public and only positive one, had entirely and justly exonerated her. But the holding of her hand by the friend half a minute too long for friendship, and the overfriendliness of looks, letters, frequency of visits, would speak within her. She had a darting view of her husband's estimation of them in his present mood. She quenched it; they were trifles, things that women of the world have to combat. The revelation to a fair-minded young woman of the majority of men being naught other than men, and some of the friendliest of men betraying confidence under the excuse of temptation, is one of the shocks to simplicity which leave her the alternative of misanthropy or philosophy. Diana had not the heart to hate her kind, so she resigned herself to pardon, and to the recognition of the state of duel between the sexes — active enough in her sphere of society. The circle hummed with it; many lived for it. Could she pretend to ignore it? Her personal experience might have instigated a less clear and less intrepid nature to take advantage of the opportunity for playing the popular innocent, who runs about with astonished eyes to find herself in so hunting a world, and wins general compassion, if not shelter in unsuspected and unlicenced places. There is perpetually the inducement to act the hypocrite before the hypocrite world, unless a woman submits to be the humbly knitting house-wife, unquestioningly worshipful of her lord; for the world is ever gracious to an hypocrisy that pays homage to the mask of virtue by copying it; the world is hostile to the face of an innocence not conventionally simpering and quite surprised; the world prefers decorum to honesty. "Let me be myself, whatever the martyrdom!" she cried, in that phase of young sensation when, to the blooming woman, the putting on of a mask appears to wither her and reduce her to the show she parades. Yet, in common with her sisterhood, she owned she had worn a sort of mask; the world demands it of them as the price of their station. That she had never worn it consentingly, was the plea for now casting it off altogether, showing herself as she was, accepting martyrdom, becoming the first martyr of the modern woman's cause — a grand position! and one imaginable to an excited mind in the dark, which does not conjure a critical humour, as light does, to correct the feverish sublimity. She was, then, this martyr, a woman capable of telling the world she knew it, and of confessing that she had behaved in disdain of its rigider rules, accord-ing to her own ideas of her immunities. O brave!

But was she holding the position by flight? It involved the challenge of consequences, not an evasion of them.

She moaned; her mental steam-wheel stopped; fatigue brought sleep.

She had sensationally led her rebellious wits to the Crossways, distilling much poison from thoughts on the way; and there, for the luxury of a still seeming indecision, she sank into oblivion.

CHAPTER XI

RECOUNTS THE JOURNEY IN A CHARIOT, WITH A CERTAIN
AMOUNT OF DIALOGUE, AND A SMALL INCIDENT ON THE
ROAD

In the morning the fight was over. She looked at the
signpost of The Crossways whilst dressing, and submitted
to follow, obediently as a puppet, the road recommended
by friends, though a voice within, that she took for the
intimations of her reason, protested that they were wrong,
that they were judging of her case in the general, and
unwisely — disastrously for her.

The mistaking of her desires for her reason was peculiar
to her situation.

"So I suppose I shall some day see The Crossways again,"
she said, to conceive a compensation in the abandonment
of freedom. The night's red vision of martyrdom was
reserved to console her secretly, among the unopened
lockers in her treasury of thoughts. It helped to sustain
her; and she was too conscious of things necessary for her
sustainment to bring it to the light of day and examine it.
She had a pitiful bit of pleasure in the gratification she
imparted to Danvers, by informing her that the journey
of the day was backward to Copsley.

"If I may venture to say so, ma'am, I am very glad,"
said her maid.

"You must be prepared for the questions of lawyers,
Danvers."

"Oh, ma'am! they'll get nothing out of me, and their
wigs won't frighten me."

"It is usually their baldness that is most frightening, my
poor Danvers."

"Nor their baldness, ma'am," said the literal maid; "I
never cared for their heads, or them. I've been in a Case
before."

"Indeed!" exclaimed her mistress; and she had a chill.

Danvers mentioned a notorious Case, adding, "They got
nothing out of me."

"In my Case you will please to speak the truth," said Diana, and beheld in the looking-glass the primming of her maid's mouth. The sight shot a sting.

"Understand that there is to be no hesitation about telling the truth of what you know of me," said Diana; and the answer was, "No, ma'am."

For Danvers could remark to herself that she *knew* little, and was not a person to hesitate. She was a maid of the world, with the quality of faithfulness, by nature, to a good mistress.

Redworth's further difficulties were confined to the hiring of a conveyance for the travellers, and hot-water bottles, together with a postillion not addicted to drunkenness. He procured a posting-chariot, an ancient and musty, of a late autumnal yellow unrefreshed by paint; the only bottles to be had were Dutch schiedam. His postillion, inspected at Storling, carried the flag of habitual inebriation on his nose, and he deemed it advisable to ride the mare in accompaniment as far as Riddlehurst, notwithstanding the postillion's vows upon his honour that he was no *drinker*. The emphasis, to a gentleman acquainted with his countrymen, was not reassuring. He had hopes of enlisting a trustier fellow at Riddlehurst, but he was disappointed; and while debating upon what to do, for he shrank from leaving two women to the conduct of that inflamed trough-snout, Brisby, despatched to Storling by an afterthought of Lady Dunstane's, rushed out of the Riddlehurst inn taproom, and relieved him of the charge of the mare. He was accommodated with a seat on a stool in the chariot, "My triumphal car," said his captive. She was very amusing about her postillion; Danvers had to beg pardon for laughing. "You are happy," observed her mistress. But Redworth laughed too, and he could not boast of any happiness beyond the temporary satisfaction, nor could she who sprang the laughter boast of that little. She said to herself, in the midst of the hilarity, "Wherever I go now, in all weathers, I am perfectly naked!" And remembering her readings of a certain wonderful old quarto book in her father's library, by an eccentric old Scottish nobleman, wherein the wearing of garments and sleeping in houses is accused as the cause of human degeneracy, she

took a forced merry stand on her return to the primitive
healthful state of man and woman, and affected scorn
of our modern ways of dressing and thinking. Whence
it came that she had some of her wildest seizures of
iridescent humour. Danvers attributed the fun to her
mistress's gladness in not having pursued her bent to quit
the country. Redworth saw deeper, and was nevertheless
amazed by the airy hawk-poise and pounce-down of her
wit, as she ranged high and low, now capriciously gener-
alizing, now dropping bolt upon things of passage — the
postillion jogging from rum to gin, the rustics baconly
agape, the horse-kneed ostlers. She touched them to the
life in similes and phrases; and next she was aloft,
derisively philosophizing, but with a comic afflatus that
dispersed the sharpness of her irony in mocking laughter.
The afternoon refreshments at the inn of the county
market-town, and the English idea of public hospitality,
as to manner and the substance provided for wayfarers,
was among the themes she made memorable to him. She
spoke of everything tolerantly, just naming it in a simple
sentence, that fell with a ring and chimed: their host's
ready acquiescence in receiving orders, his contemptuous
disclaimer of stuff he did not keep, his flat indifference to
the sheep he sheared, and the phantom half-crown flicker-
ing in one eye of the anticipatory waiter; the pervading
and confounding smell of stale beer over all the apartments;
the prevalent notion of bread, butter, tea, milk, sugar, as
matter for the exercise of a native inventive genius — these
were reviewed in quips of metaphor.

"Come, we can do better at an inn or two known to me,"
said Redworth.

"Surely this is the best that can be done for us, when we
strike them with the magic wand of a postillion?" said she.

"It depends, as elsewhere, on the individuals entertaining us."

"Yet you admit that your railways are rapidly 'polishing off' the individual."

"They will spread the metropolitan idea of comfort."

"I fear they will feed us on nothing but that big word.
It booms — a curfew bell — for every poor little light that
we would read by."

Seeing their beacon-nosed postillion preparing to mount and failing in his jump, Redworth was apprehensive, and questioned the fellow concerning potation.

"Lord, sir, they call me half a horse, but I can't 'bide water," was the reply, with the assurance that he had not "taken a pailful."

Habit enabled him to gain his seat.

"It seems to us unnecessary to heap on coal when the chimney is afire; but he may know the proper course," Diana said, convulsing Danvers; and there was discernibly to Redworth, under the influence of her phrases, a likeness of the flaming "half-horse," with the animals all smoking in the frost, to a railway engine. "Your wrinkled centaur," she named the man. Of course he had to play second to her, and not unwillingly; but he reflected passingly on the instinctive push of her rich and sparkling voluble fancy to the initiative, which women do not like in a woman, and men prefer to distantly admire. English women and men feel toward the quick-witted of their species as to aliens, having the demerits of aliens — wordiness, vanity, obscurity, shallowness, an empty glitter, the sin of posturing. A quick-witted woman exerting her wit is both a foreigner and potentially a criminal. She is incandescent to a breath of rumour. It accounted for her having detractors; a heavy counterpoise to her enthusiastic friends. It might account for her husband's discontent — the reduction of him to a state of mere masculine antagonism. What is the husband of a vanward woman? He feels himself but a diminished man. The English husband of a voluble woman relapses into a dreary mute. Ah, for the choice of places! Redworth would have yielded her the loquent lead for the smallest of the privileges due to him who now rejected all, except the public scourging of her. The conviction was in his mind that the husband of this woman sought rather to punish than be rid of her. But a part of his own emotion went to form the judgement.

Furthermore, Lady Dunstane's allusion to her "enemies" made him set down her growing crop of backbiters to the trick she had of ridiculing things English. If the English do it themselves, it is in a professionally robust, a jocose, kindly way, always with a glance at the other things, great

things, they excel in; and it is done to have the credit of
doing it.   They are keen to catch an inimical tone; they
will find occasion to chastise the presumptuous individual,
unless it be the leader of a party, therefore a power; for
they respect a power.   Redworth knew their quaintnesses;
without overlooking them he winced at the acid of an irony
that seemed to spring from aversion, and regretted it, for
her sake.   He had to recollect that she was in a sharp-
strung mood, bitterly surexcited; moreover he reminded
himself of her many and memorable phrases of enthusiasm
for England — Shakespeareland, as she would sometimes
perversely term it, to sink the country in the poet.   English
fortitude, English integrity, the English disposition to do
justice to dependents, adolescent English ingenuousness,
she was always ready to laud.   Only her enthusiasm required rousing by circumstances; it was less at the brim
than her satire.   Hence she made enemies among a placable
people.

He felt that he could have helped her under happier
conditions.   The beautiful vision she had been on the
night of the Irish Ball swept before him, and he looked at
her, smiling.

"Why do you smile?" she said.

"I was thinking of Mr. Sullivan Smith."

"Ah! my dear compatriot!   And think, too, of Lord
Larrian."

She caught her breath.   Instead of recreation, the
names brought on a fit of sadness.   It deepened; she
neither smiled nor rattled any more.   She gazed across
the hedgeways at the white meadows and bare-twigged
copses showing their last leaves in the frost.

"I remember your words: 'Observation is the most
enduring of the pleasures of life;' and so I have found
it," she said.   There was a brightness along her under-
eyelids that caused him to look away.

The expected catastrophe occurred on the descent of a
cutting in the sand, where their cordial postillion at a trot
bumped the chariot against the sturdy wheels of a waggon,
which sent it reclining for support upon a beech-tree's huge
intertwisted serpent roots, amid strips of brown bracken
and pendant weeds, while he exhibited one short stump of

leg, all boot, in air. No one was hurt. Diana disengaged herself from the shoulder of Danvers, and mildly said, —

"That reminds me, I forgot to ask why we came in a chariot."

Redworth was excited on her behalf, but the broken glass had done no damage, nor had Danvers fainted. The remark was unintelligible to him, apart from the comforting it had been designed to give. He jumped out, and held a hand for them to do the same. "I never foresaw an event more positively," said he.

"And it was nothing but a back view that inspired you all the way," said Diana.

A waggoner held the horses, another assisted Redworth to right the chariot. The postillion had hastily recovered possession of his official seat, that he might as soon as possible feel himself again where he was most intelligent, and was gay in stupidity, indifferent to what happened behind him. Diana heard him counselling the waggoner as to the common sense of meeting small accidents with a cheerful soul.

"Lord !" he cried, "I been pitched a somerset in my time, and taken up for dead, and that didn't beat me !"

Disasters of the present kind could hardly affect such a veteran. But he was painfully disconcerted by Redworth's determination not to entrust the ladies any farther to his guidance. Danvers had implored for permission to walk the mile to the town, and thence take a fly to Copsley. Her mistress rather sided with the postillion, who begged them to spare him the disgrace of riding in and delivering a box at the Red Lion.

"What'll they say? And they know Arthur Dance well there," he groaned. "What ! Arthur ! chariotin' a box ! And me a better man to his work now than I been for many a long season, fit for double the journey ! A bit of a shake always braces me up. I could read a newspaper right off, small print and all. Come along, sir, and hand the ladies in."

Danvers vowed her thanks to Mr. Redworth for refusing. They walked ahead; the postillion communicated his mixture of professional and human feelings to the waggoners, and walked his horses in the rear, meditating on the weakheartedness of gentryfolk, and the means for escaping being chaffed out of his boots at the Old Red Lion, where he was to eat, drink, and sleep that night. Ladies might be fearsome after a bit of a shake; he would not have supposed it of a gentleman. He jogged himself into an arithmetic of the number of nips of liquor he had taken to soothe him on the road, in spite of the gentleman. "For some of 'em are sworn enemies of poor men, as yonder one, ne'er a doubt."

Diana enjoyed her walk beneath the lingering brown-red of the frosty November sunset, with the scent of sand-earth strong in the air.

"I had to hire a chariot because there was no two-horse carriage," said Redworth, "and I wished to reach Copsley as early as possible."

She replied, smiling, that accidents were fated. As a certain marriage had been! The comparison forced itself on her reflections.

"But this is quite an adventure," said she, reanimated by the brisker flow of her blood. "We ought really to be thankful for it, in days when nothing happens."

Redworth accused her of getting that idea from the perusal of romances.

"Yes, our lives require compression, like romances, to be interesting, and we object to the process," she said. "Real happiness is a state of dulness. When we taste it consciously it becomes mortal — a thing of the Seasons. But I like my walk. How long these November sunsets burn, and what hues they have! There is a scientific reason, only don't tell it me. Now I understand why you always used to choose your holidays in November."

She thrilled him with her friendly recollection of his customs.

"As to happiness, the looking forward is happiness," he remarked.

"Oh, the looking back! back!" she cried.

"Forward! that is life."

"And backward, death, if you will; and still it is happiness. Death, and our postillion!"

"Ay; I wonder why the fellow hangs to the rear," said Redworth, turning about.

"It's his cunning strategy, poor creature, so that he may be thought to have delivered us at the head of the town, for us to make a purchase or two, if we go to the inn on foot," said Diana. "We'll let the manœuvre succeed."

Redworth declared that she had a head for everything, and she was flattered to hear him.

So passing from the southern into the western road, they saw the town-lights beneath an umber sky burning out sombrely over the woods of Copsley, and entered the town, the postillion following.

CHAPTER XII

BETWEEN EMMA AND DIANA

DIANA was in the arms of her friend at a late hour of the evening, and Danvers breathed the amiable atmosphere of footmen once more, professing herself perished. This maid of the world, who could endure hardships and loss of society for the mistress to whom she was attached, no sooner saw herself surrounded by the comforts befitting her station, than she indulged in the luxury of a wailful dejectedness, the better to appreciate them. She was unaffectedly astonished to find her outcries against the cold and the journeyings to and fro interpreted as a serving-woman's muffled comments on her mistress's behaviour. Lady Dunstane's maid Bartlett, and Mrs. Bridges the housekeeper, and Foster the butler, contrived to let her know that they could speak an if they would; and they expressed their pity of her to assist her to begin the speaking. She bowed in acceptance of Foster's offer of a glass of wine after supper, but treated him and the other two immediately as though they had been interrogating bigwigs.

"They wormed nothing out of me," she said to her mistress at night, undressing her. "But what a set they are! They've got such comfortable places, they've all their days and hours for talk of the doings of their superiors. They read the vilest of those town papers, and they put their two and two together of what is happening in and about. And not one of the footmen thinks of staying, because it's so dull; and they and the maids object — did one ever hear? — to the three uppers retiring, when they've done dining, to the private room to dessert."

"That is the custom?" observed her mistress.

"Foster carries the decanter, ma'am, and Mrs. Bridges the biscuits, and Bartlett the plate of fruit, and they march out in order."

"The man at the head of the procession, probably."

"Oh, yes. And the others, though they have everything except the wine and dessert, don't like it. When I was here last they were new, and had n't a word against it. Now they say it's invidious! Lady Dunstane will be left without an under-servant at Copsley soon. I was asked about your boxes, ma'am, and the moment I said they were at Dover, that instant all three peeped. They let out a mouse to me. They do love to talk!"

Her mistress could have added, "And you too, my good Danvers!" trustworthy though she knew the creature to be in the main.

"Now go, and be sure you have bedclothes enough before you drop asleep," she said; and Danvers directed her steps to gossip with Bartlett.

Diana wrapped herself in a dressing-gown Lady Dunstane had sent her, and sat by the fire, thinking of the powder of tattle stored in servants' halls to explode beneath her: and but for her choice of roads she might have been among strangers. The liking of strangers best is a curious exemplification of innocence.

"Yes, I was in a muse," she said, raising her head to Emma, whom she expected and sat armed to meet, unaccountably iron-nerved. "I was questioning whether I could be quite as blameless as I fancy, if I sit and shiver to be in England. You will tell me I have taken the right road. I doubt it. But the road is taken, and here I am. But any road that leads me to you is homeward, my darling!" She tried to melt, determining to be at least open with her.

"I have not praised you enough for coming," said Emma, when they had embraced again.

"Praise a little your 'truest friend of women.' Your letter gave the tug. I might have resisted it."

"He came straight from heaven! But, cruel Tony! where is your love?"

"It is unequal to yours, dear, I see. I could have wrestled with anything abstract and distant, from being certain — But here I am."

"But, my own dear girl, you never could have allowed this infamous charge to be undefended?"

"I think so. I've an odd apathy as to my character; rather like death, when one dreams of flying the soul. What does it matter? I should have left the flies and wasps to worry a corpse. And then — good-bye gentility! I should have worked for my bread. I had thoughts of America. I fancy I can write; and Americans, one hears, are gentle to women."

"Ah, Tony! there's the looking back. And, of all women, you!"

"Or else, dear — well, perhaps once on foreign soil, in a different air, I might — might have looked back, and seen my whole self, not shattered, as I feel it now, and come home again compassionate to the poor persecuted animal to defend her. Perhaps that was what I was running away for. I fled on the instinct, often a good thing to trust."

"I *saw* you at The Crossways."

"I remembered I had the dread that you would, though I did not imagine you would reach me so swiftly. My going there was an instinct, too. I suppose we are all instinct when we have the world at our heels. Forgive me if I generalize without any longer the right to be included in the common human sum. 'Pariah' and 'taboo' are words we borrow from barbarous tribes; they stick to me."

"My Tony, you look as bright as ever, and you speak despairingly."

"Call me enigma. I am that to myself, Emmy."

"You are not quite yourself to your friend."

"Since the blow I have been bewildered; I see nothing

upright. It came on me suddenly; stunned me. A bolt
out of a clear sky, as they say. He spared me a scene.
There had been threats, and yet the sky was clear, or
seemed. When we have a man for arbiter, he is our
sky."

Emma pressed her Tony's unresponsive hand, feeling
strangely that her friend ebbed from her.

"Has he . . . to mislead him?" she said, colouring at
the breach in the question.

"Proofs? He has the proofs he supposes."

"Not to justify suspicion?"

"He broke open my desk and took my letters."

"Horrible! But the letters?" Emma shook with a
nervous revulsion.

"You might read them."

"Basest of men! That is the unpardonable cowardice!"
exclaimed Emma.

"The world will read them, dear," said Diana, and
struck herself to ice.

She broke from the bitter frigidity in fury. "They are
letters — none very long — sometimes two short sentences
— he wrote at any spare moment. On my honour, as a
woman, I feel for him most. The letters — I would bear
any accusation rather than that exposure. Letters of a
man of his age to a young woman he rates too highly!
The world reads them. Do you hear it saying it could
have excused her for that fiddle-faddle with a younger —
a young lover? And had I thought of a lover! . . . I
had no thought of loving or being loved. I confess I was
flattered. To you, Emma, I will confess. . . . You see
the public ridicule! — and half his age, he and I would
have appeared a romantic couple! Confess, I said. Well,
dear, the stake is lighted for a trial of its effect on me.
It is this: he was never a dishonourable friend; but men
appear to be capable of friendship with women only for as
long as we keep out of pulling distance of that line where
friendship ceases. *They* may step on it; *we* must hold
back a league. I have learnt it. You will judge whether
he disrespects me. As for him, he is a man; at his worst,
not one of the worst; at his best, better than very many.
There, now, Emma, you have me stripped and burning;

there is my full confession. Except for this — yes, one
thing further — that I do rage at the ridicule, and could
choose, but for you, to have given the world cause to revile
me, or think me romantic. Something or somebody to
suffer for would really be agreeable. It is a singular fact,
I have not known what this love is, that they talk about.
And behold me marched into Smithfield! — society's here-
tic, if you please. I must own I think it hard."

Emma chafed her cold hand softly.

"It is hard; I understand it," she murmured. "And is
your Sunday visit to us in the list of offences?"

"An item."

"You gave me a happy day."

"Then it counts for me in heaven."

"He set spies on you?"

"So we may presume."

Emma went through a sphere of tenuous reflections in
a flash.

"He will rue it. Perhaps now . . . he may now be
regretting his wretched frenzy. And Tony could pardon;
she has the power of pardoning in her heart."

"Oh! certainly, dear. But tell me why it is you speak
to-night rather unlike the sedate, philosophical Emma; in
a tone — well, tolerably sentimental?"

"I am unaware of it," said Emma, who could have retorted with a like reproach. "I am anxious, I will not
say at present for your happiness, for your peace; and I
have a hope that possibly a timely word from some friend
— Lukin or another — might induce him to consider."

"To pardon *me*, do you mean?" cried Diana, flushing
sternly.

"Not pardon. Suppose a case of faults on both sides."

"You address a faulty person, my dear. But do you
know that you are hinting at a reconcilement?"

"Might it not be?"

"Open your eyes to what it involves. I trust I can
pardon. Let him go his ways, do his darkest, or repent.
But return to the roof of the ' basest of men,' who was
guilty of ' the unpardonable cowardice '? You expect me
to be superhuman. When I consent to that, I shall be out
of my woman's skin, which he has branded. Go back to

him!" She was taken with a shudder of head and limbs.
"No; I really have the power of pardoning, and I am
bound to; for among my debts to him, this present exemption, that is like liberty dragging a chain, or, say, an
escaped felon wearing his manacles, should count. I am
sensible of my obligation. The price I pay for it is an
immovable patch — attractive to male idiots, I have heard,
and a mark of scorn to females. Between the two the
remainder of my days will be lively. 'Out, out, damned
spot!' But it will not. And not on the hand — on the
forehead! We'll talk of it no longer. I have sent a note,
with an enclosure, to my lawyers. I sell The Crossways,
if I have the married woman's right to any scrap of property, for money to scatter fees."

"My purse, dear Tony!" exclaimed Emma. "My
house! You will stay with me? Why do you shake your
head? With me you are safe." She spied at the shadows
in her friend's face. "Ever since your marriage, Tony,
you have been strange in your trick of refusing to stay
with me. And you and I made our friendship the pledge
of a belief in eternity! We vowed it. Come, I do talk
sentimentally, but my heart is in it. I beg you — all the
reasons are with me — to make my house your home. You
will. You know I am rather lonely."

Diana struggled to keep her resolution from being broken
by tenderness. And doubtless poor Sir Lukin had learnt
his lesson; still, her defensive instincts could never quite
slumber under his roof; not because of any further fear
that they would have to be summoned; it was chiefly owing
to the consequences of his treacherous foolishness. For
this half-home with her friend thenceforward denied to
her, she had accepted a protector, called husband — rashly,
past credence, in the retrospect; but it had been her pro-
pelling motive; and the loathings roused by her marriage
helped to sicken her at the idea of a lengthened stay where
she had suffered the shock precipitating her to an act of
insanity.

"I do not forget you were an heiress, Emmy, and I will
come to you if I need money to keep my head up. As for
staying, two reasons are against it. If I am to fight my
battle, I must be seen; I must go about — wherever I am

received. So my field is London. That is obvious. And I shall rest better in a house where my story is not known."

Two or three questions ensued. Diana had to fortify her fictitious objection by alluding to her maid's prattle of the household below; and she excused the hapless, overfed, idle people of those regions.

To Emma it seemed a not unnatural sensitiveness. She came to a settled resolve in her thoughts, as she said, "They want a change. London is their element."

Feeling that she deceived this true heart, however lightly and necessarily, Diana warmed to her, forgiving her at last for having netted and dragged her back to front the enemy; an imposition of horrors, of which the scene and the travelling with Redworth, the talking of her case with her most intimate friend as well, had been a distempering foretaste.

They stood up and kissed, parting for the night.

An odd world, where for the sin we have not participated in we must fib and continue fibbing, she reflected. She did not entirely cheat her clearer mind, for she perceived that her step in flight had been urged both by a weak despondency and a blind desperation; also that the world of a fluid civilization is perforce artificial. But her mind was in the background of her fevered senses, and when she looked in the glass and mused on uttering the word, "Liar!" to the lovely image, her senses were refreshed, her mind somewhat relieved, the face appeared so sovereignly defiant of abasement.

Thus did a nature distraught by pain obtain some short lull of repose. Thus, moreover, by closely reading herself, whom she scourged to excess that she might in justice be comforted, she gathered an increasing knowledge of our human constitution, and stored matter for the brain.

CHAPTER XIII

TOUCHING THE FIRST DAYS OF HER PROBATION

THE result of her sleeping was, that Diana's humour, locked up over-night, insisted on an excursion, as she lay with half-buried head and open eyelids, thinking of the firm of lawyers she had to see; and to whom, and to the legal profession generally, she would be, under outward courtesies, nothing other than "the woman Warwick." She pursued the woman Warwick unmercifully through a series of interviews with her decorous and crudely-minded defenders; accurately perusing them behind their senior staidness. Her scorching sensitiveness sharpened her intelligence in regard to the estimate of discarded wives entertained by men of business and plain men of the world, and she drove the woman Warwick down their ranks, amazed by the vision of a puppet so unlike to herself in reality, though identical in situation. That woman, reciting her side of the case, gained a gradual resemblance to Danvers; she spoke primly; perpetually the creature aired her handkerchief; she was bent on softening those sugar-loaves, the hard business-men applying to her for facts. Facts were treated as unworthy of her; mere stuff of the dustheap, mutton-bones, old shoes; she swam above them in a cocoon of her spinning, sylphidine, unseizable; and between perplexing and mollifying the slaves of facts, she saw them at their heels, a tearful fry, abjectly imitative of her melodramatic performances. The spectacle was presented of a band of legal gentlemen vociferating mightily for swords and the onset, like the Austrian empress's Magyars, to vindicate her just and holy cause. Our Law-courts failing, they threatened Parliament, and for a last resort, the country! We are not going to be the woman Warwick without a stir, my brethren.

Emma, an early riser that morning, for the purpose of a private consultation with Mr. Redworth, found her lying placidly wakeful, to judge by appearances.

"You have not slept, my dear child?"

"Perfectly," said Diana, giving her hand and offering the lips. "I'm only having a warm morning bath in bed," she added, in explanation of a chill moisture that the touch of her exposed skin betrayed; for whatever the fun of the woman Warwick, there had been sympathetic feminine horrors in the frame of the sentient woman.

Emma fancied she kissed a quiet sufferer. A few remarks very soon set her wildly laughing. Both were laughing when Danvers entered the room, rather guilty, being late; and the sight of the prim-visaged maid she had been driving among the lawyers kindled Diana's comic imagination to such a pitch that she ran riot in drolleries, carrying her friend headlong on the tide.

"I have not laughed so much since you were married," said Emma.

"Nor I, dear; — proving that the bar to it was the ceremony," said Diana.

She promised to remain at Copsley three days. "Then for the campaign in Mr. Redworth's metropolis. I wonder whether I may ask him to get me lodgings: a sitting-room and two bedrooms. The Crossways has a board up for letting. I should prefer to be my own tenant; only it would give me a hundred pounds more to get a substitute's money. I should like to be at work writing instantly. Ink is my opium, and the pen my nigger, and he must dig up gold for me. It is written. Danvers, you can make ready to dress me when I ring."

Emma helped the beautiful woman to her dressing-gown and the step from her bed. She had her thoughts, and went down to Redworth at the breakfast-table, marvelling that any husband other than a madman could cast such a jewel away. The material loveliness eclipses intellectual qualities in such reflections.

"He must be mad," she said, compelled to disburden herself in a congenial atmosphere; which, however, she infrigidated by her overflow of exclamatory wonderment — a curtain that shook voluminous folds, luring Redworth to dreams of the treasure forfeited. He became rigidly practical.

"Provision will have to be made for her. Lukin must see Mr. Warwick. She will do wisely to stay with friends in town, mix in company. Women are the best allies for such cases. Who are her solicitors?"

"They are mine: Braddock, Thorpe, and Simnel."

"A good firm. She is in safe hands with them. I dare say they may come to an arrangement."

"I should wish it. She will never consent."

Redworth shrugged. A woman's "never" fell far short of outstripping the sturdy pedestrian Time, to his mind.

Diana saw him drive off to catch the coach in the valley, regulated to meet the train, and much though she liked him, she was not sorry that he had gone. She felt the better clad for it. She would have rejoiced to witness the departure on wings of all her friends, except Emma, to whom her coldness overnight had bound her anew warmly in contrition. And yet her friends were well-beloved by her; but her emotions were distraught.

Emma told her that Mr. Redworth had undertaken to hire a suite of convenient rooms, and to these she looked forward, the nest among strangers, where she could begin to write, earning bread: an idea that, with the pride of independence, conjured the pleasant morning smell of a bakery about her.

She passed three peaceable days at Copsley, at war only with the luxury of the house. On the fourth, a letter to Lady Dunstane from Redworth gave the address of the best lodgings he could find, and Diana started for London.

She had during a couple of weeks, besides the first fresh exercising of her pen, as well as the severe gratification of economy, a savage exultation in passing through the streets on foot and unknown. Save for the plunges into the office of her solicitors, she could seem to herself a woman who had never submitted to the yoke. What a pleasure it was, after finishing a number of pages, to start Eastward toward the lawyer-regions, full of imaginary cropping incidents, and from that churchyard Westward, against smoky sunsets, or in welcome fogs, an atom of the crowd! She had an affection for the crowd. They clothed her. She laughed at the gloomy forebodings of Danvers concerning the perils environing ladies in the streets after dark alone. The lights in the streets after dark, and the quick running of her blood, combined to strike sparks of fancy and inspirit the task of composition at night. This new, strange, solitary life, cut off from her adulatory society, both by the shock that made the abyss and by the utter foreignness, threw her in upon her natural forces, recasting her, and thinning away her memory of her past days, excepting girlhood, into the remote. She lived with her girlhood as with a simple little sister. They were two in one, and she corrected the dreams of the younger, protected and counselled her very sagely, advising her to love Truth and look always to Reality for her refreshment. She was ready to say, that no habitable spot on our planet was healthier and pleasanter than London. As to the perils haunting the head of Danvers, her experiences assured her of a perfect immunity from them; and the maligned thoroughfares of a great city, she was ready to affirm, contrasted favourably with certain hospitable halls.

The long-suffering Fates permitted her for a term to enjoy the generous delusion. Subsequently a sweet surprise alleviated the shock she had sustained. Emma Dunstane's carriage was at her door, and Emma entered her sitting-room, to tell her of having hired a house in the neighbourhood, looking on the park. She begged to have her for guest, sorrowfully anticipating the refusal. At least they were to be near one another.

"You really like this life in lodgings?" asked Emma, to whom the stiff furniture and narrow apartments were a dreariness, the miserably small fire of the sitting-room an aspect of cheerless winter.

"I do," said Diana; "yes," she added with some reserve, and smiled at her damped enthusiasm, "I can eat when I like, walk, work — and I am working! My legs and my pen demand it. Let me be independent! Besides, I begin to learn something of the bigger world outside the one I know, and I crush my mincing tastes. In return for that, I get a sense of strength I had not when I was a drawing-room exotic. Much is repulsive. But I am taken with a passion for reality."

They spoke of the lawyers, and the calculated period of the trial; of the husband too, and his inciting belief in the falseness of his wife. "That is his excuse," Diana said, her closed mouth meditatively dimpling the corners over thoughts of his grounds for fury. He had them, though none for the incriminating charge. The Sphinx mouth of the married woman at war and at bay must be left unriddled. She and the law differed in their interpretation of the dues of wedlock.

But matters referring to her case were secondary with Diana beside the importance of her storing impressions. Her mind required to hunger for something, and this Reality which frequently she was forced to loathe, she forced herself proudly to accept, despite her youthfulness. Her philosophy swallowed it in the lump, as the great serpent his meal; she hoped to digest it sleeping likewise. Her visits of curiosity to the Law Courts, where she stood spying and listening behind a veil, gave her a great deal of tough substance to digest. There she watched the process of the tortures to be applied to herself, and hardened her senses for the ordeal. She saw there the ribbed and shanked old skeleton world on which our fair fleshly is moulded. After all, your Fool's Paradise is not a garden to grow in. Charon's ferry-boat is not thicker with phantoms. They do not live in mind or soul. Chiefly women people it: a certain class of limp men; women for the most part: they are sown there. And put their garden under the magnifying glass of intimacy, what do we behold? A world not better than the world it curtains, only foolisher.

Her conversations with Lady Dunstane brought her at last to the point of her damped enthusiasm. She related an incident or two occurring in her career of independence, and they discussed our state of civilization plainly and gravely, save for the laughing peals her phrases occasionally provoked; as when she named the intruders and disturbers of solitarily-faring ladies, "Cupid's footpads." Her humour was created to swim on waters where a prescribed and cultivated prudery should pretend to be drowning.

"I was getting an exalted idea of English gentlemen, Emmy. 'Rich and rare were the gems she wore.' I was ready to vow that one might traverse the larger island similarly respected. I praised their chivalry. I thought it a privilege to live in such a land. I cannot describe to you how delightful it was to me to walk out and home generally protected. I might have been seriously annoyed but that one of the clerks — 'articled,' he called himself — of our lawyers happened to be by. He offered to guard me, and was amusing with his modest tiptoe air. No, I trust to the English common man more than ever. He is a man of honour. I am convinced he is matchless in any other country, except Ireland. The English gentleman trades on his reputation."

He was condemned by an afflicted delicacy, the sharpest of critical tribunals.

Emma bade her not to be too sweeping from a bad example.

"It is not a single one," said Diana. "What vexes me and frets me is, that I must be a prisoner, or allow Danvers to mount guard. And I can't see the end of it. And Danvers is no magician. She seems to know her country-men, though. She warded one of them off, by saying to me: 'This is the crossing, *my lady*.' He fled."

Lady Dunstane affixed the popular title to the latter kind of gentleman. She was irritated on her friend's behalf, and against the worrying of her sisterhood, thinking in her heart, nevertheless, that the passing of a face and figure like Diana's might inspire honourable emotions, pitiable for being hapless.

"If you were with me, dear, you would have none of these annoyances," she said, pleading forlornly.

Diana smiled to herself. "No! I should relapse into softness. This life exactly suits my present temper. My landlady is respectful and attentive; the little housemaid is a willing slave; Danvers does not despise them pugna-ciously; they make a home for me, and I am learning daily. Do you know, the less ignorant I become, the more con-siderate I am for the ignorance of others — I love them for it." She squeezed Emma's hand with more meaning than her friend apprehended. "So I win my advantage from the trifles I have to endure. They are really trifles, and I should once have thought them mountains!"

For the moment Diana stipulated that she might not have to encounter friends or others at Lady Dunstane's dinner-table, and the season not being favourable to those gatherings planned by Lady Dunstane in her project of winning sup-

porters, there was a respite, during which Sir Lukin worked
manfully at his three Clubs to vindicate Diana's name from
the hummers and hawers, gaining half a dozen hot adherents,
and a body of lukewarm, sufficiently stirred to be desirous
to see the lady.   He worked with true champion zeal,
although an interview granted him by the husband settled
his opinion as to any possibility of the two ever coming to
terms.   Also it struck him that if he by misadventure had
been a woman and the wife of such a fellow, by Jove ! . . .
— his apostrophe to the father of the gods of pagandom
signifying the amount of matter Warwick would have had
reason to complain of in earnest.   By ricochet his military
mind rebounded from his knowledge of himself to an ardent
faith in Mrs. Warwick's innocence ; for, as there was no
resemblance between them, there must, he deduced, be a
difference in their capacity for enduring the perpetual
company of a prig, a stick, a petrified poser.   Moreover,
the novel act of advocacy, and the nature of the advocacy,
had effect on him.   And then he recalled the scene in the
winter beech-woods, and Diana's wild-deer eyes ; her perfect
generosity to a traitor and fool.   How could he have
doubted her ?   Glimpses of the corrupting cause for it
partly penetrated his density : a conqueror of ladies, in mid
career, doubts them all.   Of course he had meant no harm,
nothing worse than some pretty philandering with the loveliest woman of her time.   And, by Jove ! it was worth the
rebuff to behold the Beauty in her wrath.

The reflections of Lothario, however much tending tardily
to do justice to a particular lady, cannot terminate wholesomely.   But he became a gallant partisan.   His portrayal
of Mr. Warwick to his wife and his friends was fine caricature.   " The fellow had his hand up at my first word —
stood like a sentinel under inspection. ' Understand, Sir
Lukin, that I receive you simply as an acquaintance.   As
an intermediary, permit me to state that you are taking
superfluous trouble.   The case must proceed.   It is final.
She is at liberty, in the meantime, to draw on my bankers
for the provision she may need, at the rate of five hundred
pounds per annum.'   He spoke of ' the lady now bearing my
name.'   He was within an inch of saying ' dishonouring.'   I
swear I heard the ' dis,' and he caught himself up.   He ' again

declined any attempt towards reconciliation.' It could
'only be founded on evasion of the truth to be made patent
on the day of trial.' Half his talk was lawyers' lingo.
The fellow's teeth looked like frost. If Lot's wife had a
brother, his name's Warwick. How Diana Merion, who
could have had the pick of the best of us, ever came to
marry a fellow like that, passes my comprehension, queer
creatures as women are ! He can ride ; that's about all he
can do. I told him Mrs. Warwick had no thought of reconciliation. 'Then, Sir Lukin, you will perceive that we
have no standpoint for a discussion.' I told him the point
was, for a man of honour not to drag his wife before the
public, as he had no case to stand on — less than nothing.
You should have seen the fellow's face. He shot a sneer
up to his eyelids, and flung his head back. So I said,
'Good day.' He marches me to the door, 'with his compliments to Lady Dunstane.' I could have floored him for
that. Bless my soul, what fellows the world is made of,
when here's a man, calling himself a gentleman, who, just
because he gets in a rage with his wife for one thing or
another — and past all competition the handsomest woman
of her day, and the cleverest, the nicest, the best of the
whole boiling — has her out for a public horsewhipping,
and sets all the idiots of the kingdom against her! I tried
to reason with him. He made as if he were going to sleep
standing."

Sir Lukin gratified Lady Dunstane by his honest championship of Diana. And now, in his altered mood (the
thrice indebted rogue was just cloudily conscious of a desire
to propitiate his dear wife by serving her friend), he began
a crusade against the scandal-newspapers, going with an
Irish military comrade straight to the editorial offices, and
leaving his card and a warning that the chastisement for
print of the name of the lady in their columns would be
personal and condign. Captain Carew Mahony, albeit unacquainted with Mrs. Warwick, had espoused her cause.
She was a woman, she was an Irishwoman, she was a beautiful woman. She had, therefore, three positive claims on
him as a soldier and a man. Other Irish gentlemen, animated by the same swelling degrees, were awaking to the
intimation that they might be wanted. Some words were

dropped here and there by General Lord Larrian : he regretted his age and infirmities. A goodly regiment for a
bodyguard might have been selected to protect her steps in
the public streets, when it was bruited that the General had
sent her a present of his great Newfoundland dog, Leander,
to attend on her and impose a required respect. But as it
chanced that her address was unknown to the volunteer
constabulary, they had to assuage their ardour by thinking
the dog luckier than they.

The report of the dog was a fact. He arrived one morning at Diana's lodgings, with a soldier to lead him, and a
card to introduce : the Hercules of dogs, a very ideal of the
species, toweringly big, benevolent, reputed a rescuer of
lives, disdainful of dog-fighting, devoted to his guardian's
office, with a majestic paw to give and the noblest satisfaction in receiving caresses ever expressed by mortal male
enfolded about the head, kissed, patted, hugged, snuggled,
informed that he was his new mistress's one love and
darling.

She despatched a thrilling note of thanks to Lord Larrian,
sure of her touch upon an Irish heart.

The dog Leander soon responded to the attachment of a
mistress enamoured of him. "He is my husband," she said
to Emma, and started a tear in the eyes of her smiling
friend ; "he promises to trust me, and never to have the
law of me, and to love my friends as his own ; so we are
certain to agree." In rain, snow, sunshine, through the
parks and the streets, he was the shadow of Diana, commanding, on the whole, apart from some desperate attempts
to make him serve as introducer, a civilized behaviour in the
legions of Cupid's footpads. But he helped, innocently
enough, to create an enemy.

CHAPTER XIV

GIVING GLIMPSES OF DIANA UNDER HER CLOUD BEFORE
THE WORLD AND OF HER FURTHER APPRENTICESHIP

As the day of her trial became more closely calculable,
Diana's anticipated alarms receded with the deadening of
her heart to meet the shock. She fancied she had put on
proof-armour, unconscious that it was the turning of the
inward flutterer to steel which supplied her cuirass and
shield. The necessity to brave society, in the character of
honest Defendant, caused but a momentary twitch of the
nerves. Her heart beat regularly, like a serviceable clock ;
none of her faculties abandoned her save songfulness, and
none belied her, excepting a disposition to tartness almost
venomous in the sarcastic shafts she let fly at friends inter-
ceding with Mr. Warwick to spare his wife, when she had
determined to be tried.   A strange fit of childishness overcame her powers of thinking, and was betrayed in her
manner of speaking, though to herself her dwindled humour
allowed her to appear the towering Britomart. She pouted
contemptuously on hearing that a Mr. Sullivan Smith (a
remotely recollected figure) had besought Mr. Warwick for
an interview, and gained it, by stratagem, " to bring the
man to his senses :" but an ultra-Irishman did not compromise her battle-front, as the busybody supplications of a
personal friend like Mr. Redworth did ; and that the latter,
without consulting her, should be " one of the plaintive crew
whining about the heels of the Plaintiff for a mercy she disdained and rejected " was bitter to her taste.

" He does not see that unless I go through the fire there
is no justification for this wretched character of mine ! "
she exclaimed.   Truce, treaty, withdrawal, signified publicly pardon, not exoneration by any means ; and now that
she was in armour she had no dread of the public.   So she
said.   Redworth's being then engaged upon the canvass of
a borough, added to the absurdity of his meddling with the
dilemmas of a woman.   " Dear me, Emma ! think of stepping aside from the parliamentary road to entreat a husband

to relent, and arrange the domestic alliance of a contrary couple! Quixotry is agreeable reading, a silly performance." Lady Dunstane pleaded his friendship. She had to quit the field where such darts were showering.

The first dinner-party was aristocratic, easy to encounter. Lord and Lady Crane, Lady Pennon, Lord and Lady Esquart, Lord Larrian, Mr. and Mrs. Montvert of Halford Manor, Lady Singleby, Sir Walter Capperston: friends, admirers of Diana; patrons, in the phrase of the time, of her father, were the guests. Lady Pennon expected to be amused, and was gratified, for Diana had only to open her mouth to set the great lady laughing. She petitioned to have Mrs. Warwick at her table that day week, because the marquis was dying to make her acquaintance, and begged to have all her sayings repeated to him; vowed she must be salt in the desert. "And remember, I back you through thick and thin," said Lady Pennon. To which Diana replied: "If I am salt in the desert, you are the spring;" and the old lady protested she must put that down for her book. The witty Mrs. Warwick, of whom wit was expected, had many incitements to be guilty of cheap wit; and the beautiful Mrs. Warwick, being able to pass anything she uttered, gave good and bad alike, under the impulsion to give out something, that the stripped and shivering Mrs. Warwick might find a cover in applause. She discovered the social uses of cheap wit; she laid ambushes for anecdotes, a telling form of it among a people of no conversational interlocution, especially in the circles depending for dialogue upon perpetual fresh supplies of scandal; which have plentiful crops, yet not sufficient. The old dinner and supper tables at The Crossways furnished her with an abundant store; and recollection failing, she invented. Irish anecdotes are always popular in England, as promoting, besides the wholesome shake of the sides, a kindly sense of superiority. Anecdotes also are portable, unlike the lightning flash, which will not go into the pocket; they can be carried home, they are disbursable at other tables. These were Diana's weapons. She was perforce the actress of her part. In happier times, when light of heart and natural, her vogue had not been so enrapturing. Doubtless Cleopatra in her simple Egyptian uniform would hardly have won such plaudits as her stress of barbaric Oriental splendours evoked for her on the swan and serpent Nile-barge — not from posterity at least. It is a terrible decree, that all must act who would prevail; and the more extended the audience, the greater need for the mask and buskin.

From Lady Pennon's table Diana passed to Lady Crane's, Lady Esquart's, Lady Singleby's, the Duchess of Raby's, warmly clad in the admiration she excited. She appeared at Princess Thérèse Paryli's first ball of the season, and had her circle, not of worshippers only. She did not dance. The princess, a fair Austrian, benevolent to her sisterhood, an admirer of Diana's contrasting complexion, would have had her dance once in a quadrille of her forming, but yielded to the mute expression of the refusal. Wherever Mrs. Warwick went, her arts of charming were addressed to the women. Men may be counted on for falling bowled over by a handsome face and pointed tongue; women require some wooing from their ensphered and charioted sister, particularly if she is clouded; and old women — excellent buttresses — must be suavely courted. Now, to woo the swimming matron and court the settled dowager, she had to win forgiveness for her beauty; and this was done, easily done, by forbearing to angle with it in the press of nibblers. They ranged about her, individually unnoticed. Seeming unaware of its effect where it kindled, she smote a number of musical female chords, compassion among them. A general grave affability of her eyes and smiles was taken for quiet pleasure in the scene. Her fitful intentness of look when conversing with the older ladies told of the mind within at work upon what they said, and she was careful that plain dialogue should make her comprehensible to them. Nature taught her these arts, through which her wit became extolled entirely on the strength of her reputation, and her beauty did her service by never taking aim abroad. They are the woman's arts of self-defence, as legitimately and honourably hers as the manful use of the fists with a coarser sex. If it had not been nature that taught her the practice of them in extremity, the sagacious dowagers would have seen brazenness rather than innocence — or an excusable indiscretion — in the part she was performing. They are not lightly duped by one of their sex. Few tasks are more difficult than for a young woman under a cloud to hoodwink old women of the world. They are the prey of financiers; but Time has presented them a magic ancient glass to scan their sex in.

At Princess Paryli's Ball two young men of singular elegance were observed by Diana, little though she concentered her attention on any figures of the groups. She had the woman's faculty (transiently bestowed by perfervid jealousy upon men) of distinguishing minutely in the calmest of indifferent glances. She could see without looking; and when her eyes were wide they had not to dwell to be detective. It did not escape her that the Englishman of the two hurried for the chance of an introduction, nor that he suddenly, after putting a question to a man beside him, retired. She spoke of them to Emma as they drove home. "The princess's partner in the first quadrille . . . Hungarian, I suppose? He was like a Tartar modelled by a Greek: supple as the Scythian's bow, braced as the string! He has the air of a born horseman, and valses perfectly. I won't say he was handsomer than a young Englishman there, but he had the advantage of soldierly training. How different is that quick springy figure from our young men's lounging style! It comes of military exercise and discipline."

"That was Count Jochany, a cousin of the princess, and a cavalry officer," said Emma. "You don't know the other? I am sure the one you mean must be Percy Dacier."

His retiring was explained: the Hon. Percy Dacier was the nephew of Lord Dannisburgh, often extolled to her as the promising youngster of his day, with the reserve that he wasted his youth: for the young gentleman was decorous and studious; ambitious, according to report; a politician taking to politics much too seriously and exclusively to suit his uncle's pattern for the early period of life. Uncle and nephew went their separate ways, rarely meeting, though their exchange of esteem was cordial.

Thinking over his abrupt retirement from the crowded semicircle, Diana felt her position pinch her, she knew not why.

Lady Dunstane was as indefatigable by day as by night

in the business of acting goddess to her beloved Tony, whom she assured that the service, instead of exhausting, gave her such healthfulness as she had imagined herself to have lost for ever. The word was passed, and invitations poured in to choice conversational breakfasts, private afternoon concerts, all the humming season's assemblies. Mr. Warwick's treatment of his wife was taken by implication for lunatic; wherever she was heard or seen, he had no case; a jury of some hundreds of both sexes, ready to be sworn, pronounced against him. Only the personal enemies of the lord in the suit presumed to doubt, and they exercised the discretion of a minority.

But there is an upper middle class below the aristocratic, boasting an aristocracy of morals, and eminently persuasive of public opinion, if not commanding it. Previous to the relaxation, by amendment, of a certain legal process, this class was held to represent the austerity of the country. At present a relaxed austerity is represented; and still the bulk of the members are of fair repute, though not quite on the level of their pretensions. They were then, while more sharply divided from the titular superiors they are socially absorbing, very powerful to brand a woman's character, whatever her rank might be; having innumerable agencies and avenues for that high purpose, to say nothing of the printing-press. Lady Dunstane's anxiety to draw them over to the cause of her friend set her thinking of the influential Mrs. Cramborne Wathin, with whom she was distantly connected; the wife of a potent serjeant-at-law fast mounting to the Bench and knighthood; the centre of a circle, and not strangely that, despite her deficiency in the arts and graces, for she had wealth and a cook, a husband proud of his wine-cellar, and the ambition to rule; all the rewards, together with the expectations, of the virtuous. She was a lady of incisive features bound in stale parchment. Complexion she had none, but she had spotlessness of skin, and sons and daughters just resembling her, like cheaper editions of a precious quarto of a perished type. You discerned the imitation of the type, you acknowledged the inferior compositor. Mr. Cramborne Wathin was by birth of a grade beneath his wife; he sprang (behind a curtain of horror) from tradesmen. The

Bench was in designation for him to wash out the stain, but his children suffered in large hands and feet, short legs, excess of bone, prominences misplaced. Their mother inspired them carefully with the religion she opposed to the pretensions of a nobler blood, while instilling into them that the blood they drew from her was territorial, far above the vulgar. Her appearance and her principles fitted her to stand for the Puritan rich of the period, emerging by the aid of an extending wealth into luxurious worldliness, and retaining the maxims of their forefathers for the discipline of the poor and erring.

Lady Dunstane called on her, ostensibly to let her know she had taken a house in town for the season, and in the course of the chat Mrs. Cramborne Wathin was invited to dinner. " You will meet my dear friend, Mrs. Warwick," she said, and the reply was : " Oh, I have heard of her."

The formal consultation with Mr. Cramborne Wathin ended in an agreement to accept Lady Dunstane's kind invitation.

Considering her husband's plenitude of old legal anecdotes, and her own diligent perusal of the funny publications of the day, that she might be on the level of the wits and celebrities she entertained, Mrs. Cramborne Wathin had a right to expect the leading share in the conversation to which she was accustomed. Every honour was paid to them ; they met aristocracy in the persons of Lord Larrian, of Lady Rockden, Colonel Purlby, the Pettigrews, but neither of them held the table for a moment ; the topics flew, and were no sooner up than down ; they were unable to get a shot. They had to eat in silence, occasionally grinning, because a woman labouring under a stigma would rattle-rattle, as if the laughter of the company were her due, and decency beneath her notice. Some one alluded to a dog of Mrs. Warwick's, whereupon she trips out a story of her dog's amazing intelligence.

" And pray," said Mrs. Cramborne Wathin across the table, merely to slip in a word, " what is the name of this wonderful dog ? "

" His name is Leander," said Diana.

" Oh, Leander. I don't think I hear myself calling to a dog in a name of three syllables. Two at the most."

"No, so I call Hero! if I want him to come immediately," said Diana, and the gentlemen, to Mrs. Cramborne Wathin's astonishment, acclaimed it. Mr. Redworth, at her elbow, explained the point, to her disgust.

That was Diana's offence.

If it should seem a small one, let it be remembered that a snub was intended, and was foiled; and foiled with an apparent simplicity, enough to exasperate, had there been no laughter of men to back the countering stroke. A woman under a cloud, she talked, pushed to shine; she would be heard, would be applauded. Her chronicler must likewise admit the error of her giving way to a petty sentiment of antagonism on first beholding Mrs. Cramborne Wathin, before whom she at once resolved to be herself, for a holiday, instead of acting demurely to conciliate. Probably it was an antagonism of race, the shrinking of the skin from the burr. But when Tremendous Powers are invoked, we should treat any simple revulsion of our blood as a vice. The Gods of this world's contests demand it of us, in relation to them, that the mind, and not the instincts, shall be at work. Otherwise the course of a prudent policy is never to invoke them, but avoid.

The upper class was gained by her intrepidity, her charm, and her elsewhere offending wit, however the case might go. It is chivalrous, but not, alas, inflammable in support of innocence. The class below it is governed in estimates of character by accepted patterns of conduct; yet where innocence under persecution is believed to exist, the members animated by that belief can be enthusiastic. Enthusiasm is a heaven-sent steeplechaser, and takes a flying leap of the ordinary barriers; it is more intrusive than chivalry, and has a passion to communicate its ardour. Two letters from stranger ladies reached Diana, through her lawyers and Lady Dunstane. Anonymous letters, not so welcome, being male effusions, arrived at her lodgings, one of them comical almost over the verge to pathos in its termination: "To me you will ever be the Goddess Diana —my faith in woman!"

He was unacquainted with her!

She had not the heart to think the writers donkeys. How they obtained her address was a puzzle; they stole

in to comfort her slightly. They attached her to her
position of Defendant by the thought of what would have
been the idea of her character if she had flown — a reflection emanating from inexperience of the resources of
sentimentalists.

If she had flown! She was borne along by the tide like
a butterfly that a fish may gobble unless a friendly hand
shall intervene. And could it in nature? She was past
expectation of release. The attempt to imagine living with
any warmth of blood in her vindicated character, for the
sake of zealous friends, consigned her to a cold and empty
house upon a foreign earth. She had to set her mind upon
the mysterious enshrouded Twelve, with whom the verdict
would soon be hanging, that she might prompt her human
combativeness to desire the vindication at such a price as
she would have to pay for it. When Emma Dunstane spoke
to her of the certainty of triumphing, she suggested a
possible dissentient among the fateful Twelve, merely to
escape the drumming sound of that hollow big word. The
irreverent imp of her humour came to her relief by calling
forth the Twelve, in the tone of the clerk of the Court,
and they answered to their names of trades and crafts after
the manner of Titania's elves, and were questioned as to
their fitness, by education, habits, enlightenment, to pronounce decisively upon the case in dispute, the case being
plainly stated. They replied, that the long habit of dealing with scales enabled them to weigh the value of evidence
the most delicate. Moreover, they were Englishmen, and
anything short of downright bullet facts went to favour
the woman. For thus we right the balance of legal injustice toward the sex : we conveniently wink, ma'am. A
rough, old-fashioned way for us! Is it a Breach of Promise ? — She may reckon on her damages : we have daughters
of our own. Is it a suit for Divorce ? — Well, we have
wives of our own, and we can lash, or we can spare ; that's
as it may be ; but we'll keep the couple tied, let 'em hate
as they like, if they can't furnish porkbutchers' reasons for
sundering ; because the man makes the money in this
country. — My goodness! what a funny people, sir! — It's
our way of holding the balance, ma'am. — But would it not
be better to rectify the law and the social system, dear sir?

— Why, ma'am, we find it comfortabler to take cases as they come, in the style of our fathers. — But don't you see, my good man, that you are offering scapegoats for the comfort of the majority ? — Well, ma'am, there always were scape-goats, and always will be ; we find it comes round pretty square in the end.

"And I may be the scapegoat, Emmy ! It is perfectly possible. The grocer, the porkbutcher, drysalter, stationer, tea-merchant, et caetera — they sit on me. I have studied the faces of the juries, and Mr. Braddock tells me of their composition. And he admits that they do justice roughly — a rough and tumble country ! to quote him — though he says they are honest in intention."

"More shame to the man who drags you before them — if he persists !" Emma rejoined.

"He will. I know him. I would not have him draw back now," said Diana, catching her breath. "And, dear-est, do not abuse him ; for if you do, you set me imagining guiltiness. Oh, heaven ! — suppose me publicly pardoned ! No, I have kinder feelings when we stand opposed. It is odd, and rather frets my conscience, to think of the little resentment I feel. Hardly any ! He has not cause to like his wife. I can own it, and I am sorry for him, heartily. No two have ever come together so naturally antagonistic as we two. We walked a dozen steps in stupefied union, and hit upon crossways. From that moment it was tug and tug ; he me, I him. By resisting, I made him a tyrant ; and he, by insisting, made me a rebel. And he was the maddest of tyrants — a weak one. My dear, he was also a double-dealer. Or, no, perhaps not in design. He was moved at one time by his interests ; at another by his idea of his honour. He took what I could get for him, and then turned and drubbed me for getting it."

"This is the creature you try to excuse !" exclaimed indignant Emma.

"Yes, because — but fancy all the smart things I said being called my 'sallies !' — can a woman live with it ? — because I behaved . . . I despised him too much, and I showed it. He is not a contemptible man before the world ; he is merely a very narrow one under close inspection. I could not — or did not — conceal my feeling. I showed it not only to him, to my friend. Husband grew to mean to me stifler, lung-contractor, iron mask, inquisitor, everything anti-natural. He suffered under my 'sallies': and it was the worse for him when he did not perceive their drift. He is an upright man; I have not seen marked meanness. One might build up a respectable figure in negatives. I could add a row of noughts to the single number he cherishes, enough to make a millionnaire of him; but strike away the first, the rest are wind. Which signifies, that if you do not take his estimate of himself, you will think little of his negative virtues. He is not eminently, that is to say, not saliently, selfish; not rancorous, not obtrusive — ta-ta-ta-ta. But dull! — dull as a woollen nightcap over eyes and ears and mouth. Oh! an executioner's black cap to me. Dull, and suddenly staring awake to the idea of his honour. I 'rendered' him ridiculous — I had caught a trick of 'using men's phrases.' Dearest, now that the day of trial draws nigh — you have never questioned me, and it was like you to spare me pain — but now I can speak of him and myself." Diana dropped her voice. Here was another confession. The proximity of the trial acted like fire on her faded recollection of incidents. It may be that partly the shame of alluding to them had blocked her woman's memory. For one curious operation of the charge of guiltiness upon the nearly guiltless is to make them paint themselves pure white, to the obliteration of minor spots, until the whiteness being acknowledged, or the ordeal imminent, the spots recur and press upon their consciences. She resumed, in a rapid undertone: "You know that a certain degree of independence had been, if not granted by him, conquered by me. I had the habit of it. Obedience with him is imprisonment — he is a blind wall. He received a commission, greatly to his advantage, and was absent. He seems to have received information of some sort. He returned unexpectedly, at a late hour, and attacked me at once, middling violent. My friend — and that he is! — was coming from the House for a ten minutes' talk, as usual, on his way home, to refresh him after the long sitting and bear-baiting he had nightly to endure. Now let me confess: I grew frightened; Mr. Warwick was 'off his head,' as they say — crazy, and I could not bear the thought of those two meeting. While he raged I threw open the window and put the lamp near it, to expose the whole interior — cunning as a veteran intriguer : horrible, but it had to be done to keep them apart. He asked me what madness possessed me, to sit by an open window at midnight, in view of the public, with a damp wind blowing. I complained of want of air and fanned my forehead. I heard the steps on the pavement ; I stung him to retort loudly, and I was relieved ; the steps passed on. So the trick succeeded — the trick ! It was the worst I was guilty of, but it was a trick, and it branded me trickster. It teaches me to see myself with an abyss in my nature full of infernal possibilities. I think I am hewn in black rock. A woman who can do as I did by instinct, needs to have an angel always near her, if she has not a husband she reveres."

"We are none of us better than you, dear Tony ; only some are more fortunate, and many are cowards," Emma said. "You acted prudently in a wretched situation, partly of your own making, partly of the circumstances. But a nature like yours could not sit still and moan. That marriage was to blame ! The English notion of women seems to be that we are born white sheep or black : circumstances have nothing to do with our colour. They dread to grant distinctions, and to judge of us discerningly is beyond them. Whether the fiction, that their homes are purer than elsewhere, helps to establish the fact, I do not know : there is a class that does live honestly ; and at any rate it springs from a liking for purity ; but I am sure that their method of impressing it on women has the dangers of things artificial. They narrow their understanding of human nature, and that is not the way to improve the breed."

"I suppose we women are taken to be the second thoughts of the Creator ; human nature's fringes, mere finishing touches, not a part of the texture," said Diana ; "the pretty ornamentation. However, I fancy I perceive some tolerance growing in the minds of the dominant sex. Our old lawyer, Mr. Braddock, who appears to have no distaste for conversations with me, assures me he expects the day to come when women will be encouraged to work at crafts and professions for their independence. That is the secret of the opinion of us at present — our dependency. Give us the means of independence, and we will gain it, and have a turn at judging you, my lords! You shall behold a world reversed. Whenever I am distracted by existing circumstances, I lay my finger on the material conditions, and I touch the secret. Individually, it *may* be moral with us; collectively, it is material — gross wrongs, gross hungers. I am a married rebel, and thereof comes the social rebel. I was once a dancing and singing girl. You remember the night of the Dublin Ball. A Channel sea in uproar, stirred by witches, flows between."

"You are as lovely as you were then — I could say, lovelier," said Emma.

"I have unconquerable health, and I wish I could give you the half of it, dear. I work late into the night, and I wake early and fresh in the morning. I do not sing, that is all. A few days more, and my character will be up before the Bull's Head to face him in the arena. The worst of a position like mine is, that it causes me incessantly to think and talk of myself. I believe I think less than I talk, but the subject is growing stale; as those who are long dying feel, I dare say — if they do not take it as the compensation for their departure."

The Bull's Head, or British Jury of Twelve, with the wig on it, was faced during the latter half of a week of good news. First, Mr. Thomas Redworth was returned to Parliament by a stout majority for the Borough of Orrybridge: the Hon. Percy Dacier delivered a brilliant speech in the House of Commons, necessarily pleasing to his uncle: Lord Larrian obtained the command of the Rock: the house of The Crossways was let to a tenant approved by Mr. Braddock: Diana received the opening proof-sheets of her little volume, and an instalment of the modest honorarium: and finally, the Plaintiff in the suit involving her name was adjudged to have not proved his charge.

She heard of it without a change of countenance.

She could not have wished it the reverse; she was exonerated. But she was not free; far from that; and she revenged herself on the friends who made much of her triumph and overlooked her plight, by showing no sign of satisfaction. There was in her bosom a revolt at the legal consequences of the verdict — or blunt acquiescence of the

Law in the conditions possibly to be imposed on her unless she went straight to the relieving phial ; and the burden of keeping it under, set her wildest humour alight, somewhat as Redworth remembered of her on the journey from The Crossways to Copsley. This ironic fury, coming of the contrast of the outer and the inner, would have been indulged to the extent of permanent injury to her disposition had not her beloved Emma, immediately after the tension of the struggle ceased, required her tenderest aid. Lady Dunstane chanted victory, and at night collapsed. By the advice of her physician she was removed to Copsley, where Diana's labour of anxious nursing restored her through love to a saner spirit. The hopefulness of life must bloom again in the heart whose prayers are offered for a life dearer than its own to be preserved. A little return of confidence in Sir Lukin also refreshed her when she saw that the poor creature did honestly, in his shaggy rough male fashion, reverence and cling to the flower of souls he named as his wife. His piteous groans of self-accusation during the crisis haunted her, and made the conduct and nature of men a bewilderment to her still young understanding. Save for the knot of her sensations (hardly a mental memory, but a sullen knot) which she did not disentangle to charge him with his complicity in the blind rashness of her marriage, she might have felt sisterly, as warmly as she compassionated him.

It was midwinter when Dame Gossip, who keeps the exotic world alive with her fanning whispers, related that the lovely Mrs. Warwick had left England on board the schooner-yacht *Clarissa*, with Lord and Lady Esquart, for a voyage in the Mediterranean : and (behind her hand) that the reason was urgent, inasmuch as she fled to escape the meshes of the terrific net of the marital law brutally whirled to capture her by the man her husband.

CHAPTER XV

INTRODUCES THE HON. PERCY DACIER

THE Gods of this world's contests, against whom our
poor stripped individual is commonly in revolt, are, as we
know, not miners, they are reapers; and if we appear no
longer on the surface, they cease to bruise us: they will
allow an arena character to be cleansed and made present-
able while enthusiastic friends preserve discretion. It is
of course less than magnanimity; they are not proposed to
you for your worship; they are little Gods, temporary as
that great wave, their parent human mass of the hour.
But they have one worshipful element in them, which is,
the divine insistancy upon there being two sides to a case —
to every case. And the People so far directed by them may
boast of healthfulness. Let the individual shriek, the
innocent, triumphant, have in honesty to admit the fact.
One side is vanquished according to decree of Law, but the
superior Council does not allow it to be extinguished.

Diana's battle was fought shadowily behind her for the
space of a week or so, with some advocates on behalf of the
beaten man; then it became a recollection of a beautiful
woman, possibly erring, misvalued by a husband, who was
neither a man of the world nor a gracious yokefellow, nor
anything to match her. She, however, once out of the
public flames, had to recall her scorchings to be gentle with
herself. Under a defeat, she would have been angrily self-
vindicated. The victory of the ashen laurels drove her
mind inward to gird at the hateful yoke, in compassion for
its pair of victims. Quite earnestly by such means, yet
always bearing a comical eye on her subterfuges, she
escaped the extremes of personal blame. Those advocates
of her opponent in and out of court compelled her honest
heart to search within and own to faults. But were they
not natural faults? It was her marriage; it was marriage
in the abstract: her own mistake and the world's clumsy
machinery of civilization: these were the capital offenders:
not the wife who would laugh ringingly, and would have

friends of the other sex, and shot her epigrams at the helpless despot, and was at times — yes, vixenish; a nature driven to it, but that was the word. She was too generous to recount her charges against the vanquished. If his wretched jealousy had ruined her, the secret high tribunal within her bosom, which judged her guiltless for putting the sword between their marriage tie when they stood as one, because a quarrelling couple could not in honour play the embracing, pronounced him just pardonable. She distinguished that he could only suppose, manlikely, one bad cause for the division.

To this extent she used her unerring brains, more openly than on her night of debate at The Crossways. The next moment she was off in vapour, meditating grandly on her independence of her sex and the passions. Love! she did not know it; she was not acquainted with either the criminal or the domestic God, and persuaded herself that she never could be. She was a Diana of coldness, preferring friendship; she could be the friend of men. There was another who could be the friend of women. Her heart leapt to Redworth. Conjuring up his clear trusty face, at their grasp of hands when parting, she thought of her visions of her future about the period of the Dublin Ball, and acknowledged, despite the erratic step to wedlock, a gain in having met and proved so true a friend. His face, figure, character, lightest look, lightest word, all were loyal signs of a man of honour, cold as she; he was the man to whom she could have opened her heart for inspection. Rejoicing in her independence of an emotional sex, the impulsive woman burned with a regret that at their parting she had not broken down conventional barriers and given her cheek to his lips in the anti-insular fashion with a brotherly friend. And why not when both were cold? Spirit to spirit, she did, delightfully refreshed by her capacity to do so without a throb. He had held her hand and looked into her eyes half a minute, like a dear comrade; as little arousing her instincts of defensiveness as the clearing heavens; and sisterly love for it was his due, a sister's kiss. He needed a sister, and should have one in her. Emma's recollected talk of "Tom Redworth" painted him from head to foot, brought the living man over the waters to the deck

of the yacht. A stout champion in the person of Tom
Redworth was left on British land; but for some reason
past analysis, intermixed, that is, among a swarm of sensations, Diana named her champion to herself with the formal
prefix : perhaps because she knew a man's Christian name
to be dangerous handling. They differed besides frequently
in opinion, when the habit of thinking of him as Mr. Redworth would be best. Women are bound to such small
observances, and especially the beautiful of the sisterhood,
whom the world soon warns that they carry explosives and
must particularly guard against the ignition of petty sparks.
She was less indiscreet in her thoughts than in her acts, as
is the way with the reflective daughter of impulse; though
she had fine mental distinctions : what she could offer to do
"spirit to spirit," for instance, held nothing to her mind of
the intimacy of calling the gentleman plain Tom in mere
contemplation of him. Her friend and champion was a
volunteer, far from a mercenary, and he deserved the reward, if she could bestow it unalarmed. They were to meet
in Egypt. Meanwhile England loomed the home of hostile
forces ready to shock, had she been a visible planet, and
ready to secrete a virus of her past history, had she been
making new.

She was happily away, borne by a whiter than swan's
wing on the sapphire Mediterranean. Her letters to Emma
were peeps of splendour for the invalid : her way of life on
board the yacht, and sketches of her host and hostess as
lovers in wedlock on the other side of our perilous forties ;
sketches of the bays, the towns, the people — priests, dames,
cavaliers, urchins, infants, shifting groups of supple south-
erners — flashed across the page like a web of silk, and
were dashed off, redolent of herself, as lightly as the silvery
spray of the blue waves she furrowed; telling, without allusions to the land behind her, that she had dipped in the
wells of blissful oblivion. Emma Dunstane, as is usual
with those who receive exhilarating correspondence from
makers of books, condemned the authoress in comparison,
and now first saw that she had the gift of writing. Only
one cry : "Italy, Eden of exiles!" betrayed the seeming of
a moan. She wrote of her poet and others immediately.
Thither had they fled, with adieu to England !

How many have waved the adieu! And it is England nourishing, England protecting them, England clothing them, in the honours they wear. Only the posturing lower natures, on the level of their buskins, can pluck out the pocket-knife of sentimental spite to cut themselves loose from her at heart in earnest. The higher, bleed as they may, too pressingly feel their debt. Diana had the Celtic vivid sense of country. In England she was Irish, by hereditary, and by wilful opposition. Abroad, gazing along the waters, observing, comparing, reflecting, above all, reading of the struggles at home, the things done and attempted, her soul of generosity made her, though not less Irish, a daughter of Britain. It is at a distance that striving countries should be seen if we would have them in the pure idea; and this young woman of fervid mind, a reader of public speeches and speculator on the tides of politics (desirous, further, to feel herself rather more in the pure idea), began to yearn for England long before her term of holiday exile had ended. She had been flattered by her friend, her "wedded martyr at the stake," as she named him, to believe that she could exercise a judgement in politics — could think, even speak acutely, on public affairs. The reports of speeches delivered by the men she knew or knew of, set her thrilling; and she fancied the sensibility to be as independent of her sympathy with the orators as her political notions were sovereignly above a sex devoted to trifles, and the feelings of a woman who had gone through fire. She fancied it confidently, notwithstanding a peculiar intuition that the plunge into the nobler business of the world would be a haven of safety for a woman with blood and imagination, when writing to Emma: "Mr. Redworth's great success in Parliament is good in itself, whatever his views of present questions; and I do not heed them when I look to what may be done by a man of such power in striking at unjust laws, which keep the really numerically better-half of the population in a state of slavery. If he had been a lawyer! It must be a lawyer's initiative — a lawyer's Bill. Mr. Percy Dacier also spoke well, as might have been expected, and his uncle's compliment to him was merited. Should you meet him sound him. He has read for the Bar, and is younger than Mr. Redworth. The very young men and the old are our hope. The middle-aged are hard and fast for existing facts. We pick *our* leaders on the slopes, the incline and decline of the mountain — not on the upper table-land midway, where all appears to men so solid, so tolerably smooth, save for a few excrescences, roughnesses, gradually to be levelled at their leisure; which induces one to protest that the middle-age of men is their time of delusion. It is no paradox. They may be publicly useful in a small way, I do not deny it at all. They must be near the gates of life — the opening or the closing — for their *minds* to be accessible to the urgency of the greater questions. Otherwise the world presents itself to them under too settled an aspect — unless, of course, Vesuvian Revolution shakes the land. And that touches only their nerves. I dream of some old Judge! There is one — if having caught we could keep him. But I dread so tricksy a pilot. You have guessed him — the ancient Puck! We have laughed all day over the paper telling us of his worrying the Lords. Lady Esquart congratulates her husband in being out of it. Puck *bien ridé* and bewigged might perhaps — except that at the critical moment he would be sure to plead allegiance to Oberon. However, the work will be performed by some one: I am prophetic: — when maidens are grandmothers! — when your Tony is wearing a perpetual laugh in the unhusbanded regions where there is no institution of the wedding-tie."

For the reason that she was not to participate in the result of the old Judge's or young hero's happy championship of the cause of her sex, she conceived her separateness high aloof, and actually supposed she was a contemplative, simply speculative political spirit, impersonal albeit a woman. This, as Emma, smiling at the lines, had not to learn, was always her secret pride of fancy — the belief in her possession of a disengaged intellect.

The strange illusion, so clearly exposed to her correspondent, was maintained through a series of letters very slightly descriptive, dated from the Piræus, the Bosphorus, the coasts of the Crimea, all more or less relating to the latest news of the journals received on board the yacht, and of English visitors fresh from the country she now seemed fond of calling "home." Politics, and gentle allusions to the curious exhibition of "love in marriage" shown by her amiable host and hostess : — "these dear Esquarts, who are never tired of one another, but courtly courting, tempting me to think it possible that a fortunate selection and a mutual deference may subscribe to human happiness : " — filled the paragraphs. Reviews of her first literary venture were mentioned once : "I was well advised by Mr. Redworth in putting ANTONIA for authoress. She is a buff jerkin to the stripes, and I suspect that the signature of D. A. M., written in full, would have cawed woefully to hear that her style is affected, her characters nullities, her cleverness forced, &c., &c. As it is I have much the same contempt for poor Antonia's performance. Cease penning, little fool ! She writes, ' with some comprehension of the passion of love.' I know her to be a stranger to the earliest cry. So you see, dear, that utter ignorance is the mother of the Art. Dialogues 'occasionally pointed.' She has a sister who may do better. — But why was I not apprenticed to a serviceable profession or a trade ? I perceive now that a hanger-on of the market had no right to expect a happier fate than mine has been."

On the Nile, in the winter of the year, Diana met the Hon. Percy Dacier. He was introduced to her at Cairo by Redworth. The two gentlemen had struck up a House of Commons acquaintanceship, and finding themselves bound for the same destination, had grown friendly. Redworth's arrival had been pleasantly expected. She remarked on Dacier's presence to Emma, without sketch or note of him as other than much esteemed by Lord and Lady Esquart. These, with Diana, Redworth, Dacier, the German Eastern traveller Schweizerbarth, and the French Consul and Egyptologist Duriette, composed a voyaging party up the river, of which expedition Redworth was Lady Dunstane's chief writer of the records. His novel perceptiveness and shrewdness of touch made them amusing ; and his tenderness to the Beauty's coquetry between the two foreign rivals, moved a deeper feeling. The German had a guitar, the Frenchman a voice ; Diana joined them in harmony. They complained apart severally of the accompaniment and the singer. Our English criticized them apart ; and that is at any rate to occupy a post, though it contributes nothing to entertain-

ment. At home the Esquarts had sung duets; Diana had
assisted Redworth's manly chest-notes at the piano. Each
of them declined to be vocal. Diana sang alone for the
credit of the country, Italian and French songs, Irish also.
She was in her mood of Planxty Kelly and Garryowen all
the way. "Madame est Irlandaise?" Redworth heard the
Frenchman say, and he owned to what was implied in the
answering tone of the question. " We should be dull dogs
without the Irish leaven!" So Tony in exile still managed
to do something for her darling Erin. The solitary woman
on her heights at Copsley raised an exclamation of, "Oh!
that those two had been or could be united!" She was
conscious of a mystic symbolism in the prayer.

She was not apprehensive of any ominous intervention of
another. Writing from Venice, Diana mentioned Mr.
Percy Dacier as being engaged to an heiress; "A Miss
Asper, niece of a mighty shipowner, Mr. Quintin Manx,
Lady Esquart tells me: money fabulous, and necessary to
a younger son devoured with ambition. The elder brother,
Lord Creedmore, is a common Nimrod, always absent in
Hungary, Russia, America, hunting somewhere. Mr. Dacier
will be in the Cabinet with the next Ministry." No more
of him. A new work by ANTONIA was progressing.

The Summer in South Tyrol passed like a royal procession before young eyes for Diana, and at the close of it,
descending the Stelvio, idling through the Valtelline, Como
Lake was reached, Diana full of her work, living the double
life of the author. At Bellagio one afternoon Mr. Percy
Dacier appeared. She remembered subsequently a disappointment she felt in not beholding Mr. Redworth either
with him or displacing him. If engaged to a lady, he was
not an ardent suitor; nor was he a pointedly complimentary acquaintance. His enthusiasm was reserved for Italian
scenery. She had already formed a sort of estimate of his
character, as an indifferent observer may do, and any
woman previous to the inflaming of her imagination, if
that is in store for her; and she now fell to work resetting
the puzzle it became as soon her positive conclusions had
to be shaped again. "But women never can know young
men," she wrote to Emma, after praising his good repute
as one of the brotherhood. "He drops pretty sentences

now and then: no compliments; milky nuts. Of course
he has a head, or he would not be where he is — and that
seems always to me the most enviable place a young man
can occupy." She observed in him a singular conflicting of
a buoyant animal nature with a curb of studiousness, as if
the fardels of age were piling on his shoulders before youth
had quitted its pastures. His build of limbs and his
features were those of the finely-bred English; he had the
English taste for sports, games, manly diversions; and in
the bloom of life, under thirty, his head was given to bend.
The head bending on a tall upright figure, where there was
breadth of chest, told of weights working. She recollected
his open look, larger than inquiring, at the introduction to
her; and it recurred when she uttered anything specially
taking. What it meant was past a guess, though comparing it with the frank directness of Redworth's eyes, she saw
the difference between a look that accepted her and one
that dilated on two opinions.

Her thought of the gentleman was of a brilliant young
charioteer in the ruck of the race, watchful for his chance
to push to the front; and she could have said that a dubious consort might spoil a promising career. It flattered
her to think that she sometimes prompted him, sometimes
illumined. He repeated sentences she had spoken. — "I
shall be better able to describe Mr. Dacier when you and
I sit together, my Emmy, and a stroke here and there
completes the painting. Set descriptions are good for
puppets. Living men and women are too various in the
mixture fashioning them — even the 'external presentment' — to be livingly rendered in a formal sketch. I
may tell you his eyes are pale blue, his features regular,
his hair silky, brownish, his legs long, his head rather
stooping (only the head), his mouth commonly closed;
these are the facts, and you have seen much the same in
a nursery doll. Such literary craft is of the nursery. So
with landscapes. The art of the pen (we write on darkness) is to rouse the inward vision, instead of labouring
with a Drop-scene brush, as if it were to the eye; because
our flying minds cannot contain a protracted description.
That is why the poets, who spring imagination with a
word or a phrase, paint lasting pictures. The Shake-

spearian, the Dantesque, are in a line, two at most. He
lends an attentive ear when I speak, agrees or has a quaint
pucker of the eyebrows dissenting inwardly. He lacks
mental liveliness — cheerfulness, I should say, and is
thankful to have it imparted. One suspects he would be
a dull domestic companion. He has a veritable thirst for
hopeful views of the world, and no spiritual distillery of
his own. He leans to depression. Why! The broken
reed you call your Tony carries a cargo, all of her manufacture — she reeks of secret stills; and here is a young
man — a sapling oak — inclined to droop. His nature has
an air of imploring me *que je l'arrose!* I begin to perform
Mrs. Dr. Pangloss on purpose to brighten him — the mind,
the views. He is not altogether deficient in conversational gaiety, and he shines in exercise. But the world is
a poor old ball bounding down a hill — to an Irish melody
in the evening generally, by request. So far of Mr. Percy
Dacier, of whom I have some hopes — distant, perhaps
delusive — that he may be of use to our cause. He listens.
It is an auspicious commencement."

Lugano is the Italian lake most lovingly encircled by
mountain arms, and every height about it may be scaled
with ease. The heights have their nest of waters below
for a home scene, the southern Swiss peaks, with celestial
Monta Rosa, in prospect. It was there that Diana re-
awakened, after the trance of a deadly draught, to the
glory of the earth and her share in it. She wakened
like the Princess of the Kiss; happily not to kisses; to
no sign, touch or call that she could trace backward. The
change befell her without a warning. After writing deliberately to her friend Emma, she laid down her pen and
thought of nothing; and into this dreamfulness a wine
passed, filling her veins, suffusing her mind, quickening
her soul: — and coming whence? out of air, out of the
yonder of air. She could have imagined a seraphic presence in the room, that bade her arise and live; take the
cup of the wells of youth arrested at her lips by her marriage; quit her wintry bondage for warmth, light, space,
the quick of simple being. And the strange pure ecstasy
was not a transient electrification; it came in waves on a
continuous tide; looking was living; walking flying. She

hardly knew that she slept.   The heights she had seen
rosy at eve were marked for her ascent in the dawn.   Sleep
was one wink, and fresh as the dewy field and rockflowers
on her way upward, she sprang to more and more of
heaven, insatiable, happily chirruping over her possessions.   The threading of the town among the dear common
people before others were abroad, was a pleasure: and
pleasant her solitariness threading the gardens at the base
of the rock, only she astir; and the first rough steps of
the winding footpath, the first closed buds, the sharper
air, the uprising of the mountain with her ascent; and
pleasant too was her hunger and the nibble at a little loaf
of bread.   A linnet sang in her breast, an eagle lifted her
feet.   The feet were verily winged, as they are in a season
of youth when the blood leaps to light from the pressure
of the under forces, like a source at the wellheads, and
the whole creature blooms, vital in every energy as a spirit.
To be a girl again was magical.   She could fancy her having risen from the dead.   And to be a girl, with a woman's
broader vision and receptiveness of soul, with knowledge
of evil, and winging to ethereal happiness, this was a
revelation of our human powers.

   She attributed the change to the influences of nature's
beauty and grandeur.   Nor had her woman's consciousness
to play the chrysalis in any shy recesses of her heart; she
was nowhere veiled or torpid; she was illumined, like the
Salvatore she saw in the evening beams and mounted in
the morning's; and she had not a spot of secrecy; all her
nature flew and bloomed; she was bird, flower, flowing
river, a quivering sensibility unweighted, unshrouded.
Desires and hopes would surely have weighted and
shrouded her.   She had none, save for the upper air, the
eyes of the mountain.

   Which was the dream — her past life or this ethereal
existence?   But this ran spontaneously, and the other had
often been stimulated — her vivaciousness on the Nile-
boat, for a recent example.   She had not a doubt that her
past life was the dream, or deception: and for the reason
that now she was compassionate, large of heart toward all
beneath her.   Let them but leave her free, they were forgiven, even to prayers for their wellbeing !   The plural

number in the case was an involuntary multiplying of the
single, coming of her incapacity during this elevation and
rapture of the senses to think distinctly of that One who
had discoloured her opening life. Freedom to breathe,
gaze, climb, grow with the grasses, fly with the clouds, to
muse, to sing, to be an unclaimed self, dispersed upon
earth, air, sky, to find a keener transfigured self in that
radiation — she craved no more.

Bear in mind her beauty, her charm of tongue, her
present state of white simplicity in fervour: was there
ever so perilous a woman for the most guarded and
clearest-eyed of young men to meet at early morn upon a
mountain side?

CHAPTER XVI

TREATS OF A MIDNIGHT BELL, AND OF A SCENE OF
EARLY MORNING

ON a round of the mountains rising from Osteno, South-
eastward of Lugano, the Esquart party rose from the
natural grotto and headed their carriages up and down the
defiles, halting for a night at Rovio, a little village below
the Generoso, lively with waterfalls and watercourses; and
they fell so in love with the place, that after roaming along
the flowery borderways by moonlight, they resolved to rest
there two or three days and try some easy ascents. In the
diurnal course of nature, being pleasantly tired, they had
the avowed intention of sleeping there; so they went early
to their beds, and carelessly wished one another good-
night, none of them supposing slumber to be anywhere one
of the warlike arts, a paradoxical thing you must battle
for and can only win at last when utterly beaten. Hard
by their inn, close enough for a priestly homily to have
been audible, stood a church campanile, wherein hung a
Bell, not ostensibly communicating with the demons of
the pit; in daylight rather a merry comrade. But at night,
when the children of nerves lay stretched, he threw off the
mask. As soon as they had fairly nestled, he smote their

pillows a shattering blow, loud for the retold preluding
quarters, incredibly clanging the number ten. Then he
waited for neighbouring campanili to box the ears of slumber's votaries in turn; whereupon, under pretence of excessive conscientiousness, or else oblivious of his antecedent
damnable misconduct, or perhaps in actual league and
trapdoor conspiracy with the surging goblin hosts beneath
us, he resumed his blaring strokes, a sonorous recapitula-
tion of the number; all the others likewise. It was an
alarum fit to warn of Attila or Alaric; and not simply the
maniacal noise invaded the fruitful provinces of sleep like
Hun and Vandal, the irrational repetition ploughed the
minds of those unhappy somnivolents, leaving them worse
than sheared by barbarians, disrupt, as by earthquake,
with the unanswerable question to Providence, Why! —
Why twice?

Designing slumberers are such infants. When they
have undressed and stretched themselves flat, it seems
that they have really gone back to their mothers' breasts,
and they fret at whatsoever does not smack of nature, or
custom. The cause of a repetition so senseless in its violence, and so unnecessary, set them querying and kicking
until the inevitable quarters recommenced. Then arose
an insurgent rabble in their bosoms, it might be the
loosened imps of darkness, urging them to speculate
whether the proximate monster about to dole out the
eleventh hour in uproar would again forget himself and
repeat his dreary arithmetic a second time; for they were
unaware of his religious obligation, following the hour of
the district, to inform them of the tardy hour of Rome.
They waited in suspense, curiosity enabling them to bear
the first crash callously. His performance was the same.
And now they took him for a crazy engine whose madness
had infected the whole neighbourhood. Now was the
moment to fight for sleep in contempt of him, and they
began by simulating an entry into the fortress they were
to defend, plunging on their pillows, battening down their
eyelids, breathing with a dreadful regularity. Alas! it
came to their knowledge that the Bell was in possession
and they the besiegers. Every resonant quarter was
anticipated up to the blow, without averting its murderous

abruptness; and an executioner Midnight that sounded, in addition to the reiterated quarters, four and twenty ringing hammer-strokes, with the aching pause between the twelves, left them the prey of the legions of torturers which are summed, though not described, in the title of a sleepless night.

From that period the curse was milder, but the victims raged. They swam on vasty deeps, they knocked at rusty gates, they shouldered all the weapons of black Insomnia's armoury and became her soldiery, doing her will upon themselves. Of her originally sprang the inspired teaching of the doom of men to excruciation in endlessness. She is the fountain of the infinite ocean whereon the exceedingly sensitive soul is tumbled everlastingly, with the diversion of hot pincers to appease its appetite for change.

Dacier was never the best of sleepers. He had taken to exercise his brains prematurely, not only in learning, but also in reflection; and a reflectiveness that is indulged before we have a rigid mastery of the emotions, or have slain them, is apt to make a young man more than commonly a child of nerves: nearly as much so as the dissipated, with the difference that they are hilarious while wasting their treasury, which he is not; and he may recover under favouring conditions, which is a point of vantage denied to them. Physically he had stout reserves, for he had not disgraced the temple. His intemperateness lay in the craving to rise and lead: a precocious ambition. This apparently modest young man started with an aim — and if in the distance and with but a slingstone, like the slender shepherd fronting the Philistine, all his energies were in his aim — at Government. He had hung on the fringe of an Administration. His party was out, and he hoped for higher station on its return to power. Many perplexities were therefore buzzing about his head; among them at present one sufficiently magnified and voracious to swallow the remainder. He added force to the interrogation as to why that Bell should sound its inhuman strokes twice, by asking himself why he was there to hear it! A strange suspicion of a bewitchment might have enlightened him if he had been a man accustomed to yield to the peculiar kind of sorcery issuing from that sex. He rather despised the power of women over men: and nevertheless he was there, listening to that Bell, instead of having obeyed the call of his family duties, when the latter were urgent. He had received letters at Lugano, summoning him home, before he set forth on his present expedition. The noisy alarum told him he floundered in quags, like a silly creature chasing a marsh-lamp. But was it so? Was it not, on the contrary, a serious pursuit of the secret of a woman's character? — Oh, a woman and her character! Ordinary women and their characters might set to work to get what relationship and likeness they could. They had no secret to allure. This one had: she had the secret of lake waters under rock, unfathomable in limpidness. He could not think of her without shooting at nature, and nature's very sweetest and subtlest, for comparisons. As to her sex, his active man's contempt of the petticoated secret attractive to boys and graylings, made him believe that in her he hunted the mind and the spirit: perchance a double mind, a twilighted spirit; but not a mere woman. She bore no resemblance to the bundle of women. Well, she was worth studying; she had ideas, and could give ear to ideas. Furthermore, a couple of the members of his family inclined to do her injustice. At least, they judged her harshly, owing, he thought, to an inveterate opinion they held regarding Lord Dannisburgh's obliquity in relation to women. He shared it, and did not concur in their verdict upon the woman implicated. That is to say, knowing something of her now, he could see the possibility of her innocence in the special charm that her mere sparkle of features and speech, and her freshness would have for a man like his uncle. The possibility pleaded strongly on her behalf, while the darker possibility weighted by his uncle's reputation plucked at him from below.

She was delightful to hear, delightful to see; and her friends loved her and had faith in her. So clever a woman might be too clever for her friends! . . .

The circle he moved in hummed of women, prompting novices as well as veterans to suspect that the multitude of them, and notably the fairest, yet more the cleverest, concealed the serpent somewhere.

She certainly had not directed any of her arts upon him.
Besides he was half engaged. And that was a burning
perplexity; not because of abstract scruples touching the
necessity for love in marriage. The young lady, great
heiress though she was, and willing, as she allowed him
to assume; graceful too, reputed a beauty; struck him
cold. He fancied her transparent, only Arctic. Her
transparency displayed to him all the common virtues,
and a serene possession of the inestimable and eminent
one outweighing all; but charm, wit, ardour, intercom-
municative quickness, and kindling beauty, airy grace,
were qualities that a man, it seemed, had to look for in
women spotted by a doubt of their having the chief and
priceless.

However, he was not absolutely plighted. Nor did it
matter to him whether this or that woman concealed the
tail of the serpent and trail, excepting the singular interest
this woman managed to excite, and so deeply as set him
wondering how that Resurrection Bell might be affecting
her ability to sleep. Was she sleeping? — or waking?
His nervous imagination was a torch that alternately lighted
her lying asleep with the innocent, like a babe, and tossing beneath the overflow of her dark hair, hounded by
haggard memories. She fluttered before him in either
aspect; and another perplexity now was to distinguish
within himself which was the aspect he preferred. Great
Nature brought him thus to drink of her beauty, under the
delusion that the act was a speculation on her character.

The Bell, with its clash, throb and long swoon of sound,
reminded him of her name: Diana — An attribute? or a
derision?

It really mattered nothing to him, save for her being
maligned; and if most unfairly, then that face of the vary-
ing expressions, and the rich voice, and the remembered
gentle and taking words coming from her, appealed to him
with a supplicating vividness that pricked his heart to
leap.

He was dozing when the Bell burst through the thin
division between slumber and wakefulness, recounting what
seemed innumerable peals, hard on his cranium. Gray
daylight blanched the window and the bed: his watch said

five of the morning. He thought of the pleasure of a bath
beneath some dashing sprayshowers, and jumped up to
dress, feeling a queer sensation of skin in his clothes, the
sign of a feverish night; and yawning he went into the air.
Leftward the narrow village-street led to the footway along
which he could make for the mountain-wall. He cast one
look at the head of the campanile, silly as an owlish
roysterer's glazed stare at the young Aurora, and hurried
his feet to check the yawns coming alarmingly fast, in the
place of ideas.

His elevation above the valley was about the kneecap of
the Generoso. Waters of past rain-clouds poured down
the mountain-sides like veins of metal, here and there
flinging off a shower on the busy descent; only dubiously
animate in the lack lustre of the huge bulk piled against
a yellow East that wafted fleets of pinky cloudlets overhead. He mounted his path to a level with inviting grass-
mounds where water circled, running from scoops and cups
to curves and brook-streams, and in his fancy calling to
him to hear them. To dip in them was his desire. To
roll and shiver braced by the icy flow was the spell to
break that baleful incantation of the intolerable night; so
he struck across a ridge of boulders, wreck of a landslip
from the height he had hugged, to the open space of
shadowed undulations, and soon had his feet on turf.
Heights to right and to left, and between them, aloft, a
sky the rosy wheelcourse of the chariot of morn, and
below, among the knolls, choice of sheltered nooks, where
waters whispered of secrecy to satisfy Diana herself. They
have that whisper and waving of secrecy in secret scenery;
they beckon to the bath; and they conjure classic visions
of the pudency of the Goddess irate or unsighted. The
semi-mythological state of mind, built of old images and
favouring haunts, was known to Dacier. The name of
Diana, playing vaguely on his consciousness, helped to it.
He had no definite thought of the mortal woman when the
highest grass-roll near the rock gave him view of a bowered
source and of a pool under a chain of cascades, bounded
by polished shelves and slabs. The very spot for him, he
decided at the first peep; and at the second, with fingers
instinctively loosening his waistcoat-buttons for a com-

mencement, he shouldered round and strolled away, though not at a rapid pace, nor far before he halted.

That it could be no other than she, the figure he had seen standing beside the pool, he was sure. Why had he turned? Thoughts thick and swift as a blush in the cheeks of seventeen overcame him; and queen of all, the thought bringing the picture of this mountain-solitude to vindicate a woman shamefully assailed. — She who found her pleasure in these haunts of nymph and Goddess, at the fresh cold bosom of nature, must be clear as day. She trusted herself to the loneliness here, and to the honour of men, from a like irreflective sincereness. She was unable to imagine danger where her own impelling thirst was pure. . . .

The thoughts, it will be discerned, were but flashes of a momentary vivid sensibility. Where a woman's charm has won half the battle, her character is an advancing standard and sings victory, let her do no more than take a quiet morning walk before breakfast.

But why had he turned his back on her? There was nothing in his presence to alarm, nothing in her appearance to forbid. The motive and the movement were equally quaint; incomprehensible to him; for after putting himself out of sight, he understood the absurdity of the supposition that she would seek the secluded sylvan bath for the same purpose as he. Yet now he was debarred from going to meet her. She might have an impulse to bathe her feet. Her name was Diana. . . .

Yes, and a married woman; and a proclaimed one! And notwithstanding those brassy facts, he was ready to side with the evidence declaring her free from stain; and further, to swear that her blood was Diana's!

Nor had Dacier ever been particularly poetical about women. The present Diana had wakened his curiosity, had stirred his interest in her, pricked his admiration, but gradually, until a sleepless night with its flock of raven-fancies under that dominant Bell, ended by colouring her, the moment she stood in his eyes, as freshly as the morning heavens. We are much influenced in youth by sleepless nights: they disarm, they predispose us to submit to soft occasion; and in our youth occasion is always coming.

He heard her voice. She had risen up the grass-mound, and he hung brooding half-way down. She was dressed in some texture of the hue of lavender. A violet scarf loosely knotted over the bosom opened on her throat. The loop of her black hair curved under a hat of grey beaver. Memorably radiant was her face.

They met, exchanged greetings, praised the beauty of the morning, and struck together on the Bell. She laughed: "I heard it at ten; I slept till four. I never wake later. I was out in the air by half-past. Were you disturbed?"

He alluded to his troubles with the Bell.

"It sounded like a felon's heart in skeleton ribs," he said.

"Or a proser's tongue in a hollow skull," said she.

He bowed to her conversible readiness, and at once fell into the background, as he did only with her, to perform accordant bass in their dialogue; for when a woman lightly caps our strained remarks, we gallantly surrender the leadership, lest she should too cuttingly assert her claim.

Some sweet wild cyclamen flowers were at her breast. She held in her left hand a bunch of buds and blown cups of the pale purple meadow-crocus. He admired them. She told him to look round. He confessed to not having noticed them in the grass: what was the name? Colchicum, in Botany, she said.

"These are plucked to be sent to a friend; otherwise I'm reluctant to take the life of flowers for a whim. Wild flowers, I mean. I am not sentimental about garden flowers: they are cultivated for decoration, grown for clipping."

"I suppose they don't carry the same signification," said Dacier, in the tone of a pupil to such themes.

"They carry no feeling," said she. "And that is my excuse for plucking these, where they seem to spring like our town-dream of happiness. I believe they are sensible of it too; but these must do service to my invalid friend, who cannot travel. Are you ever as much interested in the woes of great ladies as of country damsels? I am not — not unless they have natural distinction. You have met Lady Dunstane?"

The question sounded artless. Dacier answered that he thought he had seen her somewhere once, and Diana shut her lips on a rising under-smile.

"She is the *cœur d'or* of our time: the one soul I would sacrifice these flowers to."

"A bit of a blue-stocking, I think I have heard said."

"She might have been admitted to the Hotel Rambouillet, without being anything of a Précieuse. She is the woman of the largest heart now beating."

"Mr. Redworth talked of her."

"As she deserved, I am sure."

"Very warmly."

"He would!"

"He told me you were the Damon and Pythias of women."

"Her one fault is an extreme humility that makes her always play second to me; and as I am apt to gabble, I take the lead; and I am froth in comparison. I can reverence my superiors even when tried by intimacy with them. She is the next heavenly thing to heaven that I know. Court her, if ever you come across her. Or have you a man's horror of women with brains?"

"Am I expressing it?" said he.

"Do not breathe London or Paris here on me." She fanned the crocuses under her chin. "The early morning always has this — I wish I had a word! — touch . . . whisper . . . gleam . . . beat of wings — I envy poets now more than ever! — of Eden, I was going to say. Prose can paint evening and moonlight, but poets are needed to sing the dawn. That is because prose is equal to melancholy stuff. Gladness requires the finer language. Otherwise we have it coarse — anything but a reproduction. You politicians despise the little distinctions 'twixt tweedledum and tweedledee,' I fancy."

Of the poetic sort, Dacier's uncle certainly did. For himself he confessed to not having thought much on them.

"But how divine is utterance!" she said. "As we to the brutes, poets are to us."

He listened somewhat with the head of the hanged. A beautiful woman choosing to rhapsodize has her way, and is not subjected to the critical commentary within us. He wondered whether she had discoursed in such a fashion to his uncle.

"I can read good poetry," said he.

"If you would have this valley — or mountain-cleft, one should call it — described, only verse could do it for you," Diana pursued, and stopped, glanced at his face and smiled. She had spied the end of a towel peeping out of one of his pockets. "You came out for a bath! Go back, by all means, and mount that rise of grass where you first saw me; and down on the other side, a little to the right, you will find the very place for a bath, at a corner of the rock — a natural fountain; a bubbling pool in a ring of brushwood, with falling water, so tempting that I could have pardoned a push: about five feet deep. Lose no time."

He begged to assure her that he would rather stroll with her: it had been only a notion of bathing by chance when he pocketed the towel.

"Dear me," she cried, "if I had been a man I should have scurried off at a signal of release, quick as a hare I once woke up in a field with my foot on its back."

Dacier's eyebrows knotted a trifle over her eagerness to dismiss him: he was not used to it, but rather to be courted by women, and to condescend.

"I shall not long, I 'm afraid, have the pleasure of walking beside you and hearing you. I had letters at Lugano. My uncle is unwell, I hear."

"Lord Dannisburgh?"

The name sprang from her lips unhesitatingly.

His nodded affirmative altered her face and her voice.

"It is not a grave illness?"

"They rather fear it."

"You had the news at Lugano?"

He answered the implied reproach: "I can be of no service."

"But surely!"

"It 's even doubtful that he would be bothered to receive me. We hold no views in common — excepting one."

"Could I?" she exclaimed. "O that I might! If he is really ill! But if it is actually serious he would perhaps have a wish . . . I can nurse. I know I have the power to cheer him. You ought indeed to be in England."

Dacier said he had thought it better to wait for later reports. "I shall drive to Lugano this afternoon, and act on the information I get there. Probably it ends my holiday."

"Will you do me the favour to write me word? — and especially tell me if you think he would like to have me near him," said Diana. "And let him know that if he wants nursing or cheerful companionship, I am at any moment ready to come."

The flattery of a beautiful young woman to wait on him would be very agreeable to Lord Dannisburgh, Dacier conceived. Her offer to go was possibly purely charitable. But the prudence of her occupation of the post obscured whatever appeared admirable in her devotedness. Her choice of a man like Lord Dannisburgh for the friend to whom she could sacrifice her good name less falteringly than she gathered those field-flowers was inexplicable; and she herself a darker riddle at each step of his reading.

He promised curtly to write. "I will do my best to hit a flying address."

"Your Club enables me to hit a permanent one that will establish the communication," said Diana. "We shall not sleep another night at Rovio. Lady Esquart is the lightest of sleepers, and if you had a restless time, she and her husband must have been in purgatory. Besides, permit me to say, you should be with your party. The times are troublous — not for holidays! Your holiday has had a haunted look, creditably to your conscience as a politician. These Corn Law agitations!"

"Ah, but no politics here!" said Dacier.

"Politics everywhere! — in the Courts of Faëry! They are not discord to me."

"But not the last day — the last hour!" he pleaded.

"Well! only do not forget your assurance to me that you would give some thoughts to Ireland — and the cause of women. Has it slipped from your memory?"

"If I see the chance of serving you, you may trust to me."

She sent up an interjection on the misfortune of her not having been born a man

It was to him the one smart of sourness in her charm as a woman.

Among the boulder-stones of the ascent to the path, he ventured to propose a little masculine assistance in a hand stretched mutely. Although there was no great need for help, her natural kindliness checked the inclination to refuse it. When their hands disjoined she found herself reddening. She cast it on the exertion. Her heart was throbbing. It might be the exertion likewise.

He walked and talked much more airily along the descending pathway, as if he had suddenly become more intimately acquainted with her.

She listened, trying to think of the manner in which he might be taught to serve that cause she had at heart; and the colour deepened on her cheeks till it set fire to her underlying consciousness: blood to spirit. A tremor of alarm ran through her.

His request for one of the crocuses to keep as a souvenir of the morning was refused. "They are sacred; they were all devoted to my friend when I plucked them."

He pointed to a half-open one, with the petals in disparting pointing to junction, and compared it to the famous tiptoe ballet-posture, arms above head and fingers like swallows meeting in air, of an operatic danseuse of the time.

"I do not see it, because I will not see it," she said, and she found a personal cooling and consolement in the phrase. — We have this power of resisting invasion of the poetic by the commonplace, the spirit by the blood, if we please, though you men may not think that we have! — Her alarmed sensibilities bristled and made head against him as an enemy. She fancied (for the aforesaid reason — because she chose) that it was on account of the offence to her shy morning pleasure by his Londonizing. At any other moment her natural liveliness and trained social ease would have taken any remark on the eddies of the tide of converse; and so she told herself, and did not the less feel wounded, adverse, armed. He seemed somehow to have dealt a mortal blow to the happy girl she had become again. The woman she was protested on behalf of the girl, while the girl in her heart bent lowered sad eyelids

to the woman; and which of them was wiser of the truth
she could not have said, for she was honestly not aware of
the truth, but she knew she was divided in halves, with
one half pitying the other, one rebuking: and all because
of the incongruous comparison of a wild flower to an opera
dancer! Absurd indeed. We human creatures are the
silliest on earth, most certainly.

Dacier had observed the blush, and the check to her
flowing tongue did not escape him as they walked back
to the inn down the narrow street of black rooms, where
the women gossiped at the fountain and the cobbler
threaded on his doorstep. His novel excitement supplied
the deficiency, sweeping him past minor reflections. He
was, however, surprised to hear her tell Lady Esquart, as
soon as they were together at the breakfast-table, that he
had the intention of starting for England; and further
surprised, and slightly stung too, when on the poor lady's
moaning over her recollection of the midnight Bell, and
vowing she could not attempt to sleep another night in the
place, Diana declared her resolve to stay there one day
longer with her maid, and explore the neighbourhood for
the wild flowers in which it abounded. Lord and Lady
Esquart agreed to anything agreeable to her, after excusing
themselves for the necessitated flight, piteously relating
the story of their sufferings. My lord could have slept,
but he had remained awake to comfort my lady.

"True knightliness!" Diana said, in praise of these
long married lovers; and she asked them what they had
talked of during the night.

"You, my dear, partly," said Lady Esquart.

"For an opiate?"

"An invocation of the morning," said Dacier.

Lady Esquart looked at Diana and at him. She thought
it was well that her fair friend should stay. It was then
settled for Diana to rejoin them the next evening at Lugano,
thence to proceed to Luino on the Maggiore.

"I fear it is good-bye for me," Dacier said to her, as he
was about to step into the carriage with the Esquarts.

"If you have not better news of your uncle, it must be,"
she replied, and gave him her hand promptly and formally,
hardly diverting her eyes from Lady Esquart to grace the

temporary gift with a look. The last of her he saw was a waving of her arm and a finger pointing triumphantly at the Bell in the tower. It said, to an understanding unpractised in the feminine mysteries: " I can sleep through anything." What that revealed of her state of conscience and her nature, his efforts to preserve the lovely optical figure blocked his guessing. He was with her friends, who liked her the more they knew her, and he was compelled to lean to their view of the perplexing woman.

"She is a riddle to the world," Lady Esquart said, "but I know that she is good. It is the best of signs when women take to her and are proud to be her friend."

My lord echoed his wife. She talked in this homely manner to stop any notion of philandering that the young gentleman might be disposed to entertain in regard to a lady so attractive to the pursuit as Diana's beauty and delicate situation might make her seem.

"She is an exceedingly clever person, and handsomer than report, which is uncommon," said Dacier, becoming voluble on town-topics, Miss Asper incidentally among them. He denied Lady Esquart's charge of an engagement; the matter hung.

His letters at Lugano summoned him to England instantly.

"I have taken leave of Mrs. Warwick, but tell her I regret, et caetera," he said ; "and by the way, as my uncle's illness appears to be serious, the longer she is absent the better, perhaps."

"It would never do," said Lady Esquart, understanding his drift immediately. "We winter in Rome. She will not abandon us — I have her word for it. Next Easter we are in Paris ; and so home, I suppose. There will be no hurry before we are due at Cowes. We seem to have become confirmed wanderers ; for two of us at least it is likely to be our last great tour."

Dacier informed her that he had pledged his word to write to Mrs. Warwick of his uncle's condition, and the several appointed halting-places of the Esquarts between the lakes and Florence were named to him. Thus all things were openly treated ; all had an air of being on the surface ; the communications passing between Mrs. Warwick and

the Hon. Percy Dacier might have been perused by all the
world.   None but that portion of it, sage in suspiciousness,
which objects to such communications under any circumstances, could have detected in their correspondence a spark
of coming fire or that there was common warmth.   She did
not feel it, nor did he.   The position of the two interdicted
it to a couple honourably sensible of social decencies; and
who were, be it added, kept apart.   The blood is the
treacherous element in the story of the nobly civilized, of
which secret Diana, a wife and no wife, a prisoner in liberty,
a blooming woman imagining herself restored to tran-
scendent maiden ecstasies — the highest youthful poetic —
had received some faint intimation when the blush flamed
suddenly in her cheeks and her heart knelled like the
towers of a city given over to the devourer.   She had no
wish to meet him again.   Without telling herself why, she
would have shunned the meeting.   Disturbers that thwarted
her simple happiness in sublime scenery were best avoided.
She thought so the more for a fitful blur to the simplicity
of her sensations, and a task she sometimes had in restoring
and toning them, after that sweet morning time in Rovio.

CHAPTER XVII

"THE PRINCESS EGERIA"

London, say what we will of it, is after all the head of
the British giant, and if not the liveliest in bubbles, it is
past competition the largest broth-pot of brains anywhere
simmering on the hob: over the steadiest of furnaces too.
And the oceans and the continents, as you know, are perpetual and copious contributors, either to the heating
apparatus or to the contents of the pot.   Let grander
similes be sought.   This one fits for the smoky receptacle
cherishing millions, magnetic to tens of millions more, with
its caked outside of grime, and the inward substance incessantly kicking the lid, prankish, but never casting it off.
A good stew, you perceive; not a parlous boiling.   Weak

as we may be in our domestic cookery, our political has been sagaciously adjusted as yet to catch the ardours of the furnace without being subject to their volcanic activities.

That the social is also somewhat at fault, we have proof in occasional outcries over the absence of these or those particular persons famous for inspiriting. It sticks and clogs. The improvizing songster is missed, the convivial essayist, the humorous Dean, the travelled cynic, and he, the one of his day, the iridescent Irishman, whose remembered repartees are a feast, sharp and ringing, at divers tables descending from the upper to the fat citizen's, where, instead of coming in the sequence of talk, they are exposed by blasting, like fossil teeth of old Deluge sharks in monotonous walls of our chalk-quarries. Nor are these the less welcome for the violence of their introduction among a people glad to be set burning rather briskly awhile by the most unexpected of digs in the ribs. Dan Merion, to give an example. That was Dan Merion's joke with the watchman: and he said that other thing to the Marquis of Kingsbury, when the latter asked him if he had ever won a donkey-race. And old Dan is dead, and we are the duller for it! which leads to the question: Is genius hereditary? And the affirmative and negative are respectively maintained, rather against the Yes in the dispute, until a member of the audience speaks of Dan Merion's having left a daughter reputed for a sparkling wit not much below the level of his own. Why, are you unaware that the Mrs. Warwick of that scandal case of Warwick *versus* Dannisburgh was old Dan Merion's girl and his only child? It is true; for a friend had it from a man who had it straight from Mr. Braddock, of the firm of Braddock, Thorpe, and Simnel, her solicitors in the action, who told him he could sit listening to her for hours, and that she was as innocent as day; a wonderful combination of a good woman and a clever woman and a real beauty. Only her misfortune was to have a furiously jealous husband, and they say he went mad after hearing the verdict.

Diana was talked of in the London circles. A witty woman is such salt that where she has once been tasted she must perforce be missed more than any of the absent, the lowering heavens not having yet showered her like very

plentifully upon us. Then it was first heard that Percy
Dacier had been travelling with her. Miss Asper heard of
it. Her uncle, Mr. Quintin Manx, the millionnaire, was an
acquaintance of the new Judge and titled dignitary, Sir
Cramborne Wathin, and she visited Lady Wathin, at whose
table the report in the journals of the Nile-boat party was
mentioned. Lady Wathin's table could dispense with witty
women, and, for that matter, witty men. The intrusion of
the spontaneous on the stereotyped would have clashed.
She preferred, as hostess, the old legal anecdotes sure of
their laugh, and the citations from the manufactories of
fun in the Press, which were current and instantly intelligible to all her guests. She smiled suavely on an impromptu pun, because her experience of the humorous
appreciation of it by her guests bade her welcome the up-
start. Nothing else impromptu was acceptable. Mrs.
Warwick therefore was not missed by Lady Wathin. "I
have met her," she said. "I confess I am *not* one of the
fanatics about Mrs. Warwick. She has a sort of skill in
getting men to clamour. If you stoop to tickle them, they
will applaud. It is a way of winning a reputation." When
the ladies were separated from the gentlemen by the stream
of Claret, Miss Asper heard Lady Wathin speak of Mrs.
Warwick again. An illusion to Lord Dannisburgh's fit of
illness in the House of Lords led to her saying that there
was no doubt he had been fascinated, and that, in her
opinion, Mrs. Warwick was a dangerous woman. Sir
Cramborne knew something of Mr. Warwick: "Poor
man!" she added. A lady present put a question concerning Mrs. Warwick's beauty. "Yes," Lady Wathin said,
"she has good looks to aid her. Judging from what I hear
and have seen, her thirst is for notoriety. Sooner or later
we shall have her making a noise, you may be certain.
Yes, she *has* the secret of dressing well — in the French
style."

A simple newspaper report of the expedition of a Nile-
boat party could stir the Powers to take her up and turn
her on their wheel in this manner.

But others of the sons and daughters of London were
regretting her prolonged absence. The great and exclusive
Whitmonby, who had dined once at Lady Wathin's table,

and vowed never more to repeat that offence to his patience, lamented bitterly to Henry Wilmers that the sole woman worthy of sitting at a little Sunday evening dinner with the cream of the choicest men of the time was away wasting herself in that insane modern chase of the picturesque! He called her a perverted Célimène.

Redworth had less to regret than the rest of her male friends, as he was receiving at intervals pleasant descriptive letters, besides manuscript sheets of ANTONIA'S new piece of composition, to correct the proofs for the press, and he read them critically, he thought. He read them with a watchful eye to guard them from the critics. ANTONIA, whatever her faults as a writer, was not one of the order whose Muse is the Public Taste. She did at least draw her inspiration from herself, and there was much to be feared in her work, if a sale was the object. Otherwise Redworth's highly critical perusal led him flatly to admire. This was like her, and that was like her, and here and there a phrase gave him the very play of her mouth, the flash of her eyes. Could he possibly wish, or bear, to have anything altered? But she had reason to desire an extended sale of the work. Her aim, in the teeth of her independent style, was at the means of independence — a feminine method of attempting to conciliate contraries; and after despatching the last sheets to the printer, he meditated upon the several ways which might serve to assist her; the main way running thus in his mind: — We have a work of genius. Genius is good for the public. What is good for the public should be recommended by the critics. It should be. How then to come at them to get it done? As he was not a member of the honourable literary craft, and regarded its arcana altogether externally, it may be confessed of him that he deemed the Incorruptible corruptible; — not, of course, with filthy coin slid into sticky palms. Critics are human, and exceedingly, beyond the common lot, when touched; and they are excited by mysterious hints of loftiness in authorship; by rumours of veiled loveliness; whispers of a general anticipation; and also Editors can jog them. Redworth was rising to be a Railway King of a period soon to glitter with rails, iron in the concrete, golden in the visionary. He had already his

Court, much against his will. The powerful magnetic attractions of those who can help the world to fortune, was exercised by him in spite of his disgust of sycophants. He dropped words to right and left of a coming work by AN-TONIA. And who was ANTONIA? — Ah! there hung the riddle. — An exalted personage? — So much so that he dared not name her even in confidence to ladies; he named the publishers. To men he said he was at liberty to speak of her only as the most beautiful woman of her time. His courtiers of both sexes were recommended to read the new story, THE PRINCESS EGERIA.

Oddly, one great lady of his Court had heard a forthcoming work of this title spoken of by Percy Dacier, not a man to read silly fiction, unless there was meaning behind the lines: that is, rich scandal of the aristocracy, diversified by stinging epigrams to the address of discernible personages. She talked of THE PRINCESS EGERIA: nay, laid her finger on the identical Princess. Others followed her. Dozens were soon flying with the torch: a new work immediately to be published from the pen of the Duchess of Stars! — And the Princess who lends her title to the book is a living portrait of the Princess of Highest Eminence, the Hope of all Civilization. — Orders for copies of THE PRINCESS EGERIA reached the astonished publishers before the book was advertized.

Speaking to editors, Redworth complimented them with friendly intimations of the real authorship of the remarkable work appearing. He used a certain penetrative mildness of tone in saying that "he hoped the book would succeed:" it deserved to; it was original; but the originality might tell against it. All would depend upon a favourable launching of such a book. "Mrs. Warwick? Mrs. Warwick?" said the most influential of editors, Mr. Marcus Tonans; "what! that singularly handsome woman? . . . The Dannisburgh affair? . . . She's Whitmonby's heroine. If she writes as cleverly as she talks, her work is worth trumpeting." He promised to see that it went into good hands for the review, and a prompt review — an essential point; none of your long digestions of the contents.

Diana's indefatigable friend had fair assurances that her book would be noticed before it dropped dead to the public appetite for novelty. He was anxious next, notwithstanding his admiration of the originality of the conception and the cleverness of the writing, lest the Literary Reviews should fail "to do it justice:" he used the term; for if they wounded her, they would take the pleasure out of success; and he had always present to him that picture of the beloved woman kneeling at the fire-grate at The Crossways, which made the thought of her suffering any wound his personal anguish, so crucially sweet and saintly had her image then been stamped on him. He bethought him, in consequence, while sitting in the House of Commons, engaged upon the affairs of the nation, and honestly engaged, for he was a vigilant worker — that the Irish Secretary, Charles Rainer, with whom he stood in amicable relations, had an interest, to the extent of reputed ownership, in the chief of the Literary Reviews. He saw Rainer on the benches, and marked him to speak to him. Looking for him shortly afterward, the man was gone. "Off to the Opera, if he's not too late for the drop," a neighbour said, smiling queerly, as though he ought to know; and then Redworth recollected current stories of Rainer's fantastical devotion to the popular prima donna of the angelical voice. He hurried to the Opera and met the vomit, and heard in the crush-room how divine she had been that night. A fellow member of the House, tolerably intimate with Rainer, informed him, between frightful stomachic roulades of her final aria, of the likeliest place where Rainer might be found when the Opera was over: not at his Club, nor at his chambers: on one of the bridges — Westminster, he fancied.

There was no need for Redworth to run hunting the man at so late an hour, but he was drawn on by the similarity in dissimilarity of this devotee of a woman, who could worship her at a distance, and talk of her to everybody. Not till he beheld Rainer's tall figure cutting the bridge-parapet, with a star over his shoulder, did he reflect on the views the other might entertain of the nocturnal solicitation to see "justice done" to a lady's new book in a particular Review, and the absurd outside of the request was immediately smothered by the natural simplicity and pressing necessity of its inside.

He crossed the road and said, "Ah?" in recognition. "Were you at the Opera this evening?"

"Oh, just at the end," said Rainer, pacing forward. "It's a fine night. Did you hear her?"

"No; too late."

Rainer pressed ahead, to meditate by himself, as was his wont. Finding Redworth beside him, he monologuized in his depths: "They'll kill her. She puts her soul into it, gives her blood. There's no failing of the voice. You see how it wears her. She's doomed. Half a year's rest on Como . . . somewhere . . . she might be saved! She won't *refuse* to work."

"Have you spoken to her?" said Redworth.

"And next to Berlin! Vienna! A horse would be —— I? I don't know her," Rainer replied. "Some of their women stand it. She's delicately built. You can't treat a lute like a drum without destroying the instrument. We look on at a murder!"

The haggard prospect from that step of the climax checked his delivery.

Redworth knew him to be a sober man in office, a man with a head for statecraft: he had made a weighty speech in the House a couple of hours back. This Opera cantatrice, no beauty, though gentle, thrilling, winning, was his corner of romance.

"Do you come here often?" he asked.

"Yes, I can't sleep."

"London at night, from the bridge, looks fine. By the way . . ."

"It's lonely here, that's the advantage," said Rainer; "I keep silver in my pocket for poor girls going to their homes, and I'm left in peace. An hour later there's the dawn down yonder."

"By the way," Redworth interposed, and was told that after these nights of her singing she never slept till morning. He swallowed the fact, sympathized, and resumed: "I want a small favour."

"No business here, please!"

"Not a bit of it. You know Mrs. Warwick. . . . You know of her. She's publishing a book. I want you to use your influence to get it noticed quickly, if you can."

" Warwick? Oh, yes, a handsome woman. Ah, yes; the Dannisburgh affair, yes. What did I hear! — They say she 's thick with Percy Dacier at present. Who was talking of her! Yes, old Lady Dacier. So she 's a friend of yours ? "

" She 's an old friend," said Redworth, composing himself; for the dose he had taken was not of the sweetest, and no protestations could be uttered by a man of the world to repel a charge of tattlers. " The truth is, her book is clever. I have read the proofs. She *must* have an income, and she won't apply to her husband, and literature should help her, if she 's fairly treated. She 's Irish by descent; Merion's daughter, witty as her father. It 's odd you have n't met her. The mere writing of the book is extraordinarily good. If it 's put into capable hands for review! that 's all it requires. And full of life . . . bright dialogue . . . capital sketches. The book 's a piece of literature. Only it must have competent critics ! "

So he talked while Rainer ejaculated : " Warwick? Warwick ? " in the irritating tone of dozens of others. " What did I hear of her husband ? He has a post. . . . Yes, yes. Some one said the verdict in that case knocked him over — heart disease, or something."

He glanced at the dark Thames water. " Take my word for it, the groves of Academe won't compare with one of our bridges at night, if you seek philosophy. You see the London above and the London below : round us the sleepy city, and the stars in the water looking like souls of suicides. I caught a girl with a bad fit on her once. I had to lecture her! It 's when we become parsons we find out our cousin-ship with these poor peripatetics, whose 'last philosophy' is a jump across the parapet. The bridge at night is a bath for a public man. But choose another ; leave me mine."

Redworth took the hint. He stated the title of Mrs. Warwick's book, and imagined from the thoughtful cast of Rainer's head, that he was impressing THE PRINCESS EGERIA on his memory.

Rainer burst out, with clenched fists : " He beats her! The fellow lives on her and beats her; strikes that woman! He drags her about to every Capital in Europe to make money for him, and the scoundrel pays her with blows."

In the course of a heavy tirade against the scoundrel, Redworth apprehended that it was the cantatrice's husband. He expressed his horror and regret; paused, and named THE PRINCESS EGERIA and a certain Critical Review. Another outburst seemed to be in preparation. Nothing further was to be done for the book at that hour. So, with a blunt "Good night," he left Charles Rainer pacing, and thought on his walk home of the strange effects wrought by women unwittingly upon men (Englishmen); those women, or some of them, as little knowing it as the moon her traditional influence upon the tides. He thought of Percy Dacier too. In his bed he could have wished himself peregrinating a bridge.

THE PRINCESS EGERIA appeared, with the reviews at her heels, a pack of clappers, causing her to fly over editions clean as a doe the gates and hedges — to quote Mr. Sullivan Smith, who knew not a sentence of the work save what he gathered of it from Redworth, at their chance meeting on Piccadilly pavement, and then immediately he knew enough to blow his huntsman's horn in honour of the sale. His hallali rang high. "Here's another Irish girl to win their laurels! 'T is one of the blazing successes. A most enthralling work, beautifully composed. And where is she now, Mr. Redworth, since she broke away from that husband of hers, that wears the clothes of the worst tailor ever begotten by a thread on a needle, as I tell every soul of 'em in my part of the country?"

"You have seen him?" said Redworth.

"Why, sir, wasn't he on show at the Court he applied to for relief and damages? as we heard when we were watching the case daily, scarce drawing our breath for fear the innocent — and one of our own blood, would be crushed. Sure, there he stood; ay, and looking the very donkey for a woman to flip off her fingers, like the dust from my great uncle's prise of snuff! She's a glory to the old country. And better you than another, I'd say, since it wasn't an Irishman to have her: but what induced the dear lady to take *him*, is the question we're all of us asking! And it's mournful to think that somehow you contrive to get the pick of us in the girls! If ever we're united, 't will be by a trick of circumvention of that sort, pretty sure. There's a turn in the market when they shut their eyes and drop to the handiest: and London's a vortex that poor dear dull old Dublin can't compete with. I'll beg you for the address of the lady her friend, Lady Dunstane."

Mr. Sullivan Smith walked with Redworth through the park to the House of Commons, discoursing of Rails and his excellent old friend's rise to the top rung of the ladder and Beanstalk land, so elevated that one had to look up at him with watery eyes, as if one had flung a ball at the meridian sun. Arrived at famed St. Stephen's, he sent in his compliments to the noble patriot and accepted an invitation to dinner.

"And mind you read THE PRINCESS EGERIA," said Redworth.

"Again and again, my friend. The book is bought." Sullivan Smith slapped his breastpocket.

"There's a bit of Erin in it."

"It sprouts from Erin."

"Trumpet it."

"Loud as cavalry to the charge!"

Once with the title stamped on his memory, the zealous Irishman might be trusted to become an ambulant advertizer. Others, personal friends, adherents, courtiers of Redworth's, were active. Lady Pennon and Henry Wilmers, in the upper circle; Whitmonby and Westlake, in the literary, — spread the fever for this new book. The chief interpreter of public opinion caught the way of the wind and headed the gale.

Editions of the book did really run like fires in summer furze; and to such an extent that a simple literary performance grew to be respected in Great Britain, as representing Money.

CHAPTER XVIII

THE AUTHORESS

THE effect of a great success upon Diana, at her second literary venture, was shown in the transparent sedateness of a letter she wrote to Emma Dunstane, as much as in her immediate and complacent acceptance of the magical change of her fortunes. She spoke one thing and acted another, but did both with a lofty calm that deceived the admiring friend who clearly saw the authoress behind her mask, and feared lest she should be too confidently trusting to the powers of her pen to support an establishment.

"If the public were a perfect instrument to strike on, I should be tempted to take the wonderful success of my PRINCESS at her first appearance for a proof of natural aptitude in composition, and might think myself the genius. I know it to be as little a Stradivarius as I am a Paganini. It is an eccentric machine, in tune with me for the moment, because I happen to have hit it in the ringing spot. The book is a *new face* appealing to a mirror of the common surface emotions ; and the kitchen rather than the dairy offers an analogy for the real value of that 'top-skim.' I have not seen what I consider good in the book once mentioned among the laudatory notices — except by your dear hand, my Emmy. Be sure I will stand on guard against the 'vaporous generalizations,' and other 'tricks' you fear. Now that you are studying Latin for an occupation — how good and wise it was of Mr. Redworth to propose it! — I look upon you with awe as a classic authority and critic. I wish I had leisure to study with you. What I do is nothing like so solid and durable.

"THE PRINCESS EGERIA originally (I must have written word of it to you — I remember the evening off Palermo!) was conceived as a sketch ; by gradations she grew into a sort of semi-Scudéry romance, and swelled to her present portliness. That was done by a great deal of piecing, not to say puffing, of her frame. She would be healthier and have a chance of living longer if she were reduced by a reversal of the processes. But how would the judicious clippings and prickings affect our 'pensive public'? Now that I have furnished a house and have a fixed address, under the paws of creditors, I feel I am in the wizard-circle of my popularity and subscribe to its laws or waken to incubus and the desert. Have I been rash? You do not pronounce. If I have bound myself to pipe as others please, it need not be *entirely*; and I can promise you it shall not be; but still I am sensible when I lift my 'little quill' of having forced the note of a woodland wren into the popular nightingale's — which may end in the daw's, from straining; or worse, a toy-whistle.

"That is, in the field of literature. Otherwise, within me deep, I am not aware of any transmutation of the celestial into coined gold. I sound myself, and ring clear. Incessant writing is my refuge, my solace — escape out of the personal net. I delight in it, as in my early morning walks at Lugano, when I went threading the streets and by the lake away to 'the heavenly mount,' like a dim idea worming upward in a sleepy head to bright wakefulness.

"My anonymous critic, of whom I told you, is intoxicating with eulogy. The signature 'Apollonius' appears to be of literary-middle indication. He marks passages approved by you. I have also had a complimentary letter from Mr. Dacier.

"For an instance of this delight I have in writing, so strong is it that I can read pages I have written, and tear the stuff to strips (I did yesterday), and resume, as if nothing had happened. The waves within are ready for any displacement. That must be a good sign. I do not doubt of excelling my PRINCESS; and if *she* received compliments, the next may hope for more. Consider, too, the novel pleasure of earning money by the labour we delight in. It is an answer to your question whether I am happy. Yes, as the savage islander before the ship entered the bay with the fire-water. My blood is wine, and I have the slumbers of an infant. I dream, wake, forget my dream, barely dress before the pen is galloping; barely breakfast; no toilette till noon. A savage in good sooth! You see, my Emmy, I could not house with the 'companionable person' you hint at. The poles can never come together till the earth is crushed. She would find my habits intolerable, and I hers contemptible, though we might both be companionable persons. My dear, I could not even live with *myself*. My blessed little quill, which helps me divinely to live out of myself, is and must continue to be my one companion. It is my mountain height, morning light, wings, cup from the springs, my horse, my goal, my lancet and replenisher, my key of communication with the highest, grandest, holiest between earth and heaven — the vital air connecting them.

"In justice let me add that I have not been troubled by hearing of any of the mysterious legal claims, et caetera. I am sorry to hear bad reports of health. I wish him entire felicity — no step taken to bridge division! The thought of it makes me tigrish.

"A new pianist playing his own pieces (at Lady Singleby's concert) has given me exquisite pleasure and set me composing songs — not to his music, which could be rendered only by sylphs moving to 'soft recorders' in the humour of wildness, languor, bewitching caprices, giving a new sense to melody. How I wish you had been with me to hear him! It was the most Æolian thing ever caught from a night-breeze by the soul of a poet.

"But do not suppose me having headlong tendencies to the melting mood. (The above, by the way, is a Pole settled in Paris, and he is to be introduced to me at Lady Pennon's.) — What do you say to my being invited by Mr. Whitmonby to aid him in writing leading articles for the paper he is going to conduct! 'write as you talk and it will do,' he says. I am choosing my themes. To write — of politics — as I talk, seems to me like an effort to jump away from my shadow. The black dog of consciousness declines to be shaken off. If some one commanded me to *talk as I write!* I suspect it would be a way of winding me up to a sharp critical pitch rapidly.

"Not good news of Lord D. I have had messages. Mr. Dacier conceals his alarm. The PRINCESS gave *great gratification*. She did me her best service there. Is it not cruel that the interdict of the censor should force me to depend for information upon such scraps as I get from a gentleman passing my habitation on his way to the House? And he is not, he never has been, sympathetic in that direction. He sees my grief, and assumes an undertakerly air, with some notion of acting in concert, one supposes — little imagining how I revolt from that crape-hatband formalism of sorrow!

"One word of her we call our inner I. I am not drawing upon her resources for my daily needs; not wasting her at all, I trust; certainly not walling her up, to deafen her voice. It would be to fall away from you. She bids me sign myself, my beloved, ever, ever your Tony."

The letter had every outward show of sincereness in expression, and was endowed to wear that appearance by the writer's impulse to protest with so resolute a vigour as to delude herself. Lady Dunstane heard of Mr. Dacier's novel attendance at concerts. The world made a note of it; for the gentleman was notoriously without ear for music.

Diana's comparison of her hours of incessant writing to her walks under the dawn at Lugano, her boast of the similarity of her delight in both, deluded her uncorrupted conscience to believe that she was now spiritually as free as in that fair season of the new spring in her veins. She was not an investigating physician, nor was Lady Dunstane, otherwise they would have examined the material points of her conduct — indicators of the spiritual secret always. What are the patient's acts? The patient's mind was projected too far beyond them to see the forefinger they stretched at her; and the friend's was not that of a prying doctor on the look out for betraying symptoms. Lady Dunstane did ask herself why Tony should have incurred the burden of a costly household — a very costly: Sir Lukin had been at one of Tony's little dinners: — but her wish to meet the world on equal terms, after a long dependency, accounted for it in seeming to excuse. The guests on the occasion were Lady Pennon, Lady Singleby, Mr. Whitmonby, Mr. Percy Dacier, Mr. Tonans; — "Some other woman," Sir Lukin said, and himself. He reported the cookery as matching the conversation, and that was princely; the wines not less: an extraordinary fact to note of a woman. But to hear Whitmonby and Diana Warwick! How he told a story, neat as a postman's knock, and she tipped it with a remark and ran to a second, drawing in

Lady Pennon, and then Dacier, "and me!" cried Sir
Lukin; "she made us all toss the ball from hand to hand,
and all talk up to the mark; and none of us noticed that we
all went together to the drawing-room, where we talked for
another hour, and broke up fresher than we began."

"That break between the men and the women after dinner was Tony's aversion, and I am glad she has instituted
a change," said Lady Dunstane.

She heard also from Redworth of the unexampled concert of the guests at Mrs. Warwick's dinner parties. He
had met on one occasion the Esquarts, the Pettigrews, Mr.
Percy Dacier, and a Miss Paynham. Redworth had not
a word to say of the expensive household. Whatever
Mrs. Warwick did was evidently good to him. On another
evening the party was composed of Lady Pennon, Lord
Larrian, Miss Paynham, a clever Mrs. Wollasley, Mr. Henry
Wilmers, and again Mr. Percy Dacier.

When Diana came to Copsley, Lady Dunstane remarked
on the recurrence of the name of Miss Paynham in the list
of her guests.

"And Mr. Percy Dacier's too," said Diana, smiling.
"They are invited each for specific reasons. It pleases
Lord Dannisburgh to hear that a way has been found to enliven his nephew; and my little dinners are effective, I
think. He wakes. Yesterday evening he capped flying
jests with Mr. Sullivan Smith. But you speak of Miss
Paynham." Diana lowered her voice on half a dozen syllables, till the half-tones dropped into her steady look. "You
approve, Emmy?"

The answer was: "I do—true or not."

"Between us two, dear, I fear! . . . In either case, she
has been badly used. Society is big engine enough to protect itself. I incline with British juries to do rough justice
to the victims. She has neither father nor brother. I have
had no confidences: but it wears the look of a cowardly business. With two words in his ear, I could arm an Irishman
to do some work of chastisement:— he would select the
rascal's necktie for a cause of quarrel: and lords have to
stand their ground as well as commoners. They measure
the same number of feet when stretched their length.
However, vengeance with the heavens! though they seem

tardy. Lady Pennon has been very kind about it; and the Esquarts invite her to Lockton. Shoulder to shoulder, the tide may be stemmed."

"She would have gone under, but for you, dear Tony!" said Emma, folding arms round her darling's neck and kissing her. "Bring her here some day."

Diana did not promise it. She had her vision of Sir Lukin in his fit of lunacy.

"I am too weak for London now," Emma resumed. "I should like to be useful. Is she pleasant?"

"Sprightly by nature. She has worn herself with fretting."

"Then bring her to stay with me, if I cannot keep you. She will talk of you to me."

"I will bring her for a couple of days," Diana said. "I am too busy to remain longer. She paints portraits to amuse herself. She ought to be pushed, wherever she is received about London, while the season is warm. One season will suffice to establish her. She is pretty, near upon six and twenty: foolish, of course: she pays for having had a romantic head. Heavy payment, Emmy! I drive at laws, but hers is an instance of the creatures wanting simple human kindness."

"The good law will come with a better civilization; but before society can be civilized it has to be debarbarized," Emma remarked, and Diana sighed over the task and the truism.

"I should have said in younger days, because it will not look plainly on our nature and try to reconcile it with our conditions. But now I see that the sin is cowardice. The more I know of the world the more clearly I perceive that its top and bottom sin is cowardice, physically and morally alike. Lord Larrian owns to there being few heroes in an army. We must fawn in society. What is the meaning of that dread of one example of tolerance? O my dear! let us give it the right name. Society is the best thing we have, but it is a crazy vessel worked by a crew that formerly practised piracy, and now, in expiation, professes piety, fearful of a discovered Omnipotence, which is in the image of themselves and captain. Their old habits are not quite abandoned, and their new one is used as a lash to whip the exposed of us for a propitiation of the capricious potentate whom they worship in the place of the true God."

Lady Dunstane sniffed. "I smell the leading article."

Diana joined with her smile, "No, the style is rather different."

"Have you not got into a trick of composing in speaking, at times?"

Diana confessed, "I think I have at times. Perhaps the daily writing of all kinds and the nightly talking . . . I may be getting strained."

"No, Tony; but longer visits in the country to me would refresh you. I miss your lighter touches. London is a school, but, you know it, not a school for comedy nor for philosophy; that is gathered on my hills, with London distantly in view, and then occasional descents on it well digested."

"I wonder whether it is affecting me!" said Diana, musing. "A metropolitan hack! and while thinking myself free, thrice harnessed; and all my fun gone. Am I really as dull as a tract, my dear? I must be, or I should be proving the contrary instead of asking. My pitfall is to fancy I have powers equal to the first look-out of the eyes of the morning. Enough of me. We talked of Mary Paynham. If only some right good man would marry her!"

Lady Dunstane guessed at the right good man in Diana's mind. "Do you bring them together?"

Diana nodded, and then shook doleful negatives to signify no hope.

"None whatever—if we mean the same person," said Lady Dunstane, bethinking her, in the spirt of wrath she felt at such a scheme being planned by Diana to snare the right good man, that instead of her own true lover Redworth, it might be only Percy Dacier. So filmy of mere sensations are these little ideas as they flit in converse, that she did not reflect on her friend's ignorance of Redworth's love of her, or on the unlikely choice of one in Dacier's high station to reinstate a damsel.

They did not name the person.

"Passing the instance, which is cruel, I will be just to society thus far," said Diana. "I was in a boat at Rich-

mond last week, and Leander was revelling along the
mud-banks, and took it into his head to swim out to me,
and I was moved to take him on board. The ladies in the
boat objected, for he was not only wet but very muddy. I
was forced to own that their objections were reasonable.
My sentimental humaneness had no argument against
muslin dresses, though my dear dog's eyes appealed
pathetically, and he would keep swimming after us. The
analogy excuses the world for protecting itself in extreme
cases; nothing, nothing excuses its insensibility to cases
which may be pleaded. You see the pirate crew turned
pious — ferocious in sanctity." She added, half laughing:
"I am reminded by the boat, I have unveiled my anonymous
critic, and had a woeful disappointment. He wrote like a
veteran; he is not much more than a boy. I received a
volume of verse, and a few lines begging my acceptance. I
fancied I knew the writing, and wrote asking him whether
I had not to thank him, and inviting him to call. He seems
a nice lad of about two and twenty, mad for literature; and
he must have talent. Arthur Rhodes by name. I may
have a chance of helping him. He was an articled clerk
of Mr. Braddock's, the same who valiantly came to my
rescue once. He was with us in the boat."

"Bring him to me some day," said Lady Dunstane.

Miss Paynham's visit to Copsley was arranged, and it
turned out a failure. The poor young lady came in a
flutter, thinking that the friend of Mrs. Warwick would
expect her to discourse cleverly. She attempted it, to
Diana's amazement. Lady Dunstane's opposingly corresponding stillness provoked Miss Paynham to expatiate,
for she had sprightliness and some mental reserves of the
common order. Clearly, Lady Dunstane mused while
listening amiably, Tony never could have designed this
gabbler for the mate of Thomas Redworth!

Percy Dacier seemed to her the more likely one, in that
light, and she thought so still, after Sir Lukin had introduced him at Copsley for a couple of days of the hunting
season. Tony's manner with him suggested it; she had a
dash of leadership. They were not intimate in look or
tongue.

But Percy Dacier also was too good for Miss Paynham,

if that was Tony's plan for him, Lady Dunstane thought, with the relentlessness of an invalid and recluse's distaste. An aspect of penitence she had not demanded, but the silly gabbler under a stigma she could not pardon.

Her opinion of Miss Paynham was diffused in her silence.

Speaking of Mr. Dacier, she remarked, "As you say of him, Tony, he can brighten, and when you give him a chance he is entertaining. He has fine gifts. If I were a member of his family I should beat about for a match for him. He strikes me as one of the young men who would do better married."

"He is doing very well, but the wonder is that he does n't marry," said Diana. "He ought to be engaged. Lady Esquart told me that he was. A Miss Asper — great heiress; and the Daciers want money. However, there it is."

Not many weeks later Diana could not have spoken of Mr. Percy Dacier with this air of indifference without corruption of her inward guide.

CHAPTER XIX

A DRIVE IN SUNLIGHT AND A DRIVE IN MOONLIGHT

THE fatal time to come for her was in the Summer of that year.

Emma had written her a letter of unwonted bright spirits, contrasting strangely with an inexplicable oppression of her own that led her to imagine her recent placid life the pause before thunder, and to share the mood of her solitary friend she flew to Copsley, finding Sir Lukin absent, as usual. They drove out immediately after breakfast, on one of those high mornings of the bared bosom of June when distances are given to our eyes, and a soft air fondles leaf and grassblade, and beauty and peace are overhead, reflected, if we will. Rain had fallen in the night. Here and there hung a milkwhite cloud with folded sail.

The South-west left it in its bay of blue, and breathed
below. At moments the fresh scent of herb and mould
swung richly in warmth. The young beech-leaves glittered,
pools of rain-water made the roadways laugh, the grass-
banks under hedges rolled their interwoven weeds in
cascades of many-shaded green to right and left of the pair
of dappled ponies, and a squirrel crossed ahead, a lark went
up a little way to ease his heart, closing his wings when
the burst was over, startled black-birds, darting with a
clamour like a broken cockcrow, looped the wayside woods
from hazel to oak-scrub; short flights, quick spirts everywhere, steady sunshine above.

Diana held the reins. The whip was an ornament, as
the plume of feathers to the general officer. Lady Dunstane's ponies were a present from Redworth, who always
chose the pick of the land for his gifts. They joyed in
their trot, and were the very love-birds of the breed for
their pleasure of going together, so like that Diana called
them the Dromios. Through an old gravel-cutting a gateway led to the turf of the down, springy turf bordered on a
long line, clear as a racecourse, by golden gorse covers, and
leftward over the gorse the dark ridge of the fir and heath
country ran companionably to the South-west, the valley
between, with undulations of wood and meadow sunned or
shaded, clumps, mounds, promontories, away to broad
spaces of tillage banked by wooded hills, and dimmer beyond and farther, the faintest shadowiness of heights, as a
veil to the illimitable. Yews, junipers, radiant beeches,
and gleams of the service-tree or the white-beam spotted
the semicircle of swelling green Down black and silver.
The sun in the valley sharpened his beams on squares of
buttercups, and made a pond a diamond.

"You see, Tony," Emma said, for a comment on the
scene, "I could envy Italy for having you, more than you
for being in Italy."

"Feature and colour!" said Diana. "You have them
here, and on a scale that one can embrace. I should like
to build a hut on this point, and wait for such a day to
return. It brings me to life." She lifted her eyelids on
her friend's worn sweet face, and knowing her this friend
up to death, past it in her hopes, she said bravely, "It is

the Emma of days and scenes to me! It helps me to forget myself, as I do when I think of you, dearest; but the subject has latterly been haunting me, I don't know why, and ominously, as if my nature were about to horrify my soul. But I am not sentimentalizing, you are really this day and scene in my heart."

Emma smiled confidingly. She spoke her reflection: "The heart must be troubled a little to have the thought. The flower I gather here tells me that we may be happy in privation and suffering if simply we can accept beauty. I won't say expel the passions, but keep passion sober, a trotter in harness."

Diana caressed the ponies' heads with the droop of her whip: "I don't think I know him!" she said.

Between sincerity and a suspicion so cloaked and dull that she did not feel it to be the opposite of candour, she fancied she was passionless because she could accept the visible beauty, which was Emma's prescription and test; and she forced herself to make much of it, cling to it, devour it; with envy of Emma's contemplative happiness, through whose grave mind she tried to get to the peace in it, imagining that she succeeded. The cloaked and dull suspicion weighed within her nevertheless. She took it for a mania to speculate on herself. There are states of the crimson blood when the keenest wits are childish, notably in great-hearted women aiming at the majesty of their sex and fearful of confounding it by the look direct and the downright word. Yet her nature compelled her inwardly to phrase the sentence: "Emma is a wife!" The character of her husband was not considered, nor was the meaning of the exclamation pursued.

They drove through the gorse into wild land of heath and flowering hawthorn, and along by tracts of yew and juniper to another point, jutting on a furzy sand-mound, rich with the mild splendour of English scenery, which Emma stamped on her friend's mind by saying: "A cripple has little to envy in you who can fly when she has feasts like these at her doors."

They had an inclination to boast on the drive home of the solitude they had enjoyed; and just then, as the road in the wood wound under great beeches, they beheld a

London hat. The hat was plucked from its head. A clear-faced youth, rather flushed, dusty at the legs, addressed Diana.

"Mr. Rhodes!" she said, not discouragingly.

She was petitioned to excuse him; he thought she would wish to hear the news in town last night as early as possible; he hesitated and murmured it.

Diana turned to Emma: "Lord Dannisburgh!" — her paleness told the rest.

Hearing from Mr. Rhodes that he had walked the distance from town, and had been to Copsley, Lady Dunstane invited him to follow the pony-carriage thither, where he was fed and refreshed by a tea-breakfast, as he preferred walking on tea, he said. "I took the liberty to call at Mrs. Warwick's house," he informed her; "the footman said she was at Copsley. I found it on the map — I knew the direction — and started about two in the morning. I wanted a walk."

It was evident to her that he was one of the young squires bewitched whom beautiful women are constantly enlisting. There was no concealment of it, though he stirred a sad enviousness in the invalid lady by descanting on the raptures of a walk out of London in the youngest light of day, and on the common objects he had noticed along the roadside, and through the woods, more sustaining, closer with nature than her compulsory feeding on the cream of things.

"You are not fatigued?" she inquired, hoping for that confession at least; but she pardoned his boyish vaunting to walk the distance back without any fatigue at all.

He had a sweeter reward for his pains; and if the business of the chronicler allowed him to become attached to pure throbbing felicity wherever it is encountered, he might be diverted by the blissful unexpectedness of good fortune befalling Mr. Arthur Rhodes in having the honour to conduct Mrs. Warwick to town. No imagined happiness, even in the heart of a young man of two and twenty, could have matched it. He was by her side, hearing and seeing her, not less than four hours. To add to his happiness, Lady Dunstane said she would be glad to welcome him again. She thought him a pleasant specimen of the self-vowed squire.

Diana was sure that there would be a communication for her of some sort at her house in London; perhaps a message of farewell from the dying lord, now dead. Mr. Rhodes had only the news of the evening journals, to the effect that Lord Dannisburgh had expired at his residence, the Priory, Hallowmere, in Hampshire. A message of farewell from him, she hoped for: knowing him as she did, it seemed a certainty; and she hungered for that last gleam of life in her friend. She had no anticipation of the burden of the message awaiting her.

A consultation as to the despatching of the message, had taken place among the members of Lord Dannisburgh's family present at his death. Percy Dacier was one of them, and he settled the disputed point, after some time had been spent in persuading his father to take the plain view of obligation in the matter, and in opposing the dowager countess, his grandmother, by stating that he had already sent a special messenger to London. Lord Dannisburgh on his death-bed had expressed a wish that Mrs. Warwick would sit with him for an hour one night before the nails were knocked in his coffin. He spoke of it twice, putting it the second time to Percy as a formal request to be made to her, and Percy had promised him that Mrs. Warwick should have the message. He had done his best to keep his pledge, aware of the disrelish of the whole family for the lady's name, to say nothing of her presence.

"She won't come," said the earl.

"She'll come," said old Lady Dacier.

"If the woman respects herself she'll hold off it," the earl insisted because of his desire that way. He signified in mutterings that the thing was improper and absurd, a piece of sentiment, sickly senility, unlike Lord Dannisburgh. Also that Percy had been guilty of excessive folly.

To which Lady Dacier nodded her assent, remarking: "The woman is on her mettle. From what I've heard of her, she's not a woman to stick at trifles. She'll take it as a sort of ordeal by touch, and she'll come."

They joined in abusing Percy, who had driven away to another part of the country. Lord Creedmore, the heir of the house, was absent, hunting in America, or he might temporarily have been taken into favour by contrast.

Ultimately they agreed that the woman must be allowed to enter the house, but could not be received. The earl was a widower; his mother managed the family, and being hard to convince, she customarily carried her point, save when it involved Percy's freedom of action. She was one of the veterans of her sex that age to toughness; and the "hysterical fuss" she apprehended in the visit of this woman to Lord Dannisburgh's death-bed and body, did not alarm her. For the sake of the household she determined to remain, shut up in her room. Before night the house was empty of any members of the family excepting old Lady Dacier and the outstretched figure on the bed.

Dacier fled to escape the hearing of the numberless ejaculations re-awakened in the family by his uncle's extraordinary dying request. They were an outrage to the lady, of whom he could now speak as a privileged champion; and the request itself had an air of proving her stainless, a white soul and efficacious advocate at the celestial gates (reading the mind of the dying man). So he thought at one moment: he had thought so when charged with the message to her; had even thought it a natural wish that she should look once on the face she would see no more, and say farewell to it, considering that in life it could not be requested. But the susceptibility to sentimental emotion beside a death-bed, with a dying man's voice in the ear, requires fortification if it is to be maintained; and the review of his uncle's character did not tend to make this very singular request a proof that the lady's innocence was honoured in it. His epicurean uncle had no profound esteem for the kind of innocence. He had always talked of Mrs. Warwick with warm respect for her: Dacier knew that he had bequeathed her a sum of money. The inferences were either way. Lord Dannisburgh never spoke evilly of any woman, and he was perhaps bound to indemnify her materially as well as he could for what she had suffered. — On the other hand, how easy it was to be the dupe of a woman so handsome and clever. — Unlikely too that his uncle would consent to sit at the Platonic banquet with her. — Judging by himself, Dacier deemed it possible for man. He was not quick to kindle, and had lately seen much of her, had found her a Lady Egeria, helpful in counsel, prompting, inspiriting,

reviving as well-waters, and as temperately cool: not one
sign of native slipperiness. Nor did she stir the mud in
him upon which proud man is built. The shadow of the
scandal had checked a few shifty sensations rising now and
then of their own accord, and had laid them, with the lady's
benign connivance. This was good proof in her favour,
seeing that she must have perceived of late the besetting
thirst he had for her company; and alone or in the medley
equally. To see her, hear, exchange ideas with her; and to
talk of new books, try to listen to music at the opera and at
concerts, and admire her playing of hostess, were novel
pleasures, giving him fresh notions of life, and strengthening rather than disturbing the course of his life's business.

At any rate, she was capable of friendship. Why not
resolutely believe that she had been his uncle's true and
simple friend! He adopted the resolution, thanking her
for one recognized fact: — he hated marriage, and would by
this time have been in the yoke, but for the agreeable
deviation of his path to her society. Since his visit to
Copsley, moreover, Lady Dunstane's idolizing of her friend
had influenced him. Reflecting on it, he recovered from
the shock which his uncle's request had caused.

Certain positive calculations were running side by side
with the speculations in vapour. His messenger would
reach her house at about four of the afternoon. If then at
home, would she decide to start immediately? — Would she
come? That was a question he did not delay to answer.
Would she defer the visit? Death replied to that. She
would not delay it.

She would be sure to come at once. And what of the
welcome she would meet? Leaving the station in London
at six in the evening, she might arrive at the Priory, all
impediments counted, between ten and eleven at night.
Thence, coldly greeted, or not greeted, to the chamber of
death.

A pitiable and cruel reception for a woman upon such a
mission!

His mingled calculations and meditations reached that
exclamatory terminus in feeling, and settled on the picture
of Diana, about as clear as light to blinking eyes, but enough
for him to realize her being there and alone, woefully alone.

The supposition of an absolute loneliness was most possible. He had intended to drive back the next day, when the domestic storm would be over, and take the chances of her coming. It seemed now a piece of duty to return at night, a traverse of twenty rough up and down miles from Itchenford to the heathland rolling on the chalk wave of the Surrey borders, easily done after the remonstrances of his host were stopped.

Dacier sat in an open carriage, facing a slip of bright moon. Poetical impressions, emotions, any stirrings of his mind by the sensational stamp on it, were new to him, and while he swam in them, both lulled and pricked by his novel accessibility to nature's lyrical touch, he asked himself whether, if he were near the throes of death, the thought of having Diana Warwick to sit beside his vacant semblance for an hour at night would be comforting. And why had his uncle specified an hour of the night? It was a sentiment, like the request: curious in a man so little sentimental. Yonder crescent running the shadowy round of the hoop roused comparisons. Would one really wish to have her beside one in death? In life — ah! But suppose her denied to us in life. Then the desire for her companionship appears passingly comprehensible. Enter into the sentiment, you see that the hour of darkness is naturally chosen. And would even a grand old Pagan crave the presence beside his dead body for an hour of the night of a woman he did not esteem? Dacier answered no. The negative was not echoed in his mind. He repeated it, and to the same deadness.

He became aware that he had spoken for himself, and he had a fit of sourness. For who can say he is not a fool before he has been tried by a woman! Dacier's wretched tendency under vexation to conceive grotesque analogies, anti-poetic, not to say cockney similes, which had slightly chilled Diana at Rovio, set him looking at yonder crescent with the hoop, as at the shape of a white cat climbing a wheel. Men of the northern blood will sometimes lend their assent to poetical images, even to those that do not stun the mind like bludgeons and imperatively, by much repetition, command their assent; and it is for a solid exchange and interest in usury with soft poetical creatures when they are so condescending; but they are seized by the grotesque. In spite of efforts to

efface or supplant it, he saw the white cat, nothing else, even
to thinking that she had jumped cleverly to catch the wheel.
He was a true descendant of practical hard-grained fighting
Northerners, of gnarled dwarf imaginations, chivalrous
though they were, and heroes to have serviceable and valiant
gentlemen for issue. Without at all tracing back to its origin
his detestable image of the white cat on the dead circle, he
kicked at the links between his uncle and Diana Warwick,
whatever they had been; particularly at the present revival
of them. Old Lady Dacier's blunt speech, and his father's
fixed opinion, hissed in his head.

They were ignorant of his autumnal visit to the Italian
Lakes, after the winter's Nile-boat expedition; and also of
the degree of his recent intimacy with Mrs. Warwick; or
else, as he knew, he would have heard more hissing things.
Her patronage of Miss Paynham exposed her to attacks
where she was deemed vulnerable; Lady Dacier muttered
old saws as to the flocking of birds; he did not accurately
understand it, thought it indiscreet, at best. But in regard to his experience, he could tell himself that a woman
more guileless of luring never drew breath. On the contrary, candour said it had always been he who had schemed
and pressed for the meeting. He was at liberty to do it, not
being bound in honour elsewhere. Besides, despite his
acknowledgment of her beauty, Mrs. Warwick was not quite
his ideal of the perfectly beautiful woman. Constance
Asper came nearer to it. He had the English taste for red
and white, and for cold outlines: he secretly admired a
statuesque demeanour with a statue's eyes. The national
approbation of a reserved haughtiness in woman, a tempered
disdain in her slightly lifted small upperlip and drooped eyelids, was shared by him; and Constance Asper, if not exactly
aristocratic by birth, stood well for that aristocratic insular
type, which seems to promise the husband of it a casket of
all the trusty virtues, as well as the security of frigidity in
the casket. Such was Dacier's native taste; consequently
the attractions of Diana Warwick for him were, he thought,
chiefly mental, those of a Lady Egeria. She might or might
not be good, in the vulgar sense. She was an agreeable
woman, an amusing companion, very suggestive, inciting,
animating; and her past history must be left as her own.

Did it matter to him? What he saw was bright, a silver crescent on the side of the shadowy ring. Were it a question of marrying her! — That was out of the possibilities. He remembered, moreover, having heard from a man, who professed to know, that Mrs. Warwick had started in married life by treating her husband cavalierly to an intolerable degree; "Such as no Englishman could stand," the portly old informant thundered, describing it and her in racy vernacular. She might be a devil of a wife. She was a pleasant friend; just the soft bit sweeter than male friends which gave the flavour of sex without the artful seductions. He required them strong to move him.

He looked at last on the green walls of the Priory, scarcely supposing a fair watcher to be within; for the contrasting pale colours of dawn had ceased to quicken the brilliancy of the crescent, and summer daylight drowned it to fainter than a silver coin in water. It lay dispieced like a pulled rag. Eastward, over Surrey, stood the full rose of morning. The Priory clock struck four. When the summons of the bell had gained him admittance, and he heard that Mrs. Warwick had come in the night, he looked back through the doorway at the rosy colour, and congratulated himself to think that her hour of watching was at an end. A sleepy footman was his informant. Women were in my lord's dressing-room, he said. Upstairs, at the death-chamber, Dacier paused. No sound came to him. He hurried to his own room, paced about, and returned. Expecting to see no one but the dead, he turned the handle, and the two circles of a shaded lamp, on ceiling and on table, met his gaze.

CHAPTER XX

DIANA'S NIGHT-WATCH IN THE CHAMBER OF DEATH

He stepped into the room, and thrilled to hear the quiet voice beside the bed: "Who is it?"

Apologies and excuses were on his tongue. The vibration of those grave tones checked them.

" It is you," she said.

She sat in shadow, her hands joined on her lap. A
unopened book was under the lamp.

He spoke in an underbreath : " I have just come.   I wa
not sure I should find you here.   Pardon."

" There is a chair."

He murmured thanks and entered into the stillnes
observing her.

" You have been watching. . . . You must be tired."

" No."

" An hour was asked, only one."

" I could not leave him."

" Watchers are at hand to relieve you."

" It is better for him to have me."

The chord of her voice told him of the gulfs she ha
sunk in during the night.   The thought of her enduranc
became a burden.

He let fall his breath for patience, and tapped the floo
with his foot.

He feared to discompose her by speaking.   The silenc
grew more fearful, as the very speech of Death betwee
them.

" You came.   I thought it right to let you know instantly
I hoped you would come to-morrow."

" I could not delay."

" You have been sitting alone here since eleven !"

" I have not found it long."

" You must want some refreshment . . . tea ? "

" I need nothing."

" It can be made ready in a few minutes."

" I could not eat or drink."

He tried to brush away the impression of the tomb in the
heavily-curtained chamber by thinking of the summer-morn
outside ; he spoke of it, the rosy sky, the dewy grass, the piping birds.   She listened, as one hearing of a quitted sphere.

Their breathing in common was just heard if either drew
a deeper breath.   At moments his eyes wandered and shut.
Alternately in his mind Death had vaster meanings and
doubtfuller ; Life cowered under the shadow or outshone
it.   He glanced from her to the figure in the bed, and she
seemed swallowed.

He said: "It is time for you to have rest. You know your room. I will stay till the servants are up."

She replied: "No, let this night with him be mine."

"I am not intruding?" . . .

"If you wish to remain" . . .

No traces of weeping were on her face. The lamp-shade revealed it colourless, and lustreless her eyes. She was robed in black. She held her hands clasped.

"You have not suffered?"

"Oh, no."

She said it without sighing: nor was her speech mournful, only brief.

"You have seen death before?"

"I sat by my father four nights. I was a girl then. I cried till I had no more tears."

He felt a burning pressure behind his eyeballs.

"Death is natural," he said.

"It is natural to the aged. When they die honoured . . ." She looked where the dead man lay. "To sit beside the young, cut off from their dear opening life! . . ." A little shudder swept over her. "Oh! that!"

"You were very good to come. We must all thank you for fulfilling his wish."

"He knew it would be my wish."

Her hands pressed together.

"He lies peacefully!"

"I have raised the lamp on him, and wondered each time. So changeless he lies. But so like a sleep that will wake. We never see peace but in the features of the dead. Will you look? They are beautiful. They have a heavenly sweetness."

The desire to look was evidently recurrent with her. Dacier rose.

Their eyes fell together on the dead man, as thoughtfully as Death allows to the creatures of sensation.

"And after?" he said in low tones.

"I trust to my Maker," she replied. "Do you see a change since he breathed his last?"

"Not any."

"You were with him?"

"Not in the room. Two minutes later."

"Who ? . . ."

"My father. His niece, Lady Cathairn."

"If our lives are lengthened we outlive most of those we would have to close our eyes. He had a dear sister."

"She died some years back."

"I helped to comfort him for that loss."

"He told me you did."

The lamp was replaced on the table.

"For a moment, when I withdraw the light from him, I feel sadness. As if the light we lend to anything were of value to him now !"

She bowed her head deeply. Dacier left her meditation undisturbed. The birds on the walls outside were audible, tweeting, chirping.

He went to the window-curtains and tried the shutter-bars. It seemed to him that daylight would be cheerfuller for her. He had a thirst to behold her standing bathed in daylight.

"Shall I open them ?" he asked her.

"I would rather the lamp," she said.

They sat silently until she drew her watch from her girdle. "My train starts at half-past six. It is a walk of thirty-five minutes to the station. I did it last night in that time."

"You walked here in the dark alone ? "

"There was no fly to be had. The station-master sent one of his porters with me. We had a talk on the road. I like those men."

Dacier read the hour by the mantelpiece clock. "If you must really go by the early train, I will drive you."

"No, I will walk ; I prefer it."

"I will order your breakfast at once."

He turned on his heel. She stopped him. "No, I have no taste for eating or drinking."

"Pray . . ." said he, in visible distress.

She shook her head. "I could not. I have twenty minutes longer. I can find my way to the station; it is almost a straight road out of the park-gates."

His heart swelled with anger at the household for the treatment she had been subjected to, judging by her resolve not to break bread in the house.

They resumed their silent sitting. The intervals for a word to pass between them were long, and the ticking of the time-piece fronting the death-bed ruled the chamber, scarcely varied.

The lamp was raised for the final look, the leave-taking.

Dacier buried his face, thinking many things — the common multitude in insurrection.

"A servant should be told to come now," she said. "I have only to put on my bonnet and I am ready."

"You will take no . . . ?"

"Nothing."

"It is not too late for a carriage to be ordered."

"No — the walk!"

They separated.

He roused the two women in the dressing-room, asleep with heads against the wall. Thence he sped to his own room for hat and overcoat, and a sprinkle of cold water. Descending the stairs, he beheld his companion issuing from the chamber of death. Her lips were shut, her eyelids nervously tremulous.

They were soon in the warm sweet open air, and they walked without an interchange of a syllable through the park into the white hawthorn lane, glad to breathe. Her nostrils took long draughts of air, but of the change of scene she appeared scarcely sensible.

At the park-gates, she said: "There is no necessity for your coming."

His answer was: "I think of myself. I gain something every step I walk with you."

"To-day is Thursday," said she. "The funeral is . . . ?"

"Monday has been fixed. According to his directions, he will lie in the churchyard of his village — not in the family vault."

"I know," she said hastily. "They are privileged who follow him and see the coffin lowered. He spoke of this quiet little resting-place."

"Yes, it's a good end. I do not wonder at his wish for the honour you have done him. I could wish it too. But more living than dead — that is a natural wish."

"It is not to be called an honour."

"I should feel it so — an honour to me."

"It is a friend's duty. The word is too harsh; — it was his friend's desire. He did not ask it so much as he sanctioned it. For to him what has my sitting beside him been!"

"He had the prospective happiness."

"He knew well that my soul would be with him — as it was last night. But he knew it would be my poor human happiness to see him with my eyes, touch him with my hand, before he passed from our sight."

Dacier exclaimed : "How you can love!"

"Is the village church to be seen?" she asked.

"To the right of those elms; that is the spire. The black spot below is a yew. You love with the whole heart when you love."

"I love my friends," she replied.

"You tempt me to envy those who are numbered among them."

"They are not many."

"They should be grateful."

"You have some acquaintance with them all."

"And an enemy? Had you ever one? Do you know of one?"

"Direct and personal designedly? I think not. We give that title to those who are disinclined to us and add a dash of darker colour to our errors. Foxes have enemies in the dogs; heroines of melodramas have their persecuting villains. I suppose that conditions of life exist where one meets the original complexities. The bad are in every rank. The inveterately malignant I have not found. Circumstances may combine to make a whisper as deadly as a blow, though not of such evil design. Perhaps if we lived at a Court of a magnificent despot we should learn that we are less highly civilized than we imagine ourselves; but that is a fire to the passions, and the extreme is not the perfect test. Our civilization counts positive gains — unless you take the melodrama for the truer picture of us. It is always the most popular with the English. — And look, what a month June is! Yesterday morning I was with Lady Dunstane on her heights, and I feel double the age. He was fond of this wild country. We think it a desert, a blank, whither he has gone, because we will strain to see in the utter dark, and nothing can come of that but the bursting of the eyeballs."

Dacier assented: "There's no use in peering beyond the limits."

"No," said she; "the effect is like the explaining of things to a dull head — the finishing stroke to the understanding! Better continue to brood. We get to some unravelment if we are left to our own efforts. I quarrel with no priest of any denomination. That they should quarrel among themselves is comprehensible in their wisdom, for each has the specific. But they show us *their* way of solving the great problem, and we ought to thank them, though one or the other abominate us. You are advised to talk with Lady Dunstane on these themes. She is perpetually in the antechamber of death, and her soul is perennially sunshine. — See the pretty cottage under the laburnum curls! Who lives there?"

"His gamekeeper, Simon Rofe."

"And what a playground for the children, that bit of common by their garden-palings! and the pond, and the blue hills over the furzes. I hope those people will not be turned out."

Dacier could not tell. He promised to do his best for them.

"But," said she, "you are the lord here now."

"Not likely to be the tenant. Incomes are wanted to support even small estates."

"The reason is good for courting the income."

He disliked the remark; and when she said presently: "Those windmills make the landscape homely," he rejoined: "They remind one of our wheeling London gamins round the cab from the station."

"They remind you," said she, and smiled at the chance discordant trick he had, remembering occasions when it had crossed her.

"This is homelier than Rovio," she said; "quite as nice in its way."

"You do not gather flowers here."

"Because my friend has these at her feet."

"May one petition without a rival, then, for a souvenir?"

7

"Certainly, if you care to have a common buttercup."

They reached the station, five minutes in advance of the train. His coming manœuvre was early detected, and she drew from her pocket the little book he had seen lying unopened on the table, and said: "I shall have two good hours for reading."

"You will not object? . . . I must accompany you to town. Permit it, I beg. You shall not be worried to talk."

"No; I came alone and return alone."

"Fasting and unprotected! Are you determined to take away the worst impression of us? Do not refuse me this favour."

"As to fasting, I could not eat: and unprotected no woman is in England if she is a third-class traveller. That is my experience of the class; and I shall return among my natural protectors — the most unselfishly chivalrous to women in the whole world."

He had set his heart on going with her, and he attempted eloquence in pleading, but that exposed him to her humour; he was tripped.

"It is not denied that you belong to the knightly class," she said; "and it is not necessary that you should wear armour and plumes to proclaim it; and your appearance would be ample protection from the drunken sailors travelling, you say, on this line; and I may be deplorably mistaken in imagining that I could tame them. But your knightliness is due elsewhere; and I commit myself to the fortune of war. It is a battle for women everywhere; under the most favourable conditions among my dear common English. I have not my maid with me, or else I should not dare."

She paid for a third-class ticket, amused by Dacier's look of entreaty and trouble.

"Of course I obey," he murmured.

"I have the habit of exacting it in matters concerning my independence," she said; and it arrested some rumbling notions in his head as to a piece of audacity on the starting of the train. They walked up and down the platform till the bell rang and the train came rounding beneath an arch.

"Oh, by the way, may I ask?" — he said: "was it your

article in Whitmonby's journal on a speech of mine last week ? "

"The guilty writer is confessed."

" Let me thank you."

" Don't. But try to believe it written on public grounds — if the task is not too great."

" I may call ? "

" You will be welcome."

" To tell you of the funeral — the last of him ! "

" Do not fail to come."

She could have laughed to see him jumping on the steps of the third-class carriages one after another to choose her company for her. In those pre-democratic blissful days before the miry Deluge, the opinion of the requirements of poor English travellers entertained by the Seigneur Directors of the class above them, was that they differed from cattle in stipulating for seats. With the exception of that provision to suit their weakness, the accommodation extended to them resembled pens, and the seats were emphatically seats of penitence, intended to grind the sitter for his mean pittance payment and absence of aspiration to a higher state. Hard angular wood, a low roof, a shabby square of window aloof, demanding of him to quit the seat he insisted on having, if he would indulge in views of the passing scenery, — such was the furniture of dens where a refinement of castigation was practised on villain poverty by denying leathers to the windows, or else buttons to the leathers, so that the windows had either to be up or down, but refused to shelter and freshen simultaneously.

Dacier selected a compartment occupied by two old women, a mother and babe and little maid, and a labouring man. There he installed her, with an eager look that she would not notice.

" You will want the window down," he said.

She applied to her fellow-travellers for the permission ; and struggling to get the window down, he was irritated to animadvert on " these carriages " of the benevolent railway Company.

" Do not forget that the wealthy are well treated, or you may be unjust," said she, to pacify him.

His mouth sharpened its line while he tried arts and

energies on the refractory window. She told him to leave
it. "You can't breathe this atmosphere!" he cried, and
called to a porter, who did the work, remarking that it was
rather stiff.

The door was banged and fastened. Dacier had to hang on
the step to see her in the farewell. From the platform he
saw the top of her bonnet; and why she should have been
guilty of this freak of riding in an unwholesome carriage,
tasked his power of guessing. He was too English even to
have taken the explanation, for he detested the distinguishing of the races in his country, and could not therefore have
comprehended her peculiar tenacity of the sense of injury
as long as enthusiasm did not arise to obliterate it. He required a course of lessons in Irish.

Sauntering down the lane, he called at Simon Rofe's
cottage, and spoke very kindly to the gamekeeper's wife.
That might please Diana. It was all he could do at
present.

CHAPTER XXI

"THE YOUNG MINISTER OF STATE"

DESCRIPTIONS in the newspapers of the rural funeral of
Lord Dannisburgh had the effect of rousing flights of
tattlers with a twittering of the disused name of Warwick;
our social Gods renewed their combat, and the verdict of
the jury was again overhauled, to be attacked and maintained, the carpers replying to the champions that they
held to their view of it: as heads of bull-dogs are expected
to do when they have got a grip of one. It is a point of
muscular honour with them never to relax their hold.
They will tell you why:— they formed that opinion from
the first. And but for the swearing of a particular witness, upon whom the plaintiff had been taught to rely,
the verdict would have been different—to prove their
soundness of judgement. They could speak from private
positive information of certain damnatory circumstances,
derived from authentic sources. Visits of a gentleman

to the house of a married lady in the absence of the husband? Oh!—The British Lucretia was very properly not legally at home to the masculine world of that day. She plied her distaff in pure seclusion, meditating on her absent lord; or else a fair proportion of the masculine world, which had not yet, has not yet, 'doubled Cape Turk,' approved her condemnation to the sack.

There was talk in the feminine world, at Lady Wathin's assemblies. The elevation of her husband had extended and deepened her influence on the levels where it reigned before, but without, strange as we may think it now, assisting to her own elevation, much aspired for, to the smooth and lively upper pavement of Society, above its tumbled strata. She was near that distinguished surface, not on it. Her circle was practically the same as it was previous to the coveted nominal rank enabling her to trample on those beneath it. And women like that Mrs. Warwick, a woman of no birth, no money, not even honest character, enjoyed the entry undisputed, circulated among the highest:— because people took her rattle for wit!—and because also our nobility, Lady Wathin feared, had no due regard for morality. Our aristocracy, brilliant and ancient though it was, merited rebuke. She grew severe upon aristocratic scandals, whereof were plenty among the frolicsome host just overhead, as vexatious as the drawing-room party to the lodger in the floor below, who has not received an invitation to partake of the festivities, and is required to digest the noise. But if ambition is oversensitive, moral indignation is ever consolatory, for it plants us on the Judgement Seat. There indeed we may, sitting with the very Highest, forget our personal disappointments in dispensing reprobation for misconduct, however eminent the offenders.

She was Lady Wathin, and once on an afternoon's call to see her poor Lady Dunstane at her town-house, she had been introduced to Lady Pennon, a patroness of Mrs. Warwick, and had met a snub—an icy check-bow of the aristocratic head from the top of the spinal column, and not a word, not a look;—the half-turn of a head devoid of mouth and eyes! She practised that forbidding checkbow herself to perfection, so the endurance of it was

horrible. A *noli me tangere*, her husband termed it, in
his ridiculous equanimity; and he might term it what he
pleased — it was insulting. The solace she had was in
hearing that hideous Radical Revolutionary things were
openly spoken at Mrs. Warwick's evenings with her
friends: — impudently named "the elect of London."
Pleasing to reflect upon Mrs. Warwick as undermining
her supporters, to bring them some day down with a
crash! Her "elect of London" were a queer gathering,
by report of them! And Mr. Whitmonby too, no doubt
a celebrity, was the righthand man at these dinner-parties
of Mrs. Warwick. Where will not men go to be flattered
by a pretty woman! He had declined repeated, successive
invitations to Lady Wathin's table. But there of course
he would not have had "the freedom :" that is, she rejoiced
in thinking defensively and offensively, a moral wall en-
closed *her* topics. The Hon. Percy Dacier had been
brought to her Thursday afternoon by Mr. Quintin Manx,
and he had one day dined with her; and he knew Mrs.
Warwick — a little, he said. The opportunity was not lost
to convey to him, entirely in the interest of sweet Constance Asper, that the moral world entertained a settled
view of the very clever woman Mrs. Warwick certainly
was. — He had asked Diana, on their morning walk to the
station, whether she had an enemy : so prone are men,
educated by the Drama and Fiction in the belief that the
garden of civilized life must be at the mercy of the old
wild devourers, to fancy "villain whispers" an indication of
direct animosity. Lady Wathin had no sentiment of the
kind.

But she had become acquainted with the other side of
the famous Dannisburgh case — the unfortunate plaintiff;
and compassion as well as morality moved her to put on a
speaking air when Mr. Warwick's name was mentioned.
She pictured him to the ladies of her circle as "one of our
true gentlemen in his deportment and his feelings." He was,
she would venture to say, her *ideal* of an English gentleman.
"But now," she added commiseratingly, "ruined; ruined
in his health and in his prospects." A lady inquired if it
was the verdict that had thus affected him. Lady Wathin's
answer was reported over moral, or substratum, London :

"He is the victim of a fatal passion for his wife; and would take her back to-morrow were she to solicit his forgiveness." Morality had something to say against this active marital charity, attributable, it was to be feared, to weakness of character on the part of the husband. Still Mrs. Warwick undoubtedly was one of those women (of Satanic construction) who have the art of enslaving the men unhappy enough to cross their path. The nature of the art was hinted, with the delicacy of dainty feet which have to tread in mire to get to safety. Men, alas! are snared in this way. Instances too numerous for the good repute of the swinish sex, were cited, and the question of how Morality was defensible from their grossness passed without a tactical reply. There is no defence. Those women come like the Cholera Morbus — and owing to similar causes. They will prevail until the ideas of men regarding women are purified. Nevertheless the husband who could forgive, even propose to forgive, was deemed by consent generous, however weak. Though she might not have been wholly guilty, she had bitterly offended. And he despatched an emissary to her? — The theme, one may, in their language, "fear," was relished as a sugared acid. It was renewed in the late Autumn of the year, when Antonia published her new book, entitled The Young Minister of State. The signature of the authoress was now known; and from this resurgence of her name in public, suddenly a radiation of tongues from the circle of Lady Wathin declared that the repentant Mrs. Warwick *had* gone back to her husband's bosom and forgiveness! The rumour spread in spite of sturdy denials at odd corners, counting the red-hot proposal of Mr. Sullivan Smith to eat his head and boots for breakfast if it was proved correct. It filled a yawn of the Clubs for the afternoon. Soon this wanton rumour was met and stifled by another of more morbific density, heavily charged as that which led the sad Eliza to her pyre.

Antonia's hero was easily identified. The Young Minister of State could be he only who was now at all her parties, always meeting her; had been spied walking with her daily in the park near her house, on his march down to Westminster during the session; and who positively went to concerts and sat under fiddlers to be near her. It accounted moreover for his treatment of Constance Asper. What effrontery of the authoress, to placard herself with him in a book! The likeness of the hero to Percy Dacier once established became striking to glaringness — a proof of her ability, and more of her audacity; still more of her intention to flatter him up to his perdition. By the things written of him, one would imagine the conversations going on behind the scenes. She had the wiles of a Cleopatra, not without some of the Nilene's experiences. A youthful Antony-Dacier would be little likely to escape her toils. And so promising a young man! The sigh, the tear for weeping over his destruction, almost fell, such vivid realizing of the prophesy appeared in its pathetic pronouncement.

This low rumour, or malaria, began blowing in the Winter, and did not travel fast; for strangely, there was hardly a breath of it in the atmosphere of Dacier, none in Diana's. It rose from groups not so rapidly and largely mixing, and less quick to kindle; whose crazy sincereness battened on the smallest morsel of fact and collected the fictitious by slow absorption. But as guardians of morality, often doing good duty in their office, they are persistent. When Parliament assembled, Mr. Quintin Manx, a punctual member of the House, if nothing else, arrived in town. He was invited to dine with Lady Wathin. After dinner she spoke to him of the absent Constance, and heard of her being well, and expressed a great rejoicing at that. Whereupon the burly old shipowner frowned and puffed. Constance, he said, had plunged into these new spangle, candle and high singing services; was all for symbols, harps, effigies, what not. Lady Wathin's countenance froze in hearing of it. She led Mr. Quintin to a wall-sofa, and said: "Surely the dear child must have had a disappointment, for her to have taken to those foolish displays of religion! It is generally a sign."

"Well, ma'am — my lady — I let girls go their ways in such things. I don't interfere. But it's that fellow, or nobody, with her. She has fixed her girl's mind on him, and if she can't columbine as a bride, she will as a nun. Young people must be at some harlequinade."

"But it is very shocking. And he ? "

"He plays fast and loose, warm and cold. I'm ready to settle twenty times a nobleman's dowry on my niece : and she's a fine girl, a handsome girl, educated up to the brim, fit to queen it in any drawing-room. He holds her by some arts that don't hold him, it seems. He's all for politics."

"Constance can scarcely be his dupe so far, I should think."

"How do you mean ? "

"Everything points to one secret of his conduct."

"A woman ? "

Lady Wathin's head shook for her sex's pained affirmative.

Mr. Quintin in the same fashion signified the downright negative. "The fellow's as cold as a fish."

"Flattery will do anything. There is, I fear, one."

"Widow ? wife ? maid ? "

"Married, I regret to say."

"Well, if he'd get over with it," said Quintin, in whose notions the seductiveness of a married woman could be only temporary, for all the reasons pertaining to her state. At the same time his view of Percy Dacier was changed in thinking it possible that a woman could divert him from his political and social interests. He looked incredulous.

"You have heard of a Mrs. Warwick ? " said Lady Wathin.

"Warwick ! I have. I've never seen her. At my broker's in the City yesterday I saw the name on a Memorandum of purchase of Shares in a concern promising ten per cent., and not likely to carry the per annum into the plural. He told me she was a grand kind of woman, past advising."

"For what amount ? "

"Some thousands, I think it was."

"She has *no* money :" Lady Wathin corrected her emphasis : "or *ought* to have none."

"She can't have got it from *him*."

"Did you notice her Christian name ? "

"I don't recollect it, if I did. I thought the woman a donkey."

"Would you consider me a busybody were I to try to

mitigate this woman's evil influence? I love dear Constance, and should be happy to serve her."

"I want my girl married," said old Quintin. "He's one of my Parliamentary chiefs, with first-rate prospects; good family, good sober fellow — at least I thought so; by nature, I mean; barring your incantations. He suits me, she liking him."

"She admires him, I am sure."

"She's dead on end for the fellow!"

Lady Wathin felt herself empowered by Quintin Manx to undertake the release of sweet Constance Asper's knight from the toils of his enchantress. For this purpose she had first an interview with Mr. Warwick, and next she hurried to Lady Dunstane at Copsley. There, after jumbling Mr. Warwick's connubial dispositions and Mrs. Warwick's last book, and Mr. Percy Dacier's engagement to the great heiress in a gossipy hotch-potch, she contrived to gather a few items of fact, as that THE YOUNG MINISTER was probably modelled upon Mr. Percy Dacier. Lady Dunstane made no concealment of it as soon as she grew sensible of the angling. But she refused her help to any reconciliation between Mr. and Mrs. Warwick. She declined to listen to Lady Wathin's entreaties. She declined to give her reasons. — These bookworm women, whose pride it is to fancy that they can think for themselves, have a great deal of the heathen in them, as morality discovers when it wears the enlistment ribands and applies to them to win recruits for a service under the direct blessing of Providence.

Lady Wathin left some darts behind her, in the form of moral exclamations; and really intended morally. For though she did not like Mrs. Warwick, she had no wish to wound, other than by stopping her further studies of the Young Minister, and conducting him to the young lady loving him, besides restoring a bereft husband to his own. How sadly pale and worn poor Mr. Warwick appeared! The portrayal of his withered visage to Lady Dunstane had quite failed to gain a show of sympathy. And so it is ever with your book-worm women pretending to be philosophical! You sound them vainly for a manifestation of the commonest human sensibilities. They turn over the leaves of a

Latin book on their laps while you are supplicating them to assist in a work of charity!

Lady Wathin's interjectory notes haunted Emma's ear. Yet she had seen nothing in Tony to let her suppose that there was trouble of her heart below the surface; and her Tony when she came to Copsley shone in the mood of the day of Lord Dannisburgh's drive down from London with her. She was running on a fresh work; talked of composition as a trifle.

"I suppose the YOUNG MINISTER *is* Mr. Percy Dacier?" said Emma.

"Between ourselves he is," Diana replied, smiling at a secret guessed. "You know my model and can judge of the likeness."

"You write admiringly of him, Tony."

"And I do admire him. So would you, Emmy, if you knew him as well as I do now. He pairs with Mr. Redworth; he also is the friend of women. But he lifts us to rather a higher level of intellectual friendship. When the ice has melted — and it is thick at first — he pours forth all his ideas without reserve; and they are deep and noble. Ever since Lord Dannisburgh's death and our sitting together, we have been warm friends — intimate, I would say, if it could be said of one so self-contained. In that respect, no young man was ever comparable with him. And I am encouraged to flatter myself that he unbends to me more than to others."

"He is engaged, or partly, I hear; why does he not marry?"

"I wish he would!" Diana said, with a most brilliant candour of aspect.

Emma read in it, that it would complete her happiness, possibly by fortifying her sense of security; and that seemed right. Her own meditations, illumined by the beautiful face in her presence, referred to the security of Mr. Dacier.

"So, then, life is going smoothly," said Emma.

"Yes, at a good pace and smoothly: not a torrent — Thames-like, ' without o'erflowing full.' It is not Lugano and the Salvatore. Perhaps it is better: as action is better than musing."

"No troubles whatever?"

"None. Well, except an 'adorer' at times. I have to take him as my portion. An impassioned Caledonian has a little bothered me. I met him at Lady Pennon's, and have been meeting him, as soon as I put foot out of my house, ever since. If I could impress and impound him to marry Mary Paynham, I should be glad. By the way, I have consented to let her try at a portrait of me. No, I have no troubles. I have friends, the choicest of the nation; I have health, a field for labour, fairish success with it; a mind alive, such as it is. I feel like that midsummer morning of our last drive out together, the sun high, clearish, clouded enough to be cool. And still I envy Emmy on her sofa, mastering Latin, biting at Greek. What a wise recommendation that was of Mr. Redworth's! He works well in the House. He spoke excellently the other night."

"He runs over to Ireland this Easter."

"He sees for himself, and speaks with authority. He sees and feels. Englishmen mean well, but they require an extremity of misery to waken their feelings."

"It is coming, he says; and absit omen!"

"Mr. Dacier says he is the one Englishman who may always be sure of an Irish hearing; and he does not cajole them, you know. But the English defect is really not want of feeling so much as want of foresight. They will not look ahead. A famine ceasing, a rebellion crushed, they jog on as before, with their Dobbin trot and blinker confidence in 'Saxon energy.' They should study the Irish. I think it was Mr. Redworth who compared the governing of the Irish to the management of a horse: the rider should not grow restive when the steed begins to kick: calmer; firm, calm, persuasive."

"Does Mr. Dacier agree?"

"Not always. He has the inveterate national belief that Celtic blood is childish, and the consequently illogical disregard of its hold of impressions. The Irish — for I have them in my heart, though I have not been among them for long at a time — must love you to serve you, and will hate you if you have done them injury and they have not wiped it out — they with a treble revenge, or you with cordial benefits. I have told him so again and again: ventured to suggest measures."

"He listens to you, Tony?"

"He says I have brains. It ends in a compliment."

"You have inspired Mr. Redworth."

"If I have, I have lived for some good."

Altogether her Tony's conversation proved to Emma that her perusal of the model of THE YOUNG MINISTER OF STATE was an artist's, free, open, and not discoloured by the personal tincture. Her heart plainly was free and undisturbed. She had the same girl's love of her walks where wild flowers grew; if possible, a keener pleasure. She hummed of her happiness in being at Copsley, singing her Planxty Kelly and The Puritani by turns. She stood on land: she was not on the seas. Emma thought so with good reason.

She stood on land, it was true, but she stood on a cliff of the land, the seas below and about her; and she was enabled to hoodwink her friend because the assured sensation of her firm footing deceived her own soul, even while it took short flights to the troubled waters. Of her firm footing she was exultingly proud. She stood high, close to danger, without giddiness. If at intervals her soul flew out like lightning from the rift (a mere shot of involuntary fancy, it seemed to her), the suspicion of instability made her draw on her treasury of impressions of the mornings at Lugano — her loftiest, purest, dearest; and these reinforced her. She did not ask herself why she should have to seek them for aid. In other respects her mind was alert and held no sly covers, as the fiction of a perfect ignorant innocence combined with common intelligence would have us to suppose that the minds of women can do. She was honest as long as she was not directly questioned, pierced to the innermost and sanctum of the bosom. She could honestly summon bright light to her eyes in wishing the man were married. She did not ask herself why she called it up. The remorseless progressive interrogations of a Jesuit Father in pursuit of the bosom's verity might have transfixed it and shown her to herself even then a tossing vessel as to the spirit, far away from that firm land she trod so bravely.

Descending from the woody heights upon London, Diana would have said that her only anxiety concerned young Mr. Arthur Rhodes, whose position she considered precarious, and who had recently taken a drubbing for venturing to show a peep of his head, like an early crocus, in the literary market. Her ANTONIA's last book had been reviewed obediently to smart taps from the then commanding bâton of Mr. Tonans, and Mr. Whitmonby's choice picking of specimens down three columns of his paper. A Literary Review (Charles Rainer's property) had suggested that perhaps "the talented authoress might be writing too rapidly;" and another, actuated by the public taste of the period for our "vigorous homely Saxon" in one and two syllable words, had complained of a "tendency to polysyllabic phraseology." The remainder, a full majority, had sounded eulogy, with all their band-instruments, drum, trumpet, fife, trombone. Her foregoing work had raised her to Fame, which is the Court of a Queen when the lady has beauty and social influence, and critics are her dedicated courtiers, gaping for the royal mouth to be opened, and reserving the kicks of their independent manhood for infamous outsiders, whom they hoist in the style and particular service of pitchforks. They had fallen upon a little volume of verse, "like a body of barn-door hens on a stranger chick," Diana complained; and she chid herself angrily for letting it escape her forethought to propitiate them on the author's behalf. Young Rhodes was left with scarce a feather; and what remained to him appeared a preposterous ornament for the decoration of a shivering and welted poet. He laughed, or tried the mouth of laughter. ANTONIA's literary conscience was vexed at the different treatment she had met and so imperatively needed that the reverse of it would have threatened the smooth sailing of her costly household. A merry-go-round of creditors required a corresponding whirligig of receipts. She felt mercenary, debased by comparison with the well-scourged verse-mason, Orpheus of the untenanted city, who had done his publishing ingenuously for glory: a good instance of the comic-pathetic. She wrote to Emma, begging her to take him in at Copsley for a few days: — "I told you I had no troubles. I am really troubled about this poor boy. He has very little money and has embarked on literature. I cannot induce any of my friends to lend him a hand. Mr. Redworth gruffly insists on his going back to his law-clerk's office and stool, and Mr. Dacier says that no place is vacant. The reality of Lord Dannisburgh's death is brought before me by my helplessness. He would have made him an assistant private Secretary, pending a Government appointment, rather than let me plead in vain."

Mr. Rhodes with his travelling bag was packed off to Copsley, to enjoy a change of scene after his run of the gauntlet. He was very heartily welcomed by Lady Dunstane, both for her Tony's sake and his own modest worship of that luminary, which could permit of being transparent; but chiefly she welcomed him as the living proof of Tony's disengagement from anxiety, since he was her one spot of trouble, and could easily be comforted by reading with her, and wandering through the Spring woods along the heights. He had a happy time, midway in air between his accomplished hostess and his protecting Goddess. His bruises were soon healed. Each day was radiant to him, whether it rained or shone; and by his looks and what he said of himself Lady Dunstane understood that he was in the highest temper of the human creature tuned to thrilling accord with nature. It was her generous Tony's work. She blessed it, and liked the youth the better.

During the stay of Mr. Arthur Rhodes at Copsley, Sir Lukin came on a visit to his wife. He mentioned reports in the scandal-papers: one, that Mr. P. D. would shortly lead to the altar the lovely heiress Miss A., Percy Dacier and Constance Asper:—another, that a reconciliation was to be expected between the beautiful authoress Mrs. W. and her husband. "Perhaps it's the best thing she can do," Sir Lukin added.

Lady Dunstane pronounced a woman's unforgiving: "Never." The revolt of her own sensations assured her of Tony's unconquerable repugnance. In conversation subsequently with Arthur Rhodes, she heard that he knew the son of Mr. Warwick's attorney, a Mr. Fenn; and he had gathered from him some information of Mr. Warwick's

condition of health. It had been alarming; young Fenn said
it was confirmed heart-disease. His father frequently saw
Mr. Warwick, and said he was fretting himself to death.

It seemed just a possibility that Tony's natural compassionateness had wrought on her to immolate herself
and nurse to his end the man who had wrecked her life.
Lady Dunstane waited for news. At last she wrote, touching the report incidentally. There was no reply. The
silence ensuing after such a question responded forcibly.

CHAPTER XXII

BETWEEN DIANA AND DACIER: THE WIND EAST OVER
BLEAK LAND

On the third day of the Easter recess Percy Dacier
landed from the Havre steamer at Caen and drove straight-
way for the sandy coast, past fields of colza to brine-blown
meadows of coarse grass, and then to the low dunes and
long stretching sands of the ebb in semicircle: a desolate
place at that season; with a dwarf fishing-village by the
shore; an East wind driving landward in streamers every
object that had a scrap to fly. He made head to the inn,
where the first person he encountered in the passage was
Diana's maid Danvers, who relaxed from the dramatic
exaggeration of her surprise at the sight of a real English
gentleman in these woebegone regions, to inform him that
her mistress might be found walking somewhere along the
sea-shore, and had her dog to protect her. They were to
stay here a whole week, Danvers added, for a conveyance
of her private sentiments. Second thoughts however whispered to her shrewdness that his arrival could only be by
appointment. She had been anticipating something of the
sort for some time.

Dacier butted against the stringing wind, that kept him
at a rocking incline to his left for a mile. He then discerned in what had seemed a dredger's dot on the sands, a
lady's figure, unmistakably she, without the corroborating

testimony of Leander paw-deep in the low-tide water. She was out at a distance on the ebb-sands, hurtled, gyred, beaten to all shapes, in rolls, twists, volumes, like a blown banner-flag, by the pressing wind. A kerchief tied her bonnet under her chin. Bonnet and breast-ribands rattled rapidly as drummer-sticks. She stood near the little running ripple of the flat sea-water, as it hurried back from a long streaked back to a tiny imitation of spray. When she turned to the shore she saw him advancing, but did not recognize; when they met she merely looked with wide parted lips. This was no appointment.

"I had to see you," Dacier said.

She coloured to a deeper red than the rose-conjuring wind had whipped in her cheeks. Her quick intuition of the reason of his coming barred a mental evasion, and she had no thought of asking either him or herself what special urgency had brought him.

"I have been here four days."

"Lady Esquart spoke of the place."

"Lady Esquart should not have betrayed me."

"She did it inadvertently, without an idea of my profiting by it."

Diana indicated the scene in a glance. "Dreary country, do you think?"

"Anywhere!" — said he.

They walked up the sand-heap. The roaring Easter with its shrieks and whistles at her ribands was not favourable to speech. His "Anywhere!" had a penetrating significance, the fuller for the break that left it vague.

Speech between them was commanded; he could not be suffered to remain. She descended upon a sheltered pathway running along a ditch, the border of pastures where cattle cropped, raised heads, and resumed their one comforting occupation.

Diana gazed on them, smarting from the buffets of the wind she had met.

"No play of their tails to-day," she said, as she slackened her steps. "You left Lady Esquart well?"

"Lady Esquart . . . I think was well. I had to see you. I thought you would be with her in Berkshire. She told me of a little sea-side place close to Caen."

"You had to see me?"

"I miss you now if it's a day!"

"I heard a story in London . . ."

"In London there are many stories. I heard one. Is there a foundation for it?"

"No."

He breathed relieved. "I wanted to see you once before . . . if it was true. It would have made a change in my life — a gap."

"You do me the honour to like my Sunday evenings?"

"Beyond everything London can offer."

"A letter would have reached me."

"I should have had to wait for the answer. There is no truth in it?"

Her choice was to treat the direct assailant frankly or imperil her defence by the ordinary feminine evolutions, which might be taken for inviting: poor pranks always.

"There have been overtures," she said.

"Forgive me; I have scarcely the right to ask . . . speak of it."

"My friends may use their right to take an interest in my fortunes."

"I thought I might, on my way to Paris, turn aside . . . coming by this route."

"If you determined not to lose much of your time."

The coolness of her fencing disconcerted a gentleman conscious of his madness. She took instant advantage of any circuitous move; she gave him no practicable point. He was little skilled in the arts of attack, and felt that she checked his impetuousness; respected her for it, chafed at it, writhed with the fervours precipitating him here, and relapsed on his pleasure in seeing her face, hearing her voice.

"Your happiness, I hope, is the chief thought in such a case," he said.

"I am sure you would consider it."

"I can't quite forget my own."

"You compliment an ambitious hostess."

Dacier glanced across the pastures. "What was it that tempted you to this place?"

"A poet would say it looks like a figure in the shroud.

It has no features; it has a sort of grandeur belonging to death. I heard of it as the place where I might be certain of not meeting an acquaintance."

"And I am the intruder."

"An hour or two will not give you that title."

"Am I to count the minutes by my watch?"

"By the sun. We will supply you an omelette and piquette, and send you back sobered and friarly to Caen for Paris at sunset."

"Let the fare be Spartan. I could take my black broth with philosophy every day of the year under your auspices. What I should miss . . ."

"You bring no news of the world or the House?"

"None. You know as much as I know. The Irish agitation is chronic. The Corn-Law threatens to be the same."

"And your Chief — in personal colloquy?"

"He keeps a calm front. I may tell you: — there is nothing I would not confide to you: he has let fall some dubious words in private. I don't know what to think of them."

"But if he should waver?"

"It 's not wavering. It 's the openness of his mind."

"Ah! the mind. We imagine it free. The House and the country are the sentient frame governing the mind of the politician more than his ideas. He cannot think independently of them: — nor I of my natural anatomy. You will test the truth of that after your omelette and piquette, and marvel at the quitting of your line of route for Paris. As soon as the mind attempts to think independently, it is like a kite with the cord cut, and performs a series of darts and frisks, that have the look of wildest liberty till you see it fall flat to earth. The openness of his mind is most honourable to him."

"Ominous for his party."

"Likely to be good for his country."

"That is the question."

"Prepare to encounter it. In politics I am with the active minority on behalf of the inert but suffering majority. That is my rule. It leads, unless you have a despotism, to the conquering side. It is always the noblest.

I won't say, listen to me; only do believe my words have some weight. This is a question of bread."

"It involves many other questions."

"And how clearly those leaders put their case! They are admirable debaters. If I were asked to write against them, I should have but to quote them to confound my argument. I tried it once, and wasted a couple of my precious hours."

"They are cogent debaters," Dacier assented. "They make me wince now and then, without convincing me:— I own it to you. The confession is not agreeable, though it's a small matter."

"One's pride may feel a touch with the foils as keenly as the point of a rapier," said Diana.

The remark drew a sharp look of pleasure from him.

"Does the Princess Egeria propose to dismiss the individual she inspires, when he is growing most sensible of her wisdom?"

"A young Minister of State should be gleaning at large when holiday is granted him."

Dacier coloured. "May I presume on what is currently reported?"

"Parts, parts; a bit here, a bit there," she rejoined. "Authors find their models where they can, and generally hit on the nearest."

"Happy the nearest!"

"If you run to interjections I shall cite you a sentence from your latest speech in the House."

He asked for it, and to school him she consented to flatter with her recollection of his commonest words: "'Dealing with subjects of this nature emotionally does not advance us a calculable inch.'"

"I must have said that in relation to hard matter of business."

"It applies. There is my hostelry, and the spectral form of Danvers, utterly *dépaysée*. Have you spoken to the poor soul? I can never discover the links of her attachment to my service."

"She knows a good mistress. — I have but a few minutes, if you are relentless. May I . . . shall I ever be privileged to speak your Christian name?"

"My Christian name! It is Pagan. In one sphere I am Hecate. Remember that."

"I am not among the people who so regard you."

"The time may come."

"Diana!"

"Constance!"

"I break no tie. I owe no allegiance whatever to the name."

"Keep to the formal title with me. We are Mrs. Warwick and Mr. Dacier. I think I am two years younger than you; socially therefore ten in seniority; and I know how this flower of friendship is nourished and may be withered. You see already what you have done? You have cast me on the discretion of my maid. I suppose her trusty, but I am at her mercy, and a breath from her to the people beholding me as Hecate queen of Witches!. . . I have a sensation of the scirocco it would blow."

"In that event, the least I can offer is my whole life."

"We will not conjecture the event."

"The best I could hope for!"

"I see I shall have to revise the next edition of THE YOUNG MINISTER, and make an emotional curate of him. Observe Danvers. The woman is wretched; and now she sees me coming she pretends to be using her wits in studying the things about her, as I have directed. She is a riddle. I have the idea that any morning she may explode; and yet I trust her and sleep soundly. I must be free, though I vex the world's watchdogs. — So, Danvers, you are noticing how thoroughly Frenchwomen do their work."

Danvers replied with a slight mincing: "They may, ma'am; but they chatter chatter so."

"The result proves that it is not a waste of energy. They manage their fowls too."

"They've no such thing as mutton, ma'am."

Dacier patriotically laughed.

"She strikes the apology for wealthy and leisurely land-lords," Diana said.

Danvers remarked that the poor fed meagrely in France. She was not convinced of its being good for them by hearing that they could work on it sixteen hours out of the four and twenty.

Mr. Percy Dacier's repast was furnished to him half an hour later. At sunset Diana, taking Danvers beside her, walked with him to the line of the country road bearing on Caen. The wind had sunk. A large brown disk paused rayless on the western hills.

"A Dacier ought to feel at home in Normandy; and you may have sprung from this neighbourhood," said she, simply to chat. "Here the land is poorish, and a mile inland rich enough to bear repeated crops of colza, which tries the soil, I hear. As for beauty, those blue hills you see, enfold charming valleys. I meditate an expedition to Harcourt before I return. An English professor of his native tongue at the Lycée at Caen told me on my way here that for twenty shillings a week you may live in royal ease round about Harcourt. So we have our bed and board in prospect if fortune fails us, Danvers."

"I would rather die in England, ma'am," was the maid's reply.

Dacier set foot on his carriage-step. He drew a long breath to say a short farewell, and he and Diana parted.

They parted as the plainest of sincere good friends, each at heart respecting the other for the repression of that which their hearts craved; any word of which might have carried them headlong, bound together on a Mazeppa-race, with scandal for the hounding wolves, and social ruin for the rocks and torrents.

Dacier was the thankfuller, the most admiring of the two; at the same time the least satisfied. He saw the abyss she had aided him in escaping; and it was refreshful to look abroad after his desperate impulse. Prominent as he stood before the world, he could not think without a shudder of behaving like a young frenetic of the passion. Those whose aim is at the leadership of the English people know, that however truly based the charges of hypocrisy, soundness of moral fibre runs throughout the country and is the national integrity, which may condone old sins for present service, but will not have present sins to flout it. He was in tune with the English character. The passion was in him nevertheless, and the stronger for a slow growth that confirmed its union of the mind and heart. Her counsel fortified him, her suggestions opened springs;

her phrases were golden-lettered in his memory; and more, she had worked an extraordinary change in his views of life and aptitude for social converse: he acknowledged it with genial candour. Through her he was encouraged, led, excited to sparkle with the witty, feel new gifts, or a greater breadth of nature; and thanking her, he became thirstily susceptible to her dark beauty; he claimed to have found the key of her, and he prized it. She was not passionless: the blood flowed warm. Proud, chaste, she was nobly spirited; having an intellectual refuge from the besiegings of the blood; a rock-fortress. The "wife no wife" appeared to him, striking the higher elements of the man, the commonly masculine also. — Would he espouse her, had he the chance? — to-morrow! this instant! With her to back him, he would be doubled in manhood, doubled in brain and heart-energy. To call her wife, spring from her and return, a man might accept his fate to fight Trojan or Greek, sure of his mark on the enemy.

But if, after all, this imputed Helen of a decayed Paris passed, submissive to the legitimate solicitor, back to her husband?

The thought shot Dacier on his legs for a look at the blank behind him. He vowed she had promised it should not be. Could it ever be, after the ruin the meanly suspicious fellow had brought upon her? — Diana voluntarily reunited to the treacherous cur?

He sat, resolving sombrely that if the debate arose he would try what force he had to save her from such an ignominy, and dedicate his life to her, let the world wag its tongue. So the knot would be cut.

Men unaccustomed to a knot in their system find the prospect of cutting it an extreme relief, even when they know that the cut has an edge to wound mortally as well as pacify. The wound was not heavy payment for the rapture of having so incomparable a woman his own. He reflected wonderingly on the husband, as he had previously done, and came again to the conclusion that it was a poor creature, abjectly jealous of a wife he could neither master, nor equal, nor attract. And thinking of jealousy, Dacier felt none; none of individuals, only of facts: her marriage, her bondage. Her condemnation to perpetual widowhood angered him, as at an unrighteous decree. The sharp sweet bloom of her beauty, fresh in swarthiness, under the whipping Easter, cried out against that loathed inhumanity. Or he made it cry.

Being a stranger to the jealousy of men, he took the soft assurance that he was preferred above them all. Competitors were numerous: not any won her eyes as he did. She revealed nothing of the same pleasures in the shining of the others touched by her magical wand. Would she have pardoned one of them the "Diana!" bursting from his mouth?

She was not a woman for trifling, still less for secresy. He was as little the kind of lover. Both would be ready to take up their burden, if the burden was laid on them. — Diana had thus far impressed him.

Meanwhile he faced the cathedral towers of the ancient Norman city, standing up in the smoky hues of the West; and a sentence out of her book seemed fitting to the scene and what he felt. He rolled it over luxuriously as the next of delights to having her beside him. — She wrote of *"Thoughts that are bare dark outlines, coloured by some old passion of the soul, like towers of a distant city seen in the funeral waste of day."* — His bluff English anti-poetic training would have caused him to shrug at the stuff coming from another pen: he might condescendingly have criticized it, with a sneer embalmed in humour. The words were hers; she had written them; almost by a sort of anticipation, he imagined; for he at once fell into the mood they suggested, and had a full crop of the "bare dark outlines" of thoughts coloured by his particular form of passion.

Diana had impressed him powerfully when she set him swallowing and assimilating a sentence ethereally thin in substance, of mere sentimental significance, that he would antecedently have read aloud in a drawing-room, picking up the book by hazard, as your modern specimen of romantic vapouring. Mr. Dacier however was at the time in observation of the towers of Caen, fresh from her presence, animated to some conception of her spirit. He drove into the streets, desiring, half determining, to risk a drive back on the morrow.

The cold light of the morrow combined with his fear of
distressing her to restrain him. Perhaps he thought it
well not to risk his gains. He was a northerner in blood.
He may have thought it well not further to run the personal risk immediately.

CHAPTER XXIII

RECORDS A VISIT TO DIANA FROM ONE OF THE WORLD'S
GOOD WOMEN

PURE disengagement of contemplativeness had selected
Percy Dacier as the model of her YOUNG MINISTER OF
STATE, Diana supposed. Could she otherwise have dared
to sketch him? She certainly would not have done it now.

That was a reflection similar to what is entertained by
one who has dropped from a precipice to the midway ledge
over the abyss, where caution of the whole sensitive being
is required for simple self-preservation. How could she
have been induced to study and portray him! It seemed
a form of dementia.

She thought this while imagining the world to be interrogating her. When she interrogated herself, she flew to
Lugano and her celestial Salvatore, that she might be defended from a charge of the dreadful weakness of her sex.
Surely she there had proof of her capacity for pure disengagement. Even in recollection the springs of spiritual
happiness renewed the bubbling crystal play. She believed
that a divineness had wakened in her there, to strengthen
her to the end, ward her from any complicity in her sex's
culprit blushing.

Dacier's cry of her name was the cause, she chose to
think, of the excessive circumspection she must henceforth
practise; precariously footing, embracing hardest earth, the
plainest rules, to get back to safety. Not that she was personally endangered, or at least not spiritually; she could
always fly in soul to her heights. But she had now to be
on guard, constantly in the fencing attitude. And watch-

ful of herself as well. That was admitted with a ready frankness, to save it from being a necessitated and painful confession: for the voluntary acquiescence, if it involved her in her sex, claimed an individual exemption. "Women are women, and I am a woman: but I am I, and unlike them: I see we are weak, and weakness tempts: in owning the prudence of guarded steps, I am armed. It is by dissembling, feigning immunity, that we are imperilled." She would have phrased it so, with some anger at her feminine nature as well as at the subjection forced on her by circumstances.

Besides, her position and Percy Dacier's threw the fancied danger into remoteness. The world was her stepmother, vigilant to become her judge; and the world was his taskmaster, hopeful of him, yet able to strike him down for an offence. She saw their situation as he did. The course of folly must be bravely taken, if taken at all. Disguise degraded her to the reptiles.

This was faced. Consequently there was no fear of it.

She had very easily proved that she had skill and self-possession to keep him rational, and therefore they could continue to meet. A little outburst of frenzy to a reputably handsome woman could be treated as the froth of a passing wave. Men have the trick, infants their fevers.

Diana's days were spent in reasoning. Her nights were not so tuneable to the superior mind. When asleep she was the sport of elves that danced her into tangles too deliciously unravelled, and left new problems for the wise-eyed and anxious morning. She solved them with the thought that in sleep it was the mere ordinary woman who fell a prey to her tormentors; awake, she dispersed the swarm, her sky was clear. Gradually the persecution ceased, thanks to her active pen.

A letter from her legal adviser, old Mr. Braddock, informed her that no grounds existed for apprehending marital annoyance, and late in May her household had resumed its customary round.

She examined her accounts. The Debit and Credit sides presented much of the appearance of male and female in our jog-trot civilization. They matched middling well; with rather too marked a tendency to strain the leash and

run frolic on the part of friend Debit (the wanton male),
which deepened the blush of the comparison. Her father
had noticed the same funny thing in his effort to balance
his tugging accounts: "Now then for a look at Man and
Wife:" except that he made Debit stand for the portly
frisky female, Credit the decorous and contracted other
half, a prim gentleman of a constitutionally lean habit of
body, remonstrating with her. "You seem to forget that
we are married, my dear, and must walk in step or bundle
into the Bench," Dan Merion used to say.

Diana had not so much to rebuke in Mr. Debit; or not at
the first reckoning. But his ways were curious. She grew
distrustful of him, after dismissing him with a quiet admonition and discovering a series of ambush bills, which he
must have been aware of when he was allowed to pass
as an honourable citizen. His answer to her reproaches
pleaded the necessitousness of his purchases and expenditure: a capital plea; and Mrs. Credit was requested by
him, in a courteous manner, to drive her pen the faster, so
that she might wax to a corresponding size and satisfy the
world's idea of fitness in couples. She would have costly
furniture, because it pleased her taste; and a French cook,
for a like reason, in justice to her guests; and trained servants; and her tribe of pensioners; flowers she would have
profuse and fresh at her windows and over the rooms; and
the pictures and engravings on the walls were (always for
the good reason mentioned) choice ones; and she had a
love of old lace, she loved colours as she loved cheerfulness,
and silks, and satin hangings, Indian ivory carvings, count-
less mirrors, Oriental woods, chairs and desks with some
feature or a flourish in them, delicate tables with antelope
legs, of approved workmanship in the chronology of European upholstery, and marble clocks of cunning device to
symbol Time, mantel-piece decorations, illustrated editions
of her favourite authors; her bed-chambers, too, gave the
nest for sleep a dainty cosiness in aërial draperies. Hence,
more or less directly, the peccant bills. Credit was reduced
to reckon to a nicety the amount she could rely on positively: her fixed income from her investments and the letting of The Crossways: the days of half-yearly payments
that would magnify her to some proportions beside the

alarming growth of her partner, who was proud of it, and
referred her to the treasures she could summon with her
pen, at a murmur of dissatisfaction. His compliments
were sincere; they were seductive. He assured her that
she had struck a rich vein in an inexhaustible mine: by
writing only a very little faster she could double her income; counting a broader popularity, treble it; and so on
a tide of success down the widening river to a sea sheer
golden. Behold how it sparkles! Are we then to stint our
winged hours of youth for want of courage to realize the
riches we can command? Debit was eloquent, he was unanswerable.

Another calculator, an accustomed and lamentably-scru-
pulous arithmetician, had been at work for some time upon
a speculative summing of the outlay of Diana's establishment, as to its chances of swamping the income. Redworth
could guess pretty closely the cost of a household, if his
care for the holder set him venturing on averages. He
knew nothing of her ten per cent. investment and considered her fixed income a beggarly regiment to marshal
against the invader. He fancied however, in his ignorance
of literary profits, that a popular writer, selling several
editions, had come to an El Dorado. There was the mine.
It required a diligent working. Diana was often struck by
hearing Redworth ask her *when* her next book might be expected. He appeared to have an eagerness in hurrying her
to produce, and she had to say that she was not a nimble
writer. His flattering impatience was vexatious. He admired her work, yet he did his utmost to render it little
admirable. His literary taste was not that of young Arthur
Rhodes, to whom she could read her chapters, appearing to
take counsel upon them while drinking the eulogies: she
suspected him of prosaically wishing her to make money,
and though her exchequer was beginning to know the need
of it, the author's lofty mind disdained such sordidness: —
to be excused, possibly, for a failing productive energy.
She encountered obstacles to imaginative composition.
With the pen in her hand, she would fall into heavy musings; break a sentence to muse, and not on the subject.
She slept unevenly at night, was drowsy by day, unless the
open air was about her, or animating friends. Redworth's

urgency to get her to publish was particularly annoying when she felt how greatly THE YOUNG MINISTER OF STATE would have been improved had she retained the work to brood over it, polish, re-write passages, perfect it. Her musings embraced long dialogues of that work, never printed; they sprang up, they passed from memory; leaving a distaste for her present work: THE CANTATRICE: far more poetical than the preceding, in the opinion of Arthur Rhodes; and the story was more romantic; modelled on a Prima Donna she had met at the musical parties of Henry Wilmers, after hearing Redworth tell of Charles Rainer's quaint passion for the woman, or the idea of the woman. Diana had courted her, studied and liked her. The picture she was drawing of the amiable and gifted Italian, of her villain Roumanian husband, and of the eccentric, high-minded, devoted Englishman, was good in a fashion; but considering the theme, she had reasonable apprehension that her CANTATRICE would not repay her for the time and labour bestowed on it. No clever transcripts of the dialogue of the day occurred; no hair-breadth 'scapes, perils by sea and land, heroisms of the hero, fine shrieks of the heroine; no set scenes of catching pathos and humour; no distinguishable points of social satire — equivalent to a smacking of the public on the chaps, which excites it to grin with keen discernment of the author's intention. She did not appeal to the senses nor to a superficial discernment. So she had the anticipatory sense of its failure; and she wrote her best, in perverseness; of course she wrote slowly; she wrote more and more realistically of the characters and the downright human emotions, less of the wooden supernumeraries of her story, labelled for broad guffaw or deluge tears — the grappling natural links between our public and an author. Her feelings were aloof. They flowed at a hint of a scene of THE YOUNG MINISTER. She could not put them into THE CANTATRICE. And Arthur Rhodes pronounced this work poetical beyond its predecessors, for the reason that the chief characters were alive and the reader felt their pulses. He meant to say, they were poetical inasmuch as they were creations.

The slow progress of a work not driven by the author's feelings necessitated frequent consultations between Debit and Credit, resulting in altercations, recriminations, discord of the yoked and divergent couple. To restore them to their proper trot in harness, Diana reluctantly went to her publisher for an advance item of the sum she was to receive, and the act increased her distaste. An idea came that she would soon cease to be able to write at all. What then? Perhaps by selling her invested money, and ultimately The Crossways, she would have enough for her term upon earth. Necessarily she had to think that short, in order to reckon it as nearly enough. "I am sure," she said to herself, "I shall not trouble the world very long." A strange languor beset her; scarcely melancholy, for she conceived the cheerfulness of life and added to it in company; but a nerveless-ness, as though she had been left by the stream on the banks, and saw beauty and pleasure sweep along and away, while the sun that primed them dried her veins. At this time she was gaining her widest reputation for brilliancy of wit. Only to welcome guests were her evenings ever spent at home. She had no intimate understanding of the deadly wrestle of the conventional woman with her nature which she was undergoing below the surface. Perplexities she acknowledged, and the prudence of guardedness. "But as I am sure not to live very long, we may as well meet." Her meetings with Percy Dacier were therefore hardly shunned, and his behaviour did not warn her to discountenance them. It would have been cruel to exclude him from her select little dinners of eight. Whitmonby, Westlake, Henry Wilmers and the rest, she perhaps aiding, schooled him in the conversational art. She heard it said of him, that the courted discarder of the sex, hitherto a mere politician, was wonderfully humanized. Lady Pennon fell to talking of him hopefully. She declared him to be one of the men who unfold tardily, and only await the mastering passion. If the passion had come, it was controlled. His command of himself melted Diana. How could she forbid his entry to the houses she frequented? She was glad to see him. He showed his pleasure in seeing her. Remembering his tentative indiscretion on those foreign sands, she reflected that he had been easily checked: and the like was not to be said of some others. Beautiful women in her position provoke an intemperateness that contrasts touch-

ingly with the self-restraint of a particular admirer. Her
"impassioned Caledonian" was one of a host, to speak of
whom and their fits of lunacy even to her friend Emma,
was repulsive. She bore with them, foiled them, passed
them, and recovered her equanimity; but the contrast called
to her to dwell on it, the self-restraint whispered of a depth
of passion. . . .

She was shocked at herself for a singular tremble she
experienced, without any beating of the heart, on hearing
one day that the marriage of Percy Dacier and Miss Asper
was at last definitely fixed. Mary Paynham brought her
the news. She had it from a lady who had come across
Miss Asper at Lady Wathin's assemblies, and considered
the great heiress extraordinarily handsome.

"A golden miracle," Diana gave her words to say.
"Good looks and gold together are rather superhuman.
The report may be this time true."

Next afternoon the card of Lady Wathin requested Mrs.
Warwick to grant her a private interview.

Lady Wathin, as one of the order of women who can do
anything in a holy cause, advanced toward Mrs. Warwick,
unabashed by the burden of her mission, and spinally prepared, behind benevolent smilings, to repay dignity of mien
with a similar erectness of dignity. They touched fingers
and sat. The preliminaries to the matter of the interview
were brief between ladies physically sensible of antagonism
and mutually too scornful of subterfuges in one another's
presence to beat the bush.

Lady Wathin began. "I am, you are aware, Mrs. Warwick, a cousin of your friend Lady Dunstane."

"You come to me on business?" Diana said.

"It may be so termed. I have no personal interest in it.
I come to lay certain facts before you which I think you
should know. We think it better that an acquaintance, and
one of your sex, should state the case to you, instead of
having recourse to formal intermediaries, lawyers . . ."

"Lawyers?"

"Well, my husband is a lawyer, it is true. In the course
of his professional vocations he became acquainted with
Mr. Warwick. We have latterly seen a good deal of him.
He is, I regret to say, seriously unwell."

"I have heard of it."

"He has no female relations, it appears. He needs more care than he can receive from hirelings."

"Are you empowered by him, Lady Wathin?"

"I am, Mrs. Warwick. We will not waste time in apologies. He is most anxious for a reconciliation. It seems to Sir Cramborne and to me the most desireable thing for all parties concerned, if you can be induced to regard it in that light. Mr. Warwick may or may not live; but the estrangement is quite undoubtedly the cause of his illness. I touch on nothing connected with it. I simply wish that you should not be in ignorance of his proposal and his condition."

Diana bowed calmly. "I grieve at his condition. His proposal has already been made and replied to."

"Oh, but, Mrs. Warwick, an immediate and decisive refusal of a proposal so fraught with consequences! . . ."

"Ah, but, Lady Wathin, you are now outstepping the limits prescribed by the office you have undertaken."

"You will not lend ear to an intercession?"

"I will not."

"Of course, Mrs. Warwick, it is not for me to hint at things that lawyers could say on the subject."

"Your forbearance is creditable, Lady Wathin."

"Believe me, Mrs. Warwick, the step is — I speak in my husband's name as well as my own — strongly to be advised."

"If I hear one word more of it, I leave the country."

"I should be sorry indeed at any piece of rashness depriving your numerous friends of your society. We have recently become acquainted with Mr. Redworth, and I know the loss you would be to them. I have not attempted an appeal to your feelings, Mrs. Warwick."

"I thank you warmly, Lady Wathin, for what you have not done."

The aristocratic airs of Mrs. Warwick were annoying to Lady Wathin when she considered that they were borrowed, and that a pattern morality could regard the woman as ostracized: nor was it agreeable to be looked at through eyelashes under partially lifted brows. She had come to appeal to the feelings of the wife; at any rate, to discover if she had some and was better than a wild adventuress.

"Our life below is short!" she said.   To which Diana tacitly assented.

"We have our little term, Mrs. Warwick.   It is soon over."

"On the other hand, the platitudes concerning it are eternal."

Lady Wathin closed her eyes, that the like effect might be produced on her ears.   "Ah! they are the truths.   But it is not my business to preach.   Permit me to say that I feel deeply for your husband."

"I am glad of Mr. Warwick's having friends; and they are many, I hope."

"They cannot behold him perishing, without an effort on his behalf."

A chasm of silence intervened.   Wifely pity was not sounded in it.

"He will question me, Mrs. Warwick."

"You can report to him the heads of our conversation, Lady Wathin."

"Would you — it is your husband's most earnest wish; and our house is open to his wife and to him for the purpose; and it seems to us that . . . indeed it might avert a catastrophe you would necessarily deplore : — would you consent to meet him at my house ? "

"It has already been asked, Lady Wathin, and refused."

"But at my house — under our auspices ! "

Diana glanced at the clock.   "Nowhere."

"Is it not — pardon me — a wife's duty, Mrs. Warwick, at least to listen ? "

"Lady Wathin, I have listened to you."

"In the case of his extreme generosity so putting it, for the present, Mrs. Warwick, that he asks only to be heard personally by his wife!   It may preclude so much."

Diana felt a hot wind across her skin.

She smiled and said : "Let me thank you for bringing to an end a mission that must have been unpleasant to you."

"But you will meditate on it, Mrs. Warwick, will you not ? Give me that assurance ! "

"I shall not forget it," said Diana.

Again the ladies touched fingers, with an interchange of

8

the social grimace of cordiality. A few words of compassion for poor Lady Dunstane's invalided state covered Lady Wathin's retreat.

She left, it struck her ruffled sentiments, an icy libertine, whom any husband caring for his dignity and comfort was well rid of ; and if only she could have contrived allusively to bring in the name of Mr. Percy Dacier, just to show these arrant coquettes, or worse, that they were not quite so privileged to pursue their intrigues obscurely as they imagined, it would have soothed her exasperation.

She left a woman the prey of panic.

Diana thought of Emma and Redworth, and of their foolish interposition to save her character and keep her bound. She might now have been free! The struggle with her manacles reduced her to a state of rebelliousness, from which issued vivid illuminations of the one means of certain escape : an abhorrent hissing cavern, that led to a place named Liberty, her refuge, but a hectic place.

Unable to write, hating the house which held her a fixed mark for these attacks, she had an idea of flying straight to her beloved Lugano lake, and there hiding, abandoning her friends, casting off the slave's name she bore, and living free in spirit. She went so far as to reckon the cost of a small household there, and justify the violent step by an exposition of retrenchment upon her large London expenditure. She had but to say farewell to Emma, no other tie to cut! One morning on the Salvatore heights would wash her clear of the webs defacing and entangling her.

CHAPTER XXIV

INDICATES A SOUL PREPARED FOR DESPERATION

THE month was August, four days before the closing of Parliament, and Diana fancied it good for Arthur Rhodes to run down with her to Copsley. He came to her invitation joyfully, reminding her of Lady Dunstane's wish to hear some chapters of THE CANTATRICE, and the MS. was packed. They started, taking rail and fly, and winding up the distance on foot. August is the month of sober maturity and majestic foliage, songless, but a crowned and royal-robed queenly month; and the youngster's appreciation of the homely scenery refreshed Diana; his delight in being with her was also pleasant. She had no wish to exchange him for another; and that was a strengthening thought.

At Copsley the arrival of their luggage had prepared the welcome. Warm though it was, Diana perceived a change in Emma, an unwonted reserve, a doubtfulness of her eyes, in spite of tenderness; and thus thrown back on herself, thinking that if she had followed her own counsel (as she called her impulse) in old days, there would have been no such present misery, she at once, and unconsciously, assumed a guarded look. Based on her knowledge of her honest footing, it was a little defiant. Secretly in her bosom it was sharpened to a slight hostility by the knowledge that her mind had been straying. The guilt and the innocence combined to clothe her in mail, the innocence being positive, the guilt so vapoury. But she was armed only if necessary, and there was no requirement for armour. Emma did not question at all. She saw the alteration in her Tony: she was too full of the tragic apprehensiveness overmastering her to speak of trifles. She had never confided to Tony the exact nature and the growth of her malady, thinking it mortal, and fearing to alarm her dearest.

A portion of the manuscript was read out by Arthur Rhodes in the evening; the remainder next morning. Redworth perceptibly was the model of the English hero; and as to his person, no friend could complain of the sketch; his clear-eyed heartiness, manliness, wholesomeness — a word of Lady Dunstane's regarding him, — and his handsome braced figure, were well painted. Emma forgave the insistence on a certain bluntness of the nose, in consideration of the fond limning of his honest and expressive eyes, and the "light on his temples," which they had noticed together.

She could not so easily forgive the realistic picture of the man: an exaggeration, she thought, of small foibles, that even if they existed, should not have been stressed. The turn for "calculating" was shown up ridiculously; Mr.

Cuthbert Dering was calculating in his impassioned moods as well as in his cold. His head was a long division of ciphers. He had statistics for spectacles, and beheld the world through them, and the mistress he worshipped.

"I see," said Emma, during a pause; "he is a Saxon. You still affect to have the race *en grippe*, Tony."

"I give him every credit for what he is," Diana replied. "I admire the finer qualities of the race as much as anyone. You want to have them presented to you in enamel, Emmy."

But the worst was an indication that the mania for calculating in and out of season would lead to the catastrophe destructive of his happiness. Emma could not bear that. Without asking herself whether it could be possible that Tony knew the secret, or whether she would have laid it bare, her sympathy for Redworth revolted at the exposure. She was chilled. She let it pass; she merely said: "I like the writing."

Diana understood that her story was condemned.

She put on her robes of philosophy to cloak discouragement. "I am glad the writing pleases you."

"The characters are as true as life!" cried Arthur Rhodes. "The Cantatrice drinking porter from the pewter at the slips after harrowing the hearts of her audience, is dearer to me than if she had tottered to a sofa declining sustenance; and because her creatrix has infused such blood of life into her that you accept naturally whatever she does. She was exhausted, and required the porter, like a labourer in the cornfield."

Emma looked at him, and perceived the poet swamped by the admirer. Taken in conjunction with Mr. Cuthbert Dering's frenzy for calculating, she disliked the incident of the porter and the pewter.

"While the Cantatrice swallowed her draught, I suppose Mr. Dering counted the cost?" she said.

"It really might be hinted," said Diana.

The discussion closed with the accustomed pro and con upon the wart of Cromwell's nose, Realism rejoicing in it, Idealism objecting.

Arthur Rhodes was bidden to stretch his legs on a walk along the heights in the afternoon, and Emma was further

vexed by hearing Tony complain of Redworth's treatment
of the lad, whom he would not assist to any of the snug
little posts he was notoriously able to dispense.

"He has talked of Mr. Rhodes to me," said Emma.
"He thinks the profession of literature a delusion, and
doubts the wisdom of having poets for clerks."

"John-Bullish!" Diana exclaimed. "He speaks contemptuously of the poor boy."

"Only inasmuch as the foolishness of the young man in
throwing up the Law provokes his practical mind to speak."

"He might take my word for the 'young man's' ability.
I want him to have the means of living, that he may write.
He has genius."

"He may have it. I like him, and have said so. If he
were to go back to his lawstool, I have no doubt that Redworth would manage to help him."

"And make a worthy ancient Braddock of a youth of
splendid promise! Have I sketched him too Saxon?"

"It is the lens, and not the tribe, Tony."

THE CANTATRICE was not alluded to any more; but
Emma's disapproval blocked the current of composition,
already subject to chokings in the brain of the author.
Diana stayed three days at Copsley, one longer than she
had intended, so that Arthur Rhodes might have his fill of
country air.

"I would keep him, but I should be no companion for
him," Emma said.

"I suspect the gallant squire is only to be satisfied by
landing me safely," said Diana, and that small remark
grated, though Emma saw the simple meaning. When
they parted, she kissed her Tony many times. Tears were
in her eyes. It seemed to Diana that she was anxious to
make amends for the fit of alienation, and she was kissed
in return warmly, quite forgiven, notwithstanding the
deadly blank she had caused in the imagination of the
writer for pay, distracted by the squabbles of Debit and
Credit.

Diana chatted spiritedly to young Rhodes on their drive
to the train. She was profoundly discouraged by Emma's
disapproval of her work. It wanted but that one drop to
make a recurrence to the work impossible. There it must

lie! And what of the aspects of her household? — Perhaps, after all, the Redworths of the world are right, and Literature as a profession is a delusive pursuit. She did not assent to it without hostility to the world's Redworths. — "They have no sensitiveness, we have too much. We are made of bubbles that a wind will burst, and as the wind is always blowing, your practical Redworths have their crow of us."

She suggested advice to Arthur Rhodes upon the prudence of his resuming the yoke of the Law.

He laughed at such a notion, saying that he had some expectations of money to come.

"But I fear," said he, "that Lady Dunstane is very very ill. She begged me to keep her informed of your address."

Diana told him he was one of those who should know it whithersoever she went. She spoke impulsively, her sentiments of friendliness for the youth being temporarily brightened by the strangeness of Emma's conduct in deputing it to him to fulfil a duty she had never omitted. "What can she think I am going to do!"

On her table at home lay a letter from Mr. Warwick. She read it hastily in the presence of Arthur Rhodes, having at a glance at the handwriting anticipated the proposal it contained and the official phrasing.

Her gallant squire was invited to dine with her that evening, costume excused.

They conversed of Literature as a profession, of poets dead and living, of politics, which he abhorred and shied at, and of his prospects. He wrote many rejected pages, enjoyed an income of eighty pounds per annum, and eked out a subsistence upon the modest sum his pen procured him; a sum extremely insignificant; but great Nature was his own, the world was tributary to him, the future his bejewelled and expectant bride. Diana envied his youthfulness. Nothing is more enviable, nothing richer to the mind, than the aspect of a cheerful poverty. How much nobler it was, contrasted with Redworth's amassing of wealth!

When alone, she went to her bedroom and tried to write, tried to sleep. Mr. Warwick's letter was looked at. It seemed to indicate a threat; but for the moment it did not

disturb her so much as the review of her moral prostration.
She wrote some lines to her lawyers, quoting one of Mr.
Warwick's sentences. That done, his letter was dismissed.
Her intolerable languor became alternately a defeating
drowsiness and a fever. She succeeded in the effort to
smother the absolute cause: it was not suffered to show a
front; at the cost of her knowledge of a practised self-
deception. "I wonder whether the world is as bad as a
certain class of writers tell us!" she sighed in weariness,
and mused on their soundings and probings of poor humanity, which the world accepts for the very bottom-truth
if their dredge brings up sheer refuse of the abominable.
The world imagines those to be at our nature's depths who
are impudent enough to expose its muddy shallows. She
was in the mood for such a kind of writing: she could
have started on it at once but that the theme was wanting;
and it may count on popularity, a great repute for penetration. It is true of its kind, though the dredging of nature
is the miry form of art. When it flourishes we may be
assured we have been overenamelling the higher forms.
She felt, and shuddered to feel, that she could draw
from dark stores. Hitherto in her works it had been
a triumph of the good. They revealed a gaping deficiency
of the subtle insight she now possessed. "Exhibit humanity as it is, wallowing, sensual, wicked, behind the
mask," a voice called to her; she was allured by the contemplation of the wide-mouthed old dragon Ego, whose
portrait, decently painted, establishes an instant touch of
exchange between author and public, the latter detected
and confessing. Next to the pantomime of Humour and
Pathos, a cynical surgical knife at the human bosom
seems the surest talisman for this agreeable exchange; and
she could cut. She gave herself a taste of her powers.
She cut at herself mercilessly, and had to bandage the
wound in a hurry to keep in life.

Metaphors were her refuge. Metaphorically she could
allow her mind to distinguish the struggle she was undergoing, sinking under it. The banished of Eden had to put
on metaphors, and the common use of them has helped largely
to civilize us. The sluggish in intellect detest them, but our
civilization is not much indebted to that major faction.

Especially are they needed by the pedestalled woman in her conflict with the natural. Diana saw herself through the haze she conjured up. "Am I worse than other women?" was a piercing twi-thought. Worse, would be hideous isolation. The not worse, abased her sex. She could afford to say that the world was bad : not that women were.

Sinking deeper, an anguish of humiliation smote her to a sense of drowning. For what if the poetic ecstasy on her Salvatore heights had not been of origin divine? had sprung from other than spiritual founts? had sprung from the reddened sources she was compelled to conceal? Could it be? She would not believe it. But there was matter to clip her wings, quench her light, in the doubt.

She fell asleep like the wrecked flung ashore.

Danvers entered her room at an early hour for London to inform her that Mr. Percy Dacier was below, and begged permission to wait.

Diana gave orders for breakfast to be proposed to him. She lay staring at the wall until it became too visibly a reflection of her mind.

CHAPTER XXV

ONCE MORE THE CROSSWAYS AND A CHANGE OF TURNINGS

The suspicion of his having come to impart the news of his proximate marriage ultimately endowed her with sovereign calmness. She had need to think it, and she did. Tea was brought to her while she dressed; she descended the stairs revolving phrases of happy congratulation and the world's ordinary epigrams upon the marriage-tie, neatly mixed.

They read in one another's faces a different meaning from the empty words of excuse and welcome. Dacier's expressed the buckling of a strong set purpose; but, grieved by the look of her eyes, he wasted a moment to say : "You have not slept. You have heard? . . ."

"What?" said she, trying to speculate; and that was a sufficient answer.

"I had n't the courage to call last night; I passed the windows. Give me your hand, I beg."

She gave her hand in wonderment, and more wonderingly felt it squeezed. Her heart began the hammer-thump. She spoke an unintelligible something; saw herself melting away to utter weakness — pride, reserve, simple prudence, all going; crumbled ruins where had stood a fortress imposing to men. Was it love? Her heart thumped shiveringly.

He kept her hand, indifferent to the gentle tension.

"This is the point: I cannot live without you. I have gone on . . . Who was here last night? Forgive me."

"You know Arthur Rhodes."

"I saw him leave the door at eleven. Why do you torture me? There 's no time to lose now. You will be claimed. Come, and let us two cut the knot. It is the best thing in the world for me — the only thing. Be brave! I have your hand. Give it for good, and for heaven's sake don't play the sex. Be yourself. Dear soul of a woman! I never saw the soul in one but in you. I have waited: nothing but the dread of losing you sets me speaking now. And for you to be sacrificed a second time to that — ! Oh, no! You know you can trust me. On my honour, I take breath from you. You are my better in everything — guide, goddess, dearest heart! Trust me; make me master of your fate."

"But my friend!" the murmur hung in her throat. He was marvellously transformed; he allowed no space for the arts of defence and evasion.

"I wish I had the trick of courting. There 's not time; and I 'm a simpleton at the game. We can start this evening. Once away, we leave it to them to settle the matter, and then you are free, and mine to the death."

"But speak, speak! What is it?" Diana said.

"That if we delay, I 'm in danger of losing you altogether."

Her eyes lightened: "You mean that you have heard he has determined? . . ."

"There 's a process of the law. But stop it. Just this one step, and it ends. Whether intended or not, it hangs over you, and you will be perpetually tormented. Why waste your whole youth? — and mine as well! For I am

bound to you as much as if we had stood at the altar — where
we will stand together the instant you are free."

"But where have you heard?" . . .

"From an intimate friend. I will tell you — sufficiently
intimate — from Lady Wathin. Nothing of a friend, but I
see this woman at times. She chose to speak of it to
me — it does n't matter why. She is in his confidence, and
pitched me a whimpering tale. Let those people chatter.
But it 's exactly for those people that you are hanging in
chains, all your youth shrivelling. Let them shout their
worst! It 's the bark of a day; and you won't hear it;
half a year, and it will be over, and I shall bring you
back — the husband of the noblest bride in Christendom!
You don't mistrust me?"

"It is not that," said she. "But now drop my hand. I
am imprisoned."

"It 's asking too much. I 've lost you too many times.
I have the hand and I keep it. I take nothing but the
hand. It 's the hand I want. I give you mine. I love
you. Now I know what love is! — and the word carries
nothing of its weight. Tell me you do not doubt my
honour."

"Not at all. But be rational. I must think, and I cannot while you keep my hand."

He kissed it. "I keep my own against the world."

A cry of rebuke swelled to her lips at his conqueror's
tone. It was not uttered, for directness was in his character and his wooing loyal — save for bitter circumstances,
delicious to hear; and so narrow was the ring he had
wound about her senses, that her loathing of the circumstances pushed her to acknowledge within her bell of a
heart her love for him.

He was luckless enough to say: "Diana!"

It rang horridly of her husband. She drew her hand to
loosen it, with repulsing brows. "Not that name!"

Dacier was too full of his honest advocacy of the
passionate lover to take a rebuff. There lay his unconscious mastery, where the common arts of attack would
have tripped him with a quick-witted woman, and where a
man of passion, not allowing her to succumb in dignity,
would have alarmed her to the breaking loose from him.

" Lady Dunstane calls you Tony."

" She is my dearest and oldest friend."

" You and I don't count by years. You are the dearest to me on earth, Tony ! "

She debated as to forbidding that name.

The moment's pause wrapped her in a mental hurricane, out of which she came with a heart stopped, her olive cheeks ashen-hued. She had seen that the step was possible.

" Oh ! Percy, Percy, are we mad ? "

" Not mad. We take what is ours. Tell me, have I ever, ever disrespected you ? You were sacred to me ; and you are, though now the change has come. Look back on it — it is time lost, years that are dust. But look forward, and you cannot imagine our separation. What I propose is plain sense for us two. Since Rovio, I have been at your feet. Have I not some just claim for recompense ? Tell me ! Tony ! "

The sweetness of the secret name, the privileged name, in his mouth stole through her blood, melting resistance.

She had consented. The swarthy flaming of her face avowed it even more than the surrender of her hand. He gained much by claiming little : he respected her, gave her no touches of fright and shame ; and it was her glory to fall with pride. An attempt at a caress would have awakened her view of the whitherward : but she was treated as a sovereign lady rationally advised.

" Is it since Rovio, Percy ? "

" Since the morning when you refused me one little flower."

" If I had given it, you might have been saved ! "

" I fancy I was doomed from the beginning."

" I was worth a thought ? "

" Worth a life ! worth ten thousand ! "

" You have reckoned it all like a sane man : — family, position, the world, the scandal ? "

" All. I have long known that you were the mate for me. You have to weather a gale, Tony. It won't last. My dearest ! it won't last many months. I regret the trial for you, but I shall be with you, burning for the day to reinstate you and show you the queen you are."

"Yes, we two can have no covert dealings, Percy," said
Diana. They would be hateful — baseness! Rejecting
any baseness, it seemed to her that she stood in some
brightness. The light was of a lurid sort. She called on
her heart to glory in it as the light of tried love, the love
that defied the world. Her heart rose. She and he would
at a single step give proof of their love for one another:
and this kingdom of love — how different from her recent
craven languors! — this kingdom awaited her, was hers for
one word; and beset with the oceans of enemies, it was
unassailable. If only they were true to the love they
vowed, no human force could subvert it: and she doubted
him as little as of herself. This new kingdom of love,
never entered by her, acclaiming her, was well-nigh unimaginable, in spite of the many hooded messengers it had
despatched to her of late. She could hardly believe that it
had come.

"But see me as I am," she said; she faltered it through
her direct gaze on him.

"With chains to strike off? Certainly; it is done," he
replied.

"Rather heavier than those of the slave-market! I am
the deadest of burdens. It means that your enemies, personal — if you have any, and political — you have numbers,
will raise a cry. . . . Realize it. You may still be my
friend. I forgive the bit of wildness."

She provoked a renewed kissing of her hand; for magnanimity in love is an overflowing danger; and when he
said: "The burden you have to bear outweighs mine out of
all comparison. What is it to a man — a public man or
not! The woman is always the victim. That's why I
have held myself in so long:" — her strung frame softened.
She half yielded to the tug on her arm.

"Is there no talking for us without foolishness?" she
murmured. The foolishness had wafted her to sea, far
from sight of land. "Now sit, and speak soberly. Discuss
the matter. — Yes, my hand, but I must have my wits.
Leave me free to use them till we choose our path. Let it
be the brains between us, as far as it can. You ask me to
join my fate to yours. It signifies a sharp battle for you,
dear friend; perhaps the blighting of the most promising

life in England. One question is, can I countervail the
burden I shall be, by such help to you as I can afford?
Burden, is no word — I rake up a buried fever. I have
partially lived it down, and instantly I am covered with
spots. The old false charges and this plain offence make a
monster of me."

"And meanwhile you are at the disposal of the man who
falsely charged you and armed the world against you," said
Dacier.

"I can fly. The world is wide."

"Time slips. Your youth is wasted. If you escape the
man, he will have triumphed in keeping you from me. And
I thirst for you; I look to you for aid and counsel; I want
my mate. You have not to be told how you inspire me?
I am really less than half myself without you. If I am to
do anything in the world, it must be with your aid, you
beside me. Our hands are joined : one leap! Do you not
see that after . . . well, it cannot be friendship. It imposes rather more on me than I can bear. You are not the
woman to trifle; nor I, Tony, the man for it with a woman
like you. You are my spring of wisdom. You interdict
me altogether — can you? — or we unite our fates, like
these hands now. Try to get yours away!"

Her effort ended in a pressure. Resistance, nay, to hesitate at the joining of her life with his after her submission
to what was a scorching fire in memory, though it was less
than an embrace, accused her of worse than foolishness.

"Well, then," said she, "wait three days. Deliberate.
Oh! try to know yourself, for your clear reason to guide
you. Let us be something better than the crowd abusing
us, not simple creatures of impulse — as we choose to call
the animal. What if we had to confess that we took to
our heels the moment the idea struck us! Three days.
We may then pretend to a philosophical resolve. Then
come to me : or write to me."

"How long is it since the old Rovio morning, Tony?"

"An age."

"Date my deliberations from that day."

The thought of hers having to be dated possibly from an
earlier day, robbed her of her summit of feminine isolation,
and she trembled, chilled and flushed; she lost all anchorage.

"So it must be to-morrow," said he, reading her closely, "not later. Better at once. But women are not to be hurried."

"Oh! don't class me, Percy, pray! I think of you, not of myself."

"You suppose that in a day or two I might vary?"

She fixed her eyes on him, expressing certainty of his unalterable steadfastness. The look allured. It changed: her head shook. She held away and said: "No, leave me; leave me, dear, dear friend. Percy, my dearest! I will not 'play the sex.' I am yours if . . . if it is your wish. It may as well be to-morrow. Here I am useless; I cannot write, not screw a thought from my head. I dread that 'process of the Law' a second time. To-morrow, if it must be. But no impulses. Fortune is blind; she may be kind to us. The blindness of Fortune is her one merit, and fools accuse her of it, and they profit by it! I fear we all of us have our turn of folly: we throw the stake for good luck. I hope my sin is not very great. I know my position is desperate. I feel a culprit. But I am sure I have courage, perhaps brains to help. At any rate, I may say this: I bring no burden to my lover that he does not know of."

Dacier pressed her hand. "Money we shall have enough. My uncle has left me fairly supplied."

"What would he think?" said Diana, half in a glimpse of meditation.

"Think me the luckiest of the breeched. I fancy I hear him thanking you for 'making a man' of me."

She blushed. Some such phrase might have been spoken by Lord Dannisburgh.

"I have but a poor sum of money," she said. "I may be able to write abroad. Here I cannot — if I am to be persecuted."

"You shall write, with a new pen!" said Dacier. "You shall live, my darling Tony. You have been held too long in this miserable suspension, neither maid nor wife, neither woman nor stockfish. Ah! shameful. But we'll right it. The step, for us, is the most reasonable that could be considered. You shake your head. But the circumstances make it so. Courage, and we come to happiness! And

that, for you and me, means work. Look at the case of
Lord and Lady Dulac. It's identical, except that she is no
match beside you: and I do not compare her antecedents
with yours. But she braved the leap, and forced the world
to swallow it, and now, you see, she's perfectly honoured.
I know a place on a peak of the Maritime Alps, exquisite
in summer, cool, perfectly solitary, no English, snow round
us, pastures at our feet, and the Mediterranean below.
There! my Tony. To-morrow night we start. You will
meet me — shall I call here? — well, then at the railway
station, the South-Eastern, for Paris: say, twenty minutes
to eight. I have your pledge? You will come?"

She sighed it, then said it firmly, to be worthy of him.
Kind Fortune, peeping under the edge of her bandaged
eyes, appeared willing to bestow the beginning of happiness
upon one who thought she had a claim to a small taste of it
before she died. It seemed distinguishingly done, to give
a bite of happiness to the starving!

"I fancied when you were announced that you came for
congratulations upon your approaching marriage, Percy."

"I shall expect to hear them from you to-morrow evening at the station, dear Tony," said he.

The time was again stated, the pledge repeated. He
forbore entreaties for privileges, and won her gratitude.

They named once more the place of meeting and the
hour: more significant to them than phrases of intensest
love and passion. Pressing hands sharply for pledge of
good faith, they sundered.

She still had him in her eyes when he had gone. Her
old world lay shattered; her new world was up without a
dawn, with but one figure, the sun of it, to light the swinging strangeness.

Was ever man more marvellously transformed? or woman
more wildly swept from earth into the clouds? So she
mused in the hum of her tempest of heart and brain, forgetful of the years and the conditions preparing both of
them for this explosion.

She had much to do: the arrangements to dismiss her
servants, write to house-agents and her lawyer, and write
fully to Emma, write the enigmatic farewell to the Esquarts and Lady Pennon, Mary Paynham, Arthur Rhodes,

Whitmonby (stanch in friendship, but requiring friendly touches), Henry Wilmers, and Redworth. He was reserved to the last, for very enigmatical adieux: he would hear the whole story from Emma; must be left to think as he liked.

The vague letters were excellently well composed: she was going abroad, and knew not when she would return; bade her friends think the best they could of her in the meantime. Whitmonby was favoured with an anecdote, to be read as an apologue by the light of subsequent events. But the letter to Emma tasked Diana. Intending to write fully, her pen committed the briefest sentences: the tenderness she felt for Emma wakening her heart to sing that she was loved, loved, and knew love at last; and Emma's foreseen antagonism to the love and the step it involved rendered her pleadings in exculpation a stammered confession of guiltiness, ignominious, unworthy of the pride she felt in her lover. "I am like a cartridge rammed into a gun, to be discharged at a certain hour to-morrow," she wrote; and she sealed a letter so frigid that she could not decide to post it. All day she imagined hearing a distant cannonade. The light of the day following was not like earthly light. Danvers assured her there was no fog in London.

"London is insupportable; I am going to Paris, and shall send for you in a week or two," said Diana.

"Allow me to say, ma'am, that you had better take me with you," said Danvers.

"Are you afraid of travelling by yourself, you foolish creature?"

"No, ma'am, but I don't like any hands to undress and dress my mistress but my own."

"I have not lost the art," said Diana, chafing for a magic spell to extinguish the woman, to whom, immediately pitying her, she said: "You are a good faithful soul. I think you have never kissed me. Kiss me on the forehead."

Danvers put her lips to her mistress's forehead, and was asked: "You still consider yourself attached to my fortunes?"

"I do, ma'am, at home or abroad; and if you will take me with you . . ."

"Not for a week or so."

"I shall not be in the way, ma'am."

They played at shutting eyes. The petition of Danvers was declined; which taught her the more; and she was emboldened to say: "Wherever my mistress goes, she ought to have her attendant with her." There was no answer to it but the refusal.

The hours crumbled slowly, each with a blow at the passages of retreat. Diana thought of herself as another person, whom she observed, not counselling her, because it was a creature visibly pushed by the Fates. In her own mind she could not perceive a stone of solidity anywhere, nor a face that had the appearance of our common life. She heard the cannon at intervals. The things she said set Danvers laughing, and she wondered at the woman's mingled mirth and stiffness. Five o'clock struck. Her letters were sent to the post. Her boxes were piled from stairs to door. She read the labels, for her good-bye to the hated name of Warwick: — Why ever adopted! Emma might well have questioned why! Women are guilty of such unreasoning acts! But this was the close to that chapter. The hour of six went by. Between six and seven came a sound of knocker and bell at the street-door. Danvers rushed into the sitting-room to announce that it was Mr. Redworth. Before a word could be mustered, Redworth was in the room. He said: "You must come with me at once!"

CHAPTER XXVI

IN WHICH A DISAPPOINTED LOVER RECEIVES A MULTITUDE OF LESSONS

DACIER waited at the station, a good figure of a sentinel over his luggage and a spy for one among the inpouring passengers. Tickets had been confidently taken, the private division of the carriages happily secured. On board the boat she would be veiled. Landed on French soil, they threw off disguises, breasted the facts. And those? They lightened. He smarted with his eagerness.

He had come well in advance of the appointed time, for he would not have had her hang about there one minute alone.

Strange as this adventure was to a man of prominent station before the world, and electrical as the turning-point of a destiny that he was given to weigh deliberately and far-sightedly, Diana's image strung him to the pitch of it. He looked nowhere but ahead, like an archer putting hand for his arrow.

Presently he compared his watch and the terminus clock. She should now be arriving. He went out to meet her and do service. Many cabs and carriages were peered into, couples inspected, ladies and their maids, wives and their husbands — an August exodus to the Continent. Nowhere the starry she. But he had a fund of patience. She was now in some block of the streets. He was sure of her, sure of her courage. Tony and recreancy could not go together. Now that he called her Tony, she was his close comrade, known; the name was a caress and a promise, breathing of her, as the rose of sweetest earth. He counted it to be a month ere his family would have wind of the altered position of his affairs, possibly a year to the day of his making the dear woman his own in the eyes of the world. She was dear past computation, womanly, yet quite unlike the womanish women, unlike the semi-males, courteously called dashing, unlike the sentimental. His present passion for her lineaments declared her surpassingly beautiful, though his critical taste was rather for the white statue that gave no warmth. She had brains and ardour, she had grace and sweetness, a playful petulancy enlivening our atmosphere, and withal a refinement, a distinction, not to be classed; and justly might she dislike the being classed. Her humour was a perennial refreshment, a running well, that caught all the colours of light; her wit studded the heavens of the recollection of her. In his heart he felt that it was a stepping down for the brilliant woman to give him her hand; a condescension and an act of valour. She who always led or prompted when they conversed, had now in her generosity abandoned the lead and herself to him, and she deserved his utmost honouring.

But where was she? He looked at his watch, looked

at the clock. They said the same: ten minutes to the moment of the train's departure.

A man may still afford to dwell on the charms and merits of his heart's mistress while he has ten minutes to spare. The dropping minutes, however, detract one by one from her individuality and threaten to sink her in her sex entirely. It is the inexorable clock that says she is as other women. Dacier began to chafe. He was unaccustomed to the part he was performing: — and if she failed him? She would not. She would be late, though. No, she was in time! His long legs crossed the platform to overtake a tall lady veiled and dressed in black. He lifted his hat; he heard an alarmed little cry and retired. The clock said, Five minutes: a secret chiromancy in addition indicating on its face the word Fool. An odd word to be cast at him! It rocked the icy pillar of pride in the background of his nature. Certainly standing solus at the hour of eight P.M., he would stand for a fool. Hitherto he had never allowed a woman the chance to posture him in that character. He strode out, returned, scanned every lady's shape, and for a distraction watched the veiled lady whom he had accosted. Her figure suggested pleasant features. Either she was disappointed, or she was an adept. At the shutting of the gates she glided through, not without a fearful look around and at him. She disappeared. Dacier shrugged. His novel assimilation to the rat-rabble of amatory intriguers tapped him on the shoulder unpleasantly. A luckless member of the fraternity too! The bell, the clock and the train gave him his title. "And I was ready to fling down everything for the woman!" The trial of a superb London gentleman's resources in the love-passion could not have been much keener. No sign of her.

He who stands ready to defy the world, and is baffled by the absence of his fair assistant, is the fool doubled, so completely the fool that he heads the universal shout: he does not spare himself. The sole consolation he has is to revile the sex. Women! women! Whom have they not made a fool of! His uncle as much as any — and professing to know them. Him also! the man proud of escaping their wiles. "For this woman!" . . . he went on saying after he had lost sight of her in her sex's trickeries. The nearest he could get to her was to conceive that the arrant coquette was now laughing at her utter subjugation and befooling of the man popularly supposed invincible. If it were known of him! The idea of his being a puppet fixed for derision was madly distempering. He had only to ask the affirmative of Constance Asper to-morrow! A vision of his determining to do it, somewhat comforted him.

Dacier walked up and down the platform, passing his pile of luggage, solitary and eloquent on the barrow. Never in his life having been made to look a fool, he felt the red heat of the thing, as a man who has not blessedly become acquainted with the swish in boyhood finds his untempered blood turn to poison at a blow; he cannot healthily take a licking. But then it had been so splendid an insanity when he urged Diana to fly with him. Anyone but a woman would have appreciated the sacrifice.

His luggage had to be removed. He dropped his porter a lordly fee and drove home. From that astonished solitude he strolled to his Club. Curiosity mastering the wrath it was mixed with, he left his Club and crossed the park southward in the direction of Diana's house, abusing her for her inveterate attachment to the regions of Westminster. There she used to receive Lord Dannisburgh; innocently, no doubt — assuredly quite innocently; and her husband had quitted the district. Still it was rather childish for a woman to be always haunting the seats of Parliament. Her disposition to imagine that she was able to inspire statesmen came in for a share of ridicule; for when we know ourselves to be ridiculous, a retort in kind, unjust upon consideration, is balm. The woman dragged him down to the level of common men; that was the peculiar injury, and it swept her undistinguished into the stream of women. In appearance, as he had proved to the fellows at his Club, he was perfectly self-possessed, mentally distracted and bitter, hating himself for it, snapping at the cause of it. She had not merely disappointed, she had slashed his high conceit of himself, curbed him at the first animal dash forward, and he champed the bit with the fury of a thwarted racer.

Twice he passed her house. Of course no light was shown at her windows. They were scanned malignly.

He held it due to her to call and inquire whether there was any truth in the report of Mrs. Warwick's illness. Mrs. Warwick! She meant to keep the name.

A maid-servant came to the door with a candle in her hand revealing red eyelids. She was not aware that her mistress was unwell. Her mistress had left home some time after six o'clock with a gentleman. She was unable to tell him the gentleman's name. William, the footman, had opened the door to him. Her mistress's maid Mrs. Danvers had gone to the Play — with William. She thought that Mrs. Danvers might know who the gentleman was. The girl's eyelids blinked, and she turned aside. Dacier consoled her with a piece of gold, saying he would come and see Mrs. Danvers in the morning.

His wrath was partially quieted by the new speculations offered up to it. He could not conjure a suspicion of treachery in Diana Warwick; and a treachery so foully cynical! She had gone with a gentleman. He guessed on all sides; he struck at walls, as in complete obscurity.

The mystery of her conduct troubling his wits for the many hours was explained by Danvers. With a sympathy that she was at pains to show, she informed him that her mistress was not at all unwell, and related of how Mr. Redworth had arrived just when her mistress was on the point of starting for Paris and the Continent; because poor Lady Dunstane was this very day to undergo an operation under the surgeons at Copsley, and she did not wish her mistress to be present, but Mr. Redworth thought her mistress ought to be there, and he had gone down thinking she was there, and then came back in hot haste to fetch her, and was just in time, as it happened, by two or three minutes.

Dacier rewarded the sympathetic woman for her intelligence, which appeared to him to have shot so far as to require a bribe. Gratitude to the person soothing his unwontedly ruffled temper was the cause of the indiscretion in the amount he gave.

It appeared to him that he ought to proceed to Copsley for tidings of Lady Dunstane. Thither he sped by the handy railway and a timely train. He reached the park-gates at three in the afternoon, telling his flyman to wait. As he advanced by short cuts over the grass, he studied

the look of the rows of windows. She was within, and
strangely to his clouded senses she was no longer Tony,
no longer the deceptive woman he could in justice abuse.
He and she, so close to union, were divided. A hand
resembling the palpable interposition of Fate had swept
them asunder. Having the poorest right — not any — to
reproach her, he was disarmed, he felt himself a miserable
intruder; he summoned his passion to excuse him, and
gained some unsatisfied repose of mind by contemplating
its devoted sincerity; which roused an effort to feel for
the sufferer — Diana Warwick's friend. With the pair of
surgeons named, the most eminent of their day, in attendance, the case must be serious. To vindicate the breaker
of her pledge, his present plight likewise assured him of
that, and nearing the house he adopted instinctively the
funeral step and mood, just sensible of a novel small-
ness. For the fortifying testimony of his passion had to
be put aside, he was obliged to disavow it for a simpler
motive if he applied at the door. He stressed the motive,
produced the sentiment, and passed thus naturally into
hypocrisy, as lovers precipitated by their blood among the
crises of human conditions are often forced to do. He had
come to inquire after Lady Dunstane. He remembered
that it had struck him as a duty, on hearing of her dangerous illness.

The door opened before he touched the bell. Sir Lukin
knocked against him and stared.

"Ah! — who? — you?" he said, and took him by the
arm and pressed him on along the gravel. "Dacier, are
you? Redworth's in there. Come on a step, come! It's
the time for us to pray. Good God! There's mercy for
sinners. If ever there was a man! . . . But, oh, good God!
she's in their hands this minute. My saint is under the
knife."

Dacier was hurried forward by a powerful hand.
"They say it lasts about five minutes, four and a half — or
more! My God! When they turned me out of her room,
she smiled to keep me calm. She said, 'Dear husband':
— the veriest wretch and brutallest husband ever poor
woman . . . and a saint! a saint on earth! Emmy!"
Tears burst from him.

He pulled forth his watch and asked Dacier for the time.

"A minute's gone in a minute. It's three minutes and a half. Come faster. They're at their work! It's life or death. I've had death about me. But for a woman! and your wife! and that brave soul! She bears it so. Women *are* the bravest creatures afloat. If they make her shriek, it'll be only if she thinks I'm out of hearing. No: I see her. She bears it! — They may n't have begun yet. It may all be over! Come into the wood. I must pray. I must go on my knees."

Two or three steps in the wood, at the mossed roots of a beech, he fell kneeling, muttering, exclaiming.

The tempest of penitence closed with a blind look at his watch, which he left dangling. He had to talk to drug his thoughts.

"And mind you," said he, when he had rejoined Dacier and was pushing his arm again, rounding beneath the trees to a view of the house, "for a man steeped in damnable iniquity! She bears it all for me, because I begged her, for the chance of her living. It's my doing — this knife! Macpherson swears there *is* a chance. Thomson backs him. But they're at her, cutting! . . . The pain must be awful — the mere pain! The gentlest creature ever drew breath! And women fear blood — and her own! — And a head! She ought to have married the best man alive, not a —! I can't remember her once complaining of me — not once. A common donkey compared to her! All I can do is to pray. And she knows the beast I am, and has forgiven me. There is n't a blessed text of Scripture that does n't cry out in praise of her. And they cut and hack! . . ." He dropped his head. The vehement big man heaved, shuddering. His lips worked fast.

"She is not alone with them, unsupported?" said Dacier.

Sir Lukin moaned for relief. He caught his watch swinging and stared at it. "What a good fellow you were to come! Now's the time to know your friends. There's Diana Warwick, true as steel. Redworth came on her tip-toe for the Continent; he had only to mention . . . Emmy wanted to spare her. She would not have sent — wanted to spare her the sight. I offered to stand by . . . Chased me

out. Diana Warwick's there: — worth fifty of me
Dacier, I 've had my sword-blade tried by Indian horsemen,
and I know what true as steel means. She 's there. And
I know she shrinks from the sight of blood. My oath on
it, she won't quiver a muscle! Next to my wife, you may
take my word for it, Dacier, Diana Warwick is the pick of
living women. I could prove it. They go together. I
could prove it over and over. She 's the loyallest woman
anywhere. Her one error was that marriage of hers, and
how she ever pitched herself into it, none of us can guess."
After a while, he said: "Look at your watch."

"Nearly twenty minutes gone."

"Are they afraid to send out word? It 's that window!"
He covered his eyes, and muttered, sighed. He became
abruptly composed in appearance. "The worst of a black
sheep like me is, I 'm such an infernal sinner, that Providence! . . . But both surgeons gave me their word of honour that there *was* a chance. A chance! But it 's the end
of me if Emmy — Good God! no! the knife 's enough;
don't let her be killed! It would be murder. Here am I
talking! I ought to be praying. I should have sent for
the parson to help me; I can't get the proper words — bellow like a rascal trooper strung up for the cat. It must be
twenty-five minutes now. Who 's alive now!"

Dacier thought of the Persian Queen crying for news of
the slaughtered, with her mind on her lord and husband:
"Who is *not* dead?" Diana exalted poets, and here was
an example of the truth of one to nature, and of the poor
husband's depth of feeling. They said not the same thing,
but it was the same cry de profundis.

He saw Redworth coming at a quick pace.

Redworth raised his hand. Sir Lukin stopped. "He 's
waving!"

"It 's good," said Dacier.

"Speak! are you sure?"

"I judge by the look."

Redworth stepped unfalteringly.

"It 's over, all well," he said. He brushed his forehead
and looked sharply cheerful.

"My dear fellow! my dear fellow!" Sir Lukin grasped
his hand. "It 's more than I deserve. Over? She has

borne it! She would have gone to heaven and left me —! Is she safe?"

"Doing well."

"Have you seen the surgeons?"

"Mrs. Warwick."

"What did she say?"

"A nod of the head."

"You saw her?"

"She came to the stairs."

"Diana Warwick never lies. She would n't lie, not with a nod! They 've saved Emmy — do you think?"

"It looks well."

"My girl has passed the worst of it?"

"That 's over."

Sir Lukin gazed glassily. The necessity of his agony was to lean to the belief, at a beckoning, that Providence pardoned him, in tenderness for what would have been his loss. He realized it, and experienced a sudden calm: testifying to the positive pardon.

"Now, look here, you two fellows, listen half a moment," he addressed Redworth and Dacier; "I 've been the biggest scoundrel of a husband unhung, and married to a saint; and if she 's only saved to me, I 'll swear to serve her faithfully, or may a thunderbolt knock me to perdition! and thank God for his justice! Prayers are answered, mind you, though a fellow may be as black as a sweep. Take a warning from me. I 've had my lesson."

Dacier soon after talked of going. The hope of seeing Diana had abandoned him, the desire was almost extinct.

Sir Lukin could not let him go. He yearned to preach to him or anyone from his personal text of the sinner honourably remorseful on account of and notwithstanding the forgiveness of Providence, and he implored Dacier and Redworth by turns to be careful when they married of how they behaved to the sainted women their wives; never to lend ear to the devil nor to believe, as he had done, that there is no such thing as a devil, for he had been the victim of him, and he knew. The devil, he loudly proclaimed, has a multiplicity of lures, and none more deadly than when he baits with a petticoat. He had been hooked, and had found the devil in person. He begged them urgently to keep his example in memory. By following this and that wildfire he had stuck himself in a bog — a common result with those who would not see the devil at work upon them; and it required his dear suffering saint to be at death's doors, cut to pieces and gasping, to open his eyes. But, thank heaven, they were opened at last! Now he saw the beast he was: a filthy beast! unworthy of tying his wife's shoestring. No confessions could expose to them the beast he was. But let them not fancy there was no such thing as an active DEVIL about the world.

Redworth divined that the simply sensational man abased himself before Providence and heaped his gratitude on the awful Power in order to render it difficult for the promise of the safety of his wife to be withdrawn.

He said: "There is good hope;" and drew an admonition upon himself.

"Ah! my dear good Redworth," Sir Lukin sighed from his elevation of out-spoken penitence: "you will see as I do some day. It *is* the devil, think as you like of it. When you have pulled down all the Institutions of the Country, what do you expect but ruins? That Radicalism of yours has its day. You have to go through a wrestle like mine to understand it. You say, the day is fine, let's have our game. Old England pays for it! Then you'll find how you love the old land of your birth — the noblest ever called a nation! — with your Corn Law Repeals! — eh, Dacier? — You'll own it was the devil tempted you. I hear you apologizing. Pray God, it mayn't be too late!"

He looked up at the windows. "She may be sinking!"

"Have no fears," Redworth said; "Mrs. Warwick would send for you."

"She would. Diana Warwick would be sure to send. Next to my wife, Diana Warwick's . . . she'd send, never fear. I dread that room. I'd rather go through a regiment of sabres — though it's over now. And Diana Warwick stood it. The worst is over, you told me. By heaven! women are wonderful creatures. But she hasn't a peer for courage. I could trust her — most extraordinary thing, that marriage of hers! — not a soul has ever been able to explain it: — trust her to the death."

Redworth left them, and Sir Lukin ejaculated on the

merits of Diana Warwick to Dacier. He laughed scornfully: "And that's the woman the world attacks for want of virtue! Why, a fellow hasn't a chance with her, not a chance. She comes out in blazing armour if you unmask a battery. I don't know how it might be if she were in love with a fellow. I doubt her thinking men worth the trouble. I never met the man. But if she *were* to take fire, Troy'd be nothing to it. I wonder whether we might go in: I dread the house."

Dacier spoke of departing.

"No, no, wait," Sir Lukin begged him. "I was talking about women. They *are* the devil — or he makes most use of them: and you must learn to see the cloven foot under their petticoats, if you're to escape them. There's no protection in being in love with your wife; I married for love; I am, I always have been, in love with her; and I went to the deuce. The music struck up and away I waltzed. A woman like Diana Warwick might keep a fellow straight, because she's all round you; she's man and woman in brains; and legged like a deer, and breasted like a swan, and a regular sheaf of arrows in her eyes. Dark women — ah! But she has a contempt for us, you know. That's the secret of her. — Redworth's at the door. Bad? Is it bad? I never was particularly fond of that house — hated it. I love it now for Emmy's sake. I couldn't live in another — though I should be haunted. Rather her ghost than nothing — though I'm an infernal coward about the next world. But if you're right with religion you needn't fear. What I can't comprehend in Redworth is his Radicalism, and getting richer and richer."

"It's not a vow of poverty," said Dacier.

"He'll find they don't coalesce, or his children will. Once the masses are uppermost! It's a bad day, Dacier, when we've no more gentlemen in the land. Emmy backs him, so I hold my tongue. To-morrow's a Sunday. I wish you were staying here; I'd take you to church with me — we shirk it when we haven't a care. It couldn't do you harm. I've heard capital sermons. I've always had the good habit of going to church, Dacier. Now's the time for remembering them. Ah, my dear fellow, I'm not a parson. It would have been better for me if I had been."

And for you too! his look added plainly. He longed to
preach; he was impelled to chatter.

Redworth reported the patient perfectly quiet, breathing
calmly.

"Laudanum?" asked Sir Lukin. "Now there's a poison
we've got to bless! And we set up in our wisdom for knowing what is good for us!"

He had talked his hearers into a stupefied assent to anything he uttered.

"Mrs. Warwick would like to see you in two or three
minutes; she will come down," Redworth said to Dacier.

"That looks well, eh? That looks bravely," Sir Lukin
cried. "Diana Warwick would n't leave the room without
a certainty. I dread the look of those men; I shall have
to shake their hands! And so I do, with all my heart;
only — But God bless them! But we must go in, if
she's coming down."

They entered the house, and sat in the drawing-room,
where Sir Lukin took up from the table one of his wife's
Latin books, a Persius, bearing her marginal notes. He
dropped his head on it, with sobs.

The voice of Diana recalled him to the present. She
counselled him to control himself; in that case he might for
one moment go to the chamber-door and assure himself by
the silence that his wife was resting. She brought permission from the surgeons and doctor, on his promise to be
still.

Redworth supported Sir Lukin tottering out.

Dacier had risen. He was petrified by Diana's face, and
thought of her as whirled from him in a storm, bearing the
marks of it. Her underlip hung for short breaths; the big
drops of her recent anguish still gathered on her brows;
her eyes were tearless, lustreless; she looked ancient in
youth, and distant by a century, like a tall woman of the
vaults, issuing white-ringed, not of our light.

She shut her mouth for strength to speak to him.

He said: "You are not ill? You are strong?"

"I? Oh, strong. I will sit. I cannot be absent longer
than two minutes. The trial of her strength is to come.
If it were courage, we might be sure. The day is fine?"

"A perfect August day."

"I held her through it. I am thankful to heaven it was no other hand than mine. She wished to spare me. She was glad of her Tony when the time came. I thought I was a coward — I could have changed with her to save her; I am a strong woman, fit to submit to that work. I should not have borne it as she did. She expected to sink under it. All her dispositions were made for death — bequests to servants and to . . . to friends: every secret liking they had, thought of!"

Diana clenched her hands.

"I hope!" Dacier said.

"You shall hear regularly. Call at Sir William's house to-morrow. He sleeps here to-night. The suspense must last for days. It is a question of vital power to bear the shock. She has a mind so like a flying spirit that, just before the moment, she made Mr. Lanyan Thomson smile by quoting some saying of her Tony's."

"Try by-and-by to recollect it," said Dacier.

"And you were with that poor man! How did he pass the terrible time? I pitied him."

"He suffered; he prayed."

"It was the best he could do. Mr. Redworth was as he always is at the trial, a pillar. Happy the friend who knows him for one! He never thinks of himself in a crisis. He is sheer strength to comfort and aid. They will drive you to the station with Mr. Thomson. He returns to relieve Sir William to-morrow. I have learnt to admire the men of the knife! No profession equals theirs in self-command and beneficence. Dr. Bridgenorth is permanent here."

"I have a fly, and go back immediately," said Dacier.

"She shall hear of your coming. Adieu."

Diana gave him her hand. It was gently pressed.

A wonderment at the utter change of circumstances took Dacier passingly at the sight of her vanishing figure.

He left the house, feeling he dared have no personal wishes. It had ceased to be the lover's hypocrisy with him.

The crisis of mortal peril in that house enveloped its inmates, and so wrought in him as to enshroud the stripped outcrying husband, of whom he had no clear recollection, save of the man's agony. The two women, striving against

death, devoted in friendship, were the sole living images
he brought away; they were a new vision of the world and
our life.

He hoped with Diana, bled with her. She rose above
him high, beyond his transient human claims. He envied
Redworth the common friendly right to be near her. In
reflection, long after, her simplicity of speech, washed pure
of the blood-emotions, for token of her great nature, during those two minutes of their sitting together, was dearer,
sweeter to the lover than if she had shown by touch or
word that a faint allusion to their severance was in her
mind; and this despite a certain vacancy it created.

He received formal information of Lady Dunstane's
progress to convalescence. By degrees the simply official
tone of Diana's letters combined with the ceasing of them
and the absence of her personal charm to make a gentleman not remarkable for violence in the passion so calmly
reasonable as to think the dangerous presence best avoided
for a time. Subject to fits of the passion, he certainly was,
but his position in the world was a counselling spouse,
jealous of his good name. He did not regret his proposal
to take the leap; he would not have regretted it if taken.
On the safe side of the abyss, however, it wore a gruesome
look to his cool blood.

* * *

CHAPTER XXVII

CONTAINS MATTER FOR SUBSEQUENT EXPLOSION

AMONG the various letters inundating Sir Lukin Dunstane upon the report of the triumph of surgical skill
achieved by Sir William Macpherson and Mr. Lanyan
Thomson, was one from Lady Wathin, dated Adlands,
an estate of Mr. Quintin Manx's in Warwickshire, petitioning for the shortest line of reassurance as to the condition of her dear cousin, and an intimation of the period
when it might be deemed possible for a relative to call and
offer her sincere congratulations: a letter deserving a per-

sonal reply, one would suppose. She received the following,
in a succinct female hand corresponding to its terseness;
every *t* righteously crossed, every *i* punctiliously dotted, as
she remarked to Constance Asper, to whom the communication was transferred for perusal : —

"DEAR LADY WATHIN, — Lady Dunstane is gaining
strength. The measure of her pulse indicates favourably.
She shall be informed in good time of your solicitude for
her recovery. The day cannot yet be named for visits of
any kind. You will receive information as soon as the
house is open.

"I have undertaken the task of correspondence, and beg
you to believe me,

> "Very truly yours,
>
> "D. A. WARWICK."

Miss Asper speculated on the hand-writing of her rival.
She obtained permission to keep the letter, with the intention of transmitting it per post to an advertising interpreter
of character in caligraphy.

Such was the character of the fair young heiress, exhibited by her performances much more patently than the
run of a quill would reveal it.

She said, "It is rather a pretty hand, I think."

"Mrs. Warwick is a practised writer," said Lady Wathin.
"Writing is her profession, if she has any. She goes to
nurse my cousin. Her husband says she is an excellent
nurse. He says what he can for her. But you must be
in the last extremity, or she is ice. His appeal to her has
been totally disregarded. Until he drops down in the
street, as his doctor expects him to do some day, she will
continue her course; and even then . . ."

An adventuress desiring her freedom! Lady Wathin
looked. She was too devout a woman to say what she
thought. But she knew the world to be very wicked. Of
Mrs. Warwick, her opinion was formed. She would not
have charged the individual creature with a criminal
design; all she did was to stuff the person her virtue
abhorred with the wickedness of the world, and that is a
common process in antipathy.

She sympathized, moreover, with the beautiful devotedness of the wealthy heiress to her ideal of man. It had
led her to make the acquaintance of old Lady Dacier, at
the house in town, where Constance Asper had first met
Percy; Mrs. Grafton Winstanley's house, representing
neutral territory or debateable land for the occasional
intercourse of the upper class and the climbing in the
professions or in commerce; Mrs. Grafton Winstanley being on the edge of aristocracy by birth, her husband, like
Mr. Quintin Manx, a lord of fleets. Old Lady Dacier's
bluntness in speaking of her grandson would have shocked
Lady Wathin as much as it astonished, had she been less
of an ardent absorber of aristocratic manners. Percy was
plainly called a donkey, for hanging off and on with a
handsome girl of such expectations as Miss Asper. "But
what you can't do with a horse, you can't hope to do with
a donkey." She added that she had come for the purpose of seeing the heiress, of whose points of person she
delivered a judgement critically appreciative as a horse-
fancier's on the racing turf. "If a girl like that holds to
it, she's pretty sure to get him at last. It's no use to
pull his neck down to the water."

Lady Wathin delicately alluded to rumours of an
entanglement, an admiration he had, ahem.

"A married woman," the veteran nodded. "I thought
that was off? She must be a clever intriguer to keep him
so long."

"She is undoubtedly clever," said Lady Wathin, and it
was mumbled in her hearing: "The woman seems to have
a taste for our family."

They agreed that they could see nothing to be done.
The young lady must wither, Mrs. Warwick have her day.
The veteran confided her experienced why to Lady Wathin:
"All the tales you tell of a woman of that sort are sharp
sauce to the palates of men."

They might be, to the men of the dreadful gilded idle
class !

Mrs. Warwick's day appeared indefinitely prolonged,
judging by Percy Dacier's behaviour to Miss Asper.
Lady Wathin watched them narrowly when she had the
chance, a little ashamed of her sex, or indignant rather at

his display of courtliness in exchange for her open betrayal of her preference. It was almost to be wished that she would punish him by sacrificing herself to one of her many brilliant proposals of marriage. But such are women! — precisely because of his holding back he tightened the cord attaching him to her tenacious heart. This was the truth. For the rest, he was gracefully courteous; an observer could perceive the charm he exercised. He talked with a ready affability, latterly with greater social ease; evidently not acting the indifferent conqueror, or so consummately acting it as to mask the air. And yet he was ambitious, and he was not rich. Notoriously was he ambitious, and with wealth to back him, a great entertaining house, troops of adherents, he would gather influence, be propelled to leadership. The vexation of a constant itch to speak to him on the subject, and the recognition that he knew it all as well as she, tormented Lady Wathin. He gave her comforting news of her dear cousin in the Winter.

"You have heard from Mrs. Warwick?" she said.

He replied, "I had the latest from Mr. Redworth."

"Mrs. Warwick has relinquished her post?"

"When she does, you may be sure that Lady Dunstane is perfectly re-established."

"She is an excellent nurse."

"The best, I believe."

"It is a good quality in sickness."

"Proof of good all through."

"Her husband might have the advantage of it. His state is really pathetic. If she has feeling, and could only be made aware, she might perhaps be persuaded to pass from the friendly to the wifely duty."

Mr. Dacier bent his head to listen, and he bowed.

He was fast in the toils; and though we have assurance that evil cannot triumph in perpetuity, the aspect of it throning provokes a kind of despair. How strange if ultimately the lawyers once busy about the uncle were to take up the case of the nephew, and this time reverse the issue, by proving it! For poor Mr. Warwick was emphatic on the question of his honour. It excited him dangerously. He was long-suffering, but with the slightest clue terrible. The unknotting of the entanglement might thus happen:— and Constance Asper would welcome her hero still.

Meanwhile there was actually nothing to be done: a deplorable absence of motive villainy; apparently an absence of the beneficent Power directing events to their proper termination. Lady Wathin heard of her cousin's having been removed to Cowes in May, for light Solent and Channel voyages on board Lord Esquart's yacht. She heard also of heavy failures and convulsions in the City of London, quite unconscious that the Fates, or agents of the Providence she invoked to precipitate the catastrophe, were then beginning cavernously their performance of the part of villain in Diana's history.

Diana and Emma enjoyed happy quiet sailings under May breezes on the many-coloured South-western waters, heart in heart again; the physical weakness of the one, the moral weakness of the other, creating that mutual dependency which makes friendship a pulsating tie. Diana's confession had come of her letter to Emma. When the latter was able to examine her correspondence, Diana brought her the heap for perusal, her own sealed scribble, throbbing with all the fatal might-have-been, under her eyes. She could have concealed and destroyed it. She sat beside her friend, awaiting her turn, hearing her say at the superscription: "Your writing, Tony?" and she nodded. She was asked: "Shall I read it?" She answered: "Read." They were soon locked in an embrace. Emma had no perception of coldness through those brief dry lines; her thought was of the matter.

"The danger is over now?" she said.

"Yes, that danger is over now."

"You have weathered it?"

"I love him."

Emma dropped a heavy sigh in pity of her, remotely in compassion for Redworth, the loving and unbeloved. She was too humane and wise of our nature to chide her Tony for having her sex's heart. She had charity to bestow on women; in defence of them against men and the world, it was a charity armed with the weapons of battle. The wife madly stripped before the world by a jealous husband,

and left chained to the rock, her youth wasting, her blood arrested, her sensibilities chilled and assailing her under their multitudinous disguises, and for whom the world is merciless, called forth Emma's tenderest commiseration; and that wife being Tony, and stricken with the curse of love, in other circumstances the blessing, Emma bled for her.

"But nothing desperate?" she said.

"No; you have saved me."

"I would knock at death's doors again, and pass them, to be sure of that."

"Kiss me; you may be sure. I would not put my lips to your cheek if there were danger of my faltering."

"But you love him."

"I do: and because I love him I will not let him be fettered to me."

"You will see him."

"Do not imagine that his persuasions undermined your Tony. I am subject to panics."

"Was it your husband?"

"I had a visit from Lady Wathin. She knows him. She came as peacemaker. She managed to hint at his authority. Then came a letter from him — of supplication, interpenetrated with the hint: a suffused atmosphere. Upon that, unexpected by me, my — let me call him so once, forgive me! — lover came. Oh! he loves me, or did then. Percy! He had been told that I should be claimed. I felt myself the creature I am — a wreck of marriage. But I fancied I could serve him: — I saw golden. My vanity was the chief traitor. Cowardice of course played a part. In few things that we do, where self is concerned, will cowardice not be found. And the hallucination colours it to seem a lovely heroism. That was the second time Mr. Redworth arrived. I am always at crossways, and he rescues me; on this occasion unknowingly."

"There's a divinity" . . . said Emma. "When I think of it I perceive that Patience is our beneficent fairy god-mother, who brings us our harvest in the long result."

"My dear, does she bring us our labourers' rations, to sustain us for the day?" said Diana.

"Poor fare, but enough."

"I fear I was born godmotherless."

"You have stores of patience, Tony; only now and then fits of desperation."

"My nature's frailty, the gap in it: we will give it no fine names — they cover our pitfalls. I am open to be carried on a tide of unreasonableness when the coward cries out. But I can say, dear, that after one rescue, a similar temptation is unlikely to master me. I do not subscribe to the world's decrees for love of the monster, though I am beginning to understand the dues of allegiance. We have ceased to write letters. You may have faith in me."

"I have, with my whole soul," said Emma.

So the confession closed; and in the present instance there were not any forgotten chambers to be unlocked and ransacked for addenda confessions.

The subjects discoursed of by the two endeared the hours to them. They were aware that the English of the period would have laughed a couple of women to scorn for venturing on them, and they were not a little hostile in consequence, and shot their epigrams profusely, applauding the keener that appeared to score the giant bulk of their intolerant enemy, who holds the day, but not the morrow. Us too he holds for the day, to punish us if we have temporal cravings. He scatters his gifts to the abject; tossing to us rebels bare dog-biscuit. But the life of the spirit is beyond his region; we have our morrow in his day when we crave nought of him. Diana and Emma delighted to discover that they were each the rebel of their earlier and less experienced years, each a member of the malcontent minor faction, the salt of earth, to whom their salt must serve for nourishment, as they admitted, relishing it determinedly, not without gratification.

Sir Lukin was busy upon his estate in Scotland. They summoned young Arthur Rhodes to the island, that he might have a taste of the new scenes. Diana was always wishing for his instruction and refreshment; and Redworth came to spend a Saturday and Sunday with them, and showed his disgust of the idle boy, as usual, at the same time consulting them on the topic of furniture for the Berkshire mansion he had recently bought, rather

vaunting the Spanish pictures his commissioner in Madrid
was transmitting. The pair of rebels, vexed by his treatment of the respectful junior, took him for an incarnation
of their enemy, and pecked and worried the man astonishingly. He submitted to it like the placable giant.
Yes, he was a Liberal, and furnishing and decorating
the house in the stability of which he trusted. Why not?
We must accept the world as it is, try to improve it by
degrees. — Not so: humanity will not wait for you, the
victims are shrieking beneath the bricks of your enormous edifice, behind the canvas of your pictures. "But
you may really say that luxurious yachting is an odd kind
of insurgency," avowed Diana. "It's the tangle we
are in."

"It's the coat we have to wear; and why fret at it for
being comfortable?"

"I don't half enough, when I think of my shivering
neighbours."

"Money is of course a rough test of virtue," said Redworth. "We have no other general test."

Money! The ladies proclaimed it a mere material test;
Diana, gazing on sunny sea, with an especial disdain.
And name us your sort of virtue. There is more virtue
in poverty. He denied that. Inflexibly British, he declared money, and also the art of getting money, to be
hereditary virtues, deserving of their reward. The reward
a superior wealth and its fruits? Yes, the power to enjoy
and spread enjoyment: and let idleness envy both! He
abused idleness, and by implication the dilettante insurgency fostering it. However, he was compensatingly
heterodox in his view of the Law's persecution of women;
their pertinacious harpings on the theme had brought him
to that; and in consideration of the fact, as they looked
from yacht to shore, of their being rebels participating
largely in the pleasures of the tyrant's court, they allowed
him to silence them, and forgave him.

Thoughts upon money and idleness were in confusion
with Diana. She had a household to support in London,
and she was not working; she could not touch THE
CANTATRICE while Emma was near. Possibly, she again
ejaculated, the Redworths of the world were right: the

fruitful labours were with the mattock and hoe, or the
mind directing them.   It was a crushing invasion of mate-
rialism, so she proposed a sail to the coast of France, and
thither they flew, touching Cherbourg, Alderney, Sark,
Guernsey, and sighting the low Brittany rocks.   Memorable days to Arthur Rhodes.   He saw perpetually the
one golden centre in new scenes.   He heard her voice, he
treasured her sayings; her gestures, her play of lip and
eyelid, her lift of head, lightest movements, were imprinted
on him, surely as the heavens are mirrored in the quiet
seas, firmly and richly as earth answers to the sprinkled
grain.   For he was blissfully athirst, untroubled by a
hope.   She gave him more than she knew of: a present
that kept its beating heart into the future; a height of
sky, a belief in nobility, permanent through manhood
down to age.   She was his foam-born Goddess of those
leaping waters; differently hued, crescented, a different
influence.   He had a happy week, and it charmed Diana
to hear him tell her so.   In spite of Redworth, she had
faith in the fruit-bearing powers of a time of simple happiness, and shared the youth's in reflecting it.   Only the
happiness must be simple, that of the glass to the lovely
face: no straining of arms to retain, no heaving of the
bosom in vacancy.

His poverty and capacity for pure enjoyment led her to
think of him almost clingingly when hard news reached
her from the quaint old City of London, which despises
poverty and authorcraft and all mean adventurers, and
bows to the lordly merchant, the mighty financier, Redworth's incarnation of the virtues.   Happy days on board
the yacht *Clarissa!*   Diana had to recall them with effort.
They who sow their money for a promising high percentage
have built their habitations on the sides of the most erup-
tive mountain in Europe.   Ætna supplies more certain
harvests, wrecks fewer vineyards and peaceful dwellings.
The greed of gain is our volcano.   Her wonder leapt up
at the slight inducement she had received to embark her
money in this Company: a South-American mine, collapsed
almost within hearing of the trumpets of prospectus, after
two punctual payments of the half-yearly interest.   A Mrs.
Ferdinand Cherson, an elder sister of the pretty Mrs.

Fryar-Gunnett, had talked to her of the cost of things one afternoon at Lady Singleby's garden-party, and spoken of the City as the place to help to swell an income, if only you have an acquaintance with some of the chief City men. The great mine was named, and the rush for allotments. She knew a couple of the Directors. They vowed to her that ten per cent. was a trifle; the fortune to be expected out of the mine was already clearly estimable at forties and fifties. For their part they anticipated cent. per cent. Mrs. Cherson said she wanted money, and had therefore invested in the mine. It seemed so consequent, the cost of things being enormous! She and her sister Mrs. Fryar-Gunnett owned husbands who did their bidding, because of their having the brains, it might be understood. Thus five thousand pounds invested would speedily bring five thousand pounds per annum. Diana had often dreamed of the City of London as the seat of magic; and taking the City's contempt for authorcraft and the intangible as, from its point of view, justly founded, she had mixed her dream strangely with an ancient notion of the City's probity. Her broker's shaking head did not damp her ardour for shares to the full amount of her ability to purchase. She remembered her satisfaction at the allotment; the golden castle shot up from this fountain mine. She had a frenzy for mines and fished in some English with smaller sums. "I am now a miner," she had exclaimed, between dismay at her audacity and the pride of it. Why had she not consulted Redworth? He would peremptorily have stopped the frenzy in its first intoxicating effervescence. She, like Mrs. Cherson, like all women who have plunged upon the cost of things, wanted money. She naturally went to the mine. Address him for counsel in the person of dupe, she could not; shame was a barrier. Could she tell him that the prattle of a woman, spendthrift as Mrs. Cherson, had induced her to risk her money? Latterly the reports of Mrs. Fryar-Gunnett were not of the flavour to make association of their names agreeable to his hearing.

She had to sit down in the buzz of her self-reproaches and amazement at the behaviour of that reputable City, shrug, and recommence the labour of her pen. Material misfortune had this one advantage; it kept her from speculative thoughts of her lover, and the meaning of his absence and silence.

Diana's perusal of the incomplete CANTATRICE was done with the cold critical eye interpreting for the public. She was forced to write on nevertheless, and exactly in the ruts of the foregoing matter. It propelled her. No longer perversely, of necessity she wrote her best, convinced that the work was doomed to unpopularity, resolved that it should be at least a victory in style. A fit of angry cynicism now and then set her composing phrases as baits for the critics to quote, condemnatory of the attractiveness of the work. Her mood was bad. In addition, she found Whitmonby cool; he complained of the coolness of her letter of adieu; complained of her leaving London so long. How could she expect to be his Queen of the London Salon if she lost touch of the topics? He made no other allusion. They were soon on amicable terms, at the expense of flattering arts that she had not hitherto practised. But Westlake revealed unimagined marvels of the odd corners of the masculine bosom. He was the man of her circle the neatest in epigram, the widest of survey, an Oriental traveller, a distinguished writer, and if not personally bewitching, remarkably a gentleman of the world. He was wounded; he said as much. It came to this: admitting that he had no claims, he declared it to be unbearable for him to see another preferred. The happier was unmentioned, and Diana scraped his wound by rallying him. He repeated that he asked only to stand on equal terms with the others; her preference of one was past his tolerance. She told him that since leaving Lady Dunstane she had seen but Whitmonby, Wilmers, and him. He smiled sarcastically, saying he had never had a letter from her, except the formal one of invitation.

"Powers of blarney, have you forsaken a daughter of Erin?" cried Diana. "Here is a friend who has a craving for you, and I talk sense to him. I have written to none of my set since I last left London."

She pacified him by doses of cajolery new to her tongue. She liked him, abhorred the thought of losing any of her friends, so the cajoling sentences ran until Westlake betrayed an inflammable composition, and had to be put out, and smoked sullenly. Her resources were tried in restoring him to reason. The months of absence from London appeared to have transformed her world. Tonans was moderate. The great editor rebuked her for her prolonged absence from London, not so much because it discrowned her as Queen of the Salon, but candidly for its rendering her service less to him. Everything she knew of men and affairs was to him stale.

"How do you get to the secrets?" she asked.

"By sticking to the centre of them," he said.

"But how do you manage to be in advance and act the prophet?"

"Because I will have them at any price, and that is known."

She hinted at the peccant City Company.

"I think I have checked the mining mania, as I did the railway," said he; "and so far it was a public service. There's no checking of maniacs."

She took her whipping within and without. "On another occasion I shall apply to you, Mr. Tonans."

"Ah, there was a time when you could have been a treasure to me," he rejoined; alluding of course to the Dannisburgh days.

In dejection, as she mused on those days, and on her foolish ambition to have a London house where her light might burn, she advised herself, with Redworth's voice, to quit the house, arrest expenditure, and try for happiness by burning and shining in the spirit: devoting herself, as Arthur Rhodes did, purely to literature. It became almost a decision.

Percy she had still neither written to nor heard from, and she dared not hope to meet him. She fancied a wish to have tidings of his marriage: it would be peace, if in desolation. Now that she had confessed and given her pledge to Emma, she had so far broken with him as to render the holding him chained a cruelty, and his reserve whispered of a rational acceptance of the end between them. She thanked him for it; an act whereby she was instantly melted to such softness that a dread of him haunted her. Coward, take up your burden for armour!

she called to her poor dungeoned self wailing to have common nourishment. She knew how prodigiously it waxed on crumbs ; nay, on the imagination of small morsels. By way of chastizing it, she reviewed her life, her behaviour to her husband, until she sank backward to a depth deprived of air and light. That life with her husband was a dungeon to her nature deeper than any imposed by present conditions. She was then a revolutionary to reach to the breath of day. She had now to be only not a coward, and she could breathe as others did. "Women who sap the moral laws pull down the pillars of the temple on their sex," Emma had said. Diana perceived something of her personal debt to civilization. Her struggles passed into the doomed CANTATRICE occupying days and nights under pressure for immediate payment ; the silencing of friend Debit, ridiculously calling himself Credit, in contempt of sex and conduct, on the ground that he was he solely by virtue of being she. He had got a trick of singing operatic solos in the form and style of the delightful tenor Tellio, and they were touching in absurdity, most real in unreality. Exquisitely trilled, after Tellio's manner,

> "The tradesmen all beseech ye,
>   The landlord, cook and maid,
>   Complete THE CANTATRICE,
>   That they may soon be paid,"

provoked her to laughter in pathos. He approached, posturing himself operatically, with perpetual new verses, rhymes to Danvers, rhymes to Madame Sybille, the cook. Seeing Tellio at one of Henry Wilmers' private concerts, Diana's lips twitched to dimples at the likeness her familiar had assumed. She had to compose her countenance to talk to him ; but the moment of song was the trial. Lady Singleby sat beside her, and remarked : "You have always fun going on in you !" She partook of the general impression that Diana Warwick was too humorous to nurse a downright passion.

Before leaving, she engaged Diana to her annual garden-party of the closing season, and there the meeting with Percy occurred, not unobserved. Had they been overheard, very little to implicate them would have been gathered.

He walked in full view across the lawn to her, and they presented mask to mask.

"The beauty of the day tempts you at last, Mrs. Warwick."

"I have been finishing a piece of work."

Lovely weather, beautiful dresses: agreed. Diana wore a yellow robe with a black bonnet, and he commented on the becoming hues; for the first time, he noticed her dress! Lovely women? Dacier hesitated. One he saw. But surely he must admire Mrs. Fryar-Gunnett? And who steps beside her, transparently fascinated, with visage at three-quarters to the rays within her bonnet? Can it be Sir Lukin Dunstane? and beholding none but his charmer!

Dacier withdrew his eyes thoughtfully from the spectacle, and moved to woo Diana to a stroll. She could not restrain her feet; she was out of the ring of her courtiers for the moment. He had seized his opportunity.

"It is nearly a year!" he said.

"I have been nursing nearly all the time, doing the work I do best."

"Unaltered?"

"A year must leave its marks."

"Tony!"

"You speak of a madwoman, a good eleven months dead. Let her rest. Those are the conditions."

"Accepted, if I may see her."

"Honestly accepted?"

"Imposed fatally, I have to own. I have felt with you: you are the wiser. But, admitting that, surely we can meet. I may see you?"

"My house has not been shut."

"I respected the house. I distrusted myself."

"What restores your confidence?"

"The strength I draw from you."

One of the Beauties at a garden-party is lucky to get as many minutes as had passed in quietness. Diana was met and captured. But those last words of Percy's renewed her pride in him by suddenly building a firm faith in herself. Noblest of lovers! she thought, and brooded on the little that had been spoken, the much conveyed, for a proof of perfect truthfulness.

The world had watched them. It pronounced them discreet if culpable; probably cold to the passion both. Of Dacier's coldness it had no doubt, and Diana's was presumed from her comical flights of speech. She was given to him because of the known failure of her other adorers. He in the front rank of politicians attracted her with the lustre of his ambition; she him with her mingling of talent and beauty. An astute world; right in the main, owing to perceptions based upon brute nature; utterly astray in particulars, for the reason that it takes no count of the soul of man or woman. Hence its glee at a catastrophe; its poor stock of mercy. And when no catastrophe follows, the prophet, for the honour of the profession, must decry her as cunning beyond aught yet revealed of a serpent sex.

Save for a word or two, the watchman might have overheard and trumpeted his report of their interview at Diana's house. After the first pained breathing, when they found themselves alone in that room where they had plighted their fortunes, they talked allusively to define the terms imposed on them by Reason. The thwarted step was unmentioned; it was a past madness. But Wisdom being recognized, they could meet. It would be hard if that were denied! They talked very little of their position; both understood the mutual acceptance of it; and now that he had seen her and was again under the spell, Dacier's rational mind, together with his delight in her presence, compelled him honourably to bow to the terms. Only, as these were severe upon lovers, the innocence of their meetings demanded indemnification in frequency.

"Come whenever you think I can be useful," said Diana.

They pressed hands at parting, firmly and briefly, not for the ordinary dactylology of lovers, but in sign of the treaty of amity.

She soon learnt that she had tied herself to her costly household.

CHAPTER XXVIII

DIALOGUE ROUND THE SUBJECT OF A PORTRAIT, WITH
SOME INDICATIONS OF THE TASK FOR DIANA

An enamoured Egeria who is not a princess in her
worldly state nor a goddess by origin has to play one of
those parts which strain the woman's faculties past naturalness. She must never expose her feelings to her lover;
she must make her counsel weighty; otherwise she is little
his nymph of the pure wells, and what she soon may be,
the world will say. She has also, most imperatively, to
dazzle him without the betrayal of artifice, where simple
spontaneousness is beyond conjuring. But feelings that
are constrained becloud the judgement besides arresting
the fine jet of delivery wherewith the mastered lover is
taught through his ears to think himself prompted, and
submit to be controlled, by a creature super-feminine. She
must make her counsel so weighty in poignant praises as to
repress impulses that would rouse her own; and her betraying impulsiveness was a subject of reflection to Diana after
she had given Percy Dacier, metaphorically, the key of her
house. Only as his true Egeria could she receive him.
She was therefore grateful, she thanked and venerated this
noblest of lovers for his not pressing to the word of love,
and so strengthening her to point his mind, freshen his
moral energies and inspirit him. His chivalrous acceptance of the conditions of their renewed intimacy was a radiant knightliness to Diana, elevating her with a living image
for worship : — he so near once to being the absolute lord
of her destinies ! How to reward him, was her sole dangerous thought. She prayed and strove that she might give
him of her best, to practically help him; and she had
reason to suppose she could do it, from the visible effect of
her phrases. He glistened in repeating them; he had fallen
into the habit; before witnesses too; in the presence of
Miss Paynham, who had taken earnestly to the art of painting, and obtained her dear Mrs. Warwick's promise of a
few sittings for the sketch of a portrait, near the close of

the season. "A very daring thing to attempt," Miss Paynham said, when he was comparing her first outlines and the beautiful breathing features. "Even if one gets the face, the lips will seem speechless, to those who know her."

"If they have no recollection," said Dacier.

"I mean, the endeavour should be to represent them at the moment of speaking."

"Put it into the eyes." He looked at the eyes.

She looked at the mouth. "But it is the mouth, more than the eyes."

He looked at the face. "Where there is character, you have only to study it to be sure of a likeness."

"That is the task, with one who utters jewels, Mr. Dacier."

"Bright wit, I fear, is above the powers of your art."

"Still I feel it could be done. See — now — that!"

Diana's lips had opened to say: "Confess me a model model: I am dissected while I sit for portrayal. I must be for a moment like the frog of the two countrymen who were disputing as to the manner of his death, when he stretched to yawn, upon which they agreed that he had defeated the truth for both of them. I am not quite inanimate."

"Irish countrymen," said Dacier.

"The story adds, that blows were arrested; so confer the nationality as you please."

Diana had often to divert him from a too intent perusal of her features with sparkles and stories current or invented to serve the immediate purpose.

Miss Paynham was Mrs. Warwick's guest for a fortnight, and observed them together. She sometimes charitably laid down her pencil and left them, having forgotten this or that. They were conversing of general matters with their usual crisp precision on her return, and she was rather like the two countrymen, in debating whether it was excess of coolness or discreetness; though she was convinced of their inclinations, and expected love some day to be leaping up. Diana noticed that she had no reminder for leaving the room when it was Mr. Redworth present. These two had become very friendly, according to her hopes; and Miss Paynham was extremely solicitous to draw suggestions from Mr. Redworth and win his approval.

"Do I appear likely to catch the mouth now, do you think, Mr. Redworth?"

He remarked, smiling at Diana's expressive dimple, that the mouth was difficult to catch. He did not gaze intently. Mr. Redworth was the genius of friendship, "the friend of women," Mrs. Warwick had said of him. Miss Paynham discovered it, as regarded herself. The portrait was his commission to her, kindly proposed, secretly of course, to give her occupation and the chance of winning a vogue with the face of a famous Beauty. So many, however, were Mrs. Warwick's visitors, and so lively the chatter she directed, that accurate sketching was difficult to an amateurish hand. Whitmonby, Sullivan Smith, Westlake, Henry Wilmers, Arthur Rhodes, and other gentlemen, literary and military, were almost daily visitors when it became known that the tedium of the beautiful sitter required beguiling, and there was a certainty of finding her at home. On Mrs. Warwick's Wednesday numerous ladies decorated the group. Then was heard such a rillet of dialogue without scandal or politics, as nowhere else in Britain; all vowed it subsequently; for to the remembrance it seemed magical. Not a breath of scandal, and yet the liveliest flow. Lady Pennon came attended by a Mr. Alexander Hepburn, a handsome Scot, at whom Dacier shot one of his instinctive keen glances, before seeing that the hostess had mounted a transient colour. Mr. Hepburn, in settling himself on his chair rather too briskly, contrived the next minute to break a precious bit of China standing by his elbow; and Lady Pennon cried out, with sympathetic anguish: "Oh, my dear, what a trial for you!"

"Brittle is foredoomed," said Diana, unruffled.

She deserved compliments, and would have had them if she had not wounded the most jealous and petulant of her courtiers.

"Then the Turk is a sapient custodian!" said Westlake, vexed with her flush at the entrance of the Scot.

Diana sedately took his challenge. "*We*, Mr. Westlake, have the philosophy of ownership."

Mr. Hepburn penitentially knelt to pick up the fragments, and Westlake murmured over his head: "As long as it is we who are the cracked."

"Did we not start from China?"

"We were consequently precipitated to Stamboul."

"You try to elude the lesson."

"I remember my first pædagogue telling me so when he rapped the book on my cranium."

"The mark of the book is not a disfigurement."

It was gently worded, and the shrewder for it. The mark of the book, if not a disfigurement, was a characteristic of Westlake's fashion of speech. Whitmonby nodded twice, for signification of a palpable hit in that bout; and he noted within him the foolishness of obtruding the remotest allusion to our personality when crossing the foils with a woman. She is down on it like the lightning, quick as she is in her contracted circle; politeness guarding her from a riposte.

Mr. Hepburn apologized very humbly, after regaining his chair. Diana smiled and said: "Incidents in a drawing-room are prize-shots at Dulness."

"And in a dining-room too," added Sullivan Smith. "I was one day at a dinner-party, apparently of undertakers hired to mourn over the joints and the birds in the dishes, when the ceiling came down, and we all sprang up merry as crickets. It led to a pretty encounter and a real prize-shot."

"Does that signify a duel?" asked Lady Pennon.

"'Twould be the vulgar title, to bring it into discredit with the populace, my lady."

"Rank me one of the populace then! I hate duelling and rejoice that it is discountenanced."

"The citizens, and not the populace, I think Mr. Sullivan Smith means," Diana said. "The citizen is generally right in morals. My father also was against the practice, when it raged at its 'prettiest.' I have heard him relate a story of a poor friend of his, who had to march out for a trifle, and said, as he accepted the invitation, 'It's all nonsense!' and walking to the measured length, 'It's all nonsense, you know!' and when lying on the ground, at his last gasp, 'I told you it was all nonsense!'"

Sullivan Smith leaned over to Whitmonby and Dacier amid the ejaculations, and whispered: "A lady's way of telling the story!—and excuseable to her:—she had to

Jonah the adjective. What the poor fellow said was " . . . he murmured the sixty-pounder adjective, as in the belly of the whale, to rightly emphasize his noun.

Whitmonby nodded to the superior relish imparted by the vigour of masculine veracity in narration. "A story for its native sauce piquante," he said.

"Nothing without it!"

They had each a dissolving grain of contempt for women compelled by their delicacy to spoil that kind of story which demands the piquant accompaniment to flavour it racily and make it passable. For to see insipid mildness complacently swallowed as an excellent thing, knowing the rich smack of savour proper to the story, is your anecdotal gentleman's annoyance. But if the anecdote had supported him, Sullivan Smith would have let the expletive rest.

Major Carew Mahoney capped Mrs. Warwick's tale of the unfortunate duellist with another, that confessed the practice absurd, though he approved of it; and he cited Lord Larrian's opinion: "It keeps men braced to civil conduct."

"I would not differ with the dear old lord; but no! the pistol is the sceptre of the bully," said Diana.

Mr. Hepburn, with the widest of eyes on her in perpetuity, warmly agreed; and the man was notorious among men for his contrary action.

"Most righteously our Princess Egeria distinguishes her reign by prohibiting it," said Lady Singleby.

"And how," Sullivan Smith sighed heavily, "how, I'd ask, are ladies to be protected from the bully?"

He was beset: "So it was all for us? all in consideration for our benefit?"

He mournfully exclaimed: "Why, surely!"

"That is the funeral apology of the Rod, at the close of every barbarous chapter," said Diana.

"Too fine in mind, too fat in body; that is a consequence with men, dear madam. The conqueror stands to his weapons, or he loses his possessions."

"Mr. Sullivan Smith jumps at his pleasure from the special to the general, and will be back, if we follow him, Lady Pennon. It is the trick men charge to women, showing that they can resemble us."

Lady Pennon thumped her knee. "Not a bit. There's no resemblance, and they know nothing of us."

"Women are a blank to them, I believe," said Whitmonby, treacherously bowing; and Westlake said: "Traces of a singular scrawl have been observed when they were held in close proximity to the fire."

"Once, on the top of a coach," Whitmonby resumed, "I heard a comely dame of the period when summers are ceasing threatened by her husband with a divorce, for omitting to put sandwiches in their luncheon-basket. She made him the inscrutable answer: 'Ah, poor man! you will go down ignorant to your grave!' We laughed, and to this day I cannot tell you why."

"That laugh was from a basket lacking provision;—and I think we could trace our separation to it," Diana said to Lady Pennon, who replied: "They expose themselves; they get no nearer to the riddle."

Miss Courtney, a rising young actress, encouraged by a smile from Mrs. Warwick, remarked: "On the stage, we have each our parts equally."

"And speaking parts; not personæ mutæ."

"The stage has advanced in verisimilitude," Henry Wilmers added slyly; and Diana rejoined: "You recognize a verisimilitude of the mirror when it is in advance of reality. Flatter the sketch, Miss Paynham, for a likeness to be seen. Probably there are still Old Conservatives who would prefer the personation of us by boys."

"I don't know," Westlake affected dubiousness. "I have heard that a step to the riddle is gained by a serious contemplation of boys."

"Serious?"

"That is the doubt."

"The doubt throws its light on the step!"

"I advise them not to take any leap from their step," said Lady Pennon.

"It would be a way of learning that we are no wiser than our sires; but perhaps too painful a way," Whitmonby observed. "Poor Mountford Wilts boasted of knowing women; and he married. To jump into the mouth of the enigma, is not to read it."

"You are figures of conceit when you speculate on us, Mr. Whitmonby."

"An occupation of our leisure, my lady, for your amusement."

"The leisure of the humming-top, a thousand to the minute, with the pretence that it sleeps!" Diana said.

"The sacrilegious hand to strip you of your mystery is withered as it stretches," exclaimed Westlake. "The sage and the devout are in accord for once."

"And whichever of the two I may be, I'm one of them, happy to do my homage blindfold!" Sullivan Smith waved the sign of it.

Diana sent her eyes over him and Mr. Hepburn, seeing Dacier. "That rosy mediævalism seems the utmost we can expect." An instant she saddened, foreboding her words to be ominous, because of suddenly thirsting for a modern cry from him, the silent. She quitted her woman's fit of earnestness, and took to the humour that pleased him. "Aslauga's knight, at his blind man's buff of devotion, catches the hem of the tapestry and is found by his lady kissing it in a trance of homage five hours long! Sir Hilary of Agincourt, returned from the wars to his castle at midnight, hears that the châtelaine is away dancing, and remains with all his men mounted in the courtyard till the grey morn brings her back! Adorable! We had a flag flying in those days. Since men began to fret the riddle, they have hauled it down half-mast. Soon we shall behold a bare pole and hats on around it. That is their solution."

A smile circled at the hearing of Lady Singleby say: "Well! I am all for our own times, however literal the men."

"We are two different species!" thumped Lady Pennon, swimming on the theme. "I am sure, I read what they write of women! And their heroines!"

Lady Esquart acquiesced: "We are utter fools or horrid knaves."

"Nature's original hieroglyphs — which have that appearance to the peruser," Westlake assented.

"And when they would decipher us, and they hit on one of our 'arts,' the literary pirouette they perform is memorable." Diana looked invitingly at Dacier. "But I for one discern a possible relationship and a likeness."

"I think it exists — behind a curtain," Dacier replied.

"Before the era of the Nursery. Liberty to grow; independence is the key of the secret."

"And what comes after the independence?" he inquired.

Whitmonby, musing that some distraction of an earnest incentive spoilt Mrs. Warwick's wit, informed him: "The two different species then break their shallow armistice and join the shock of battle for possession of the earth, and we are outnumbered and exterminated, to a certainty. So I am against independence."

"Socially a Mussulman, subject to explosions!" Diana said. "So the eternal duel between us is maintained, and men will protest that they are for civilization. Dear me, I should like to write a sketch of the women of the future — don't be afraid! — the far future. What a different earth you will see!"

And very different creatures! the gentlemen unanimously surmised. Westlake described the fairer portion, no longer the weaker; frightful hosts.

Diana promised him a sweeter picture, if ever she brought her hand to paint it.

"You would be offered up to the English national hangman, Jehoiachim Sneer," interposed Arthur Rhodes, evidently firing a gun too big for him, of premeditated charging, as his patroness perceived; but she knew him to be smarting under recent applications of the swish of Mr. Sneer, and that he rushed to support her. She covered him by saying: "If he has to be encountered, he kills none but the cripple," wherewith the dead pause ensuing from a dose of outlandish speech in good company was bridged, though the youth heard Westlake mutter unpleasantly: "Jehoiachim," and had to endure a stare of Dacier's, who did not conceal his want of comprehension of the place he occupied in Mrs. Warwick's gatherings.

"They know nothing of us whatever!" Lady Pennon harped on her dictum.

"They put us in a case and profoundly study the captive creature," said Diana: "but would any *man* understand this? . . ." She dropped her voice and drew in the heads of Lady Pennon, Lady Singleby, Lady Esquart and Miss Courtney: "Real woman's nature speaks. A maid of mine had a 'follower.' She was a good girl; I was anxious about her and asked her if she could trust him. 'Oh, yes, ma'am,' she replied, 'I can; he's quite like a female.' I longed to see the young man, to tell him he had received the highest of eulogies."

The ladies appreciatingly declared that such a tale was beyond the understandings of men. Miss Paynham primmed her mouth, admitting to herself her inability to repeat such a tale: an act that she deemed not "quite like a lady." She had previously come to the conclusion that Mrs. Warwick, with all her generous qualities, was deficient in delicate sentiment — owing perhaps to her coldness of temperament. Like Dacier also, she failed to comprehend the patronage of Mr. Rhodes: it led to suppositions; indefinite truly, and not calumnious at all; but a young poet, rather good-looking and well built, is not the same kind of wing-chick as a young actress, like Miss Courtney — Mrs. Warwick's latest shieldling: he is hardly enrolled for the reason that was assumed to sanction Mrs. Warwick's maid in the encouragement of her follower. Miss Paynham sketched on, with her thoughts in her bosom: a damsel castigatingly pursued by the idea of sex as the direct motive of every act of every person surrounding her; deductively therefore that a certain form of the impelling passion, mild or terrible, or capricious, or it might be less pardonable, was unceasingly at work among the human couples up to decrepitude. And she too frequently hit the fact to doubt her gift of reading into them. Mr. Dacier was plain, and the state of young Mr. Rhodes; and the Scottish gentleman was at least a vehement admirer. But she penetrated the breast of Mr. Thomas Redworth as well, mentally tore his mask of friendship to shreds. He was kind indeed in commissioning her to do the portrait. His desire for it, and his urgency to have the features exactly given, besides the infrequency of his visits of late, when a favoured gentleman was present, were the betraying signs. Deductively, moreover, the lady who inspired the passion in numbers of gentlemen and set herself to win their admiration with her lively play of dialogue, must be coquettish; she could hold them only by coldness. Anecdotes, epigrams, drolleries, do not bubble to the lips of a woman who is under an emotional spell:

rather they prove that she has the spell for casting. It
suited Mr. Dacier, Miss Paynham thought: it was cruel
to Mr. Redworth; at whom, of all her circle, the beautiful woman looked, when speaking to him, sometimes
tenderly.

"Beware the silent one of an assembly!" Diana had
written. She did not think of her words while Miss Paynham continued mutely sketching. The silent ones, with
much conversation around them, have their heads at work,
critically perforce; the faster if their hands are occupied;
and the point they lean to do is the pivot of their thoughts.
Miss Paynham felt for Mr. Redworth.

Diana was unaware of any other critic present than him
she sought to enliven, not unsuccessfully, notwithstanding
his English objection to the pitch of the converse she led,
and a suspicion of effort to support it : — just a doubt, with
all her easy voluble run, of the possibility of naturalness in
a continuous cleverness. But he signified pleasure, and in
pleasing him she was happy : in the knowledge that she
dazzled, was her sense of safety. Percy hated scandal; he
heard none. He wanted stirring, cheering; in her house
he had it. He came daily, and as it was her wish that
new themes, new flights of converse, should delight him
and show her exhaustless, to preserve her ascendancy, she
welcomed him without consulting the world. He was
witness of Mr. Hepburn's presentation of a costly China
vase, to repair the breach in her array of ornaments, and
excuse a visit. Judging by the absence of any blow within,
he saw not a sign of coquetry. Some such visit had been
anticipated by the prescient woman, so there was no reddening. She brought about an exchange of sentences between him and her furious admirer, sparing either of them
a glimpse of which was the sacrifice to the other, amusing
them both. Dacier could allow Mr. Hepburn to outsit
him; and he left them, proud of his absolute confidence
in her.

She was mistaken in imagining that her social vivacity,
mixed with comradeship of the active intellect, was the
charm which kept Mr. Percy Dacier temperate when he
well knew her to distinguish him above her courtiers. Her
powers of dazzling kept him tame; they did not stamp her

mark on him. He was one of the order of highly polished
men, ignorant of women, who are impressed for long terms
by temporary flashes, that hold them bound until a fresh
impression comes, to confirm or obliterate the preceding.
Affairs of the world he could treat competently; he had a
head for high politics and the management of men; the
feminine half of the world was a confusion and a vexation
to his intelligence, characterless; and one woman at last
appearing decipherable, he fancied it must be owing to her
possession of character, a thing prized the more in women
because of his latent doubt of its existence. Character, that
was the mark he aimed at; that moved him to homage as
neither sparkling wit nor incomparable beauty, nor the unusual combination, did. To be distinguished by a woman
of character (beauty and wit for jewellery), was his minor
ambition in life, and if Fortune now gratified it, he owned
to the flattery. It really seemed by every test that she had
the quality. Since the day when he beheld her by the bedside of his dead uncle, and that one on the French sea-sands,
and again at Copsley, ghostly white out of her wrestle with
death, bleeding holy sweat of brow for her friend, the print
of her features had been on him as an index of depth of
character, imposing respect and admiration — a sentiment
imperilled by her consent to fly with him. Her subsequent
reserve until they met — by an accident that the lady at
any rate was not responsible for, proved the quality positively. And the nature of her character, at first suspected,
vanquished him more, by comparison, than her vivid intellect, which he originally, and still lingeringly, appreciated
in condescension, as a singular accomplishment, thrilling at
times, now and then assailably feminine. But, after her
consent to a proposal that caused him retrospective worldly
shudders, and her composed recognition of the madness, a
character capable of holding him in some awe was real
majesty, and it rose to the clear heights, with her mental
attributes for satellites. His tendency to despise women
was wholesomely checked by the experience to justify him
in saying, Here is a worthy one! She was health to him,
as well as trusty counsel. Furthermore, where he respected,
he was a governed man, free of the common masculine craze
to scale fortresses for the sake of lowering flags. Whilst

under his impression of her character, he submitted honourably to the ascendancy of a lady whose conduct suited him and whose preference flattered; whose presence was very refreshing; whose letters were a stimulant. Her letters were really running well-waters, not a lover's delusion of the luminous mind of his lady. They sparkled in review and preserved their integrity under critical analysis. The reading of them hurried him in pursuit of her from house to house during the autumn; and as she did not hint at the shadow his coming cast on her, his conscience was easy. Regarding their future, his political anxieties were a mountainous defile, curtaining the outlook. They met at Lockton, where he arrived after a recent consultation with his Chief, of whom, and the murmurs of the Cabinet, he spoke to Diana openly, in some dejection.

"They might see he has been breaking with his party for the last four years," she said. "The plunge to be taken is tremendous."

"But will he? He appears too despondent for a header."

"We cannot dance on a quaking floor."

"No; it's exactly that quake of the floor which gives 'much qualms,' to me as well," said Dacier.

"A treble Neptune's power!" she rejoined, for his particular delectation. "Enough if he hesitates. I forgive him his nausea. He awaits the impetus, and it will reach him, and soon. He will not wait for the mob at his heels, I am certain. A Minister who does that, is a post, and goes down with the first bursting of the dam. He has tried compromise and discovered that it does not appease the Fates; is not even a makeshift-mending at this hour. He is a man of nerves, very sensitively built; as quick — quicker than a woman, I could almost say, to feel the tremble of the air — forerunner of imperative changes."

Dacier brightened fondly. "You positively describe him; paint him to the life, without knowing him!"

"I have seen him; and if I paint, whose are the colours?"

"Sometimes I repeat you to him, and I get all the credit," said Dacier.

"I glow with pride to think of speaking anything that you repeat," said Diana, and her eyes were proudly lustreful.

Their love was nourished on these mutual flatteries.

Thin food for passion! The innocence of it sanctioned the meetings and the appointments to meet. When separated they were interchanging letters, formally worded in the apostrophe and the termination, but throbbingly full : or Diana thought so of Percy's letters, with grateful justice ; for his manner of opening his heart in amatory correspond-ence was to confide important secret matters, up to which mark she sprang to reply in counsel. He proved his affec-tion by trusting her ; his respect by his tempered style : — "A Greenland style of writing," she had said of an unhappy gentleman's epistolary compositions resembling it ; and now the same official baldness was to her mind Italianly rich ; it called forth such volumes.

Flatteries that were thin food for passion appeared the simplest exchanges of courtesy, and her meetings with her lover, judging by the nature of the discourse they held, so consequent to their joint interest in the great crisis antici-pated, as to rouse her indignant surprise and a turn for downright rebellion when the Argus world signified the fact of its having one eye, or more, wide open.

Debit and Credit, too, her buzzing familiars, insisted on an audience at each ear, and at the house-door, on her return to London.

CHAPTER XXIX

SHOWS THE APPROACHES OF THE POLITICAL AND THE DOMESTIC CRISIS IN COMPANY

THERE was not much talk of Diana between Lady Dunstane and her customary visitor Tom Redworth now. She was shy in speaking of the love-stricken woman, and more was in his mind for thought than for speech. She sometimes wondered how much he might know, ending with the re-flection that little passing around was unknown to him. He had to shut his mind against thought, against all medi-tation upon Mrs. Warwick ; it was based scientifically when speculating and calculating, on the material element — a talisman. Men and women crossing the high seas of life he had found most readable under that illuminating inquiry, as to their means. An inspector of seaworthy ships proceeds in like manner. Whence would the money come? He could not help the bent of his mind; but he could avoid subjecting her to the talismanic touch. The girl at the Dublin Ball, the woman at the fire-grate of The Crossways, both in one were his Diana. Now and then, hearing an ugly whisper, his manful sympathy with the mere woman in her imprisoned liberty, defended her desperately from charges not distinctly formulated within him:— "She's not made of stone." That was a height of self-abnegation to shake the poor fellow to his roots; but, then, he had no hopes of his own; and he stuck to it. Her choice of a man like Dacier, too, of whom Redworth judged highly, showed nobility. She irradiated the man; but no baseness could be in such an alliance. If allied, they were bound together for good. The tie — supposing a villain world not wrong — was only not the sacred tie because of impediments. The tie!— he deliberated, and said stoutly No. Men of Redworth's nature go through sharp contests, though the duration of them is short, and the tussle of his worship of this woman with the materialistic turn of his mind was closed by the complete shutting up of the latter under lock and bar; so that a man, very little of an idealist, was able to sustain her in the pure imagination — where she did almost belong to him. She was his, in a sense, because she might have been his — but for an incredible extreme of folly. The dark ring of the eclipse cast by some amazing foolishness round the shining crescent perpetually in secret claimed the whole sphere of her, by what might have been, while admitting her lost to him in fact. To Thomas Redworth's mind the lack of perfect sanity in his conduct at any period of manhood, was so entirely past belief that he flew at the circumstances confirming the charge, and had wrestles with the angel of reality, who did but set him dreaming backward, after flinging him.

He heard at Lady Wathin's that Mrs. Warwick was in town for the winter. "Mr. Dacier is also in town," Lady Wathin said, with an acid indication of the needless mention of it. "We have not seen him." She invited Redworth to meet a few friends at dinner. "I think you admire Miss Asper: in my idea a very saint among young women; and you know what the young women of our day are. She will be present. She is, you are aware, England's greatest heiress. Only yesterday, hearing of that poor man Mr. Warwick's desperate attack of illness — heart! — and of his having no relative or friend to soothe his pillow, — he is lying in absolute loneliness, — she offered to go and nurse him! Of course it could not be done. It is not her place. The beauty of the character of a dear innocent young girl, with every gratification at command, who could make the offer, strikes me as unparalleled. She was perfectly sincere — she *is* sincerity. She asked at once, Where is he? She wished me to accompany her on a first visit. I saw a tear."

Redworth had called at Lady Wathin's for information of the state of Mr. Warwick, concerning which a rumour was abroad. No stranger to the vagrant compassionateness of sentimentalists; — rich, idle, conscience-pricked or praise-catching; — he was unmoved by the tale that Miss Asper had proposed to go to Mr. Warwick's sick-bed in the uniform of a Sister of Charity: — "Speaking French!" Lady Wathin exclaimed; and his head rocked, as he said: "An Englishman would not be likely to know better."

"She speaks exquisite French — all European languages, Mr. Redworth. She does not pretend to *wit*. To my thinking, depth of sentiment is a far more feminine accomplishment. It assuredly will be found a greater treasure."

The modest man (modest in such matters) was led by degrees to fancy himself sounded regarding Miss Asper: a piece of sculpture glacially decorative of the domestic mansion in person, to his thinking; and as to the nature of it — not a Diana, with all her faults!

If Diana had any faults, in a world and a position so heavily against her! He laughed to himself, when alone, at the neatly implied bitter reproach cast on the wife by the forsaken young lady, who proposed to nurse the abandoned husband of the woman bereaving her of the man she loved. Sentimentalists enjoy these tricks, the conceiving or the doing of them — the former mainly, which are cheaper, and equally effective. Miss Asper might be defi-

cient in wit; this was a form of practical wit, occasionally
exhibited by creatures acting on their instincts. Warwick
he pitied, and he put compulsion on himself to go and see
the poor fellow, the subject of so sublime a generosity.
Mr. Warwick sat in an arm-chair, his legs out straight on
the heels, his jaw dragging hollow cheeks, his hands loosely
joined; improving in health, he said. A demure woman
of middle age was in attendance. He did not speak of his
wife. Three times he said disconnectedly, "I hear reports,"
and his eyelids worked. Redworth talked of general
affairs, without those consolatory efforts, useless between
men, which are neither medicine nor good honest water:
— he judged by personal feelings. In consequence, he left
an invalid the sourer for his visit.

Next day he received a briefly-worded summons from Mrs.
Warwick.

Crossing the park on the line to Diana's house, he met
Miss Paynham, who grieved to say that Mrs. Warwick
could not give her a sitting; and in a still mournfuller tone,
imagined he would find her at home, and alone by this
time. "I left no one but Mr. Dacier there," she observed.

"Mrs. Warwick will be disengaged to-morrow, no doubt,"
he said consolingly.

Her head performed the negative. "They talk politics,
and she becomes animated, loses her pose. I will per-
severe, though I fear I have undertaken a task too much
for me."

"I am deeply indebted to you for the attempt." Redworth bowed to her and set his face to the Abbey-towers,
which wore a different aspect in the smoked grey light
since his two minutes of colloquy. He had previously
noticed that meetings with Miss Paynham produced a
similar effect on him, a not so very impressionable man.
And how was it done? She told him nothing he did not
know or guess.

Diana was alone. Her manner, after the greeting,
seemed feverish. She had not to excuse herself for abruptness when he heard the nature of the subject. Her counsellor and friend was informed, in feminine style, that she
had requested him to call, for the purpose of consulting
him with regard to a matter she had decided upon; and it

was, the sale of The Crossways. She said that it would have gone to her heart once; she supposed she had lost her affection for the place, or had got the better of her superstitions. She spoke lamely as well as bluntly. The place was hers, she said; her own property. Her husband could not interdict a sale.

Redworth addressed himself to her smothered antagonism. "Even if he had rights, as they are termed . . . I think you might count on their not being pressed."

"I have been told of illness." She tapped her foot on the floor.

"His present state of health is unequal to his ordinary duties."

"Emma Dunstane is fully supplied with the latest intelligence, Mr. Redworth. You know the source."

"I mention it simply . . ."

"Yes, yes. What I have to protest is, that in this respect I am free. The Law has me fast, but leaves me its legal view of my small property. I have no authority over me. I can do as I please in this, without a collision, or the dread of one. It is the married woman's perpetual dread when she ventures a step. Your Law originally presumed her a China-footed animal. And more, I have a claim for maintenance."

She crimsoned angrily.

Redworth showed a look of pleasure, hard to understand. "The application would be sufficient, I fancy," he said.

"It should have been offered."

"Did you not decline it?"

"I declined to apply for it. I thought — But, Mr. Redworth, another thing, concerning us all: I want very much to hear your ideas of the prospects of the League; because I know you have ideas. The leaders are terrible men; they fascinate me. They appear to move with an army of facts. They are certainly carrying the country. I am obliged to think them sincere. Common agitators would not hold together, as they do. They gather strength each year. If their statistics are not illusory — an army of phantoms instead of one of facts; — and they knock at my head without admission, I have to confess; — they must win."

"Ultimately, it is quite calculable that they will win,"
said Redworth; and he was led to discourse of rates and
duties and prohibitive tariffs to a woman surprisingly athirst,
curious for every scrap of intelligence relating to the power,
organization, and schemes of the League. "Common sense
is the secret of every successful civil agitation," he said
"Rap it unremittingly on crowds of the thickest of human
heads, and the response comes at last to sweep all before it.
You may reckon that the country will beat the landlords —
for that is our question. Is it one of your political themes?"

"I am not presumptuous to such a degree: — a poor
scholar," Diana replied. "Women striving to lift their
heads among men deserve the sarcasm."

He denied that any sarcasm was intended, and the lesson
continued. When she had shaped in her mind some portion of his knowledge of the subject, she reverted casually
to her practical business. Would he undertake to try to
obtain a purchaser of The Crossways, at the price he might
deem reasonable? She left the price entirely to his judgement. And now she had determined to part with the old
place, the sooner the better! She said that smiling; and
Redworth smiled, outwardly and inwardly. Her talk of
her affairs was clearer to him than her curiosity for the
mysteries of the League. He gained kind looks besides
warm thanks by the promise to seek a purchaser; especially
by his avoidance of prying queries. She wanted just this
excellent automaton fac-totum; and she referred him to
Mr. Braddock for the title-deeds et caetera — the chirping
phrase of ladies happily washing their hands of the mean
details of business.

"How of your last work?" he asked her.

Serenest equanimity rejoined: "As I anticipated, it is not
popular. The critics are of one mind with the public. You
may have noticed, they rarely flower above that rocky surface. THE CANTATRICE sings them a false note. My next
will probably please them less."

Her mobile lips and brows shot the faint upper-wreath of
a smile hovering. It was designed to display her philosophy

"And what is the name of your next?" said he.

"I name it THE MAN OF TWO MINDS, if you can allow
that to be in nature."

" Contra-distinguished from the woman ? "

" Oh ! you must first believe the woman to have one."

" You are working on it ? "

" By fits.   And I forgot, Mr. Redworth : I have mislaid
my receipts, and must ask you for the address of your wine-
merchant ; — or, will you ? Several dozen of the same wines.
I can trust him to be in awe of you, and the good repute of
my table depends on his honesty."

Redworth took the definite order for a large supply of
wine.

She gave him her hand : a lost hand, dear to hold, need-
ing to be guided, he feared.   For him, it was merely a hand,
cut off from the wrist ; and he had performed that executive
part !   A wiser man would now have been the lord of
it. . . .   So he felt, with his burning wish to protect and
cherish the beloved woman, while saying : " If we find a
speedy bidder for The Crossways, you will have to thank
our railways."

" You ! " said Diana, confident in his ability to do everything of the practical kind.

Her ingenuousness tickled him.   He missed her comic
touches upon men and things, but the fever shown by her
manner accounted for it.

As soon as he left her, she was writing to the lover who
had an hour previously been hearing her voice ; the note of
her theme being Party ; and how to serve it, when to sacrifice it to the Country.   She wrote, carolling bars of the Puritani marches ; and such will passion do, that her choice of
music was quite in harmony with her theme.   The mar-
tially-amorous melodies of Italian Opera in those days
fostered a passion challenged to intrepidity from the heart
of softness ; gilding at the same time, and putting warm
blood even into dull arithmetical figures which might be
important to her lover, her hero fronting battle.   She con-
densed Redworth's information skilfully, heartily giving it
and whatever she had imbibed, as her own, down to the
remark : " Common sense in questions of justice, is a weapon
that makes way into human heads and wins the certain
majority, if we strike with it incessantly."   Whether anything she wrote was her own, mattered little : the savour of
Percy's praise, which none could share with her, made it

instantly all her own. Besides she wrote to strengthen him;
she naturally laid her friends and the world under contribution; and no other sort of writing was possible. Percy
had not a common interest in fiction; still less for high
comedy. He liked the broad laugh when he deigned to
open books of that sort; puns and strong flavours and har-
lequin surprises; and her work would not admit of them,
however great her willingness to force her hand for his
amusement: consequently her inventiveness deadened. She
had to cease whipping it. "My poor old London cabhorse
of a pen shall go to grass!" she sighed, looking to the sale
of The Crossways for money; looking no farther.

Those marshalled battalions of Debit and Credit were in
hostile order, the weaker simply devoted to fighting for
delay, when a winged messenger bearing the form of old
Mr. Braddock descended to her with the reconciling news
that a hermit bachelor, an acquaintance of Mr. Redworth's
— both of whom wore a gloomy hue in her mind immediately — had offered a sum for the purchase of The Crossways. Considering the out-of-the-way district, Mr. Braddock
thought it an excellent price to get. She thought the reverse, but confessed that double the sum would not have
altered her opinion. Double the sum scarcely counted for
the service she required of it for much more than a year.
The money was paid shortly after into her Bank, and then
she enjoyed the contemptuous felicity of tossing meat to her
lions, tigers, wolves, and jackals, who, but for the fortunate
intervention, would have been feeding on her. These me-
nagerie beasts of prey were the lady's tradesmen, Debit's
hungry brood. She had a rapid glimpse of a false position
in regarding that legitimate band so scornfully: another
glimpse likewise of a day to come when they might not be
stopped at the door. She was running a race with something; — with what? It was unnamed; it ran in a shroud.

At times she surprised her heart violently beating when
there had not been a thought to set it in motion. She traced
it once to the words "next year," incidentally mentioned.
"Free," was a word that checked her throbs, as at a question of life or death. Her solitude, excepting the hours of
sleep, if then, was a time of irregular breathing. The something unnamed, running beside her, became a dreadful

familiar; the race between them past contemplation for
ghastliness. "But this is your Law!" she cried to the
world, while blinding her eyes against a peep of the shrouded
features.

Singularly, she had but to abandon hope, and the shadowy
figure vanished, the tragic race was ended. How to live
and think, and not to hope: the slave of passion had this
problem before her.

Other tasks were supportable, though one seemed hard
at moments and was not passive; it attacked her. The
men and women of her circle derisively, unanimously, dis-
believed in an innocence that forfeited reputation. Women
were complimentarily assumed to be not such gaping idiots.
And as the weeks advanced, a change came over Percy.
The gentleman had grown restless at covert congratulations,
hollow to his knowledge, however much caressing vanity,
and therefore secretly a wound to it. One day, after sitting
silent, he bluntly proposed to break "this foolish trifling;"
just in his old manner, though not so honourably; not very
definitely either. Her hand was taken.

"I feared that dumbness!" Diana said, letting her hand
go, but keeping her composure. "My friend Percy, I am
not a lion-tamer, and if you are of those animals, we break
the chapter. Plainly you think that where there appears
to be a choice of fools, the woman is distinctly designed for
the person. Drop my hand, or I shall repeat the fable of
the Goose with the Golden Eggs."

"Fables are applicable only in the school-room," said he;
and he ventured on "Tony!"

"I vowed an oath to my dear Emma — as good as to the
heavens! and that of itself would stay me from being insane again." She released herself. "Signor Percy, you
teach me to suspect you of having an idle wish to pluck
your plaything to pieces : — to boast of it ? Ah ! my friend,
I fancied I was of more value to you. You must come less
often ; even to not at all, if you are one of those idols with
feet of clay which leave the print of their steps in a room;
or fall and crush the silly idolizer."

"But surely you know . . . " said he. "We can't have
to wait long." He looked full of hopeful meanings.

"A reason!" . . . She kept down her breath. A long-drawn sigh followed, through parted lips. She had a sensation of horror. "And I cannot propose to nurse him — Emma will not hear of it," she said. "I dare not. Hypocrite to that extreme? Oh, no! But I must hear nothing. As it is, I am haunted. Now let this pass. Tony me no Tonies; I am *atony* to such whimpering business now we are in the van of the struggle. All round us it sounds like war. Last night I had Mr. Tonans dining here; he wished to meet you; and you must have a private meeting with Mr. Whitmonby: he will be useful; others as well. You are wrong in affecting contempt of the Press. It perches you on a rock; but the swimmer in politics knows what draws the tides. Your own people, your set, your class, are a drag to you, like inherited superstitions to the wakening brain. The greater the glory! For you see the lead you take? You are saving your class. They should lead, and will, if they prove worthy in the crisis. Their curious error is to believe in the stability of a monumental position."

"Perfectly true!" cried Dacier; and the next minute, heated by approbation, was begging for her hand earnestly. She refused it.

"But you say things that catch me!" he pleaded. "Remember, it was nearly mine. It soon will be mine. I heard yesterday from Lady Wathin . . . well, if it pains you!"

"Speak on," said Diana, resigned to her thirsty ears.

"He is not expected to last through the autumn."

"The calculation is hers?"

"Not exactly: — judging from the symptoms."

Diana flashed a fiery eye into Dacier's, and rose. She was past danger of melting, with her imagination darkened by the funeral image; but she craved solitude, and had to act the callous, to dismiss him.

"Good. Enough for the day. Now leave me, if you please. When we meet again, stifle that raven's croak. I am not a 'Sister of Charity,' but neither am I a vulture hovering for the horse in the desert to die. A poor simile! — when it is my own and not another's breath that I want. Nothing in nature, only gruesome German stories will fetch comparisons for the yoke of this Law of yours. It seems the nightmare dream following an ogre's supper."

She was not acting the shiver of her frame.

To-morrow was open to him, and prospect of better fortune, so he departed, after squeezing the hand she ceremoniously extended.

But her woman's intuition warned her that she had not maintained the sovereign impression which was her security. And hope had become a flame in her bosom that would no longer take the common extinguisher. The race she ran was with a shrouded figure no more, but with the figure of the shroud; she had to summon paroxysms of a pity hard to feel, images of sickness, helplessness, the vaults, the last human silence — for the stilling of her passionate heart. And when this was partly effected, the question, Am I going to live? renewed her tragical struggle. Who was it under the vaults, in the shroud, between the planks? and with human sensibility to swell the horror! Passion whispered of a vaster sorrow needed for herself; and the hope conjuring those frightful complexities was needed to soothe her. She pitied the man, but she was an enamoured woman. Often of late she had been sharply stung, relaxed as well, by the observations of Danvers assisting at her toilette. Had she beauty and charm, beauty and rich health in the young summer blooming of her days? — and all doomed to waste? No insurgency of words arose in denunciation of the wrong done to her nature. An undefined heavy feeling of wrong there was, just perceptive enough to let her know, without gravely shaming, that one or another must be slain for peace to come; for it is the case in which the world of the Laws overloading her is pitiless to women, deaf past ear-trumpets, past intercession; detesting and reviling them for a feeble human cry, and for one apparent step of revolt piling the pelted stones on them. It will not discriminate shades of hue, it massacres all the shadowed. They are honoured, after a fashion, at a certain elevation. Descending from it, and purely to breathe common air (thus in her mind), they are scourged and outcast. And alas! the very pleading for them excites a sort of ridicule in their advocate. How? She was utterly, even desperately, nay personally, earnest, and her humour closed her lips; though comical views of the scourged and outcast coming from the opposite party — the huge bully world —

she would not have tolerated. Diana raged at a prevailing
strength on the part of that huge bully world, which seemed
really to embrace the atmosphere. Emma had said: "The
rules of Christian Society are a blessed Government for us
women. We owe it so much that there is not a brick of
the fabric we should not prop." Emma's talk of obedience
to the Laws, being Laws, was repeated by the rebel, with
an involuntary unphrased comparison of the vessel in dock
and the vessel at sea.

When Dacier next called to see Mrs. Warwick, he heard
that she had gone to Copsley for a couple of weeks. The
lesson was emphasized by her not writing:— and was it
the tricky sex, or the splendid character of the woman,
which dealt him this punishment? Knowing how much
Diana forfeited for him, he was moved to some enthusiasm,
despite his inclination to be hurt.

She, on her return to London, gained a considerable increase of knowledge as to her position in the eye of the
world; and unlike the result of her meditations derived
from the clamouring tradesmen, whom she could excuse,
she was neither illuminated nor cautioned by that dubious
look; she conscientiously revolted. Lady Pennon hinted
a word for her government. "A good deal of what you
so capitally call 'Green tea talk' is going on, my dear."
Diana replied, without pretending to misunderstand: "Gossip is a beast of prey that does not wait for the death of the
creature it devours. They are welcome to my shadow, if
the liberty I claim casts one, and it feeds them." To which
the old lady rejoined: "Oh! I am with you through thick
and thin. I presented you at Court, and I stand by you.
Only, walk carefully. Women have to walk with a train.
You are too famous not to have your troops of watchers."

"But I mean to prove," said Diana, "that a woman can
walk with her train independent of the common reserves
and artifices."

"Not on highways, my dear!"

Diana, praising the speaker, referred the whole truth in
that to the material element of her metaphor.

She was more astonished by Whitmonby's candid chid-
ing; but with him she could fence, and men are easily
diverted. She had sent for him, to bring him and Percy

Dacier together to a conference. Unaware of the project, he took the opportunity of their privacy to speak of the great station open to her in London being imperilled; and he spoke of "tongues," and ahem! A very little would have induced him to fill that empty vocable with a name.

She had to pardon the critic in him for an unpleasant review of her hapless CANTATRICE; and as a means of evasion, she mentioned the poor book and her slaughter of the heroine, that he had complained of.

"I killed her; I could not let her live. You were unjust in accusing the authoress of heartlessness."

"If I did, I retract," said he. "She steers too evidently from the centre of the vessel. She has the organ in excess."

"Proof that it is not squandered."

"The point concerns direction."

"Have I made so bad a choice of my friends?"

"It is the common error of the sprightly to suppose that in parrying a thrust they blind our eyes."

"The world sees always what it desires to see, Mr. Whitmonby."

"The world, my dear Mrs. Warwick, is a blundering machine upon its own affairs, but a cruel sleuth-hound to rouse in pursuit."

"So now you have me chased by sight and scent. And if I take wing?"

"Shots! volleys!—You are lawful game. The choice you have made of your friends, should oblige you to think of them."

"I imagine I do. Have I offended any, or one?"

"I will not say that. You know the commotion in a French kitchen when the guests of the house declined a particular dish furnished them by command. The cook and his crew were loyal to their master, but, for the love of their Art, they sent him notice. It is ill serving a mad sovereign."

Diana bowed to the compact little apologue.

"I will tell you another story, traditional in our family from my great-grandmother, a Spanish woman," she said. "A cavalier serenaded his mistress, and rascal mercenaries fell upon him before he could draw sword. He battered his guitar on their pates till the lattice opened with a cry, and startled them to flight. 'Thrice blessed and beloved!' he called to her above, in reference to the noise, 'it was merely a diversion of the accompaniment.' Now there was loyal service to a sovereign!"

"You are certainly an angel!" exclaimed Whitmonby. "I swallow the story, and leave it to digestion to discover the appositeness. Whatever tuneful instrument one of your friends possesses shall solace your slumbers or batter the pate of your enemy. But discourage the habitual serenader."

"The musician you must mean is due here now, by appointment to meet you," said Diana, and set him momentarily agape with the name of Mr. Percy Dacier.

That was the origin of the alliance between the young statesman and a newspaper editor. Whitmonby, accepting proposals which suited him, quitted the house, after an hour of political talk, no longer inclined to hint at the "habitual serenader," but very ready to fall foul of those who did, as he proved when the numbers buzzed openly. Times were masculine; the excitement on the eve of so great a crisis, and Diana's comprehension of it and fine heading cry, put that weak matter aside. Moreover, he was taught to suppose himself as welcome a guest as Dacier; and the cook could stand criticism; the wines — wonderful to say of a lady's table — were trusty; the talk, on the political evenings and the social and anecdotal supper-nights, ran always in perfect accord with his ideal of the conversational orchestra: an improvized harmony, unmatched elsewhere. She did not, he considered, so perfectly assort her dinner-guests; that was her one fault. She had therefore to strain her adroitness to cover their deficiencies and fuse them. But what other woman could have done it! She led superbly. If an Irishman was present, she kept him from overflooding, managed to extract just the flavour of him, the smack of salt. She did even, at Whitmonby's table, on a red-letter Sunday evening, in concert with him and the Dean, bring down that cataract, the Bodleian, to the levels of interchanging dialogue by seasonable touches, inimitably done, and never done before. Sullivan Smith, unbridled in the middle of dinner, was docile to her. "Irishmen," she said, pleading on their behalf to Whitmonby, who pronounced the race too raw for an Olympian feast, "are invaluable if you hang them up to smoke and cure;" and the master of social converse could not deny that they were responsive to her magic. The supper-nights were mainly devoted to Percy's friends. He brought as many as he pleased, and as often as it pleased him; and it was her pride to provide Cleopatra banquets for the lover whose anxieties were soothed by them, and to whom she sacrificed her name willingly in return for a generosity that certain chance whispers of her heart elevated to the pitch of measureless.

So they wore through the Session and the Autumn, clouds heavier, the League drumming, the cry of Ireland "ominously Banshee," as she wrote to Emma.

CHAPTER XXX

IN WHICH THERE IS A TASTE OF A LITTLE DINNER AND AN AFTERTASTE

"BUT Tony lives!" Emma Dunstane cried, on her solitary height, with the full accent of envy marking the verb; and when she wrote enviously to her friend of the life among bright intelligences, and of talk worth hearing, it was a happy signification that health, frail though it might be, had grown importunate for some of the play of life. Diana sent her word to name her day, and she would have her choicest to meet her dearest. They were in the early days of December, not the best of times for improvized gatherings. Emma wanted, however, to taste them as they cropped; she was also, owing to her long isolation, timid at a notion of encountering the pick of the London world, prepared by Tony to behold "a wonder more than worthy of them," as her friend unadvisedly wrote. That was why she came unexpectedly, and for a mixture of reasons, went to an hotel. Fatality designed it so. She was reproached, but she said: "You have to write or you entertain at night;

I should be a clog and fret you. My hotel is Maitland's; excellent; I believe I am to lie on the pillow where a crowned head reposed! You will perceive that I am proud as well as comfortable. And I would rather meet your usual set of guests."

"The reason why I have been entertaining at night is, that Percy is harassed and requires enlivening," said Diana. "He brings his friends. My house is open to them, if it amuses him. What the world says, is past a thought. I owe him too much."

Emma murmured that the world would soon be pacified.

Diana shook her head. "The poor man is better; able to go about his affairs; and I am honestly relieved. It lays a spectre. As for me, I do not look ahead. I serve as a kind of secretary to Percy. I labour at making abstracts by day, and at night preside at my supper-table. You would think it monotonous; no incident varies the course we run. I have not time to ask whether it is happiness. It seems to bear a resemblance."

Emma replied: "He may be everything you tell me. He should not have chosen the last night of the Opera to go to your box and sit beside you till the fall of the curtain. The presence at the Opera of a man notoriously indifferent to music was enough in itself."

Diana smiled with languor. "You heard of that? But the Opera was The Puritani, my favourite. And he saw me sitting in Lady Pennon's box alone. We were compromised neck-deep already. I can kiss you, my own Emmy, till I die; but what the world says, is what the wind says. Besides he has his hopes. . . . If I am blackened ever so thickly, he can make me white. Dear me! if the world knew that he comes here almost nightly! It will; and does it matter? I am his in soul; the rest is waste-paper — a half-printed sheet."

"Provided he is worthy of such devotion!"

"He is absolute worthiness. He is the prince of men: I dread to say, mine! for fear. But Emmy will not judge him to-morrow by contrast with more voluble talkers. — I can do anything but read poetry now. That kills me! — See him through me. In nature, character, intellect, he has no rival. Whenever I despond — and it comes now

and then — I rebuke myself with this one admonition:
Simply to have known him!   Admit that for a woman to
find one who is worthy among the opposite creatures, is a
happy termination of her quest, and in some sort dis-
misses her to the Shades, an uncomplaining ferry-bird.
If my end were at hand I should have no cause to lament
it.   We women miss life only when we have to confess we
have never met the man to reverence."

Emma had to hear a very great deal of Mr. Percy.
Diana's comparison of herself to "the busy bee at a
window-pane," was more in her old manner; and her
friend would have hearkened to the marvels of the gentleman less unrefreshed, had it not appeared to her that her
Tony gave in excess for what was given in return.   She
hinted her view.

"It is expected of our sex," Diana said.

The work of busy bee at a window-pane had at any rate
not spoilt her beauty, though she had voluntarily, profit-
lessly, become this man's drudge, and her sprightly fancy,
her ready humour and darting look all round in discussion,
were rather deadened.

But the loss was not perceptible in the circle of her
guests.   Present at a dinner little indicating the last, were
Whitmonby, in lively trim for shuffling, dealing, cutting,
trumping or drawing trumps; Westlake, polishing epigrams under his eyelids; Henry Wilmers, who timed an
anecdote to strike as the passing hour without freezing
the current; Sullivan Smith, smoked, cured and ready to
flavour; Percy Dacier, pleasant listener, measured speaker;
and young Arthur Rhodes, the neophyte of the hostess's
training; of whom she had said to Emma, "The dear boy
very kindly serves to frank an unlicenced widow;" and
whom she prompted and made her utmost of, with her
natural tact.   These she mixed and leavened.   The talk
was on high levels and low; an enchantment to Emma
Dunstane: now a story; a question opening new routes;
sharp sketches of known personages; a paradox shot by
laughter as soon as uttered; and all so smoothly; not a
shadow of the dominant holder-forth or a momentary prospect of dead flats; the mellow ring of appositeness being
the concordant note of deliveries running linked as they

flashed, and a tolerant philosophy of the sage in the world recurrently the keynote.

Once only had Diana to protect her nurseling. He cited a funny line from a recent popular volume of verse, in perfect à propos, looking at Sullivan Smith; who replied, that the poets had become too many for him, and he read none now. Diana said: "There are many Alexanders, but Alexander of Macedon is not dwarfed by the number." She gave him an opening for a smarter reply, but he lost it in a comment — against Whitmonby's cardinal rule: "The neatest turn of the wrist that ever swung a hero to crack a crown!" and he bowed to young Rhodes: "I'll read your versicler to-morrow morning early." The latter expressed a fear that the hour was too critical for poetry.

"I have taken the dose at a very early hour," said Whitmonby, to bring conversation to the flow again, "and it effaced the critical mind completely."

"But did not silence the critical nose," observed Westlake.

Wilmers named the owner of the longest nose in Europe.

"Potentially, indeed a critic!" said Diana.

"Nights beside it must be fearful, and good matter for a divorce, if the poor dear lady could hale it to the doors of the Vatican!" Sullivan Smith exclaimed. "But there's character in noses."

"Calculable by inches?" Dacier asked.

"More than in any other feature," said Lady Dunstane. "The Riffords are all prodigiously gifted and amusing: *suspendens omnia naso*. It should be prayed for in families."

"Totum ut te faciant, Fabulle, nasum," rejoined Whitmonby. "Lady Isabella was reading the tale of the German princess, who had a sentinel stationed some hundred yards away to whisk off the flies, and she owned to me that her hand instinctively travelled upward."

"Candour is the best concealment, when one has to carry a saddle of absurdity," said Diana. "Touchstone's 'poor thing, but mine own,' is godlike in its enveloping fold."

"The most comforting sermon ever delivered on property in poverty," said Arthur Rhodes.

Westlake assented. "His choice of Audrey strikes me as an exhibition of the sure instinct for pasture of the philosophical jester in a forest."

"With nature's woman, if he can find her, the urban seems equally at home," said Lady Dunstane.

"Baron Pawle is an example," added Whitmonby. "His cook is a pattern wife to him. I heard him say at table that she was responsible for all except the wines. 'I wouldn't have them on my conscience, with a Judge!' my lady retorted."

"When poor Madame de Jacquières was dying," said Wilmers, "her confessor sat by her bedside, prepared for his ministrations. '*Pour commencer, mon ami, jamais je n'ai fais rien hors nature.*'"

Lord Wadaster had uttered something tolerably similar: "I am a sinner, and in good society." Sir Abraham Hartiston, a minor satellite of the Regent, diversified this: "I am a sinner, and go to good society." Madame la Comtesse de la Roche-Aigle, the cause of many deaths, declared it unwomanly to fear anything save "*les revenants.*" Yet the countess could say the pretty thing: "Foot on a flower, then think of me!"

"Sentimentality puts up infant hands for absolution," said Diana.

"But tell me," Lady Dunstane inquired generally, "why men are so much happier than women in laughing at their spouses?"

They are humaner, was one dictum; they are more frivolous, ironically another.

"It warrants them for blowing the bugle-horn of masculine superiority night and morning from the castle-walls," Diana said.

"I should imagine it is for joy of heart that they still have cause to laugh!" said Westlake.

On the other hand, are women really pained by having to laugh at their lords? Curious little speeches flying about the great world, affirmed the contrary. But the fair speakers were chartered libertines, and their laugh admittedly had a biting acid. The parasite is concerned in the majesty of the tree.

"We have entered Botany Bay," Diana said to Emma;

who answered: "A metaphor is the Deus ex machinâ of an argument;" and Whitmonby, to lighten a shadow of heaviness, related allusively an anecdote of the Law-Courts. Sullivan Smith begged permission to "black cap" it with Judge FitzGerald's sentence upon a convicted criminal: "Your plot was perfect but for One above." Dacier cited an execrable impromptu line of the Chief of the Opposition in Parliament. The Premier, it was remarked, played him like an angler his fish on the hook; or say, Mr. Serjeant Rufus his witness in the box.

"Or a French journalist an English missionary," said Westlake; and as the instance was recent it was relished.

The talk of Premiers offered Whitmonby occasion for a flight to the Court of Vienna and Kaunitz. Wilmers told a droll story of Lord Busby's missing the Embassy there. Westlake furnished a sample of the tranquil sententiousness of Busby's brother Robert during a stormy debate in the House of Commons.

"I remember," Dacier was reminded, "hearing him say, when the House resembled a Chartist riot, ' Let us stand aside and meditate on Life. If Youth could know, in the season of its reaping of the Pleasures, that it is but sowing Doctor's bills!'"

Latterly a malady had supervened, and Bob Busby had retired from the universal to the special; — his mysterious case.

"Assure him, that is endemic. He may be cured of his desire for the exposition of it," said Lady Dunstane.

Westlake chimed with her: "Yes, the charm in discoursing of one's case is over when the individual appears no longer at odds with Providence."

"But then we lose our Tragedy," said Whitmonby.

"Our Comedy too," added Diana. "We must consent to be Busbied for the sake of the instructive recreations."

"A curious idea, though," said Sullivan Smith, "that some of the grand instructive figures were in their day colossal bores!"

"So you see the marvel of the poet's craft at last?" Diana smiled on him, and he vowed: "I'll read nothing else for a month." Young Rhodes bade him beware of a deluge in proclaiming it.

They rose from table at ten, with the satisfaction of knowing that they had not argued, had not wrangled, had never stagnated, and were digestingly refreshed; as it should be among grown members of the civilized world, who mean to practise philosophy, making the hour of the feast a balanced recreation and a regeneration of body and mind.

"Evenings like these are worth a pilgrimage," Emma said, embracing Tony outside the drawing-room door. "I am so glad I came: and if I am strong enough, invite me again in the Spring. To-morrow early I start for Copsley, to escape this London air. I shall hope to have you there soon."

She was pleased by hearing Tony ask her whether she did not think that Arthur Rhodes had borne himself well; for it breathed of her simply friendly soul.

The gentlemen followed Lady Dunstane in a troop, Dacier yielding perforce the last adieu to young Rhodes.

Five minutes later Diana was in her dressing-room, where she wrote at night, on the rare occasions now when she was left free for composition. Beginning to dwell on THE MAN OF TWO MINDS, she glanced at the woman likewise divided, if not similarly; and she sat brooding. She did not accuse her marriage of being the first fatal step: her error was the step into Society without the wherewithal to support her position there. Girls of her kind, airing their wings above the sphere of their birth, are cryingly adventuresses. As adventuresses they are treated. Vain to be shrewish with the world! Rather let us turn and scold our nature for irreflectively rushing to the cream and honey! Had she subsisted on her small income in a country cottage, this task of writing would have been holiday. Or better, if, as she preached to Mary Paynham, she had apprenticed herself to some productive craft. The simplicity of the life of labour looked beautiful. What will not look beautiful contrasted with the fly in the web? She had chosen to be one of the flies of life.

Instead of running to composition, her mind was eloquent with a sermon to Arthur Rhodes, in Redworth's vein; more sympathetically, of course. "For I am not one of the lecturing Mammonites!" she could say.

She was far from that. Penitentially, in the thick of her disdain of the arrogant money-getters, she pulled out a drawer where her bank-book lay, and observed it contemplatively; jotting down a reflection before the dread book of facts was opened: "Gaze on the moral path you should have taken, you are asked for courage to commit a sanctioned suicide, by walking back to it stripped — a skeleton self." She sighed forth: "But I have no courage: I never had!"

The book revealed its tale in a small pencilled computation of the bank-clerk's, on the peccant side. Credit presented many pages blanks. She seemed to have withdrawn from the struggle with such a partner.

It signified an immediate appeal to the usurers, unless the publisher could be persuaded, with three parts of the book in his hands, to come to the rescue. Work! roared old Debit, the sinner turned slavedriver.

Diana smoothed her wrists, compressing her lips not to laugh at the simulation of an attitude of combat. She took up her pen.

And strange to think, she could have flowed away at once on the stuff that Danvers delighted to read! — wicked princes, rogue noblemen, titled wantons, daisy and lily innocents, traitorous marriages, murders, a gallows dangling a corpse dotted by a moon, and a woman bowed beneath. She could have written, with the certainty that in the upper and the middle as well as in the lower classes of the country, there would be a multitude to read that stuff, so cordially, despite the gaps between them, are they one in their literary tastes. And why should they not read it? Her present mood was a craving for excitement; for incident, wild action, the primitive machinery of our species; any amount of theatrical heroics, pathos, and clown-gabble. A panorama of scenes came sweeping round her.

She was, however, harnessed to a different kind of vehicle, and had to drag it. The sound of the house-door shutting, imagined perhaps, was a fugitive distraction. Now to animate The Man of Two Minds!

He is courting, but he is burdened with the task of tasks. He has an ideal of womanhood and of the union of couples: a delicacy extreme as his attachment: and he must induce the lady to school herself to his ideal, not allowing her to suspect him less devoted to her person; while she, an exacting idol, will drink any quantity of idealization as long as he starts it from a full acceptance of her acknowledged qualities. Diana could once have tripped the scene along airily. She stared at the opening sentence, a heavy bit of moralized manufacture, fit to yoke beside that on her view of her bank-book.

"It has come to this — I have no head," she cried.

And is our public likely to muster the slightest taste for comic analysis that does not tumble to farce? The doubt reduced her whole MS. to a leaden weight, composed for sinking. Percy's addiction to burlesque was a further hindrance, for she did not perceive how her comedy could be strained to gratify it.

There was a knock, and Danvers entered.

"You have apparently a liking for late hours," observed her mistress. "I told you to go to bed."

"It is Mr. Dacier," said Danvers.

"He wishes to see me?"

"Yes, ma'am. He apologized for disturbing you."

"He must have some good reason."

What could it be! Diana's glass approved her appearance. She pressed the black swell of hair above her temples, rather amazed, curious, inclined to a beating of the heart.

CHAPTER XXXI

A CHAPTER CONTAINING GREAT POLITICAL NEWS AND THEREWITH AN INTRUSION OF THE LOVE-GOD.

DACIER was pacing about the drawing-room, as in a place too narrow for him.

Diana stood at the door. "Have you forgotten to tell me anything I ought to know?"

He came up to her and shut the door softly behind her, holding her hand. "You are near it. I returned . . .

But tell me first: — You were slightly under a shadow this evening, dejected."

"Did I show it?"

She was growing a little suspicious, but this cunning touch of lover-like interest dispersed the shade.

"To me you did."

"It was unpardonable to let it be seen."

"No one else could have observed it."

Her woman's heart was thrilled; for she had concealed the dejection from Emma.

"It was nothing," she said; "a knot in the book I am writing. We poor authors are worried now and then. But you?"

His face rippled by degrees brightly, to excite a reflection in hers.

"Shall I tune you with good news? I think it will excuse me for coming back."

"Very good news?"

"Brave news, as far as it goes."

"Then it concerns you!"

"Me, you, the country."

"Oh! do I guess?" cried Diana. "But speak, pray; I burn."

"What am I to have for telling it?"

"Put no price. You know my heart. I guess — or fancy. It relates to your Chief?"

Dacier smiled in a way to show the lock without the key; and she was insensibly drawn nearer to him, speculating on the smile.

"Try again," said he, keenly appreciating the blindness to his motive of her studious dark eyes, and her open-lipped breathing.

"Percy! I must be right."

"Well, you are. He has decided!"

"Oh! that is the bravest possible. When did you hear?"

"He informed me of his final decision this afternoon."

"And you were charged with the secret all the evening, and betrayed not a sign! I compliment the diplomatic statesman. But when will it be public?"

"He calls Parliament together the first week of next month."

"The proposal is — ? No more compromises!"

"Total!"

Diana clapped hands; and her aspect of enthusiasm was intoxicating. "He is a wise man and a gallant Minister! And while you were reading me through, I was blind to you," she added meltingly.

"I have not made too much of it?" said he.

"Indeed you have not."

She was radiant with her dark lightnings, yet visibly subject to him under the spell of the news he had artfully lengthened out to excite and overbalance her: — and her enthusiasm was all pointed to his share in the altered situation, as he well knew and was flattered in knowing.

"So Tony is no longer dejected? I thought I could freshen you and get my excuse."

"Oh! a high wind will make a dead leaf fly like a bird. I soar. Now I do feel proud. I have longed for it — to have you leading the country: not tugged at like a waggon with a treble team uphill. We two are a month in advance of all England. You stand by him? — only to hear it, for I am sure of it!"

"We stand or fall together."

Her glowing look doated on the faithful lieutenant.

"And if the henchman is my hero I am but a waiting-woman. But I must admire his leader."

"Tony!"

"Ah! no," she joined her hands, wondering whither her armed majesty had fled; "no softness! no payments! Flatter me by letting me think you came to a head — not a silly woman's heart, with one name on it, as it has not to betray. I have been frank; you need no proofs . . ." The supplicating hands left her figure an easy prey to the storm, and were crushed in a knot on her bosom. She could only shrink. "Ah! Percy . . . you undo my praise of you — my pride in receiving you."

They were speechless perforce.

"You see, Tony, my dearest, I am flesh and blood after all."

"You drive me to be ice and door-bolts!"

Her eyes broke over him reproachfully.

"It is not so much to grant," he murmured.

"It changes everything between us."

"Not me. It binds me the faster."

"It makes me a loathsome hypocrite."

"But, Tony! is it so much ?"

"Not if you value it low."

"But how long do you keep me in this rag-puppet's state of suspension ?"

"Patience."

"Dangling and swinging day and night !"

"The rag-puppet shall be animated and repaid if I have life. I wish to respect my hero. Have a little mercy. Our day will come: perhaps as wonderfully as this wonderful news. My friend, drop your hands. Have you forgotten who I am ? I want to think, Percy !"

"But you are mine."

"You are abasing your own."

"No, by heaven !"

"Worse, dear friend ; you are lowering yourself to the woman who loves you."

"You must imagine me superhuman."

"I worship you — or did."

"Be reasonable, Tony. What harm ! Surely a trifle of recompense ? Just to let me feel I live ! You own you love me. Then I am your lover."

"My dear friend Percy, when I have consented to be your paramour, this kind of treatment of me will not want apologies."

The plain speaking from the wound he dealt her was effective with a gentleman who would never have enjoyed his privileges had he been of a nature unsusceptible to her distinct wish and meaning.

He sighed. "You know how my family bother me. The woman I want, the only woman I could marry, I can't have."

"You have her in soul."

"Body and soul, it must be ! I believe you were made without fire."

"Perhaps. The element is omitted with some of us : happily, some think. Now we can converse. There seems to be a measurement of distances required before men and women have a chance with their brains : — or before a man will understand that he can be advised and seconded. When will the Cabinet be consulted?"

"Oh, a few days. Promise me . . ."

"Any honourable promise!"

"You will not keep me waiting longer than the end of the Session?"

"Probably there will be an appeal to the country."

"In any case, promise me: have some compassion."

"Ah, the compassion! You do not choose your words, Percy, or forget who is the speaker."

"It is Tony who forgets the time she has kept her lover dangling. Promise, and I will wait."

"You hurt my hand, sir."

"I could crack the knuckles. Promise!"

"Come to me to-morrow."

"To-morrow you are in your armour — triple brass! All creation cries out for now. We are mounted on barbs and you talk of ambling."

"Arthur Rhodes might have spoken that."

"Rhodes!" he shook off the name in disgust. "Pet him as much as you like; don't . . ." he was unable to phrase his objection.

She cooled him further with eulogies of the chevaleresque manner of speaking which young Mr. Rhodes could assume; till for very wrath of blood — not jealousy: he had none of any man, with her; and not passion; the little he had was a fitful gust — he punished her coldness by taking what hastily could be gathered.

Her shape was a pained submission; and she thought: Where is the woman who ever knows a man! — as women do think when one of their artifices of evasion with a lover, or the trick of imposingness, has apparently been subduing him. But the pain was less than previously, for she was now mistress of herself, fearing no abysses.

Dacier released her quickly, saying: "If I come to-morrow, shall I have the promise?"

She answered: "Be sure I shall not lie."

"Why not let me have it before I go?"

"My friend, to tell you the truth, you have utterly distracted me."

"Forgive me if I did hurt your hand."

"The hand? You might strike it off."

"I can't be other than a mortal lover, Tony. There's the fact."

"No; the fault is mine when I am degraded. I trust you: there's the error."

The trial for Dacier was the sight of her quick-lifting bosom under the mask of cold language: an attraction and repulsion in union; a delirium to any lover impelled to trample on weak defences. But the evident pain he inflicted moved his pity, which helped to restore his conception of the beauty of her character. She stood so nobly meek. And she was never prudish, only self-respecting. Although the great news he imparted had roused an ardent thirst for holiday and a dash out of harness, and he could hardly check it, he yielded her the lead.

"Trust me you may," he said. "But you know we are one. The world has given you to me, me to you. Why should we be asunder? There's no reason in it."

She replied: "But still I wish to burn a little incense in honour of myself, or else I cannot live. It is the truth. You make Death my truer friend, and at this moment I would willingly go out. You would respect me more dead than alive. I could better pardon you too."

He pleaded for the red mouth's pardon, remotely irritated by the suspicion that she swayed him overmuch: and he had deserved the small benevolences and donations of love, crumbs and heavenly dews!

"Not a word of pardon," said Diana. "I shall never count an iota against you 'in the dark backward and abysm of Time.' This news is great, and I have sunk beneath it. Come to-morrow. Then we will speak upon whatever you can prove rátional. The hour is getting late."

Dacier took a draught of her dark beauty with the crimson he had kindled over the cheeks. Her lips were firmly closed, her eyes grave; dry, but seeming to waver tearfully in their heavy fulness. He could not doubt her love of him; and although chafing at the idea that she swayed him absurdly — beyond the credible in his world of wag-tongues — he resumed his natural soberness, as a garment, not very uneasily fitting: whence it ensued — for so are we influenced by the garb we put on us — that his manly sentiment of revolt in being condemned to play second, was repressed by the refreshment breathed on him from her lofty character, the pure jewel proffered to his inward ownership.

"Adieu for the night," he said, and she smiled. He pressed for a pressure of her hand. She brightened her smile instead, and said only: "Good night, Percy."

CHAPTER XXXII

WHEREIN WE BEHOLD A GIDDY TURN AT THE SPECTRAL CROSSWAYS

DANVERS accompanied Mr. Dacier to the house-door. Climbing the stairs, she found her mistress in the drawing-room still.

"You must be cold, ma'am," she said, glancing at the fire-grate.

"Is it a frost?" said Diana.

"It's midnight and midwinter, ma'am."

"Has it struck midnight?"

The mantel-piece clock said five minutes past.

"You had better go to bed, Danvers, or you will lose your bloom. Stop; you are a faithful soul. Great things are happening and I am agitated. Mr. Dacier has told me news. He came back purposely."

"Yes, ma'am," said Danvers. "He had a great deal to tell?"

"Well, he had." Diana coloured at the first tentative impertinence she had heard from her maid. "What is the secret of you, Danvers? What attaches you to me?"

"I'm sure I don't know, ma'am. I'm romantic."

"And you think me a romantic object?"

"I'm sure I can't say, ma'am. I'd rather serve you than any other lady; and I wish you was happy."

"Do you suppose I am unhappy?"

"I'm sure — but if I may speak, ma'am: so handsome and clever a lady! and young! I can't bear to see it."

"Tush, you silly woman. You read your melting tales and imagine. I must go and write for money: it is my profession. And I haven't an idea in my head. This news disturbs me. Ruin if I don't write; so I must. — I can't!"

Diana beheld the ruin. She clasped the great news for succour. Great indeed: and known but to her of all the outer world. She was ahead of all — ahead of Mr. Tonans!

The visionary figure of Mr. Tonans petrified by the great news, drinking it, and confessing her ahead of him in the race for secrets, arose toweringly. She had not ever seen the Editor in his den at midnight. With the rumble of his machinery about him, and fresh matter arriving and flying into the printing-press, it must be like being in the very furnace-hissing of Events: an Olympian Council held in Vulcan's smithy. Consider the bringing to the Jove there news of such magnitude as to stupefy him! He, too, who had admonished her rather sneeringly for staleness in her information. But this news, great though it was, and throbbing like a heart plucked out of a breathing body, throbbed but for a brief term, a day or two; after which, great though it was, immense, it relapsed into a common organ, a possession of the multitude, merely historically curious.

"You are not afraid of the streets at night?" Diana said to her maid, as they were going upstairs.

"Not when we're driving, ma'am," was the answer.

THE MAN OF TWO MINDS faced his creatrix in the dressing-room, still delivering that most ponderous of sentences — a smothering pillow!

I have mistaken my vocation, thought Diana: I am certainly the flattest proser who ever penned a line.

She sent Danvers into the bedroom on a trifling errand, unable to bear the woman's proximity, and oddly unwilling to dismiss her.

She pressed her hands on her eyelids. Would Percy have humiliated her so if he had respected her? He took advantage of the sudden loss of her habitual queenly initiative at the wonderful news to debase and stain their inti-

macy. The lover's behaviour was judged by her sensations: she felt humiliated, plucked violently from the
throne where she had long been sitting securely, very
proudly. That was at an end. If she was to be better than
the loathsomest of hypocrites, she must deny him his
admission to the house. And then what was her life!

Something that was pressing her low, she knew not how,
and left it unquestioned, incited her to exaggerate the
indignity her pride had suffered. She was a dethroned
woman. Deeper within, an unmasked actress, she said.
Oh, she forgave him! But clearly he took her for the same
as other women consenting to receive a privileged visitor.
And sounding herself to the soul, was she so magnificently
better? Her face flamed. She hugged her arms at her
breast to quiet the beating, and dropped them when she
surprised herself embracing the memory. He had brought
political news, and treated her as — name the thing! Not
designedly, it might be: her position invited it. "The
world had given her to him." The world is always a
prophet of the mire; but the world is no longer an utterly
mistaken world. She shook before it.

She asked herself why Percy or the world should think
highly of an adventuress, who was a denounced wife, a
wretched author, and on the verge of bankruptcy. She was
an adventuress. When she held The Crossways she had
at least a bit of solid footing: now gone. An adventuress without an idea in her head: witness her dullard,
The Man of Two Minds, at his work of sermonizing his
mistress.

The tremendous pressure upon our consciousness of the
material cause, when we find ourselves cast among the
breakers of moral difficulties and endeavour to elude that
mud-visaged monster, chiefly by feigning unconsciousness,
was an experience of Diana's, in the crisis to which she was
wrought. Her wits were too acute, her nature too direct,
to permit of a lengthened confusion. She laid the scourge
on her flesh smartly. — I gave him these privileges because
I am weak as the weakest, base as my enemies proclaim
me. I covered my woman's vile weakness with an air of
intellectual serenity that he, choosing his moment, tore
away, exposing me to myself, as well as to him, the most

ordinary of reptiles. I kept up a costly household for the sole purpose of seeing him and having him near me. Hence this bitter need of money!—Either it must be money or disgrace. Money would assist her quietly to amend and complete her work. Yes, and this want of money, in a review of the last two years, was the material cause of her recklessness. It was, her revived and uprising pudency declared, the principal, the only cause. Mere want of money.

And she had a secret worth thousands! The secret of a day, no more: anybody's secret after some four and twenty hours.

She smiled at the fancied elongation and stare of the features of Mr. Tonans in his editorial midnight den.

What if he knew it and could cap it with something novel and stranger? Hardly. But it was an inciting suggestion.

She began to tremble as a lightning-flash made visible her fortunes recovered, disgrace averted, hours of peace for composition stretching before her: a summer afternoon's vista.

It seemed a duel between herself and Mr. Tonans, and she sure of her triumph — Diana victrix!

"Danvers!" she called.

"Is it to undress, ma'am?" said the maid, entering to her.

"You are not afraid of the streets, you tell me. I have to go down to the City, I think. It is urgent. Yes, I must go. If I were to impart the news to you, your head would be a tolling bell for a month."

"You will take a cab, ma'am."

"We must walk out to find one. I must go, though I should have to go on foot. Quick with bonnet and shawl; muffle up warmly. We have never been out so late: but does it matter? You're a brave soul, I'm sure, and you shall have your fee."

"I don't care for money, ma'am."

"When we get home you shall kiss me."

Danvers clothed her mistress in furs and rich wrappings: Not paid for! was Diana's desperate thought, and a wrong one; but she had to seem the precipitated bankrupt and succeeded. She was near being it. The boiling of her secret carried her through the streets rapidly and unobservantly except of such small things as the glow of the lights on the pavements and the hushed cognizance of the houses, in silence to a thoroughfare where a willing cabman was met. The destination named, he nodded alertly: he had driven gentlemen there at night from the House of Commons, he said.

"*Our* Parliament is now sitting, and you drive ladies," Diana replied.

"I hope I know one, never mind the hour," said he of the capes.

He was bidden to drive rapidly.

"Complexion a tulip: you do not often see a pale cabman," she remarked to Danvers, who began laughing, as she always expected to do on an excursion with her mistress.

"Do you remember, ma'am, the cabman taking us to the coach, when you thought of going to the continent?"

"And I went to The Crossways? I have forgotten him."

"He declared you was so beautiful a lady he would drive you to the end of England for nothing."

"It must have been when I was paying him. Put it out of your mind, Danvers, that there are individual cabmen. They are the painted flowers of our metropolitan thoroughfares, and we gather them in rows."

"They have their feelings, ma'am."

"Brandied feelings are not pathetic to me."

"I like to think kindly of them," Danvers remarked, in reproof of her inhumanity; adding: "They may overturn us!" at which Diana laughed.

Her eyes were drawn to a brawl of women and men in the street. "Ah! that miserable sight!" she cried. "It is the everlasting nightmare of London."

Danvers humped, femininely injured by the notice of it. She wondered her mistress should deign to.

Rolling on between the blind and darkened houses, Diana transferred her sensations to them, and in a fit of the nerves imagined them beholding a funeral convoy without followers.

They came in view of the domed cathedral, hearing, in a pause of the wheels, the bell of the hour. "Faster! faster! my dear man," Diana murmured, and they entered a small still square of many lighted windows.

"This must be where the morrow is manufactured," she said. "Tell the man to wait. — Or rather it's the mirror of yesterday: we have to look backward to see forward in life."

She talked her cool philosophy to mask her excitement from herself.

Her card, marked: "*Imperative — two minutes*," was taken up to Mr. Tonans. They ascended to the editorial ante-room. Doors opened and shut, hasty feet traversed the corridors, a dull hum in dumbness told of mighty business at work. Diana received the summons to the mighty head of the establishment. Danvers was left to speculate. She heard the voice of Mr. Tonans: "Not more than two!" This was not a place for compliments. Men passed her, hither and yonder, cursorily noticing the presence of a woman. She lost, very strangely to her, the sense of her sex and became an object — a disregarded object. Things of more importance were about. Her feminine self-esteem was troubled; all idea of attractiveness expired. Here was manifestly a spot where women had dropped from the secondary to the cancelled stage of their extraordinary career in a world either blowing them aloft like soap-bubbles or quietly shelving them as supernumeraries. A gentleman — sweet vision! — shot by to the editor's door, without even looking cursorily. He knocked. Mr. Tonans appeared and took him by the arm, dictating at a great rate; perceived Danvers, frowned at the female, and requested him to wait in the room, which the gentleman did, not once casting eye upon a woman. At last her mistress returned to her, escorted so far by Mr. Tonans, and he refreshingly bent his back to bow over her hand: so we have the satisfaction of knowing that we are not such poor creatures after all! Suffering in person, Danvers was revived by the little show of homage to her sex.

They descended the stairs.

"You are not an Editor of a paper, but you may boast

hat you have been near the nest of one," Diana said,
when they resumed their seats in the cab. She breathed
deeply from time to time, as if under a weight, or relieved
of it, but she seemed animated, and she dropped now and
again a funny observation or the kind that tickled Danvers
and caused the maid to boast of her everywhere as better
than a Play.

At home, Danvers busied her hands to supply her mistress a cup of refreshing tea and a plate of biscuits. Diana
had stunned herself with the strange weight of the expedition, and had not a thought. In spite of tea at that hour,
she slept soundly through the remainder of the night,
dreamlessly till late into the morning.

CHAPTER XXXIII

EXHIBITS THE SPRINGING OF A MINE IN A NEWSPAPER
ARTICLE

THE powers of harmony would seem to be tried to their
shrewdest pitch when Politics and Love are planted together
in a human breast. This apparently opposite couple can
nevertheless chant a very sweet accord, as was shown by
Dacier on his homeward walk from Diana's house. Let
Love lead, the God will make music of any chamber-com-
rade. He was able to think of affairs of State while feeling the satisfied thirst of the lover whose pride, irritated
by confidential wild eulogies of the beautiful woman, had
recently clamoured for proofs of his commandership. The
impression she stamped on him at Copsley remained, but
it could not occupy the foreground for ever. He did not
object to play second to her sprightly wits in converse, if
he had some warm testimony to his mastery over her
blood. For the world had given her to him, enthusiastic
friends had congratulated him : she had exalted him for
true knightliness ; and he considered the proofs well earned,
though he did not value them low. They were little by
comparison. They lighted, instead of staining, her unparalleled high character.

She loved him. Full surely did she love him, or such
a woman would never have consented to brave the world;
once in their project of flight, and next, even more endear-
ingly when contemplated, in the sacrifice of her good name;
not omitting that fervent memory of her pained submission,
but a palpitating submission, to his caress. She was in his
arms again at the thought of it. He had melted her, and
won the confession of her senses by a surprise, and he
owned that never had woman been so vigilantly self-
guarded or so watchful to keep her lover amused and
aloof. Such a woman deserved long service. But then
the long service deserved its time of harvest. Her surging
look of reproach in submission pointed to the golden time,
and as he was a man of honour, pledged to her for life, he
had no remorse, and no scruple in determining to exact her
dated promise, on this occasion deliberately. She was the
woman to be his wife ; she was his mind's mate : they had
hung apart in deference to mere scruples too long. During
the fierce battle of the Session she would be his help, his
fountain of counsel; and she would be the rosy gauze-veiled
more than cold helper and adviser, the being which would
spur her womanly intelligence to acknowledge, on this
occasion deliberately, the wisdom of the step. They had
been so close to it ! She might call it madness then : now
it was wisdom. Each had complete experience of the other,
and each vowed the step must be taken.

As to the secret communicated, he exulted in the pardonable cunning of the impulse turning him back to her house
after the guests had gone, and the dexterous play of his
bait on the line, tempting her to guess and quit her queenly
guard. Though it had not been distinctly schemed, the
review of it in that light added to the enjoyment. It had
been dimly and richly conjectured as a hoped result. Small
favours from her were really worth, thrice worth, the
utmost from other women. They tasted the sweeter for
the winning of them artfully — an honourable thing in
love. Nature, rewarding the lover's ingenuity and enter-
prise, inspires him with old Greek notions of right and
wrong : and love is indeed a fluid mercurial realm, continu-
ally shifting the principles of rectitude and larceny. As

long as he means nobly, what is there to condemn him? Not she in her heart. She was the presiding divinity.

And she, his Tony, that splendid Diana, was the woman the world abused! Whom will it not abuse?

The slough she would have to plunge in before he could make her his own with the world's consent, was already up to her throat. She must, and without further hesitation, be steeped, that he might drag her out, washed of the imputed defilement, and radiant, as she was in character. Reflection now said this; not impulse.

Her words rang through him. At every meeting she said things to confound his estimate of the wits of women, or be remembered for some spirited ring they had:— *A high wind will make a dead leaf fly like a bird.* He murmured it and flew with her. She quickened a vein of imagination that gave him entrance to a strangely brilliant sphere, above his own, where she sustaining, he too could soar; and he did, scarce conscious of walking home, undressing, falling asleep.

The act of waking was an instantaneous recovery of his emotional rapture of the overnight; nor was it a bar to graver considerations. His Chief had gone down to a house in the country; his personal business was to see and sound the followers of their party — after another sight of his Tony. She would be sure to counsel sagaciously; she always did. She had a marvellous intuition of the natures of the men he worked with, solely from his chance descriptions of them: it was as though he started the bird and she transfixed it. And she should not have matter to ruffle her smooth brows: that he swore to. She should sway him as she pleased, be respected after her prescribed manner. The promise must be exacted; nothing besides the promise. — You see, Tony, you cannot be less than Tony to me now, he addressed the gentle phantom of her. Let me have your word, and I am your servant till the Session ends. — Tony blushes her swarthy crimson: Diana, fluttering, rebukes her; but Diana is the appeasable Goddess; Tony is the woman, and she loves him. The glorious Goddess need not cut them adrift; they can show her a book of honest pages.

Dacier could truthfully say he had worshipped, done knightly service to the beloved woman, homage to the

aureole encircling her. Those friends of his, covertly
congratulating him on her preference, doubtless thought
him more privileged than he was; but they did not know
Diana; and they were welcome, if they would only believe,
to the knowledge that he was at the feet of this most sovereign woman. He despised the particular Satyr-world which,
whatever the nature or station of the woman, crowns the
desecrator, and bestows the title of Fool on the worshipper.
He could have answered veraciously that she had kept him
from folly.

Nevertheless the term to service must come. In the
assurance of the approaching term he stood braced against
a blowing world; happy as men are when their muscles are
strung for a prize they pluck with the energy and aim of
their whole force.

Letters and morning papers were laid for him to peruse
in his dressing-room. He read his letters before the bath.
Not much public news was expected at the present season.
While dressing, he turned over the sheets of Whitmonby's
journal. Dull comments on stale tidings. Foreign news,
Home news, with the leaders on them, identically dull.
Behold the effect of Journalism: a witty man, sparkling
overnight, gets into his pulpit and proses; because he must
say something, and he really knows nothing. Journalists
have an excessive overestimate of their influence. They
cannot, as Diana said, comparing them with men on the
Parliamentary platform, cannot feel they are aboard the
big vessel; they can only strive to raise a breeze, or find
one to swell; and they cannot measure the stoutness or the
greatness of the good ship England. Dacier's personal
ambition was inferior to his desire to extend and strengthen
his England. Parliament was the field, Government the
office. How many conversations had passed between him
and Diana on that patriotic dream! She had often filled
his drooping sails; he owned it proudly: — and while the
world, both the hoofed and the rectilinear portions, were
biting at her character! Had he fretted her self-respect?
He blamed himself, but a devoted service must have its
term.

The paper of Mr. Tonans was reserved for perusal at
breakfast. He reserved it because Tonans was an opponent,

tricksy and surprising now and then, amusing too; unlikely
to afford him serious reflections. The recent endeavours of
his journal to whip the Government-team to a right-about-
face were annoying, preposterous. Dacier had admitted
to Diana that Tonans merited the thanks of the country
during the discreditable Railway mania, when his articles
had a fine exhortative and prophetic twang, and had done
marked good. Otherwise, as regarded the Ministry, the
veering gusts of Tonans were objectionable : he "raised the
breeze" wantonly as well as disagreeably. Anyone can
whip up the populace if he has the instruments; and
Tonans frequently intruded on the Ministry's prerogative
to govern. The journalist was bidding against the statesman. But such is the condition of a rapidly Radicalizing
country! We must take it as it is.

With a complacent, What now, Dacier fixed his indifferent
eyes on the first column of the leaders.

He read, and his eyes grew horny. He jerked back at
each sentence, electrified, staring. The article was shorter
than usual. Total Repeal was named; the precise date
when the Minister intended calling Parliament together to
propose it. The "Total Repeal" might be guess-work —
an editor's bold stroke : but the details, the date, were
significant of positive information. The Minister's definite
and immediate instructions were exactly stated.

Where could the fellow have got hold of that ? Dacier
asked the blank ceiling.

He frowned at vacant corners of the room in an effort to
conjure some speculation indicative of the source.

Had his Chief confided the secret to another and a
traitor? Had they been overheard in his library when
the project determined on was put in plain speech ?

The answer was no, impossible, to each question.

He glanced at Diana. She ? But it was past midnight
when he left her. And she would never have betrayed
him, never, never. To imagine it a moment was an
injury to her.

Where else could he look ? It had been specially mentioned in the communication as a secret by his Chief, who
trusted him and no others. Up to the consultation with
the Cabinet, it was a thing to be guarded like life itself.

Not to a soul except Diana would Dacier have breathed syllable of any secret — and one of this weight!

He ran down the article again. There were the facts; undeniable facts; and they detonated with audible roaring and rounding echoes of them over England. How did they come there? As well inquire how man came on the face of the earth.

He had to wipe his forehead perpetually. Think as he would in exaltation of Diana to shelter himself, he was the accused. He might not be the guilty, but he had opened his mouth; and though it was to her only, and she, as Dunstane had sworn, true as steel, he could not escape condemnation. He had virtually betrayed his master. Diana would never betray her lover, but the thing was in the air as soon as uttered: and off to the printing-press! Dacier's grotesque fancy under annoyance pictured a stream of small printer's devils in flight from his babbling lips.

He consumed bits of breakfast, with a sour confession that a newspaper-article had hit him at last, and stunningly.

Hat and coat were called for. The state of aimlessness in hot perplexity demands a show of action. Whither to go first was as obscure as what to do. Diana said of the Englishman's hat and coat, that she supposed they were to make him a walking presentment of the house he had shut up behind him. A shot of the eye at the glass confirmed the likeness, but with a ruefully wry-faced repudiation of it internally: — Not so shut up! the reverse of that — a common babbler.

However, there was no doubt of Diana. First he would call on her. The pleasantest dose in perturbations of the kind is instinctively taken first. She would console, perhaps direct him to guess how the secret had leaked. — But so suddenly, immediately! It was inexplicable.

Sudden and immediate consequences were experienced. On the steps of his house his way was blocked by the arrival of Mr. Quintin Manx, who jumped out of a cab, bellowing interjections and interrogations in a breath. Was there *anything* in that article? He had read it at breakfast, and it had choked him. Dacier was due at a house and could not wait: he said, rather sharply, he was not responsible for newspaper articles. Quintin Manx, a senior gentleman and junior landowner, vowed that no Minister intending to sell the country should treat him as a sheep. The shepherd might go; he would not carry his flock with him.   But was there a twinkle of probability in the story? . . . that article! Dacier was unable to inform him; he was very hurried, had to keep an appointment.

"If I let you go, will you come and lunch with me at two?" said Quintin.

To get rid of him, Dacier nodded and agreed.

"Two o'clock, mind!" was bawled at his heels as he walked off with his long stride, unceremoniously leaving the pursy gentleman of sixty to settle with his cabman far to the rear.

CHAPTER XXXIV

IN WHICH IT IS DARKLY SEEN HOW THE CRIMINAL'S JUDGE MAY BE LOVE'S CRIMINAL

WHEN we are losing balance on a precipice we do not think much of the thing we have clutched for support. Our balance is restored and we have not fallen; that is the comfortable reflection: we stand as others do, and we will for the future be warned to avoid the dizzy stations which cry for resources beyond a common equilibrium, and where a slip precipitates us to ruin.

When, further, it is a woman planted in a burning blush, having to idealize her feminine weakness, that she may not rebuke herself for grovelling, the mean material acts by which she sustains a tottering position are speedily swallowed in the one pervading flame.   She sees but an ashen curl of the path she has traversed to safety, if anything.

Knowing her lover was to come in the morning, Diana's thoughts dwelt wholly upon the way to tell him, as tenderly as possible without danger to herself, that her time for entertaining was over until she had finished her book; indefinitely, therefore.   The apprehension of his complaining pricked the memory that she had something to forgive.   He had sunk her in her own esteem by compelling her to see her

woman's softness. But how high above all other men her
experience of him could place him notwithstanding!   He
had bowed to the figure of herself, dearer than herself, that
she set before him: and it was a true figure to the world;
a too fictitious to any but the most knightly of lovers. She
forgave; and a shudder seized her. — Snake! she rebuked
the delicious run of fire through her veins; for she was not
like the idol women of imperishable type, who are never
for a twinkle the prey of the blood: statues created by
man's common desire to impress upon the sex his possessing pattern of them as domestic decorations.

When she entered the room to Dacier and they touched
hands, she rejoiced in her coolness, without any other feeling or perception active. Not to be unkind, not too kind:
this was her task. She waited for the passage of commonplaces.

"You slept well, Percy?"

"Yes; and you?"

"I don't think I even dreamed."

They sat. She noticed the cloud on him and waited for
his allusion to it, anxious concerning him simply.

Dacier flung the hair off his temples. Words of Titanic
formation were hurling in his head at journals and journalists. He muttered his disgust at them.

"Is there anything to annoy you in the papers to-day?"
she asked, and thought how handsome his face was in anger.

The paper of Mr. Tonans was named by him. "You
have not seen it?"

"I have not opened it yet."

He sprang up. "The truth is, those fellows can now afford to buy right and left, corrupt every soul alive! There
must have been a spy at the keyhole. I'm pretty certain
— I could swear it was not breathed to any ear but mine;
and there it is this morning in black and white."

"*What* is?" cried Diana, turning to him on her chair.

"The thing I told you last night."

Her lips worked, as if to spell the thing. "Printed, do
you say?" she rose.

"Printed. In a leading article, loud as a trumpet; a hue
and cry running from end to end of the country. And my
Chief has already had the satisfaction of seeing the secret

he confided to me yesterday roared in all the thoroughfares this morning. They've got the facts: his decision to propose it, and the date — the whole of it! But who could have betrayed it?"

For the first time since her midnight expedition she felt a sensation of the full weight of the deed. She heard thunder.

She tried to disperse the growing burden by an inward summons to contempt of the journalistic profession, but nothing would come. She tried to minimize it, and her brain succumbed. Her views of the deed last night and now throttled reason in two contending clutches. The enormity swelled its dimensions, taking shape, and pointing magnetically at her. She stood absolutely, amazedly, bare before it.

"Is it of such very great importance?" she said, like one supplicating him to lessen it.

"A secret of State? If you ask whether it is of great importance to me, relatively it is of course. Nothing greater. Personally my conscience is clear. I never mentioned it — could n't have mentioned it — to any one but you. I'm not the man to blab secrets. He spoke to me because he knew he could trust me. To tell you the truth, I'm brought to a dead stop. I can't make a guess. I'm certain, from what he said, that he trusted me only with it: perfectly certain. I know him well. He was in his library, speaking in his usual conversational tone, deliberately, not overloud. He stated that it was a secret between us."

"Will it affect him?"

"This article? Why, naturally it will. You ask strange questions. A Minister coming to a determination like that! It affects him vitally. The members of the Cabinet are not so devoted. . . . It affects us all — the whole Party; may split it to pieces! There's no reckoning the upset right and left. If it were false, it could be refuted; we could despise it as a trick of journalism. It's true. There's the mischief. Tonans did not happen to call here last night? — absurd! I left later than twelve."

"No, but let me hear," Diana said hurriedly, for the sake of uttering the veracious negative and to slur it over. "Let me hear . . ." She could not muster an idea.

Her delicious thrilling voice was a comfort to him. He lifted his breast high and thumped it, trying to smile. "After all, it's pleasant being with you, Tony. Give me your hand — you may : I'm bothered — confounded by this morning surprise. It was like walking against the muzzle of a loaded cannon suddenly unmasked. One can't fathom the mischief it will do. And I shall be suspected, and can't quite protest myself the spotless innocent. Not even to one's heart's mistress ! to the wife of the bosom ! I suppose I'm no Roman. You won't give me your hand ? Tony, you might, seeing I am rather . . ."

A rush of scalding tears flooded her eyes.

"Don't touch me," she said, and forced her sight to look straight at him through the fiery shower. "I have done positive *mischief?*"

"You, my dear Tony ?" He doated on her face. "I don't blame you, I blame myself. These things should never be breathed. Once in the air, the devil has hold of them. Don't take it so much to heart. The thing's bad enough to bear as it is. Tears ! Let me have the hand. I came, on my honour, with the most honest intention to submit to your orders : but if I see you weeping in sympathy !"

"Oh ! for heaven's sake," she caught her hands away from him, "don't be generous. Whip me with scorpions. And don't touch me," cried Diana. "Do you understand ? You did not name it as a secret. I did not imagine it to be a secret of immense, *immediate* importance."

"But — *what?*" shouted Dacier stiffening.

He wanted her positive meaning, as she perceived, having hoped that it was generally taken and current, and the shock to him over.

"I had . . . I had not a suspicion of doing harm, Percy."

"But what harm have you done ? No riddles !"

His features gave sign of the break in their common ground, the widening gulf.

"I went . . . it was a curious giddiness : I can't account for it. I thought . . ."

"*Went?* You went where ?"

"Last night. I would speak intelligibly : my mind has gone. Ah ! you look. It is not so bad as my feeling."

"But where did you go last night? What! — to Tonans?"

She drooped her head: she saw the track of her route cleaving the darkness in a demoniacal zig-zag and herself in demon's grip.

"Yes," she confronted him. "I went to Mr. Tonans."

"Why?"

"I went to him —"

"You went alone?"

"I took my maid."

"Well?"

"It was late when you left me . . . ."

"Speak plainly!"

"I am trying: I will tell you all."

"At once, if you please."

"I went to him — why? There is no accounting for it. He sneered constantly at any stale information."

"You gave him constant information?"

"No: in our ordinary talk. He railed at me for being 'out of it.' I must be childish: I went to show him — oh! my vanity! I think I must have been possessed."

She watched the hardening of her lover's eyes. They penetrated, and through them she read herself insufferably.

But it was with hesitation still that he said: "Then you betrayed me?"

"Percy! I had not a suspicion of mischief."

"You went straight to this man?"

"Not thinking . . ."

"You sold me to a journalist!"

"I thought it was a secret of a day. I don't think you — no, you did not tell me to keep it secret. A word from you would have been enough. I was in extremity."

Dacier threw his hands up and broke away. He had an impulse to dash from the room, to get a breath of different air. He stood at the window, observing tradesmen's carts, housemaids, blank doors, dogs, a beggar fifer. Her last words recurred to him. He turned: "You were in extremity, you said. What is the meaning of that? What extremity?"

Her large dark eyes flashed powerlessly; her shape appeared to have narrowed; her tongue, too, was a feeble penitent.

"You ask a creature to recall her acts of insanity."

"There must be some signification in your words, I suppose."

"I will tell you as clearly as I can. You have the right to be my judge. I was in extremity — that is, I saw no means . . . I could not write : it was ruin coming."

"Ah ? — you took payment for playing spy ? "

"I fancied I could retrieve . . . Now I see the folly, the baseness. I was blind."

"Then you sold me to a journalist for money ? "

The intolerable scourge fetched a stifled scream from her and drove her pacing, but there was no escape; she returned to meet it.

The room was a cage to both of them, and every word of either was a sting.

"Percy, I did not imagine he would use it — make use of it as he has done."

"Not ? And when he paid for it ? "

"I fancied it would be merely of general service — if any."

"Distributed ; I see : not leading to the exposure of the communicant ! "

"You are harsh ; but I would not have you milder."

The meekness of such a mischief-doer was revolting and called for the lash.

"Do me the favour to name the sum. I am curious to learn what my imbecility was counted worth."

"No sum was named."

"Have I been bought for a song ? "

"It was a suggestion — no definite . . . nothing stipulated."

"You were to receive money ! "

"Leave me a bit of veiling ! No, you shall behold me the thing I am. Listen . . . I was poor . . ."

"You might have applied to me."

"For money ! That I could not do."

"Better than betraying me, believe me."

"I had no thought of betraying. I hope I could have died rather than consciously betray."

"Money ! My whole fortune was at your disposal."

"I was beset with debts, unable to write, and, last night

when you left me, abject. It seemed to me that you disrespected me . . ."

"Last night!" Dacier cried with lashing emphasis.

"It is evident to me that I have the reptile in me, Percy.
Or else I am subject to lose my reason. I went . . . I
went like a bullet: I cannot describe it; I was mad. I
need a strong arm, I want help. I am given to think that
I do my best and can be independent; I break down. I
went blindly — now I see it — for the chance of recovering
my position, as the gambler casts; and he wins or loses.
With me it is the soul that is lost. No exact sum was
named; thousands were hinted."

"You are hardly practical on points of business."

"I was insane."

"I think you said you slept well after it," Dacier
remarked.

"I had so little the idea of having done evilly, that I
slept without a dream."

He shrugged: — the consciences of women are such
smooth deeps, or running shallows.

"I have often wondered how your newspaper men got
their information," he said, and muttered: "Money —
women!" adding: "Idiots to prime them! And I one of
the leaky vessels! Well, we learn. I have been rather
astonished at times of late at the scraps of secret knowledge displayed by Tonans. If he flourishes his thousands!
The wonder is, he does n't corrupt the Ministers' wives.
Perhaps he does. Marriage will become a danger-sign to
Parliamentary members. Foreign women do these tricks
. . . women of a well-known stamp. It is now a full year, I
think, since I began to speak to you of secret matters — and
congratulated myself, I recollect, on your thirst for them."

"Percy, if you suspect that I have uttered one word
before last night, you are wrong. I cannot paint my temptation or my loss of sense last night. Previously I was
blameless. I thirsted, yes; but in the hope of helping
you."

He looked at her. She perceived how glitteringly loveless his eyes had grown. It was her punishment; and
though the enamoured woman's heart protested it excessive, she accepted it.

"I can never trust you again," he said.

"I fear you will not," she replied.

His coming back to her after the departure of the guests last night shone on him in splendid colours of single-minded loverlike devotion. "I came to speak to my own heart. I thought it would give you pleasure; thought I could trust you utterly. I had not the slightest conception I was imperilling my honour! . . ."

He stopped. Her bloodless fixed features revealed an intensity of anguish that checked him. Only her mouth, a little open for the sharp breath, appeared dumbly beseeching. Her large eyes met his like steel to steel, as of one who would die fronting the weapon.

He strangled a loathsome inclination to admire.

"So good bye," he said.

She moved her lips.

He said no more. In half a minute he was gone.

To her it was the plucking of life out of her breast.

She pressed her hands where heart had been. The pallor and cold of death took her body.

CHAPTER XXXV

REVEALS HOW THE TRUE HEROINE OF ROMANCE COMES FINALLY TO HER TIME OF TRIUMPH

THE shutting of her house-door closed for Dacier that woman's history in connection with himself. He set his mind on the consequences of the act of folly — the trusting a secret to a woman. All were possibly not so bad: none should be trusted.

The air of the street fanned him agreeably as he revolved the horrible project of confession to the man who had put faith in him. Particulars might be asked. She would be unnamed, but an imagination of the effect of naming her placarded a notorious woman in fresh paint : two members of the same family her victims !

And last night, no later than last night, he had swung round at this very corner of the street to give her the fullest proof of his affection. He beheld a dupe trotting into a carefully-laid pitfall. She had him by the generosity of his confidence in her. Moreover, the recollection of her recent feeble phrasing, when she stood convicted of the treachery, when a really clever woman would have developed her resources, led him to doubt her being so finely gifted. She was just clever enough to hoodwink. He attributed the dupery to a trick of imposing the idea of her virtue upon men. Attracted by her good looks and sparkle, they entered the circle of her charm, became delightfully intimate, suffered a rebuff, and were from that time prepared to serve her purpose. How many other wretched dupes had she dangling? He spied at Westlake, spied at Redworth, at old Lord Larrian, at Lord Dannisburgh, at Arthur Rhodes, dozens. Old and young were alike to her if she saw an end to be gained by keeping them hooked. Tonans too, and Whitmonby. Newspaper editors were especially serviceable. Perhaps "a young Minister of State" held the foremost rank in that respect: if completely duped and squeezeable, he produced more substantial stuff.

The background of ice in Dacier's composition was brought to the front by his righteous contempt of her treachery. No explanation of it would have appeased him. She was guilty, and he condemned her. She stood condemned by all the evil likely to ensue from her misdeed. Scarcely had he left her house last night when she was away to betray him! — He shook her from him without a pang. Crediting her with the one merit she had — that of not imploring for mercy — he the more easily shook her off. Treacherous, she had not proved theatrical. So there was no fuss in putting out her light, and it was done. He was justified by the brute facts. Honourable, courteous, kindly gentleman, highly civilized, an excellent citizen and a patriot, he was icy at an outrage to his principles, and in the dominion of Love a sultan of the bow-string and chopper period, sovereignly endowed to stretch a finger for the scimitared Mesrour to make the erring woman head and trunk with one blow: and away with those remnants! This internally he did. Enough that the brute facts justified him.

St. James's park was crossed, and the grass of the Green park, to avoid inquisitive friends. He was obliged to walk; exercise, action of any sort, was imperative, and but for some engagement he would have gone to his fencing-rooms for a bout with the master. He remembered his engagement and grew doubly embittered. He had absurdly pledged himself to lunch with Quintin Manx; that was, to pretend to eat while submitting to be questioned by a political dullard strong on his present right to overhaul and rail at his superiors. The house was one of a block along the North-Western line of Hyde park. He kicked at the subjection to go there, but a promise was binding, though he gave it when stunned. He could have silenced Mr. Manx with the posing interrogation: Why have I so long consented to put myself at the mercy of a bore? For him, he could not answer it, though Manx, as leader of the Shipping interest, was influential. The man had to be endured, like other doses in politics.

Dacier did not once think of the great ship-owner's niece till Miss Constance Asper stepped into her drawing-room to welcome him. She was an image of repose to his mind. The calm pure outline of her white features refreshed him as the Alps the Londoner newly alighted at Berne; smoke, wrangle, the wrestling city's wickedness, behind him.

"My uncle is very disturbed," she said. "Is the news — if I am not very indiscreet in inquiring?"

"I have a practice of never paying attention to newspaper articles," Dacier replied.

"I am only affected by living with one who does," Miss Asper observed, and the lofty isolation of her head above politics gave her a moral attractiveness in addition to physical beauty. Her water-colour sketches were on her uncle's walls: the beautiful in nature claimed and absorbed her. She dressed with a pretty rigour, a lovely simplicity, picturesque of the nunnery. She looked indeed a high-born young lady-abbess.

"It's a dusty game for ladies," Dacier said, abhorring the women defiled by it.

And when one thinks of the desire of men to worship women, there is a pathos in a man's discovery of the fair young creature undefiled by any interest in public affairs, virginal amid her bower's environments.

The angelical beauty of a virgin mind and person captivated him, by contrast. His natural taste was to admire it, shunning the lures and tangles of the women on high seas, notably the married: who, by the way, contrive to ensnare us through wonderment at a cleverness caught from their traffic with the masculine world: often — if we did but know! — a parrot repetition of the last male visitor's remarks. But that which the fair maiden speaks, though it may be simple, is her own.

She too is her own: or vowed but to one. She is on all sides impressive in purity. The world worships her as its perfect pearl: and we are brought refreshfully to acknowledge that the world is right.

By contrast, the white radiation of Innocence distinguished Constance Asper celestially. As he was well aware, she had long preferred him — the reserved among many pleading pressing suitors. Her steady faithfulness had fed on the poorest crumbs.

He ventured to express the hope that she was well.

"Yes," she answered, with eyelids lifted softly to thank him for his concern in so humble a person.

"You look a little pale," he said.

She coloured like a sea-water shell. "I am inclined to paleness by nature."

Her uncle disturbed them. Lunch was ready. He apologized for the absence of Mrs. Markland, a maternal aunt of Constance, who kept house for them. Quintin Manx fell upon the meats, and then upon the Minister. Dacier found himself happily surprised by the accession of an appetite. He mentioned it, to escape from the worrying of his host, as unusual with him at midday: and Miss Asper, supporting him in that effort, said benevolently: "Gentlemen should eat; they have so many fatigues and troubles." She herself did not like to be seen eating in public. Her lips opened to the morsels, as with a bird's bill, though with none of the pecking eagerness we complacently observe in poultry.

"But now, I say, positively, how about that article?" said Quintin.

Dacier visibly winced, and Constance immediately said: "Oh! spare us politics, dear uncle."

Her intercession was without avail, but by contrast with the woman implicated in the horrible article, it was a carol of the seraphs.

"Come, you can say whether there's anything in it," Dacier's host pushed him.

"I should not say it if I could," he replied.

The mild sweetness of Miss Asper's look encouraged him.

He was touched to the quick by hearing her say: "You ask for Cabinet secrets, uncle. All secrets are holy, but secrets of State are under a seal next to divine."

Next to divine! She was the mouthpiece of his ruling principle.

"I'm not prying into secrets," Quintin persisted; "all I want to know is, whether there's any foundation for that article — all London's boiling about it, I can tell you — or it's only newspaper's humbug."

"Clearly the oracle for you is the Editor's office," rejoined Dacier.

"A pretty sort of answer I should get."

"It would at least be complimentary."

"How do you mean?"

"The net was cast for you — and the sight of a fish in it!"

Miss Asper almost laughed. "Have you heard the choir at St. Catherine's?" she asked.

Dacier had not. He repented of his worldliness, and drinking persuasive claret, said he would go to hear it next Sunday.

"Do," she murmured.

"Well, you seem to be a pair against me," her uncle grumbled. "Anyhow I think it's important. People have been talking for some time, and I don't want to be taken unawares; I won't be a yoked ox, mind you."

"Have you been sketching lately?" Dacier asked Miss Asper.

She generally filled a book in the autumn, she said.

"May I see it?"

"If you wish."

They had a short tussle with her uncle and escaped. He

was conducted to a room midway upstairs: an heiress's conception of a saintly little room; and more impressive in purity, indeed it was, than a saint's, with the many cruci- fixes, gold and silver emblems, velvet prie-Dieu chairs, jewel-clasped sacred volumes: every invitation to meditate in luxury on an ascetic religiousness.

She depreciated her sketching powers. "I am impatient with my imperfections. I am therefore doomed not to advance."

"On the contrary, that is the state guaranteeing ultimate excellence," he said, much disposed to drone about it.

She sighed: "I fear not."

He turned the leaves, comparing her modesty with the performance. The third of the leaves was a subject in- stantly recognized by him. It represented the place he had inherited from Lord Dannisburgh.

He named it.

She smiled: "You are good enough to see a likeness? My aunt and I were passing it last October, and I waited for a day, to sketch."

"You have taken it from my favourite point of view."

"I am glad."

"How much I should like a copy!"

"If you will accept that?"

"I could not rob you."

"I can make a duplicate."

"The look of the place pleases you?"

"Oh! yes; the pines behind it; the sweet little village church; even the appearance of the rustics; — it is all im- pressively old English. I suppose you are very seldom there?"

"Does it look like a home to you?"

"No place more!"

"I feel the loneliness."

"Where I live I feel no loneliness!"

"You have heavenly messengers near you."

"They do not always come."

"Would you consent to make the place less lonely to me?"

Her bosom rose. In deference to her maidenly under- standing, she gazed inquiringly.

"If you love it!" said he.

"The place?" she said, looking soft at the possessor.

"Constance!"

"Is it true?"

"As you yourself. Could it be other than true? This hand is mine?"

"Oh! Percy."

Borrowing the world's poetry to describe them, the long prayed-for Summer enveloped the melting snows.

So the recollection of Diana's watch beside his uncle's death-bed was wiped out. Ay, and the hissing of her treachery silenced. This maidenly hand put him at peace with the world, instead of his defying it for a worthless woman — who could not do better than accept the shelter of her husband's house, as she ought to be told, if her friends wished her to save her reputation.

Dacier made his way downstairs to Quintin Manx, by whom he was hotly congratulated and informed of the extent of the young lady's fortune: on the strength of which it was expected that he would certainly speak a private word in elucidation of that newspaper article.

"I know nothing of it," said Dacier, but promised to come and dine.

Alone in her happiness Constance Asper despatched various brief notes under her gold-symbolled crest to sisterly friends; one to Lady Wathin, containing the single line: —

"Your prophesy is confirmed."

Dacier was comfortably able to face his Club after the excitement of a proposal, with a bride on his hands. He was assaulted concerning the article, and he parried capitally. Say that her lips were rather cold: at any rate, they invigorated him. Her character was guaranteed — not the hazy idea of a dupe. And her fortune would be enormous; a speculation merely due to worldly prudence and prospective ambition.

At the dinner-table of four, in the evening, conversation would have seemed dull to him, by contrast, had it not been for the presiding grace of his bride, whose habitually eminent feminine air of superiority to the repast was throned by her appreciative receptiveness of his looks and utterances. Before leaving her, he won her consent to a very early marriage; on the plea of a possibly approaching Session, and also that they had waited long. The consent, notwithstanding the hurry of preparations it involved, besides the annihilation of her desire to meditate on so solemn a change in her life and savour the congratulation of her friends and have the choir of St. Catherine's rigorously drilled in her favourite anthems, was beautifully yielded to the pressure of circumstances.

There lay on his table at night a letter; a bulky letter. No need to tear it open for sight of the signature: the superscription was redolent of that betraying woman. He tossed it unopened into the fire.

As it was thick, it burned sullenly, discolouring his name on the address, as she had done, and still offering him a last chance of viewing the contents. She fought on the consuming fire to have her exculpation heard.

But was she not a shameless traitor? She had caught him by his love of his country and hope to serve it. She had wound into his heart to bleed him of all he knew and sell the secrets for money. A wonderful sort of eloquence lay there, on those coals, no doubt. He felt a slight movement of curiosity to glance at two or three random sentences: very slight. And why read them now? They were valueless to him, mere outcries. He judged her by the brute facts. She and her slowly-consuming letter were of a common blackness. Moreover, to read them when he was plighted to another woman would be senseless. In the discovery of her baseness, she had made a poor figure. Doubtless during the afternoon she had trimmed her intuitive Belial art of making "the worse appear the better cause:" queer to peruse, and instructive in an unprofitable department of knowledge — the tricks of the sex.

He said to himself, with little intuition of the popular taste: She wouldn't be a bad heroine of Romance! He said it derisively of the Romantic. But the right worshipful heroine of Romance was the front-face female picture he had won for his walls. Poor Diana was the flecked heroine of Reality: not always the same; not impeccable; not an ignorant-innocent, nor a guileless: good under good leading; devoted to the death in a grave crisis; often wrestling with her terrestrial nature nobly; and a growing soul; but not one whose purity was carved in marble for the assurance to an Englishman that his possession of the changeless thing defies time and his fellows, is the pillar of his home and universally enviable. Your fair one of Romance cannot suffer a mishap without a plotting villain, perchance many of them, to wreak the dread iniquity: she cannot move without him; she is the marble block, and if she is to have a feature, he is the sculptor; she depends on him for life, and her human history at least is married to him far more than to the rescuing lover. No wonder, then, that men should find her thrice cherishable featureless, or with the most moderate possible indication of a countenance. Thousands of the excellent simple creatures do; and every reader of her tale. On the contrary, the heroine of Reality is that woman whom you have met or heard of once in your course of years, and very probably despised for bearing in her composition the motive principle; at best, you say, a singular mixture of good and bad; anything but the feminine ideal of man. Feature to some excess, you think, distinguishes her. Yet she furnishes not any of the sweet sensual excitement pertaining to her spotless rival pursued by villainy. She knocks at the doors of the mind, and the mind must open to be interested in her. Mind and heart must be wide open to excuse her sheer descent from the pure ideal of man.

Dacier's wandering reflections all came back in crowds to the judicial Bench of the Black Cap. He felt finely, apart from the treason, that her want of money degraded her: him too, by contact. Money she might have had to any extent: upon application for it, of course. How was he to imagine that she wanted money! Smilingly as she welcomed him and his friends, entertaining them royally, he was bound to think she had means. A decent propriety bound him not to think of the matter at all. He naturally supposed she was capable of conducting her affairs. And — money! It soiled his memory: though the hour at Rovio was rather pretty, and the scene at Copsley touching: other times also, short glimpses of the woman were taking. The flood of her treachery effaced them. And why reflect? Constance called to him to look her way.

Diana's letter died hard. The corners were burnt to

black tissue, with an edge or two of discoloured paper. A small frayed central heap still resisted, and in kindness to the necessity for privacy, he impressed the fire-tongs to complete the execution. After which he went to his desk and worked, under the presidency of Constance.

CHAPTER XXXVI

IS CONCLUSIVE AS TO THE HEARTLESSNESS OF WOMEN WITH BRAINS

HYMENÆAL rumours are those which might be backed to run a victorious race with the tale of evil fortune ; and clearly for the reason that man's livelier half is ever alert to speed them. They travel with an astonishing celerity over the land, like flames of the dry beacon-faggots of old time in announcement of the invader or a conquest, gathering as they go : wherein, to say nothing of their vastly wider range, they surpass the electric wires. Man's nuptial half is kindlingly concerned in the launch of a new couple ; it is the business of the fair sex : and man himself (very strangely, but nature quickens him still) lends a not unfavouring eye to the preparations of the matrimonial vessel for its oily descent into the tides, where billows will soon be rising, captain and mate soon discussing the fateful question of who is commander. We consent, it appears, to hope again for mankind ; here is another chance ! Or else, assuming the happiness of the pair, that pomp of ceremonial, contrasted with the little wind-blown candle they carry between them, catches at our weaker fibres. After so many ships have foundered, some keel up, like poisoned fish, at the first drink of water, it is a gallant spectacle, let us avow ; and either the world perpetuating it is heroical or nature incorrigible in the species. Marriages are unceasing. Friends do it, and enemies ; the unknown contractors of this engagement, or armistice, inspire an interest. It certainly is both exciting and comforting to hear that man and woman are ready to join in a mutual affirmative, say Yes together again. It sounds like the end of the war.

The proclamation of the proximate marriage of a young
Minister of State and the greatest heiress of her day; —
notoriously "*The* young Minister of State" of a famous
book written by the beautiful, now writhing, woman madly
enamoured of him — and the heiress whose dowry could
purchase a Duchy; this was a note to make the gossips of
England leap from their beds at the midnight hour and
wag tongues in the market-place. It did away with the
political hubbub over the Tonans article, and let it noise
abroad like nonsense. The Hon. Percy Dacier espouses
Miss Asper; and she rescues him from the snares of a siren,
he her from the toils of the Papists. She would have gone
over to them, she was going when, luckily for the Protest-
ant Faith, Percy Dacier intervened with his proposal.
Town and country buzzed the news; and while that dreary
League trumpeted about the business of the nation, a people
suddenly become Oriental chattered of nothing but the
blissful union to be celebrated in princely state, with every
musical accessory, short of Operatic.

Lady Wathin was an active agent in this excitement.
The excellent woman enjoyed marriages of High Life:
which, as there is presumably wealth to support them, are
manifestly under *sanction:* and a marriage that she could
consider one of her own contrivance, had a delicate flavour
of a marriage in the family; not quite equal to the seeing
a dear daughter of her numerous progeny conducted to
the altar, but excelling it in the pomp that bids the heavens
open. She and no other spread the tidings of Miss Asper's
debating upon the step to Rome at the very instant of
Percy Dacier's declaration of his love; — and it was a
beautiful struggle, that of the half-dedicated nun and her
deep-rooted earthly passion, love prevailing! She sent
word of to Lady Dunstane: "You know the interest I
have always taken in dear Constance Asper," &c.; inviting
her to come on a visit a week before the end of the month,
that she might join in the ceremony of a wedding "likely
to be the grandest of our time." Pitiful though it was, to
think of the bridal pair having but eight or ten days at
the outside, for a honeymoon, the beauty of their "mutual
devotion to duty" was urged by Lady Wathin upon all
hearers.

Lady Dunstane declined the invitation. She waited to hear from her friend, and the days went by; she could only sorrow for her poor Tony, divining her state. However little of wrong in the circumstances, they imposed a silence on her decent mind, and no conceivable shape of writing would transmit condolences. She waited, with a dull heart-ache : by no means grieving at Dacier's engagement to the heiress; until Redworth animated her, as the bearer of rather startling intelligence, indirectly relating to the soul she loved. An accident in the street had befallen Mr. Warwick. Redworth wanted to know whether Diana should be told of it, though he had no particulars to give; and some-what to his disappointment, Lady Dunstane said she would write. She delayed, thinking the accident might not be serious; and the information of it to Diana surely would be so. Next day at noon her visitor was Lady Wathin, evidently perturbed and anxious to say more than she dared : but she received no assistance. After beating the air in every direction, especially dwelling on the fond reciprocal affection of the two devoted lovers, to be united within three days' time, Lady Wathin said at last : "And is it not shocking ! I talk of a marriage and am appalled by a death. That poor man died last night in the hospital. I mean poor Mr. Warwick. He was recovering, getting strong and well, and he was knocked down at a street-crossing and died last night. It is a warning to us ! "

"Mr. Redworth happened to hear of it at his Club, near which the accident occurred, and he called at the hospital. Mr. Warwick was then alive," said Lady Dunstane; add-ing : "Well, if prevention is better than cure, as we hear ! Accidents are the specific for averting the maladies of age, which are a certain crop ! "

Lady Wathin's eyelids worked and her lips shut fast at the coldhearted remark void of meaning.

She sighed. "So ends a life of misery, my dear ! "

"You are compassionate."

"I hope so. But . . . Indeed I must speak, if you will let me. I think of the living."

Lady Dunstane widened her eyes. "Of Mrs. Warwick ? "

"She has now the freedom she desired. I think of others. Forgive me, but Constance Asper is to me as a daughter. I have perhaps no grounds for any apprehension. Love so ardent, so sincere, was never shown by bridegroom elect : and it is not extraordinary to those acquainted with dear Constance. But one may be a worshipped saint and experience defection. The terrible stories one hears of a power of fascination almost . . . !" Lady Wathin hung for the word.

"Infernal," said Lady Dunstane, whose brows had been bent inquiringly. "Have no fear. The freedom you allude to will not be used to interfere with any entertainment in prospect. It was *freedom* my friend desired. Now that her jewel is restored to her, she is not the person to throw it away, be sure. And pray, drop the subject."

"One may rely . . . you think ? "

"Oh ! Oh ! "

"This release coming just before the wedding ! . . ."

"I should hardly suppose the man to be the puppet you depict, or indicate."

"It is because men — so many — are not puppets that one is conscious of alarm."

"Your previous remark," said Lady Dunstane, "sounded superstitious. Your present one has an antipodal basis. But, as for your alarm, check it : and spare me further. My friend has acknowledged powers. Considering that she does not use them, you should learn to respect her."

Lady Wathin bowed stiffly. She refused to partake of lunch, having, she said, satisfied her conscience by the performance of a duty and arranged with her flyman to catch a train. Her cousin Lady Dunstane smiled loftily at everything she uttered, and she felt that if a woman like this Mrs. Warwick could put division between blood-relatives, she could do worse, and was to be dreaded up to the hour of the nuptials.

"I meant no harm in coming," she said, at the shaking of hands.

"No, no ; I understand," said her hostess : "you are hen-hearted over your adopted brood. The situation is perceptible and your intention creditable."

As one of the good women of the world, Lady Wathin in departing was indignant at the tone and dialect of a younger woman not modestly concealing her possession of the larger brain. Brains in women she both dreaded and detested; she believed them to be devilish. Here were instances: — they had driven poor Sir Lukin to evil courses, and that poor Mr. Warwick straight under the wheels of a cab. Sir Lukin's name was trotting in public with a naughty Mrs. Fryar-Gunnett's: Mrs. Warwick might still trim her arts to baffle the marriage. Women with brains, moreover, are all heartless: they have no pity for distress, no horror of catastrophes, no joy in the happiness of the deserving. Brains in men advance a household to station; but brains in women divide it and are the wrecking of society. Fortunately Lady Wathin knew she could rally a powerful moral contingent, the aptitude of which for a one-minded cohesion enabled it to crush those fractional daughters of mischief. She was a really good woman of the world, heading a multitude; the same whom you are accustomed to hear exalted; lucky in having had a guided girlhood, a thick-curtained prudence; and in having stock in the moral funds, shares in the sentimental tramways. Wherever the world laid its hoards or ran its lines, she was found, and forcible enough to be eminent; though at fixed hours of the day, even as she washed her hands, she abjured worldliness: a performance that cleansed her. If she did not make morality appear loveable to the objects of her dislike, it was owing to her want of brains to see the origin, nature and right ends of morality. But a world yet more deficient than she, esteemed her cordially for being a bulwark of the present edifice; which looks a solid structure when the microscope is not applied to its components.

Supposing Percy Dacier a dishonourable tattler as well as an icy lover, and that Lady Wathin, through his bride, had become privy to the secret between him and Diana? There is reason to think that she would have held it in terror over the baneful woman, but not have persecuted her: for she was by no means the active malignant of theatrical plots. No, she would have charged it upon the possession of brains by women, and have had a further motive for inciting the potent dignitary her husband to employ his authority to repress the sex's exercise of those fell weapons, hurtful alike to them and all coming near them.

So extreme was her dread of Mrs. Warwick, that she

drove from the London railway station to see Constance and be reassured by her tranquil aspect.

Sweet Constance and her betrothed Percy were together, examining a missal.

Lady Dunstane despatched a few words of the facts to Diana. She hoped to hear from her; rather hoped, for the moment, not to see her. No answer came. The great day of the nuptials came and passed. She counted on her husband's appearance the next morning, as the good gentleman made a point of visiting her, to entertain the wife he adored, whenever he had a wallet of gossip that would overlay the blank of his absence. He had been to the church of the wedding — he did not say with whom: — all the world was there; and he rapturously described the ceremony, stating that it set women weeping and caused him to behave like a fool.

"You are impressionable," said his wife.

He murmured something in praise of the institution of marriage — when celebrated impressively, it seemed.

"Tony calls the social world 'the theatre of appetites,' as we have it at present," she said; "and the world at a wedding is, one may reckon, in the second act of the hungry tragi-comedy."

"Yes, there's the breakfast," Sir Lukin assented. Mrs. Fryar-Gunnett was much more intelligible to him: in fact, quite so, as to her speech.

Emma's heart now yearned to her Tony. Consulting her strength, she thought she might journey to London, and on the third morning after the Dacier-Asper marriage, she started.

Diana's door was open to Arthur Rhodes when Emma reached it.

"Have you seen her?" she asked him.

His head shook dolefully. "Mrs. Warwick is unwell; she has been working too hard."

"You also, I'm afraid."

"No." He could deny that, whatever the look of him.

"Come to me at Copsley soon," said she, entering to Danvers in the passage.

"My mistress is upstairs, my lady," said Danvers. "She is lying on her bed."

"She is ill?"

"She has been lying on her bed ever since."

"Since what?" Lady Dunstane spoke sharply.

Danvers retrieved her indiscretion. "Since she heard of the accident, my lady."

"Take my name to her. Or no: I can venture."

"I am not allowed to go in and speak to her. You will find the room quite dark, my lady, and very cold. It is her command. My mistress will not let me light the fire; and she has not eaten or drunk of anything since. . . . She will die, if you do not persuade her to take nourishment: a little, for a beginning. It wants the beginning."

Emma went upstairs, thinking of the enigmatical maid, that she must be a good soul after all. Diana's bedroom door was opened slowly.

"You will not be able to see at first, my lady," Danvers whispered. "The bed is to the left, and a chair. I would bring in a candle, but it hurts her eyes. She forbids it."

Emma stepped in. The chill thick air of the unlighted London room was cavernous. She almost forgot the beloved of her heart in the thought that a living woman had been lying here more than two days and nights, fasting. The proof of an uttermost misery revived the circumstances within her to render her friend's presence in this desert of darkness credible. She found the bed by touch, silently, and distinguished a dark heap on the bed; she heard no breathing. She sat and listened; then she stretched her hand and met her Tony's. It lay open. It was the hand of a drowned woman.

Shutters and curtains and the fireless grate gave the room an appalling likeness to the vaults.

So like to the home of death it seemed, that in a few minutes the watcher had lost count of time and kept but a wormy memory of the daylight. She dared not speak, for some fear of startling; for the worse fear of never getting answer. Tony's hand was lifeless. Her clasp of it struck no warmth.

She stung herself with bitter reproaches for having let common mundane sentiments, worthy of a Lady Wathin, bar her instant offer of her bosom to the beloved who suffered in this depth of mortal agony. Tony's love of

a man, as she should have known, would be wrought of
the elements of our being: when other women named Happiness, she said Life; in division, Death. Her body lying
still upon the bed here was a soul borne onward by the
river of Death.

The darkness gave sight after a while, like a curtain
lifting on a veil: the dead light of the underworld. Tony
lay with her face up, her underlip dropped; straight from
head to feet. The outline of her face, without hue of it,
could be seen: sign of the hapless women that have souls
in love. Hateful love of men! Emma thought, and was
moved to feel at the wrist for her darling's pulse. He has
killed her! the thought flashed, as, with pangs chilling
her frame, the pressure at the wrist continued insensible
of the faintest beat. She clasped it, trembling, in pain to
stop an outcry.

"It is Emmy," said the voice.

Emma's heart sprang to heaven on a rush of thanks.

"My Tony," she breathed softly.

She hung for a further proof of life in the motionless
body. "Tony!" she said.

The answer was at her hand, a thread-like return of her
clasp.

"It is Emmy come to stay with you, never to leave
you."

The thin still answer was at her hand a moment; the
fingers fell away. A deep breath was taken twice to say:
"Don't talk to me."

Emma retained the hand. She was warned not to press
it by the deadness following its effort to reply.

But Tony lived; she had given proof of life. Over this
little wavering taper in the vaults Emma cowered, cherishing the hand, silently hoping for the voice.

It came: "Winter."

"It is a cold winter, Tony."

"My dear will be cold."

"I will light the fire."

Emma lost no time in deciding to seek the match-box.
The fire was lit and it flamed; it seemed a revival in the
room. Coming back to the bedside, she discerned her
Tony's lack-lustre large dark eyes and her hollow cheeks:

her mouth open to air as to the drawing-in of a sword; rather as to the releaser than the sustainer. Her feet were on the rug her maid had placed to cover them. Emma leaned across the bed to put them to her breast, beneath her fur mantle, and held them there despite the half-animate tug of the limbs and the shaft of iciness they sent to her very heart. When she had restored them to some warmth, she threw aside her bonnet and lying beside Tony, took her in her arms, heaving now and then a deep sigh.

She kissed her cheek.

"It is Emmy."

"Kiss her."

"I have no strength."

Emma laid her face on the lips. They were cold; even the breath between them cold.

"Has Emmy been long . . . ?"

"Here, dear? I think so. I am with my darling."

Tony moaned. The warmth and the love were bringing back her anguish.

She said: "I have been happy. It is not hard to go."

Emma strained to her. "Tony will wait for her soul's own soul to go, the two together."

There was a faint convulsion in the body. "If I cry, I shall go in pain."

"You are in Emmy's arms, my beloved."

Tony's eyes closed for forgetfulness under that sensation. A tear ran down from her, but the pain was lax and neighboured sleep, like the pleasure.

So passed the short winter day, little spoken.

Then Emma bethought her of a way of leading Tony to take food, and she said: "I shall stay with you; I shall send for clothes; I am rather hungry. Don't stir, dear. I will be mistress of the house."

She went below to the kitchen, where a few words in the ear of a Frenchwoman were sufficient to waken immediate comprehension of what was wanted, and smart service: within ten minutes an appetizing bouillon sent its odour over the bedroom. Tony, days back, had said her last to the act of eating; but Emma sipping at the spoon and expressing satisfaction, was a pleasant picture. The bouillon smelt pleasantly.

"Your servants love you," Emma said.

"Ah, poor good souls."

"They crowded up to me to hear of you. Madame of course at the first word was off to her pots. And we English have the habit of calling ourselves the practical people! — This bouillon is consummate. — However, we have the virtues of barbarians; we can love and serve for love. I never tasted anything so good. I could become a glutton."

"Do," said Tony.

"I should be ashamed to ' drain the bowl ' all to myself: a solitary toper is a horrid creature, unless he makes a song of it."

"Emmy makes a song of it to me."

"But ' pledge me ' is a noble saying, when you think of humanity's original hunger for the whole. It is there that our civilizing commenced, and I am particularly fond of hearing the call. It is grandly historic. So pledge me, Tony. We two can feed from one spoon; it is a closer bond than the loving cup. I want you just to taste it and excuse my gluttony."

Tony murmured, "No." The spoon was put to her mouth. She sighed to resist. The stronger will compelled her to move her lips. Emma fed her as a child, and nature sucked for life.

The first effect was a gush of tears.

Emma lay with her that night, when the patient was the better sleeper. But during the night at intervals she had the happiness of feeling Tony's hand travelling to make sure of her.

CHAPTER XXXVII

AN EXHIBITION OF SOME CHAMPIONS OF THE STRICKEN LADY

CLOSE upon the hour of ten every morning the fortuitous meeting of two gentlemen at Mrs. Warwick's housedoor was a signal for punctiliously stately greetings, the salutation of the raised hat and a bow of the head from a position of military erectness, followed by the remark: "I trust you are well, sir:" to which the reply: "I am very well, sir, and trust you are the same," was deemed a complimentary fulfilment of their mutual obligation in presence. Mr. Sullivan Smith's initiative imparted this exercise of formal manners to Mr. Arthur Rhodes, whose renewed appearance, at the minute of his own arrival, he viewed, as he did not conceal, with a disappointed and a reproving eye. The inquiry after the state of Mrs. Warwick's health having received its tolerably comforting answer from the footman, they left their cards in turn, then descended the doorsteps, faced for the performance of the salute, and departed their contrary ways.

The pleasing intelligence refreshed them one morning, that they would be welcomed by Lady Dunstane. Thereupon Mr. Sullivan Smith wheeled about to Mr. Arthur Rhodes and observed to him: "Sir, I might claim, by right of seniority, to be the foremost of us two in offering my respects to the lady, but the way is open to you."

"Sir," said Mr. Arthur Rhodes, "permit me to defer to your many superior titles to that distinction."

"The honour, sir, lies rather in the bestowing than in the taking."

"I venture to think, sir, that though I cannot speak pure Castilian, I require no lesson from a Grandee of Spain in acknowledging the dues of my betters."

"I will avow myself conquered, sir, by your overpowering condescension," said Mr. Sullivan Smith; "and I entreat you to ascribe my acceptance of your brief retirement to the urgent character of the business I have at heart."

He laid his fingers on the panting spot, and bowed.

Mr. Arthur Rhodes, likewise bowing, deferentially fell to rearward.

"If I mistake not," said the Irish gentleman, "I am indebted to Mr. Rhodes; and we have been joint participators in the hospitality of Mrs. Warwick's table."

The English gentleman replied: "It was there that I first had the pleasure of an acquaintance which is graven on my memory, as the words of the wise king on tablets of gold and silver."

Mr. Sullivan Smith gravely smiled at the unwonted match he had found in ceremonious humour, in Saxonland, and saying: "I shall not long detain you, Mr. Rhodes," he passed through the doorway.

Arthur waited for him, pacing up and down, for a quarter of an hour, when a totally different man reappeared in the same person, and was the Sullivan Smith of the rosy beaming features and princely heartiness. He was accosted: "Now, my dear boy, it's your turn to try if you have a chance, and good luck go with ye. I've said what I could on your behalf, for you're one of ten thousand in this country, you are."

Mr. Sullivan Smith had solemnified himself to proffer a sober petition within the walls of the newly widowed lady's house; namely, for nothing less than that sweet lady's now unfettered hand: and it had therefore been perfectly natural to him, until his performance ended with the destruction of his hopes, to deliver himself in the high Castilian manner. Quite unexpected, however, was the reciprocal loftiness of tone spontaneously adopted by the young English squire, for whom, in consequence, he conceived a cordial relish; and as he paced in the footsteps of Arthur, anxious to quiet his curiosity by hearing how it had fared with one whom he had to suppose the second applicant, he kept ejaculating: "Not a bit! The fellow can't be Saxon! And she had a liking for him. She's nigh coming of the age when a woman takes to the chicks. Better he than another, if it's to be any one. For he's got fun in him; he carries his own condiments, instead of borrowing from the popular castors, as is their way over here. But I might have known there's always sure to

be salt and savour in the man she covers with her wing.
Excepting, if you please, my dear lady, a bad shot you
made at a rascal cur, no more worthy of you than Beelze-
bub of Paradise. No matter! The daughters of Erin
must share the fate of their mother Isle, that their tears
may shine in the burst of sun to follow. For personal and
patriotic motives, I would have cheered her and been like
a wild ass combed and groomed and tamed by the adorable
creature. But her friend says there's not a whisk of a
chance for me, and I must roam the desert, kicking up,
and worshipping the star I hail brightest. They know me
not, who think I can't worship. Why, what were I without my star? At best a pickled porker."

Sullivan Smith became aware of a ravishing melodious-
ness in the soliloquy, as well as a clean resemblance in the
simile. He would certainly have proceeded to improvize
impassioned verse, if he had not seen Arthur Rhodes on
the pavement. "So, here's the boy. Query, the face he
wears."

"How kind of you to wait," said Arthur.

"We'll call it sympathy, for convenience," rejoined
Sullivan Smith. "Well, and what next?"

"You know as much as I do. Thank heaven, she is
recovering."

"Is that all?"

"Why, what more?"

Arthur was jealously inspected.

"You look open-hearted, my dear boy." Sullivan Smith
blew the sound of a reflective ahem. "Excuse me for
cornemusing in your company," he said. "But seriously,
there was only one thing to pardon your hurrying to the
lady's door at such a season, when the wind tells tales to
the world. She's down with a cold, you know."

"An influenza," said Arthur.

The simplicity of the acquiescence was vexatious to a
champion desirous of hostilities, to vindicate the lady, in
addition to his anxiety to cloak her sad plight.

"She caught it from contact with one of the inhabitants
of this country. 'T is the fate of us Irish, and we're condemned to it for the sin of getting tired of our own. I
begin to sneeze when I land at Holyhead. Unbutton a

waistcoat here, in the hope of meeting a heart, and you 're
lucky in escaping a pulmonary attack of no common
severity, while the dog that infected you scampers off, to
celebrate his honeymoon mayhap. Ah, but call at her
house in shoals, the world 'll soon be saying it 's worse
than a coughing cold. If you came to lead her out of it
in triumph, the laugh 'd be with you, and the lady well
covered. D' ye understand? "

The allusion to the dog's honeymoon had put Arthur
Rhodes on the track of the darting cracker-metaphor.

"I think I do," he said. "She will soon be at Copsley
— Lady Dunstane's house, on the hills — and there we can
see her."

"And that 's next to the happiness of consoling — if only
it had been granted! She 's not an ordinary widow, to be
caught when the tear of lamentation has opened a practicable path or water-way to the poor nightcapped jewel
within. So, and you 're a candid admirer, Mr. Rhodes!
Well, and I 'll be one with you; for there 's not a star in
the firmament more deserving of homage than that lady."

"Let 's walk in the park and talk of her," said Arthur.
"There 's no sweeter subject to me."

His boyish frankness rejoiced Sullivan Smith.

"As long as you like! — nor to me!" he exclaimed.
"And that ever since I first beheld her on the night of a
Ball in Dublin: before I had listened to a word of her
speaking: and she bore her father's Irish name: — none of
your Warwicks and your . . . But let the cur go barking. He can't tell what he 's lost; perhaps he does n't
care. And after inflicting his hydrophobia on her tender
fame! Pooh, sir; you call it a civilized country, where
you and I and dozens of others are ready to start up as
brothers of the lady, to defend her, and are paralyzed by
the Law. 'T is a law they 've instituted for the protection
of dirty dogs — their majority!"

"I owe more to Mrs. Warwick than to any soul I
know," said Arthur.

"Let 's hear," quoth Sullivan Smith; proceeding: "She 's
the Arabian Nights in person, that 's sure; and Shakespeare's Plays, tragic and comic; and the Book of Celtic
History; and Erin incarnate — down with a cold, no matter

where; but we know where it was caught. So there's a pretty library for who's to own her now she's enfranchized by circumstances; — and a poetical figure too!"

He subsided for his companion to rhapsodize.

Arthur was overcharged with feeling, and could say only: "It would be another world to me if I lost her."

"True; but what of the lady?"

"No praise of mine could do her justice."

"That may be, but it's negative of yourself, and not a portrait of the object. Has n't she the brain of Socrates — or better, say Minerva, on the bust of Venus, and the remainder of her finished off to an exact resemblance of her patronymic Goddess of the bow and quiver?"

"She has a wise head and is beautiful."

"And chaste."

Arthur reddened: he was prepared to maintain it, could not speak it.

"She is to us in this London, what the run of water was to Theocritus in Sicily: the nearest to the visibly divine," he said, and was applauded.

"Good, and on you go. Top me a few superlatives on that, and I'm your echo, my friend. Is n't the seeing and listening to her like sitting under the silvery canopy of a fountain in high Summer?"

"All the comparisons are yours," Arthur said enviously.

"Mr. Rhodes, you are a poet, I believe, and all you require to loosen your tongue is a drop of Bacchus, so if you will do me the extreme honour to dine with me at my Club this evening, we'll resume the toast that should never be uttered dry. You reprove me justly, my friend."

Arthur laughed and accepted. The Club was named, and the hour, and some items of the little dinner: the birds and the year of the wines.

It surprised him to meet Mr. Redworth at the table of his host. A greater surprise was the partial thaw in Redworth's bearing toward him. But, as it was partial, and he a youth and poor, not even the genial influences of Bacchus could lift him to loosen his tongue under the repressing presence of the man he knew to be his censor, though Sullivan Smith encouraged him with praises and opportunities. He thought of the many occasions when

Mrs. Warwick's art of management had produced a tacit harmony between them. She had no peer. The dinner failed of the pleasure he had expected from it. Redworth's bluntness killed the flying metaphors, and at the end of the entertainment he and Sullivan Smith were drumming upon politics.

"Fancies he has the key of the Irish difficulty!" said the latter, clapping hand on his shoulder, by way of blessing, as they parted at the Club-steps.

Redworth asked Arthur Rhodes the way he was going, and walked beside him.

"I suppose you take exercise; don't get colds and that kind of thing," he remarked in the old bullying fashion; and changed it abruptly. "I am glad to have met you this evening. I hope you'll dine with me one day next week. Have you seen Mrs. Warwick lately?"

"She is unwell; she has been working too hard," said Arthur.

"Seriously unwell, do you mean?"

"Lady Dunstane is at her house, and speaks of her recovering."

"Ah. You've not seen her?"

"Not yet."

"Well, good-night."

Redworth left him, and only when moved by gratitude to the lad for his mention of Mrs. Warwick's "working too hard," as the cause of her illness, recollected the promised dinner and the need for having his address.

He had met Sullivan Smith accidentally in the morning and accepted the invitation to meet young Rhodes, because these two, of all men living, were for the moment dearest to him, as Diana Warwick's true and simple champions; and he had intended a perfect cordiality toward them both; the end being a semi-wrangle with the patriot, and a patronizing bluntness with the boy; who, by the way, would hardly think him sincere in the offer of a seat at his table. He owned himself incomplete. He never could do the thing he meant, in the small matters not leading to fortune. But they led to happiness! Redworth was guilty of a sigh: for now Diana Warwick stood free; doubly free, he was reduced to reflect in a wavering dubiousness. Her

more than inclination for Dacier, witnessed by him, and
the shot of the world, flying randomly on the subject, had
struck this cuirassier, making light of his armour, without
causing any change of his habitual fresh countenance. As
for the scandal, it had never shaken his faith in her nature.
He thought of the passion. His heart struck at Diana's,
and whatever might by chance be true in the scandal
affected him little, if but her heart were at liberty. That
was the prize he coveted, having long read the nature of
the woman and wedded his spirit to it. She would complete him.

Of course, infatuated men argue likewise, and scandal
does not move them. At a glance, the lower instincts and
the higher spirit appear equally to have the philosophy of
overlooking blemishes. The difference between appetite
and love is shown when a man, after years of service, can
hear and see, and admit the possible, and still desire in
worship; knowing that we of earth are begrimed and must
be cleansed for presentation daily on our passage through ·
the miry ways, but that our souls, if flame of a soul shall
have come of the agony of flesh, are beyond the baser mis-
chances: partaking of them indeed, but sublimely. Now
Redworth believed in the soul of Diana. For him it
burned, and it was a celestial radiance about her, un-
quenched by her shifting fortunes, her wilfulnesses, and,
it might be, errors. She was a woman and weak; that is,
not trained for strength. She was a soul; therefore perpetually pointing to growth in purification. He felt it,
and even discerned it of her, if he could not have phrased
it. The something sovereignly characteristic that aspired
in Diana enchained him. With her, or rather with his
thought of her soul, he understood the right union of
women and men, from the roots to the flowering heights
of that rare graft. She gave him comprehension of the
meaning of love: a word in many mouths, not often explained. With her, wound in his idea of her, he perceived
it to signify a new start in our existence, a finer shoot of
the tree stoutly planted in good gross earth; the senses
running their live sap, and the minds companioned, and
the spirits made one by the whole-natured conjunction.
In sooth, a happy prospect for the sons and daughters of

Earth, divinely indicating more than happiness: the speeding of us, compact of what we are, between the ascetic rocks and the sensual whirlpools, to the creation of certain nobler races, now very dimly imagined.

Singularly enough, the man of these feelings was far from being a social rebel. His Diana conjured them forth in relation to her, but was not on his bosom to enlighten him generally. His notions of citizenship tolerated the female Pharisees, as ladies offering us an excellent social concrete where quicksands abound, and without quite justifying the Lady Wathins and Constance Aspers of the world, whose virtues he could set down to accident or to acid blood, he considered them supportable and estimable where the Mrs. Fryar-Gunnetts were innumerable, threatening to become a majority; as they will constantly do while the sisterhood of the chaste are wattled in formalism and throned in sourness.

Thoughts of Diana made phantoms of the reputable and their reverse alike. He could not choose but think of her. She was free; and he too; and they were as distant as the horizon sail and the raft-floating castaway. Her passion for Dacier might have burnt out her heart. And at present he had no claim to visit her, dared not intrude. He would have nothing to say, if he went, save to answer questions upon points of business: as to which, Lady Dunstane would certainly summon him when he was wanted.

Riding in the park on a frosty morning, he came upon Sir Lukin, who looked gloomy and inquired for news of Diana Warwick, saying that his wife had forbidden him to call at her house just yet. "She's got a cold, you know," said Sir Lukin; adding, "confoundedly hard on women! — eh? Obliged to keep up a show. And I'd swear, by all that's holy, Diana Warwick hasn't a spot, not a spot, to reproach herself with. I fancy I ought to know women by this time. And look here, Redworth, last night — that is, I mean, yesterday evening, I broke with a woman — a lady of my acquaintance, you know, because she would go on scandal-mongering about Diana Warwick. I broke with her. I told her I'd have out any man who abused Diana Warwick, and I broke with her. By Jove! Redworth, those women can prove spitfires.

They 've bags of venom under their tongues, barley-sugar though they look — and that 's her colour. But I broke with her for good. I doubt if I shall ever call on her again. And in point of fact, I won't."

Mrs. Fryar-Gunnett was described in the colouring of the lady.

Sir Lukin, after some further remarks, rode on, and Redworth mused on a moral world that allows a woman of Mrs. Fryar-Gunnett's like to hang on to it, and to cast a stone at Diana; forgetful, in his championship, that Diana was not disallowed a similar licence.

When he saw Emma Dunstane, some days later, she was in her carriage driving, as she said, to Lawyerland, for an interview with old Mr. Braddock, on her friend's affairs. He took a seat beside her. "No, Tony is *not* well," she replied to his question, under the veil of candour. "She is recovering, but she — you can understand — suffered a shock. She is not able to attend to business, and certain things have to be done."

"I used to be her man of business," Redworth observed.

"She speaks of your kind services. This is mere matter for lawyers."

"She is recovering?"

"You may see her at Copsley next week. You can come down on Wednesdays or Saturdays?"

"Any day. Tell her I want her opinion upon the state of things."

"It will please her; but you will have to describe the state of things."

Emma feared she had said too much. She tried candour again for concealment. "My poor Tony has been struck down low. I suppose it is like losing a diseased limb: — she has her freedom, at the cost of a blow to the system."

"She may be trusted for having strength," said Redworth.

"Yes." Emma's mild monosyllable was presently followed by an exclamation: "One has to experience the irony of Fate to comprehend how cruel it is!" Then she remembered that such language was peculiarly abhorrent to him.

"Irony of Fate!" he echoed her, "I thought you were above that literary jargon."

"And I thought I was: or thought it could be put in a dialect practically explicable," she answered, smiling at the lion roused.

"Upon my word," he burst out, "I should like to write a book of Fables, showing how donkeys get into grinding harness, and dogs lose their bones, and fools have their sconces cracked, and all run jabbering of the irony of Fate, to escape the annoyance of tracing the causes. And what are they? nine times out of ten, plain want of patience, or some debt for indulgence. There's a subject:— let some one write, Fables in illustration of the irony of Fate: and I'll undertake to tack-on my grandmother's maxims for a moral to each of 'em. We prate of that irony when we slink away from the lesson — the rod we conjure. And you to talk of Fate! It's the seed we sow, individually or collectively. I'm bound-up in the prosperity of the country, and if the ship is wrecked, it ruins my fortune, but not me, unless I'm bound-up in myself. At least I hope that's my case."

He apologized for intruding Mr. Thomas Redworth.

His hearer looked at him, thinking he required a more finely pointed gift of speech for the ironical tongue, but relishing the tonic directness of his faculty of reason while she considered that the application of the phrase might be brought home to him so as to render "my Grandmother's moral" a conclusion less comfortingly, if quite intelligibly, summary. And then she thought of Tony's piteous instance; and thinking with her heart, the tears insisted on that bitter irony of the heavens, which bestowed the long-withheld and coveted boon when it was empty of value or was but as a handful of spices to a shroud.

Perceiving the moisture in her look, Redworth understood that it was foolish to talk rationally. But on her return to her beloved, the real quality of the man had overcome her opposing state of sentiment, and she spoke of him with an iteration and throb in the voice that set a singular query whirring round Diana's ears. Her senses were too heavy for a suspicion.

CHAPTER XXXVIII

CONVALESCENCE OF A HEALTHY MIND DISTRAUGHT

FROM an abandonment that had the last pleasure of life in a willingness to yield it up, Diana rose with her friend's help in some state of fortitude, resembling the effort of her feet to bear the weight of her body. She plucked her courage out of the dust to which her heart had been scattered, and tasked herself to walk as the world does. But she was indisposed to compassionate herself in the manner of the burdened world. She lashed the creature who could not raise a head like others, and made the endurance of torture a support, such as the pride of being is to men. She would not have seen any similarity to pride in it; would have deemed it the reverse. It was in fact the painful gathering of the atoms composing pride. For she had not only suffered; she had done wrongly: and when that was acknowledged, by the light of her sufferings the wrong-doing appeared gigantic, chorussing eulogies of the man she had thought her lover: and who was her lover once, before the crime against him. In the opening of her bosom to Emma, he was painted a noble figure; one of those that Romance delights to harass for the sake of ultimately the more exquisitely rewarding. He hated treachery: she had been guilty of doing what he most hated. She glorified him for the incapacity to forgive; it was to her mind godlike. And her excuses of herself?

At the first confession, she said she had none, and sullenly maintained that there was none to exonerate. Little by little her story was related — her version of the story: for not even as woman to woman, friend to great-hearted friend, pure soul to soul, could Diana tell of the state of shivering abjection in which Dacier had left her on the fatal night; of the many causes conducing to it, and of the chief. That was an unutterable secret, bound by all the laws of feminine civilization not to be betrayed. Her excessive self-abasement and exaltation of him who had struck her down, rendered it difficult to be understood; and not till Emma had revolved it and let it ripen in the mind some days could she perceive with any clearness her Tony's motives, or mania. The very word Money thickened the riddle: for Tony knew that her friend's purse was her own to dip in at her pleasure; yet she, to escape so small an obligation, had committed the enormity for which she held the man blameless in spurning her.

"You see what I am, Emmy," Diana said.

"What I do not see, is that he had grounds for striking so cruelly."

"I proved myself unworthy of him."

But does a man pretending to love a woman cut at one blow, for such a cause, the ties uniting her to him? Unworthiness of that kind is not commonly the capital offence in love. — Tony's deep prostration and her resplendent picture of her judge and executioner, kept Emma questioning within herself. Gradually she became enlightened enough to distinguish in the man a known, if not common, type of the externally soft and polished, internally hard and relentless, who are equal to the trials of love only as long as favouring circumstances and seemings nurse the fair object of their courtship.

Her thoughts recurred to the madness driving Tony to betray the secret; and the ascent unhelped to get a survey of it and her and the conditions, was mountainous. She toiled up but to enter the regions of cloud; sure nevertheless that the obscurity was penetrable and excuses to be discovered somewhere. Having never wanted money herself, she was unable perfectly to realize the urgency of the need: she began, however, to comprehend that the very eminent gentleman, before whom all human creatures were to bow in humility, had for an extended term considerably added to the expenses of Tony's household, by inciting her to give those little dinners to his political supporters, and bringing comrades perpetually to supper-parties, careless of how it might affect her character and her purse. Surely an honourable man was bound to her in honour? Tony's remark: "I have the reptile in me, dear," — her exaggeration of the act, in her resigned despair, — was surely no justification for his breaking from her, even though he had discovered a vestige of the common "reptile," to leave her with a stain on her name? — There would not have been a question about it if Tony had not exalted him so loftily, refusing, in visible pain, to hear him blamed.

Danvers had dressed a bed for Lady Dunstane in her mistress's chamber, where often during the night Emma caught a sound of stifled weeping or the long falling breath of wakeful grief. One night she asked whether Tony would like to have her by her side.

"No, dear," was the answer in the dark; "but you know my old pensioners, the blind fifer and his wife; I've been thinking of them."

"They were paid as they passed down the street yesterday, my love."

"Yes, dear, I hope so. But he flourishes his tune so absurdly. I've been thinking, that is the part I have played, instead of doing the female's duty of handing round the tin-cup for pennies. I won't cry any more."

She sighed and turned to sleep, leaving Emma to disburden her heart in tears.

For it seemed to her that Tony's intellect was weakened. She not merely abased herself and exalted Dacier preposterously, she had sunk her intelligence in her sensations: a state that she used to decry as the sin of mankind, the origin of error and blood.

Strangely too, the proposal came from her, or the suggestion of it, notwithstanding her subjectedness to the nerves, that she should show her face in public. She said: "I shall have to run about, Emmy, when I can fancy I am able to rattle up to the old mark. At present, I feel like a wrestler who has had a fall. As soon as the stiffness is over, it's best to make an appearance, for the sake of one's backers, though I shall never be in the wrestling ring again."

"That is a good decision — when you feel quite yourself, dear Tony," Emma replied.

"I dare say I have disgraced my sex, but not as they suppose. I feel my new self already, and can make the poor brute go through fire on behalf of the old. What is the task? — merely to drive a face!"

"It is not known."

"It will be known."

"But this is a sealed secret."

"Nothing is a secret that has been spoken. It's in the air, and I have to breathe to live by it. And I would rather it were out. 'She betrayed him.' Rather that, than have them think — anything! They will exclaim, How could she! I have been unable to answer it to you — my own heart. How? Oh! our weakness is the swiftest dog to hunt us; we cannot escape it. But I have the answer for them, that I trust with my whole soul none of them would have done the like."

"None, my Tony, would have taken it to the soul as you do."

"I talk, dear. If I took it honestly, I should be dumb, soon dust. The moment we begin to speak, the guilty creature is running for cover. She could not otherwise exist. I am sensible of evasion when I open my lips."

"But Tony has told me all."

"I think I have. But if you excuse my conduct, I am certain I have not."

"Dear girl, accounting for it is not the same as excusing."

"Who can account for it! I was caught in a whirl — Oh! nothing supernatural: my weakness; which it pleases me to call a madness — shift the ninety-ninth! When I drove down that night to Mr. Tonans, I am certain I had my clear wits, but I felt like a bolt. I saw things, but at too swift a rate for the conscience of them. Ah! let never Necessity draw the bow of our weakness: it is the soul that is winged to its perdition. I remember I was writing a story, named THE MAN OF TWO MINDS. I shall sign it *By The Woman of Two Natures*. If ever it is finished. Capacity for thinking should precede the act of writing. It should; I do not say that it does. Capacity for assimilating the public taste and reproducing it is the commonest. The stuff is perishable, but it pays us for our labour, and in so doing saves us from becoming tricksters. Now I can see that Mr. Redworth had it in that big head of his — the authoress outliving her income!"

"He dared not speak."

"Why did he not dare?"

"Would it have checked you?"

"I was a shot out of a gun, and I am glad he did not stand in my way. What power charged the gun, is another question. Dada used to say, that it is the devil's master-stroke to get us to accuse him. 'So fare ye well, old Nickie Ben.' My dear, I am a black sheep; a creature with a spotted reputation; I must wash and wash; and not with water — with sulphur-flames." She sighed. "I am down there where they burn. You should have let me lie and die. You were not kind. I was going quietly."

"My love!" cried Emma, overborne by a despair that she traced to the woman's concealment of her bleeding heart, — "you live for me. Do set your mind on that. Think of what you are bearing, as your debt to Emma. Will you?"

Tony bowed her head mechanically.

"But I am in love with King Death, and must confess it," she said. "That hideous eating you forced on me, snatched me from him. And I feel that if I had gone, I should have been mercifully forgiven by everybody."

"Except by me," said Emma, embracing her. "Tony would have left her friend for her last voyage in mourning. And my dearest will live to know happiness."

"I have no more belief in it, Emmy."

"The mistake of the world is to think happiness possible to the senses."

"Yes; we distil that fine essence *through* the senses; and the act is called the pain of life. It is the death of them. So much I understand of what our existence must be. But I may grieve for having done so little."

"That is the sound grief, with hope at the core — not in love with itself and wretchedly mortal, as we find self is under every shape it takes; especially the chief one."

"Name it."

"It is best named Amor."

There was a writhing in the frame of the hearer, for she did want Love to be respected; not shadowed by her misfortune. Her still-flushed senses protested on behalf of the eternalness of the passion, and she was obliged to think Emma's cold condemnatory intellect came of the no-knowledge of it.

A letter from Mr. Tonans, containing an enclosure, was a

sharp trial of Diana's endurance of the irony of Fate. She had spoken of the irony in allusion to her freedom. Now that, according to a communication from her lawyers, she was independent of the task of writing, the letter which paid the price of her misery bruised her heavily.

"Read it and tear it all to strips," she said in an abhorrence to Emma, who rejoined: "Shall I go at once and see him?"

"Can it serve any end? But throw it into the fire. Oh! no simulation of virtue. There was not, I think, a stipulated return for what I did. But I perceive clearly — I can read only by events — that there was an understanding. You behold it. I went to him to sell it. He thanks me, says I served the good cause well. I have not that consolation. If I had thought of the cause — of anything high, it would have arrested me. On the fire with it!"

The letter and square slip were consumed. Diana watched the blackening papers.

"So they cease their sinning, Emmy; and as long as I am in torment, I may hope for grace. We talked of the irony. It means, the pain of fire."

"I spoke of the irony to Redworth," said Emma; "incidentally, of course."

"And he fumed?"

"He is really not altogether the Mr. Cuthbert Dering of your caricature. He is never less than acceptably rational. I won't repeat his truisms; but he said, or I deduced from what he said, that a grandmother's maxims would expound the enigma."

"Probably the simple is the deep, in relation to the mysteries of life," said Diana, whose wits had been pricked to a momentary activity by the letter. "He behaves wisely; so perhaps we are bound to take his words for wisdom. Much nonsense is talked and written, and he is one of the world's reserves, who need no more than enrolling, to make a sturdy phalanx of common sense. It's a pity they are not enlisted and drilled to express themselves." She relapsed. "But neither he nor any of them could understand my case!"

"He puts the idea of an irony down to the guilt of impatience, Tony."

"Could there be a keener irony than that? A friend of Dada's waited patiently for a small fortune, and when it arrived, he was a worn-out man, just assisted to go decently to his grave."

"But he may have gained in spirit by his patient waiting."

"Oh! true. We are warmer if we travel on foot sunward, but it is a discovery that we are colder if we take to ballooning upward. The material good reverses its benefits the more nearly we clasp it. All life is a lesson that we live to enjoy but in the spirit. I will brood on your saying."

"It is your own saying, silly Tony, as the only things worth saying always are!" exclaimed Emma, as she smiled happily to see her friend's mind reviving, though it was faintly and in the dark.

CHAPTER XXXIX

OF NATURE WITH ONE OF HER CULTIVATED DAUGHTERS AND A SHORT EXCURSION IN ANTI-CLIMAX

A MIND that after a long season of oblivion in pain returns to wakefulness without a keen edge for the world, is much in danger of souring permanently. Diana's love of nature saved her from the dire mischance during a two months' residence at Copsley, by stupefying her senses to a state like the barely conscious breathing on the verge of sleep. February blew South-west for the pairing of the birds. A broad warm wind rolled clouds of every ambiguity of form in magnitude over peeping azure, or skimming upon lakes of blue and lightest green, or piling the amphitheatre for majestic sunset. Or sometimes those daughters of the wind flew linked and low, semi-purple, threatening the shower they retained and teaching gloom to rouse a songful nest in the bosom of the viewer. Sometimes they were April, variable to soar with rain-skirts and sink with sun-shafts. Or they drenched wood and field for a day and opened on the high South-western star. Daughters of the wind, but shifty daughters of this wind of the dropping sun, they have to be watched to be loved in their transformations.

Diana had Arthur Rhodes and her faithful Leander for walking companions. If Arthur said: "Such a day would be considered melancholy by London people," she thanked him in her heart, as a benefactor who had revealed to her things of the deepest. The simplest were her food. Thus does Nature restore us, by drugging the brain and making her creature confidingly animal for its new growth. She imagined herself to have lost the power to think; certainly she had not the striving or the wish. Exercise of her limbs to reach a point of prospect, and of her ears and eyes to note what bird had piped, what flower was out on the banks, and the leaf of what tree it was that lay beneath the budding, satiated her daily desires. She gathered unknowingly a sheaf of landscapes, images, keys of dreamed horizons, that opened a world to her at any chance breath altering shape or hue: a different world from the one of her old ambition. Her fall had brought her renovatingly to earth, and the saving naturalness of the woman recreated her childlike, with shrouded recollections of her strange taste of life behind her; with a tempered fresh blood to enjoy aimlessly, and what would erewhile have been a barrenness to her sensibilities.

In time the craving was evolved for positive knowledge, and shells and stones and weeds were deposited on the library-table at Copsley, botanical and geological books comparingly examined, Emma Dunstane always eager to assist; for the samples wafted her into the heart of the woods. Poor Sir Lukin tried three days of their society, and was driven away headlong to Club-life. He sent down Redworth, with whom the walks of the zealous inquirers were profitable, though Diana, in acknowledging it to herself, reserved a decided preference for her foregone ethereal mood, larger, and untroubled by the presence of a man. The suspicion Emma had sown was not excited to an alarming activity; but she began to question: could the best of men be simply a woman's friend? — was not long service rather less than a proof of friendship? She could be blind when her heart was on fire for another. Her passion for her liberty, however, received no ominous warning to look to the defences. He was the same blunt speaker, and knotted his brows as queerly as ever at Arthur, in a transparent calculation of how this fellow meant to gain his livelihood. She wilfully put it to the credit of Arthur's tact that his elder was amiable, without denying her debt to the good man for leaving her illness and her appearance unmentioned. He forebore even to scan her features. Diana's wan contemplativeness, in which the sparkle of meaning slowly rose to flash, as we see a bubble rising from the deeps of crystal waters, caught at his heart while he talked his matter-of-fact. But her instinct of a present safety was true. She and Arthur discovered — and it set her first meditating whether she did know the man so very accurately — that he had printed, for private circulation, when at Harrow School, a little book, a record of his observations in nature. Lady Dunstane was the casual betrayer. He shrugged at the nonsense of a boy's publishing; anybody's publishing he held for a doubtful proof of sanity. His excuse was, that he had not published opinions. Let us observe, and assist in our small sphere; not come mouthing to the footlights!

"We retire," Diana said, for herself and Arthur.

"The wise thing, is to avoid the position that enforces publishing," said he, to the discomposure of his raw junior.

In the fields he was genially helpful; commending them to the study of the South-west wind, if they wanted to forecast the weather and understand the climate of our country. "We have no Seasons, or only a shuffle of them. Old calendars give seven months of the year to the South-west, and that's about the average. Count on it, you may generally reckon what to expect. When you don't have the excess for a year or two, you are drenched the year following." He knew every bird by its flight and its pipe, habits, tricks, hints of sagacity homely with the original human ; and his remarks on the sensitive life of trees and herbs were a spell to his thirsty hearers. Something of astronomy he knew; but in relation to that science, he sank his voice, touchingly to Diana, who felt drawn to kinship

with him when he had a pupil's tone. An allusion by
Arthur to the poetical work of Aratus, led to a memorably
pleasant evening's discourse upon the long reading of the
stars by these our mortal eyes. Altogether the mind of
the practical man became distinguishable to them as that
of a plain brother of the poetic. Diana said of him to
Arthur: "He does not supply me with similes; he points
to the source of them." Arthur, with envy of the man
of positive knowledge, disguised an unstrung heart in
agreeing.

Redworth alluded passingly to the condition of public
affairs. Neither of them replied. Diana was wondering
how one who perused the eternal of nature should lend a
thought to the dusty temporary of the world. Subsequently
she reflected that she was asking him to confine his great
male appetite to the nibble of bread which nourished her
immediate sense of life. Her reflections were thin as mist,
coming and going like the mist, with no direction upon her
brain, if they sprang from it. When he had gone, welcome
though Arthur had seen him to be, she rebounded to a
broader and cheerfuller liveliness. Arthur was flattered by
an idea of her casting off incubus — a most worthy gentleman, and a not perfectly sympathetic associate. Her eyes
had their lost light in them, her step was brisker; she
challenged him to former games of conversation, excursions in blank verse here and there, as the mood dictated.
They amused themselves, and Emma too. She revelled in
seeing Tony's younger face and hearing some of her natural
outbursts. That Dacier never could have been the man for
her, would have compressed and subjected her, and inflicted
a further taste of bondage in marriage, she was assured.
She hoped for the day when Tony would know it, and
haply that another, whom she little comprehended, was her
rightful mate.

March continued South-westerly and grew rainier, as
Redworth had foretold, bidding them look for gales and
storm, and then the change of wind. It came, after wet-
tings of a couple scorning the refuge of dainty townsfolk
under umbrellas, and proud of their likeness to dripping
wayside wildflowers. Arthur stayed at Copsley for a week
of the Crisp North-easter; and what was it, when he had

taken his leave, that brought Tony home from her solitary
walk in dejection ?   It could not be her seriously regretting
the absence of the youthful companion she had parted with
gaily, appointing a time for another meeting on the heights,
and recommending him to repair idle hours with strenuous
work.   The fit passed and was not explained.   The winds
are sharp with memory.   The hard shrill wind crowed to
her senses of an hour on the bleak sands of the French
coast : the beginning of the curtained misery, inscribed as
her happiness.   She was next day prepared for her term in
London with Emma, who promised her to make an expedition at the end of it by way of holiday, to see The Crossways, which Mr. Redworth said was not tenanted.

"You won't go through it like a captive ?" said Emma.

"I don't like it, dear," Diana put up a comic mouth.
"The debts we owe ourselves are the hardest to pay.   That
is the discovery of advancing age : and I used to imagine it
was quite the other way.   But they are the debts of honour,
imperative.   I shall go through it grandly, you will see.
If I am stopped at my first recreancy and turned directly
the contrary way, I think I have courage."

"You will not fear to meet . . . anyone ?" Emma said.

"The world and all it contains ! I am robust, eager for
the fray, an Amazon, a brazen-faced hussy.   Fear and I
have parted.   I shall not do you discredit.   Besides you
intend to have me back here with you?   And besides
again, I burn to make a last brave appearance.   I have not
outraged the world, dear Emmy, whatever certain creatures
in it may fancy."

She had come out of her dejectedness with a shrewder
view of Dacier; equally painful, for it killed her romance,
and changed the garden of their companionship in imagination to a waste.   Her clearing intellect prompted it, whilst
her nature protested, and reviled her to uplift him.   He
had loved her.   "I shall die knowing that a man did love
me once," she said to her widowed heart, and set herself
blushing and blanching.   But the thought grew inveterate :
"He could not bear much."   And in her quick brain it shot
up a crop of similitudes for the quality of that man's love.
She shuddered, as at a swift cleaving of cold steel.   He had
not given her a chance; he had not replied to her letter

written with the pen dipped in her heart's blood; he must
have gone straight away to the woman he married. This
after almost justifying the scandalous world : — after . . .
She realized her sensations of that night when the house-
door had closed on him; her feeling of lost sovereignty,
degradation, feminine danger, friendlessness : and she was
unaware, and never knew, nor did the world ever know,
what cunning had inspired the frosty Cupid to return to
her and be warmed by striking a bargain for his weighty
secret. She knew too well that she was not of the snows
which do not melt, however high her conceit of herself
might place her. Happily she now stood out of the sun,
in a bracing temperature, Polar; and her compassion for
women was deeply sisterly in tenderness and understanding.
She spoke of it to Emma as her gain.

"I have not seen that you required to suffer to be con-
siderate," Emma said.

"It is on my conscience that I neglected Mary Paynham,
among others — and because you did not take to her,
Emmy."

"The reading of it appears to me, that she has neglected
you."

"She was not in my confidence, and so I construe it as
delicacy. One never loses by believing the best."

"If one is not duped."

"Expectations dupe us, not trust. The light of every
soul burns upward. Of course, most of them are candles in
the wind. Let us allow for atmospheric disturbance. Now
I thank you, dear, for bringing me back to life. I see that
I was really a selfish suicide, because I feel I have power
to do some good, and belong to the army. When we are
beginning to reflect, as I do now, on a recovered basis of
pure health, we have the world at the dawn and know we
are young in it, with great riches, great things gained and
greater to achieve. Personally I behold a queer little
wriggling worm for myself; but as one of the active world
I stand high and shapely; and the very thought of doing
work, is like a draught of the desert-springs to me. Instead of which, I have once more to go about presenting
my face to vindicate my character. Mr. Redworth would
admit no irony in that ! At all events, it is anti-climax."

"I forgot to tell you, Tony, you have been proposed for," said Emma; and there was a rush of savage colour over Tony's cheeks.

Her apparent apprehensions were relieved by hearing the name of Mr. Sullivan Smith.

"My poor dear countryman! And he thought me worthy, did he? Some day, when we are past his repeating it, I'll thank him."

The fact of her smiling happily at the narration of Sullivan Smith's absurd proposal by mediatrix, proved to Emma how much her nature thirsted for the smallest support in her self-esteem.

The second campaign of London was of bad augury at the commencement, owing to the ridiculous intervention of a street-organ, that ground its pipes in a sprawling roar of one of the Puritani marches, just as the carriage was landing them at the door of her house. The notes were harsh, dissonant, drunken, interlocked and horribly torn asunder, intolerable to ears not keen to extract the tune through dreadful memories. Diana sat startled and paralyzed. The melody crashed a revival of her days with Dacier, as in gibes; and yet it reached to her heart. She imagined a Providence that was trying her on the threshold, striking at her feebleness. She had to lock herself in her room for an hour of deadly abandonment to misery, resembling the run of poison through her blood, before she could bear to lift eyes on her friend; to whom subsequently she said: "Emmy, there are wounds that cut sharp as the enchanter's sword, and we don't know we are in halves till some rough old intimate claps us on the back, merely to ask us how we are! I have to join myself together again, as well as I can. It's done, dear; but don't notice the cement."

"You will be brave," Emma petitioned.

"I long to show you I will."

The meeting with those who could guess a portion of her story, did not disconcert her. To Lady Pennon and Lady Singleby, she was the brilliant Diana of her nominal luminary issuing from cloud. Face and tongue, she was the same; and once in the stream, she soon gathered its current topics and scattered her arrowy phrases. Lady Pennon ran

about with them, declaring that the beautiful speaker, if
ever down, was up, and up to her finest mark. Mrs. Fryar-
Gunnett had then become the blazing regnant antisocial
star; a distresser of domesticity, the magnetic attraction
in the spirituous flames of that wild snapdragon bowl, called
the Upper class; and she was angelically blonde, a straw-
coloured Beauty. "A lovely wheatsheaf, if the head were
ripe," Diana said of her.

"Threshed, says her fame, my dear," Lady Pennon replied, otherwise allusive.

"A wheatsheaf of contention for the bread of wind,"
said Diana, thinking of foolish Sir Lukin; thoughtless of
talking to a gossip.

She would have shot a lighter dart, had she meant it to
fly and fix.

Proclaim, ye classics, what minor Goddess, or primal, Iris
or Ate, sped straight away on wing to the empty wheat-
sheaf-ears of the golden-visaged Amabel Fryar·Gunnett,
daughter of Demeter in the field to behold, of Aphrodite
in her rosy incendiarism for the many of men; filling that
pearly concave with a perversion of the uttered speech,
such as never lady could have repeated, nor man, if less
than a reaping harvester: which verily for women to hear,
is to stamp a substantial damnatory verification upon the
delivery of the saying: —

"Mrs. Warwick says of you, that you're a bundle of
straws for everybody and bread for nobody."

Or, stranger speculation, through what, and what number
of conduits, curious, and variously colouring, did it reach
the fair Amabel of the infant-in-cradle smile, in that de-
formation of the original utterance! To pursue the thing,
would be to enter the subtersensual perfumed caverns of a
Romance of Fashionable Life, with no hope of coming back
to light, other than by tail of lynx, like the great Arabian
seaman, at the last page of the final chapter. A prospec-
tively popular narrative indeed! and coin to reward it, and
applause. But I am reminded that a story properly closed
on the marriage of the heroine Constance and her young
Minister of State, has no time for conjuring chemists' bou-
quet of aristocracy to lure the native taste. When we have
satisfied English sentiment, our task is done, in every

branch of art, I hear: and it will account to posterity for the condition of the branches. Those yet wakeful eccentrics interested in such a person as Diana, to the extent of remaining attentive till the curtain falls, demand of me to gather-up the threads concerning her: which my gardener sweeping his pile of dead leaves before the storm and night, advises me to do speedily. But it happens that her resemblance to her sex and species of a civilized period plants the main threads in her bosom. Rogues and a policeman, or a hurried change of front of all the actors, are not a part of our slow machinery.

Nor is she to show herself to advantage. Only those who read her woman's blood and character with the head, will care for Diana of the Crossways now that the knot of her history has been unravelled. Some little love they must have for her likewise: and how it can be quickened on behalf of a woman who never sentimentalizes publicly, and has no dolly-dolly compliance, and muses on actual life, and fatigues with the exercise of brains, and is in sooth an alien: a princess of her kind and time, but a foreign one, speaking a language distinct from the mercantile, trafficking in ideas: — this is the problem. For to be true to her, one cannot attempt at propitiation. She said worse things of the world than that which was conveyed to the boxed ears of Mrs. Fryar-Gunnett. Accepting the war declared against her a second time, she performed the common mental trick in adversity of setting her personally known innocence to lessen her generally unknown error: but anticipating that this might become known, and the other not; and feeling that the motives of the acknowledged error had served to guard her from being the culprit of the charge she writhed under, she rushed out of a meditation compounded of mind and nerves, with derision of the world's notion of innocence and estimate of error. It was a mood lasting through her stay in London, and longer, to the discomfort of one among her friends; and it was worthy of The Anti-climax Expedition, as she called it.

For the rest, her demeanour to the old monster world exacting the servility of her, in repayment for its tolerating countenance, was faultless. Emma beheld the introduction to Mrs. Warwick of his bride, by Mr. Percy Dacier. She

had watched their approach up the Ball-room, thinking,
how differently would Redworth and Tony have looked.
Differently, had it been Tony and Dacier: but Emma could
not persuade herself of a possible harmony between them,
save at the cost of Tony's expiation of the sin of the
greater heart in a performance equivalent to Suttee. Perfectly an English gentleman of the higher order, he seemed
the effigy of a tombstone one, fixed upright, and civilly
proud of his effigy bride. So far, Emma considered them
fitted. She perceived his quick eye on her corner of the
room; necessarily, for a man of his breeding, without a
change of expression. An emblem pertaining to her creed
was on the heroine's neck; also dependant at her waist.
She was white from head to foot; a symbol of purity. Her
frail smile appeared deeply studied in purity. Judging
from her look and her reputation, Emma divined that the
man was justly mated with a devious filmy sentimentalist,
likely to "*fiddle harmonics on the sensual strings*" for him
at a mad rate in the years to come. Such fiddling is indeed
the peculiar diversion of the opulent of a fatly prosperous
people; who take it, one may concede to them, for an inspired elimination of the higher notes of life: the very
highest. That saying of Tony's ripened with full significance to Emma now. Not sensualism, but sham spiritual-
ism, was the meaning; and however fine the notes, they
come skilfully evoked of the under-brute in us. Reasoning
it so, she thought it a saying for the penetration of the
most polished and deceptive of the later human masks.
She had besides, be it owned, a triumph in conjuring a sentence of her friend's, like a sword's edge, to meet them;
for she was boiling angrily at the ironical destiny which
had given to those Two a beclouding of her beloved, whom
she could have rebuked in turn for her insane caprice of
passion.

But when her beloved stood-up to greet Mrs. Percy Dacier,
all idea save tremulous admiration of the valiant woman,
who had been wounded nigh to death, passed from Emma's
mind. Diana tempered her queenliness to address the favoured lady with smiles and phrases of gentle warmth, of
goodness of nature; and it became a halo rather than a
personal eclipse that she cast.

Emma looked at Dacier. He wore the prescribed conventional air, subject in half a minute to a rapid blinking of the eyelids. His wife could have been inimically imagined fascinated and dwindling. A spot of colour came to her cheeks. She likewise began to blink.

The happy couple bowed, proceeding; and Emma had Dacier's back for a study. We score on that flat slate of man, unattractive as it is to hostile observations, and unprotected, the device we choose. Her harshest, was the positive thought that he had taken the woman best suited to him. Doubtless, he was a man to prize the altar-candle above the lamp of day. She fancied the back-view of him shrunken and straitened: perhaps a mere hostile fancy: though it was conceivable that he should desire as little of these meetings as possible. Eclipses are not courted.

The specially womanly exultation of Emma Dunstane in her friend's noble attitude, seeing how their sex had been struck to the dust for a trifling error, easily to be overlooked by a manful lover, and had asserted its dignity in physical and moral splendour, in self-mastery and benignness, was unshared by Diana. As soon as the business of the expedition was over, her orders were issued for the sale of the lease of her house and all it contained. "I would sell Danvers too," she said, "but the creature declines to be treated as merchandize. It seems I have a faithful servant; very much like my life, not quite to my taste; the one thing out of the wreck! — with my dog!"

Before quitting her house for the return to Copsley, she had to grant Mr. Alexander Hepburn, post-haste from his Caledonia, a private interview. She came out of it noticeably shattered. Nothing was related to Emma, beyond the remark: "I never knew till this morning the force of No in earnest." The weighty little word — woman's native watchdog and guardian, if she calls it to her aid *in earnest* — had encountered and withstood a fiery ancient host, astonished at its novel power of resistance.

Emma contented herself with the result. "Were you much supplicated?"

"An Operatic Fourth-Act," said Diana, by no means feeling so flippantly as she spoke.

She received, while under the impression of this man's

honest, if primitive, ardour of courtship, or effort to capture, a characteristic letter from Westlake, choicely phrased, containing presumeably an application for her hand, in the generous offer of his own. Her reply to a pursuer of that sort was easy. Comedy, after the barbaric attack, refreshed her wits and reliance on her natural fencing weapons. To Westlake, the unwritten No was conveyed in a series of kindly ironic subterfuges, that played it like an impish flea across the pages, just giving the bloom of the word; and rich smiles come to Emma's life in reading the dexterous composition: which, however, proved so thoroughly to Westlake's taste, that a second and a third exercise in the comedy of the negative had to be despatched to him from Copsley.

CHAPTER XL

IN WHICH WE SEE NATURE MAKING OF A WOMAN A MAID AGAIN, AND A THRICE WHIMSICAL

On their way from London, after leaving the station, the drive through the valley led them past a field, where cricketers were at work bowling and batting under a vertical sun: not a very comprehensible sight to ladies, whose practical tendencies, as observers of the other sex, incline them to question the gain of such an expenditure of energy. The dispersal of the alphabet over a printed page is not less perplexing to the illiterate. As soon as Emma Dunstane discovered the Copsley head gamekeeper at one wicket, and, actually, Thomas Redworth facing him, bat in hand, she sat up, greatly interested. Sir Lukin stopped the carriage at the gate, and reminded his wife that it was the day of the year for the men of his estate to encounter a valley Eleven. Redworth, like the good fellow he was, had come down by appointment in the morning out of London, to fill the number required, Copsley being weak this year. Eight of their wickets had fallen for a lamentable figure of twenty-nine runs; himself clean-bowled the first ball. But

Tom Redworth had got fast hold of his wicket, and already scored fifty to his bat. "There! grand hit!" Sir Lukin cried, the ball flying hard at the rails. "Once a cricketer, always a cricketer, if you've legs to fetch the runs. And Pullen's not doing badly. His business is to stick. We shall mark them a hundred yet. I do hate a score on our side without the two 00's." He accounted for Redworth's mixed colours by telling the ladies he had lent him his flannel jacket; which, against black trousers, looked odd but not ill.

Gradually the enthusiasm of the booth and bystanders converted the flying of a leather ball into a subject of honourable excitement.

"And why are you doing nothing?" Sir Lukin was asked; and he explained:

"My stumps are down: I'm married." He took his wife's hand prettily.

Diana had a malicious prompting. She smothered the wasp, and said: "Oh! look at that!"

"Grand hit again! Oh! good! good!" cried Sir Lukin, clapping to it, while the long-hit-off ran spinning his legs into one for an impossible catch; and the batsmen were running and stretching bats, and the ball flying away, flying back, and others after it, and still the batsmen running, till it seemed that the ball had escaped control and was leading the fielders on a coltish innings of its own, defiant of bowlers.

Diana said merrily: "Bravo our side!"

"Bravo, old Tom Redworth!" rejoined Sir Lukin. "Four, and a three! And capital weather, have n't we! Hope we shall have same sort day next month — return match, my ground. I've seen Tom Redworth score — old days — over two hundred t' his bat. And he used to bowl too. But bowling wants practice. And, Emmy, look at the old fellows lining the booth, pipe in mouth and cheering. They do enjoy a day like this. We'll have a supper for fifty at Copsley's :— it's fun. By Jove! we must have reached up to near the hundred."

He commissioned a neighbouring boy to hie to the booth for the latest figures, and his emissary taught lightning a lesson.

Diana praised the little fellow.

"Yes, he's a real English boy," said Emma.

"We've thousands of 'em, thousands, ready to your hand!" exclaimed Sir Lukin; "and a confounded Radicalized country . . ." he muttered gloomily of "lets us be kicked! . . . any amount of insult, meek as gruel! . . . making of the finest army the world has ever seen! You saw the papers this morning? Good heaven! how a nation with an atom of self-respect can go on standing that sort of bullying from foreigners! We do. We're insulted and we're threatened, and we call for a hymn!— Now then, my man, what is it?"

The boy had flown back. "Ninety-two marked, sir; ninety-nine runs; one more for the hundred."

"Well reckoned; and mind you're up at Copsley for the return-match.— And Tom Redworth says, they may bite their thumbs to the bone— they don't hurt us. I tell him, he has no sense of national pride. He says, we're not prepared for war. We never are! And whose the fault? Says, we're a peaceful people, but 'ware who touches us! He doesn't feel a kick.— Oh! clever snick! Hurrah for the hundred!— Two— three. No, don't force the running, you fools!— though they're wild with the ball: ha!— no! —all right!" The wicket stood. Hurrah!

The heat of the noonday sun compelled the ladies to drive on.

"Enthusiasm has the privilege of not knowing monotony," said Emma. "He looks well in flannels."

"Yes, he does," Diana replied, aware of the reddening despite her having spoken so simply. "I think the chief advantage men have over us is in their amusements."

"Their recreations."

"That is the better word." Diana fanned her cheeks and said she was warm. "I mean, the permanent advantage. For you see that age does not affect them."

"Tom Redworth is not a patriarch, my dear."

"Well, he is what would be called mature."

"He can't be more than thirty-two or three; and that, for a man of his constitution, means youth."

"Well, I can imagine him a patriarch playing cricket."

"I should imagine you imagine the possible chances. He is the father who would play with his boys."

"And lock up his girls in the nursery." Diana murmured of the extraordinary heat.

Emma begged her to remember his heterodox views of the education for girls.

"He bats admirably," said Diana. "I wish I could bat half as well."

"Your batting is with the tongue."

"Not so good. And a solid bat, or bludgeon, to defend the poor stumps, is surer. But there is the difference of cricket:— when your stumps are down, you are idle, at leisure; not a miserable prisoner."

"Supposing all marriages miserable."

"To the mind of me," said Diana, and observed Emma's rather saddened eyelids for a proof that schemes to rob her of dear liberty were certainly planned.

They conversed of expeditions to Redworth's Berkshire mansion, and to The Crossways, untenanted at the moment, as he had informed Emma, who fancied it would please Tony to pass a night in the house she loved; but as he was to be of the party she coldly acquiesced.

The woman of flesh refuses pliancy when we want it of her, and will not, until it is her good pleasure, be bent to the development called a climax, as the puppet-woman, mother of Fiction and darling of the multitude! ever amiably does, at a hint of the Nuptial Chapter. Diana in addition sustained the weight of brains. Neither with waxen optics nor with subservient jointings did she go through her pathways of the world. Her direct individuality rejected the performance of simpleton, and her lively blood, the warmer for its containment, quickened her to penetrate things and natures; and if as yet, in justness to the loyal male friend, she forbore to name him conspirator, she read both him and Emma, whose inner bosom was revealed to her, without an effort to see. But her characteristic chasteness of mind, — not coldness of the blood, — which had supported an arduous conflict, past all existing rights closely to depict, and which barbed her to pierce to the wishes threatening her freedom, deceived her now to think her flaming in blushes came of her relentless divination on behalf of her recovered treasure: whereby the clear reading of others distracted the view of herself. For one may be the cleverest alive, and still hoodwinked while blood is young and warm.

The perpetuity of the contrast presented to her reflections, of Redworth's healthy, open, practical, cheering life, and her own freakishly interwinding, darkly penetrative, simulacrum of a life, cheerless as well as useless, forced her humiliated consciousness by degrees, in spite of pride, to the knowledge that she was engaged in a struggle with him; and that he was the stronger; — it might be, the worthier: she thought him the handsomer. He throve to the light of day, and she spun a silly web that meshed her in her intricacies. Her intuition of Emma's wishes led to this; he was constantly before her. She tried to laugh at the image of the concrete cricketer, half-flannelled, and red of face: the "lucky calculator," as she named him to Emma, who shook her head, and sighed. The abstract, healthful and powerful man, able to play besides profitably working, defied those poor efforts. Consequently, at once she sent up a bubble to the skies, where it became a spheral realm, of far too fine an atmosphere for men to breathe in it; and thither she transported herself at will, whenever the contrast, with its accompanying menace of a tyrannic subjugation, overshadowed her. In the above, the kingdom composed of her shattered romance of life and her present aspirings, she was free and safe. Nothing touched her there — nothing that Redworth did. She could not have admitted there her ideal of a hero. It was the sublimation of a virgin's conception of life, better fortified against the enemy. She peopled it with souls of the great and pure, gave it illimitable horizons, dreamy nooks, ravishing landscapes, melodies of the poets of music. Higher and more celestial than the Salvatore, it was likewise, now she could assure herself serenely, independent of the horrid blood-emotions. Living up there, she had not a feeling.

The natural result of this habit of ascending to a superlunary home, was the loss of an exact sense of how she was behaving below. At the Berkshire mansion, she wore a supercilious air, almost as icy as she accused the place of being. Emma knew she must have seen in the library a row of her literary ventures, exquisitely bound; but there was no allusion to the books. Mary Paynham's portrait of

Mrs. Warwick hung staring over the fireplace, and was criticized, as though its occupancy of that position had no significance.

"He thinks she has a streak of genius," Diana said to Emma.

"It may be shown in time," Emma replied, for a comment on the work. "He should know, for the Spanish pictures are noble acquisitions."

"They are, doubtless, good investments."

He had been foolish enough to say, in Diana's hearing, that he considered the purchase of the Berkshire estate a good investment. It had not yet a name. She suggested various titles for Emma to propose: "The Funds;" or "Capital Towers;" or "Dividend Manor;" or "Railholm;" blind to the evidence of inflicting pain. Emma, from what she had guessed concerning the purchaser of The Crossways, apprehended a discovery there which might make Tony's treatment of him unkinder, seeing that she appeared actuated contrariously; and only her invalid's new happiness in the small excursions she was capable of taking to a definite spot, of some homely attractiveness, moved her to follow her own proposal for the journey. Diana pleaded urgently, childishly in tone, to have Arthur Rhodes with them, "so as to be sure of a sympathetic companion for a walk on the Downs." At The Crossways, they were soon aware that Mr. Redworth's domestics were in attendance to serve them. Manifestly the house was his property, and not much of an investment! The principal bed-room, her father's once, and her own, devoted now to Emma's use, appalled her with a resemblance to her London room. She had noticed some of her furniture at "Dividend Manor," and chosen to consider it in the light of a bargain from a purchase at the sale of her goods. Here was her bed, her writing-table, her chair of authorship, desks, books, ornaments, water-colour sketches. And the drawing-room was fitted with her brackets and étagères, holding every knick-knack she had possessed and scattered, small bronzes, antiques, ivory junks, quaint ivory figures Chinese and Japanese, bits of porcelain, silver incense-urns, dozens of dainty sundries. She had a shamed curiosity to spy for an omission of one of them; all were there. The Crossways had been turned into a trap.

Her reply to this blunt wooing, conspired, she felt justified in thinking, between him and Emma, was emphatic in muteness. She treated it as if unobserved. At night, in bed, the scene of his mission from Emma to her under this roof, barred her customary ascent to her planetary kingdom. Next day she took Arthur after breakfast for a walk on the Downs and remained absent till ten minutes before the hour of dinner. As to that young gentleman, he was near to being caressed in public. Arthur's opinions, his good sayings, were quoted; his excellent companionship on really poetical walks, and perfect sympathy, praised to his face. Challenged by her initiative to a kind of language that threw Redworth out, he declaimed: " We pace with some who make young morning stale."

" Oh! stale as peel of fruit long since consumed," she chimed.

And so they proceeded ; and they laughed, Emma smiled a little, Redworth did the same beneath one of his questioning frowns — a sort of fatherly grimace.

A suspicion that this man, when infatuated, was able to practise the absurdest benevolence, the burlesque of chivalry, as a *man*-admiring sex esteems it, stirred very naughty depths of the woman in Dania, labouring under her perverted mood. She put him to proof, for the chance of arming her wickedest to despise him. Arthur was petted, consulted, cited, flattered all round; all but caressed. She played, with a reserve, the maturish young woman smitten by an adorable youth ; and enjoyed doing it because she hoped for a visible effect — more paternal benevolence — and could do it so dispassionately. Coquetry, Emma thought, was most unworthily shown; and it was of the worst description. Innocent of conspiracy, she had seen the array of Tony's lost household treasures: she wondered at a heartlessness that would not even utter common thanks to the friendly man for the compliment of prizing her portrait and the things she had owned; and there seemed an effort to wound him.

The invalided woman, charitable with allowances for her erratic husband, could offer none for the woman of a long widowhood, that had become a trebly sensitive maidenhood; abashed by her knowledge of the world, animated by her

abounding blood; cherishing her new freedom, dreading the
menacer; feeling, that though she held the citadel, she was
daily less sure of its foundations, and that her hope of some
last romance in life was going; for in him shone not a
glimpse.   He appeared to Diana as a fatal power, attracting
her without sympathy, benevolently overcoming: one of
those good men, strong men, who subdue and do not kindle.
The enthralment revolted a nature capable of accepting
subjection only by burning.   In return for his moral excellence, she gave him the moral sentiments: esteem, gratitude,
abstract admiration, perfect faith.   But the man?   She could
not now say she had never been loved; and a flood of tenderness rose in her bosom, swelling from springs that she
had previously reproved with a desperate severity: the unhappy, unsatisfied yearning to be more than loved, to love.
It was alive, out of the wreck of its first trial.   This, the
secret of her natural frailty, was bitter to her pride: chastely-
minded as she was, it whelmed her.   And then her comic
imagination pictured Redworth dramatically making love.
And to a widow!   It proved him to be senseless of romance.
Poetic men take aim at maidens.   His devotedness to a
widow was charged against him by the widow's shudder at
antecedents distasteful to her soul, a discoloration of her
life.   She wished to look entirely forward, as upon a world
washed clear of night, not to be cast back on her antecedents
by practical wooings or words of love; to live spiritually;
free of the shower at her eyelids attendant on any idea of
her loving.   The woman who talked of the sentimentalist's
"fiddling harmonics," herself stressed the material chords,
in her attempt to escape out of herself and away from her
pursuer.

Meanwhile she was as little conscious of what she was
doing as of how she appeared.   Arthur went about with
the moony air of surcharged sweetness, and a speculation
on it, alternately tiptoe and prostrate.   More of her intoxicating wine was administered to him, in utter thoughtlessness of consequences to one who was but a boy and a friend,
almost of her own rearing.   She told Emma, when leaving
The Crossways, that she had no desire to look on the place
again: she wondered at Mr. Redworth's liking such a solitude.   In truth, the look back on it let her perceive that

her husband haunted it, and disfigured the man, of real
generosity, as her heart confessed, but whom she accused
of a lack of prescient delicacy, for not knowing she would
and must be haunted there. Blaming him, her fountain of
colour shot up, at a murmur of her unjustness and the poor
man's hopes.

A week later, the youth she publicly named "her Arthur"
came down to Copsley with news of his having been recommended by Mr. Redworth for the post of secretary to an
old Whig nobleman famous for his patronage of men of
letters. And besides, he expected to inherit, he said, and
gazed in a way to sharpen her instincts. The wine he had
drunk of late from her flowing vintage was in his eyes.
They were on their usual rambles out along the heights.
"Accept, by all means, and thank Mr. Redworth," said she,
speeding her tongue to intercept him. "Literature is a
good stick and a bad horse. Indeed, I ought to know.
You can always write ; I hope you will."

She stepped fast, hearing : "Mrs. Warwick — Diana!
May I take your hand ? "

This was her pretty piece of work ! "Why should you ?
If you speak my Christian name, no : you forfeit any pretext. And pray, don't loiter. We are going at the pace of
the firm of Potter and Dawdle, and you know they never got
their shutters down till it was time to put them up again."

Nimble-footed as she was, she pressed ahead too fleetly
for amorous eloquence to have a chance. She heard
"Diana! " twice, through the rattling of her discourse and
flapping of her dress.

"Christian names are coin that seem to have an indifferent valuation of the property they claim," she said in
the Copsley garden; "and as for hands, at meeting and
parting, here is the friendliest you could have. Only don't
look rueful. My dear Arthur, spare me that, or I shall
blame myself horribly."

His chance had gone, and he composed his face. No
hope in speaking had nerved him; merely the passion to
speak. Diana understood the state, and pitied the naturally modest young fellow, and chafed at herself as a senseless incendiary, who did mischief right and left, from
seeking to shun the apparently inevitable. A side-thought

intruded, that he would have done his wooing poetically — not in the burly storm, or bull-Saxon, she apprehended. Supposing it imperative with her to choose ? She looked up, and the bird of broader wing darkened the whole sky, bidding her know that she had no choice.

Emma was requested to make Mr. Redworth acquainted with her story, all of it: — "So that this exalted friendship of his may be shaken to a common level. He has an unbearably high estimate of me, and it hurts me. Tell him all; and more than even you have known: — but for his coming to me, on the eve of your passing under the surgeon's hands, I should have gone — flung the world my glove! A matter of minutes. Ten minutes later ! The train was to start for France at eight, and I was awaited. I have to thank heaven that the man was one of those who can strike icily. Tell Mr. Redworth what I say. You two converse upon every subject. One may be too loftily respected — in my case. By and by — for he is a tolerant reader of life and women, I think — we shall be humdrum friends of the lasting order."

Emma's cheeks were as red as Diana's. "I fancy Tom Redworth has not much to learn concerning any person he cares for," she said. "You like him ? I have lost touch of you, my dear, and ask."

"I like him : that I can say. He is everything I am not. But now I am free, the sense of being undeservedly over-esteemed imposes fetters, and I don't like them. I have been called a Beauty. Rightly or other, I have had a Beauty's career; and a curious caged beast's life I have found it. Will you promise me to speak to him ? And also, thank him for helping Arthur Rhodes to a situation."

At this, the tears fell from her. And so enigmatical had she grown to Emma, that her bosom friend took them for a confessed attachment to the youth.

Diana's wretched emotion shamed her from putting any inquiries whether Redworth had been told. He came repeatedly, and showed no change of face, always continuing in the form of huge hovering griffin ; until an idea, instead of the monster bird, struck her. Might she not, after all, be cowering under imagination ? The very maidenly idea wakened her womanliness — to reproach her remainder of pride, not to see more accurately. It was the reason why she resolved, against Emma's extreme entreaties, to take lodgings in the South valley below the heights, where she could be independent of fancies and perpetual visitors, but near her beloved at any summons of urgency : which Emma would not habitually send because of the coming of a particular gentleman. Dresses were left at Copsley for a dining and sleeping there upon occasion, and poor Danvers, despairing over the riddle of her mistress, was condemned to the melancholy descent. "It's my belief," she confided to Lady Dunstane's maid Bartlett, "she'll hate men all her life after that Mr. Dacier."

If women were deceived, and the riddle deceived herself, there is excuse for a plain man like Redworth in not having the slightest clue to the daily shifting feminine maze he beheld. The strange thing was, that during her maiden time she had never been shifty or flighty, invariably limpid and direct.

CHAPTER XLI

CONTAINS A REVELATION OF THE ORIGIN OF THE TIGRESS IN DIANA

An afternoon of high summer blazed over London through the City's awning of smoke, and the three classes of the population, relaxed by the weariful engagement with what to them was a fruitless heat, were severally bathing their ideas in dreams of the contrast possible to embrace : breezy seas or moors, aërial Alps, cool beer. The latter, if confessedly the lower comfort, is the readier at command ; and Thomas Redworth, whose perspiring frame was directing his inward vision to fly for solace to a trim new yacht, built on his lines, beckoning from Southampton Water, had some of the amusement proper to things plucked off the levels, in the conversation of a couple of journeymen close ahead of him, as he made his way from a quiet street of brokers' offices to a City Bank. One asked the other if he had ever tried any of that cold stuff they were now selling out of barrows, with cream. His companion answered, that he had not got much opinion of stuff of the sort; and what was it like?

"Well, it's cheap, it ain't bad; it's cooling. But it ain't refreshing."

"Just what I reckoned all that newfangle rubbish."

Without a consultation, the conservatives in beverage filed with a smart turn about, worthy of veterans at parade on the drill-ground, into a public-house; and a dialogue chiefly remarkable for absence of point, furnished matter to the politician's head of the hearer. Provided that their beer was unadulterated! Beer they would have; and why not, in weather like this? But how to make the publican honest! And he was not the only trickster preying on the multitudinous poor copper crowd, rightly to be protected by the silver and the golden. Revelations of the arts practised to plump them with raw-earth and minerals in the guise of nourishment, had recently knocked at the door of the general conscience and obtained a civil reply from the footman. Repulsive as the thought was to one still holding to Whiggish Liberalism, though flying various Radical kites, he was caught by the decisive ultra-torrent, and whirled to admit the necessity for the interference of the State, to stop the poisoning of the poor. Upper classes have never legislated systematically in their interests; and quid . . . rabidæ tradis ovile lupæ? says one of the multitude. We may be seeing fangs of wolves where fleeces waxed. The State that makes it a vital principle to concern itself with the helpless poor, meets instead of waiting for Democracy; which is a perilous flood but when it is dammed. Or else, in course of time, luxurious yachting, my friend, will encounter other reefs and breakers than briny ocean's! Capital, whereat Diana Warwick aimed her superbest sneer, has its instant duties. She theorized on the side of poverty, and might do so: he had no right to be theorizing on the side of riches. Across St. George's Channel, the cry for humanity in Capital was an agony. He ought to be there, doing, not cogitating. The post of Irish Secretary must be won by real service founded on absolute local knowledge. Yes, and sympathy, if you like; but sympathy is for proving, not prating. . . .

These were the meditations of a man in love; veins, arteries, headpiece in love, and constantly brooding at a solitary height over the beautiful coveted object; only too bewildered by her multifarious evanescent feminine evasions, as of colours on a ruffled water, to think of pouncing: for he could do nothing to soften, nothing that seemed to please her: and all the while, the motive of her mind impelled him in reflection beyond practicable limits: even pointing him to apt quotations! Either he thought within her thoughts, or his own were at her disposal. Nor was it sufficient for him to be sensible of her influence, to restrain the impetus he took from her. He had already wedded her morally, and much that he did, as well as whatever he debated, came of Diana; more than if they had been coupled, when his downright practical good sense could have spoken. She held him suspended, swaying him in that posture; and he was not a whit ashamed of it. The beloved woman was throned on the very highest of the man.

Furthermore, not being encouraged, he had his peculiar reason for delay, though now he could offer her wealth. She had once in his hearing derided the unpleasant hiss of the ungainly English matron's title of Mrs. There was no harm in the accustomed title, to his taste; but she disliking it, he did the same, on her special behalf; and the prospect, funereally draped, of a title sweeter-sounding to her ears, was above his horizon. Bear in mind, that he underwent the reverse of encouragement. Any small thing to please her was magnified, and the anticipation of it nerved the modest hopes of one who deemed himself and any man alive deeply her inferior.

Such was the mood of the lover condemned to hear another malignant scandal defiling the name of the woman he worshipped. Sir Lukin Dunstane, extremely hurried, bumped him on the lower step of the busy Bank, and said: "Pardon!" and "Ha! Redworth! making money?"

"Why, what are you up to down here?" he was asked, and he answered: "Down to the Tower, to an officer quartered there. Not bad quarters, but an infernal distance. Business."

Having cloaked his expedition to the distance with the comprehensive word, he repeated it; by which he feared he had rendered it too significant, and he said: "No, no; nothing particular; " and that caused the secret he contained to swell in his breast rebelliously, informing the candid creature of the fact of his hating to lie: whereupon thus he poured himself out, in the quieter bustle of an alley, off the main thoroughfare. "You're a friend of hers. I'm sure you care for her reputation; you're an old friend of hers, and she's my wife's dearest friend: and I'm fond of her too; and I ought to be, and ought to know, and do know: — pure? Strike off my fist if there's a spot on her character! And a scoundrel like that fellow Wroxeter! — Damnedest rage I ever was in! — Swears . . . down at Lockton . . . when she was a girl. Why, Redworth, I can tell you, when Diana Warwick was a girl! — "

Redworth stopped him. "Did he say it in your presence?"

Sir Lukin was drawn-up by the harsh question. "Well, no; not exactly." He tried to hesitate, but he was in the hot vein of a confidence and he wanted advice. "The cur said it to a woman — hang the woman! And she hates Diana Warwick: I can't tell why — a regular snake's hate. By Jove! how women can hate!"

"Who is the woman?" said Redworth.

Sir Lukin complained of the mob at his elbows. "I don't like mentioning names here."

A convenient open door of offices invited him to drag his receptacle, and possible counsellor, into the passage, where immediately he bethought him of a postponement of the distinct communication; but the vein was too hot. "I say, Redworth, I wish you'd dine with me. Let's drive up to my Club. — Very well, two words. And I warn you, I shall call him out, and make it appear it's about another woman, who'll like nothing so much, if I know the Jezebel. Some women are *hussies*, let 'em be handsome as houris. And she's a fire-ship; by heaven, she is! Come, you're a friend of my wife's, but you're a man of the world and my friend, and you know how fellows are tempted, Tom Redworth. — Cur though he is, he's likely to step out and receive a lesson. — Well, he's the favoured cavalier for the present . . . h'm . . . Fryar-Gunnett. Swears he told her, circumstantially; and it was down at Lockton, when Diana Warwick was a girl. Swears she'll spit her venom at her, so that

Diana Warwick sha'n't hold her head up in London Society, what with that cur Wroxeter, Old Dannisburgh, and Dacier. And it does count a list, does n't it? — confound the handsome hag! She's jealous of a dark rival. I've been down to Colonel Hartswood at the Tower, and he thinks Wroxeter deserves horsewhipping, and we may manage it. I know you're dead against duelling; and so am I, on my honour. But you see there are cases where a lady must be protected; and anything new, left to circulate against a lady who has been talked of twice — Oh, by Jove! it must be stopped. If she has a male friend on earth, it must be stopped on the spot."

Redworth eyed Sir Lukin curiously through his wrath.

"We'll drive up to your Club," he said.

"Hartswood dines with me this evening, to confer," rejoined Sir Lukin. "Will you meet him?"

"I can't," said Redworth, "I have to see a lady, whose affairs I have been attending to in the City; and I'm engaged for the evening. You perceive, my good fellow," he resumed, as they rolled along, "this is a delicate business. You have to consider your wife. Mrs. Warwick's name won't come up, but another woman's will."

"I meet Wroxeter at a gambling-house he frequents, and publicly call him cheat — slap his face, if need be."

"Sure to!" repeated Redworth. "No stupid pretext will quash the woman's name. Now, such a thing as a duel would give pain enough."

"Of course; I understand," Sir Lukin nodded his clear comprehension. "But what is it you advise, to trounce the scoundrel, and silence him?"

"Leave it to me for a day. Let me have your word that you won't take a step: positively — neither you nor Colonel Hartswood. I'll see you by appointment at your Club." Redworth looked up over the chimneys. "We're going to have a storm and a gale, I can tell you."

"Gale and storm!" cried Sir Lukin; "what has that got to do with it?"

"Think of something else for a time."

"And that brute of a woman — deuced handsome she is! — if you care for fair women, Redworth: — she's a Venus jumped slap out of the waves, and the Devil for sire — *that* you learn : — running about, sowing her lies. She's a yellow witch. Oh! but she's a shameless minx. And a black-leg cur like Wroxeter! Any woman intimate with a fellow like that, stamps herself. I loathe her. Sort of woman who swears in the morning you're the only man on earth; and next day — that evening — engaged! — fee to Polly Hopkins — and it's a gentleman, a nobleman, my lord! — been going on behind your back half the season! — and she is n't hissed when she abuses a lady, a saint in comparison! You know the world, old fellow : — Brighton, Richmond, visits to a friend as deep in the bog. How Fryar-Gunnett — a man, after all — can stand it! And drives of an afternoon for an airing — by heaven! You're out of that mess, Redworth: not much taste for the sex ; and you're right, you're lucky. Upon my word, the corruption of society in the present day is awful; it's appalling. — I rattled at her : and oh! dear me, perks on her hind heels and defies me to prove: and *she's* no pretender, but hopes she's as good as any of my 'chaste Dianas.' My dear old friend, it's when you come upon women of that kind you have a sickener. And I'm bound by the best there is in a man — honour, gratitude, all the list — to defend Diana Warwick."

"So, you see, for your wife's sake, your name can't be hung on a woman of that kind," said Redworth. "I'll call here the day after to-morrow at three P. M."

Sir Lukin descended and vainly pressed Redworth to run up into his Club for refreshment. Said he roguishly : "Who's the lady ?"

The tone threw Redworth on his frankness.

"The lady I've been doing business for in the City, is Miss Paynham."

"I saw her once at Copsley ; good-looking. Cleverish ?"

"She has ability."

Entering his Club, Sir Lukin was accosted in the reading-room by a cavalry officer, a Colonel Launay, an old Harrovian, who stood at the window and asked him whether it was not Tom Redworth in the cab. Another, of the same School, standing squared before a sheet of one of the evening newspapers, heard the name and joined them, saying : "Tom Redworth is going to be married, some fellow told me."

"He 'll make a deuced good husband to any woman — if it 's true," said Sir Lukin, with Miss Paynham ringing in his head. "He 's a cool-blooded old boy, and likes women for their intellects."

Colonel Launay hummed in meditative emphasis. He stared at vacancy with a tranced eye, and turning a similar gaze on Sir Lukin, as if through him, burst out: "Oh, by George, I say, what a hugging that woman 'll get!"

The cocking of ears and queries of Sir Lukin put him to the test of his right to the remark; for it sounded of occult acquaintance with interesting subterranean facts; and there was a communication, in brief syllables and the dot language, crudely masculine. Immensely surprised, Sir Lukin exclaimed: "Of course! when fellows live quietly and are careful of themselves. Ah! you may think you know a man for years, and you don't: you don't know more than an inch or two of him. Why, of course, Tom Redworth 'd be uxorious — the very man! And tell us what has become of the Firefly now? One never sees her. Did n't complain?"

"Very much the contrary."

Both gentlemen were grave, believing their knowledge in the subterranean world of a wealthy city to give them a positive cognizance of female humanity; and the substance of Colonel Launay 's communication had its impressiveness for them.

"Well, it 's a turn right-about-face for me," said Sir Lukin. "What a world we live in! I fancy I 've hit on the woman he means to marry; — had an idea of another woman once; but he 's one of your friendly fellows with women. That 's how it was I took him for a fish. Great mistake, I admit. But Tom Redworth 's a man of morals after all; and when those men do break loose for a plunge — ha! Have you ever boxed with him? Well, he keeps himself in training, I can tell you."

Sir Lukin 's round of visits drew him at night to Lady Singleby 's, where he sighted the identical young lady of his thoughts, Miss Paynham, temporarily a guest of the house; and he talked to her of Redworth, and had the satisfaction to spy a blush, a rageing blush: which avowal presented her to his view as an exceedingly good-looking girl; so that he began mentally to praise Redworth for a manly superiority to small trifles and the world's tattle.

"You saw him to-day," he said.

She answered: "Yes. He goes down to Copsley to-morrow."

"I think not," said Sir Lukin.

"I have it from him." She closed her eyelids in speaking.

"He and I have some rather serious business in town."

"Serious?"

"Don't be alarmed: not concerning him."

"Whom, then? You have told me so much — I have a right to know."

"Not an atom of danger, I assure you?"

"It concerns Mrs. Warwick!" said she.

Sir Lukin thought the guess extraordinary. He preserved an impenetrable air. But he had spoken enough to set that giddy head spinning.

Nowhere during the night was Mrs. Fryar-Gunnett visible. Earlier than usual, she was riding next day in the Row, alone for perhaps two minutes, and Sir Lukin passed her, formally saluting. He could not help the look behind him, she sat so bewitchingly on horseback! He looked, and behold, her riding-whip was raised erect from the elbow. It was his horse that wheeled; compulsorily he was borne at a short canter to her side.

"Your commands?"

The handsome Amabel threw him a sombre glance from the corners of her uplifted eyelids; and snakish he felt it; but her colour and the line of her face went well with sullenness; and, her arts of fascination cast aside, she fascinated him more in seeming homelier, girlish. If the trial of her beauty of a woman in a temper can bear the strain, she has attractive lures indeed; irresistible to the amorous idler: and when, in addition, being the guilty person, she plays the injured, her show of temper on the taking face pitches him into perplexity with his own emotions, creating a desire to strike and be stricken, howl and set howling, which is of the happier augury for tender reconcilement on the terms of the gentleman on his kneecap.

"You've been doing a pretty thing!" she said, and

briefly she named her house and half an hour, and flew. Sir Lukin was left to admire the figure of the horsewoman. Really, her figure had an air of vindicating her successfully, except for the poison she spat at Diana Warwick. And what pretty thing had he been doing? He reviewed dozens of speculations until the impossibility of seizing one determined him to go to Mrs. Fryar-Gunnett at the end of the half-hour — " Just to see what these women have to say for themselves."

Some big advance drops of Redworth's thunderstorm drawing gloomily overhead, warned him to be quick and get his horse into stables. Dismounted, the sensational man was irresolute, suspecting a female trap. But curiosity combined with the instinctive turning of his nose in the direction of the lady's house, led him thither, to an accompaniment of celestial growls, which impressed him, judging by that naughty-girl face of hers and the woman's tongue she had, as a likely prelude to the scene to come below.

CHAPTER XLII

THE PENULTIMATE: SHOWING A FINAL STRUGGLE FOR LIBERTY AND RUN INTO HARNESS

THE prophet of the storm had forgotten his prediction; which, however, was of small concern to him, apart from the ducking he received midway between the valley and the heights of Copsley; whither he was bound, on a mission so serious that, according to his custom in such instances, he chose to take counsel of his active legs : an adviseable course when the brain wants clearing and the heart fortifying. Diana's face was clearly before him through the deluge; now in single features, the dimple running from her mouth, the dark bright eyes and cut of eyelids, and nostrils alive under their lightning; now in her whole radiant smile, or musefully listening, nursing a thought. Or she was obscured, and he felt the face. The individuality of it had him by the heart, beyond his powers of visioning. On his arrival, he stood in the hall, adrip like one of the trees of the lawn, laughing at Lady Dunstane's anxious exclamations. His portmanteau had come and he was expected; she hurried out at the first ringing of the bell, to greet and reproach him for walking in such weather.

"Diana has left me," she said, when he reappeared in dry clothing. "We are neighbours; she has taken cottage-lodgings at Selshall, about an hour's walk:— one of her wild dreams of independence. Are you disappointed?"

"I am," Redworth confessed.

Emma coloured. "She requires an immense deal of humouring at present. The fit will wear off; only we must wait for it. Any menace to her precious liberty makes her prickly. She is passing the day with the Pettigrews, who have taken a place near her village for a month. She promised to dine and sleep here, if she returned in time. What is your news?"

"Nothing; the world wags on."

"You have nothing special to tell her?"

"Nothing;" he hummed; "nothing, I fancy, that she does not know."

"You said you were disappointed."

"It's always a pleasure to see her."

"Even in her worst moods, I find it so."

"Oh! moods!" quoth Redworth.

"My friend, they are to be reckoned with women."

"Certainly; what I meant was, that I don't count them against women."

"Good; but my meaning was . . . I think I remember your once comparing them and the weather; and you spoke of the 'one point more variable in women.' You may forestall your storms. There is no calculating the effect of a few little words at a wrong season."

"With women! I suppose not. I have no pretension to a knowledge of the sex."

Emma imagined she had spoken plainly enough, if he had immediate designs; and she was not sure of that, and wished rather to shun his confidences while Tony was in her young widowhood, revelling in her joy of liberty. By and by, was her thought: perhaps next year. She dreaded Tony's refusal of the yoke, and her iron-hardness to the dearest of men proposing it: and moreover, her further to be apprehended holding to the refusal, for the sake of consistency, if it was once uttered. For her own sake, she shrank from hearing intentions, that distressing the good man, she would have to discountenance. His candour in confessing disappointment, and his open face, his excellent sense too, gave her some assurance of his not being foolishly impetuous. After he had read to her for an hour, as his habit was on evenings and wet days, their discussion of this and that in the book lulled any doubts she had of his prudence, enough to render it even a dubious point whether she might be speculating upon a wealthy bachelor in the old-fashioned ultra-feminine manner; the which she so abhorred that she rejected the idea. Consequently, Redworth's proposal to walk down to the valley for Diana, and bring her back, struck her as natural when a shaft of western sunshine from a whitened edge of raincloud struck her windows. She let him go without an intimated monition or a thought of one; thinking simply that her Tony would be more likely to come, having him for escort. Those are silly women who are always imagining designs and intrigues and future palpitations in the commonest actions of either sex. Emma Dunstane leaned to the contrast between herself and them.

Danvers was at the house about sunset, reporting her mistress to be on her way, with Mr. Redworth. The maid's tale of the dreadful state of the lanes, accounted for their tardiness; and besides the sunset had been magnificent. Diana knocked at Emma's bedroom door, to say, outside, hurriedly in passing, how splendid the sunset had been, and beg for an extra five minutes. Taking full fifteen, she swam into the drawing-room, lively with kisses on Emma's cheeks, and excuses, referring her misconduct in being late to the seductions of "Sol" in his glory. Redworth said he had rarely seen so wonderful a sunset. The result of their unanimity stirred Emma's bosom to match-making regrets; and the walk of the pair together, alone under the propitious flaming heavens, appeared to her now as an opportunity lost. From sisterly sympathy, she fancied she could understand Tony's liberty-loving reluctance: she had no comprehension of the backwardness of the man beholding the dear woman handsomer than in her maiden or her married time: and sprightlier as well. She chatted deliciously, and drew Redworth to talk his best on his choicer subjects, playing over them like a fire-wisp, determined at once to flounder him and to make him shine. Her tender esteem for the man was transparent through it all; and Emma, whose evening had gone happily between them, said to her, in their privacy, before parting: 'You seemed to have been inspired by 'Sol,' my dear. You do like him, don't you?"

Diana vowed she adored him; and with a face of laughter in rosy suffusion, put Sol for Redworth, Redworth for Sol; but, watchful of Emma's visage, said finally: "If you mean the mortal man, I think him up to almost all your hyperboles — as far as men go; and he departed to his night's rest, which I hope will be good, like a king. Not to admire him, would argue me senseless, heartless. I do; I have reason to."

"And you make him the butt of your ridicule, Tony."

"No; I said 'like a king;' and he is one. He has, to me, morally the grandeur of your Sol sinking, Cæsar stabbed, Cato on the sword-point. He is Roman, Spartan, Imperial; English, if you like, the pick of the land. It is an honour to call him friend, and I do trust he will choose the pick among us, to make her a happy woman — if she's for running in harness. There, I can't say more."

Emma had to be satisfied with it, for the present.

They were astonished at breakfast by seeing Sir Lukin ride past the windows. He entered with the veritable appetite of a cavalier who had ridden from London fasting; and why he had come at that early hour, he was too hungry to explain. The ladies retired to read their letters by the morning's post; whereupon Sir Lukin called to Redworth: "I met that woman in the park yesterday, and had to stand a volley. I went beating about London for you all the afternoon and evening. She swears you rated her like a scullery wench, and threatened to ruin Wroxeter. Did you see him? She says, the story's true in one particular, that he did snatch a kiss, and got mauled. Not so much to pay for it! But what a ruffian — eh?"

"I saw him," said Redworth. "He's one of the new set of noblemen who take bribes to serve as baits for transactions in the City. They help to the ruin of their order, or are signs of its decay. We won't judge it by him. He favoured me with his ' word of honour ' that the thing you heard was entirely a misstatement, and so forth: — apologized, I suppose. He mumbled something."

"A thorough cur!"

"He professed his readiness to fight, if either of us was not contented."

"He spoke to the wrong man. I've half a mind to ride back and have him out for that rascal ' osculation ' — and the lady unwilling! — and she a young one, a girl, under the protection of the house! By Jove! Redworth, when you come to consider the scoundrels men can be, it stirs a fellow's bile. There's a deal of that sort of villany going — and succeeding sometimes! He deserves the whip or a bullet."

"A sermon from Lukin Dunstane might punish him."

"Oh! I'm a sinner, I know. But, go and tell one woman of another woman, and that a lie! That's beyond me."

"The gradations of the deeps are perhaps measureable to those who are in them."

"The sermon's at me — pop!" said Sir Lukin. "By the way, I'm coming round to think Diana Warwick was right when she used to jibe at me for throwing up my commission. Idleness is the devil — or mother of him. I manage my estates; but the truth is, it does n't occupy my mind."

"Your time."

"My mind, I say."

"Whichever you please."

"You're crusty to-day, Redworth. Let me tell you, I *think* — and hard too, when the fit 's on me. However, you did right in stopping — I'll own — a piece of folly, and shutting the mouths of those two; though it caused me to come in for a regular drencher. But a pretty woman in a right-down termagant passion is good theatre; because it can't last, at that pace; and you're sure of your agreeable tableau. Not that I trust her ten minutes out of sight — or any woman, except one or two; my wife and

Diana Warwick. Trust those you've tried, old boy.
Diana Warwick ought to be taught to thank you; though
I don't know how it's to be done."

"The fact of it is," Redworth frowned and rose, "I've
done mischief. I had no right to mix myself in it. I'm
seldom caught off my feet by an impulse; but I was. I
took the fever from you."

He squared his figure at the window, and looked up on
a driving sky.

"Come, let's play open cards, Tom Redworth," said Sir
Lukin, leaving the table and joining his friend by the
window. "You moral men are doomed to be marrying
men, always; and quite right. Not that one doesn't hear
a roundabout thing or two about you: no harm. Very
much the contrary: — as the world goes. But you're the
man to marry a wife; and if I guess the lady, she's a sensible girl and won't be jealous. I'd swear she only waits
for asking."

"Then you don't guess the lady," said Redworth.

"Mary Paynham?"

The desperate half-laugh greeting the name convinced
more than a dozen denials.

Sir Lukin kept edging round for a full view of the friend
who shunned inspection. "But is it? . . . can it be? it
must be, after all! . . . why, of course it is! But the
thing staring us in the face is just what we never see.
Just the husband for her! — and she's the wife! Why,
Diana Warwick's the very woman, of course! I remember
I used to think so before she was free to wed."

"She is not of that opinion." Redworth blew a heavy
breath; and it should be chronicled as a sigh; but it was
hugely masculine.

"Because you didn't attack, the moment she was free;
that's what upset my calculations," the sagacious gentleman continued, for a vindication of his acuteness: then
seizing the reply: "Refuses? You don't mean to say
you're the man to take a refusal? and from a green widow
in the blush? Did you see her cheeks when she was peeping at the letter in her hand? She colours at half a word
— takes the lift of a finger for Hymen coming. And lots
of fellows are after her; I know it from Emmy. But

you're not the man to be refused. You're her friend — her champion. That woman Fryar-Gunnett would have it you were the favoured lover, and sneered at my talk of old friendship. Women are always down dead on the facts; can't put them off a scent!"

"There's the mischief!" Redworth blew again. "I had no right to be championing Mrs. Warwick's name. Or the world won't give it, at all events. I'm a blundering donkey. Yes, she wishes to keep her liberty. And, upon my soul, I'm in love with everything she wishes! I've got the habit."

"Habit be hanged!" cried Sir Lukin. "You're in love with the woman. I know a little more of you now, Mr. Tom. You're a fellow in earnest about what you do. You're feeling it now, on the rack, by heaven! though you keep a bold face. Did she speak positively? — sort of feminine of 'you're the monster, not the man?' or measured little doctor's dose of pity? — worse sign! You're not going?"

"If you'll drive me down in half an hour," said Redworth.

"Give me an hour," Sir Lukin replied, and went straight to his wife's blue-room.

Diana was roused from a meditation on a letter she held, by the entrance of Emma in her bed-chamber, to whom she said: "I have here the very craziest bit of writing! — but what is disturbing you, dear?"

Emma sat beside her, panting and composing her lips to speak. "Do you love me? I throw policy to the winds, if only I can batter at you for your heart and find it! Tony, do you love me? But don't answer: give me your hand. You have rejected him!"

"He has told you?"

"No. He is not the man to cry out for a wound. He heard in London — Lukin has had the courage to tell me, after his fashion: — Tom Redworth heard an old story, coming from one of the baser kind of women: grossly false, he knew. I mention only Lord Wroxeter and Lockton. He went to man and woman both, and had it refuted, and stopped their tongues, on peril; as he of all men is able to do when he wills it."

Observing the quick change in Tony's eyes, Emma exclaimed: "How you looked disdain when you asked whether he had told me! But why are you the handsome tigress to him, of all men living! The dear fellow, dear to me at least! since the day he first saw you, has worshipped you and striven to serve you: — and harder than any Scriptural service to have the beloved woman to wife. I know nothing to compare with it, for he is a man of warmth. He is one of those rare men of honour who can command their passion; who venerate when they love: and those are the men that women select for punishment! Yes, you! It is to the woman he loves that he cannot show himself as he is, because he is at her feet. You have managed to stamp your spirit on him; and as a consequence, he defends you now, for flinging him off. And now his chief regret is, that he has caused his name to be coupled with yours. I suppose he had some poor hope, seeing you free. Or else the impulse to protect the woman of his heart and soul was too strong. I have seen what he suffered, years back, at the news of your engagement."

"Oh, for God's sake, don't," cried Tony, tears running over, and her dream of freedom, her visions of romance, drowning.

"It was like the snapping of the branch of an oak, when the trunk stands firm," Emma resumed, in her desire to scourge as well as to soften. "But similes applied to him will strike you as incongruous." Tony swayed her body, for a negative, very girlishly and consciously. "He probably did not woo you in a poetic style, or the courtly by prescription." Again Tony swayed; she had to hug herself under the stripes, and felt as if alone at sea, with her dear heavens pelting. "You have sneered at him for his calculating — to his face: and it was when he was comparatively poor that he calculated — to his cost! — that he dared not ask you to marry a man who could not offer you a tithe of what he considered fit for the peerless woman. Peerless, I admit. There he was not wrong. But if he had valued you half a grain less, he might have won you. You talk much of chivalry; you conceive a superhuman ideal, to which you fit a very indifferent wooden model, while the man of all the world the most chivalrous! . . .

He is a man quite other from what you think him: anything but a 'Cuthbert Dering' or a 'Man of Two Minds.' He was in the drawing-room below, on the day I received your last maiden letter from The Crossways — now his property, in the hope of making it yours."

"I behaved abominably there!" interposed Tony, with a gasp.

"Let it pass. At any rate, that was the prick of a needle, not the blow of a sword."

"But marriage, dear Emmy! marriage! Is marriage to be the end of me?"

"What amazing apotheosis have you in prospect? And are you steering so particularly well by yourself?"

"Miserably! But I can dream. And the thought of a husband cuts me from any dreaming. It's all dead flat earth at once!"

"Would you have rejected him when you were a girl?"

"I think so."

"The superior merits of another? . . ."

"Oh, no, no, no, *no!* I might have accepted him: and I might not have made him happy. I wanted a hero, and the jewelled garb and the feather did not suit him."

"No; he is not that description of lay-figure. You have dressed it, and gemmed it, and — made your discovery. Here is a true man; and if you can find me any of your heroes to match him, I will thank you. He came on the day I speak of, to consult me as to whether, with the income he then had . . . Well, I had to tell him you were engaged. The man has never wavered in his love of you since that day. He has had to bear something."

This was an electrical bolt into Tony's bosom, shaking her from self-pity and shame to remorseful pity of the suffering lover; and the tears ran in streams, as she said: "He bore it, Emmy, he bore it." She sobbed out: "And he went on building a fortune and batting! Whatever he undertakes he does perfectly — approve of the pattern or not. Oh! I have no doubt he had his nest of wishes piping to him all the while: only it seems quaint, dear, quaint, and against everything we've been reading of lovers! Love was his bread and butter!" Her dark eyes showered. "And to tell you what you do not know of him, his way of making love is really," she sobbed, "pretty. It . . . it took me by surprise; I was expecting a bellow and an assault of horns; and if, dear: — you will say, what boarding-school girl have you got with you! and I feel myself getting childish: — if Sol in his glory had not been so m . . . majestically m . . . magnificent, nor seemed to show me the king . . . kingdom of my dreams, I might have stammered the opposite word to the one he heard. Last night, when he took my hand kindly before going to bed, I had a fit for dropping on my knees to him. I saw him bleed, and he held himself right royally. I told you he did; — Sol in his moral grandeur! How infinitely above the physical monarch — is he not, Emmy? What one dislikes, is the devotion of all that grandeur to win a widow. It should be a maiden princess. You feel it so, I am sure. And here am I, as if a maiden princess were I, demanding romantic accessories of rubious vapour in the man condescending to implore the widow to wed him. But, tell me, does he know everything of his widow — everything? I shall not have to go through the frightful chapter?"

"He is a man with his eyes awake; he knows as much as any husband could require to know," said Emma; adding: "My darling! he trusts you. It is the soul of the man that loves you, as it is mine. You will not tease him? Promise me. Give yourself frankly. You see it clearly before you."

"I see compulsion, my dear. What I see, is a regiment of Proverbs, bearing placards instead of guns, and each one a taunt at women, especially at widows. They march; they form square; they enclose me in the middle, and I have their inscriptions to digest. Read that crazy letter from Mary Paynham while I am putting on my bonnet. I perceive I have been crying like a raw creature in her teens. I don't know myself. An advantage of the darker complexions is our speedier concealment of the traces."

Emma read Miss Paynham's letter, and returned it with the comment: "Utterly crazy." Tony said: "Is it not? I am to 'Pause before I trifle with a noble heart too long.' She is to 'have her happiness in the constant prayer for ours;' and she is 'warned by one of those intimations

never failing her, that he runs a serious danger.' It reads
like a Wizard's Almanack. And here: 'Homogeneity of
sentiment the most perfect, is unable to contend with the
fatal charm, which exercised by an indifferent person, must
be ascribed to original predestination.' She should be
under the wing of Lady Wathin. There is the mother for
such chicks! But I'll own to you, Emmy, that after the
perusal, I did ask myself a question as to my likeness of
late to the writer. I have drivelled . . . I was shuddering over it when you came in. I have sentimentalized up
to thin smoke. And she tells a truth when she says I
am not to 'count social cleverness' — she means volu-
bility — 'as a warrant for domineering a capacious intelligence:' — because of the gentleman's modesty. Agreed:
I have done it; I am contrite. I am going into slavery
to make amends for presumption. Banality, thy name is
marriage!"

"Your business is to accept life as we have it," said
Emma; and Tony shrugged. She was precipitate in going
forth to her commonplace fate, and scarcely looked at the
man requested by Emma to escort her to her cottage. After
their departure, Emma fell into laughter at the last words
with the kiss of her cheeks: "Here goes old Ireland!"
But, from her look and from what she had said upstairs,
Emma could believe that the singular sprite of girlishness
invading and governing her latterly, had yielded place to
the woman she loved.

CHAPTER XLIII

NUPTIAL CHAPTER; AND OF HOW A BARELY WILLING WOMAN
WAS LED TO BLOOM WITH THE NUPTIAL SENTIMENT

EMMA watched them on their way through the park, till
they rounded the beechwood, talking, it could be surmised,
of ordinary matters; the face of the gentleman turning at
times to his companion's, which steadily fronted the gale.
She left the ensuing to a prayer for their good direction,
with a chuckle at Tony's evident feeling of a ludicrous

posture, and the desperate rush of her agile limbs to have
it over. But her prayer throbbed almost to a supplication
that the wrong done to her beloved by Dacier — the wound
to her own sisterly pride rankling as an injury to her sex,
might be cancelled through the union of the woman noble
in the sight of God with a more manlike man.

Meanwhile the feet of the couple were going faster than
their heads to the end of the journey. Diana knew she
would have to hoist the signal — and how? The prospect was dumbfoundering. She had to think of appeasing
her Emma. Redworth, for his part, actually supposed she
had accepted his escorting in proof of the plain friendship
offered him over-night.

"What do your 'birds' do in weather like this?" she
said.

"Cling to their perches and wait patiently. It's the
bad time with them when you don't hear them chirp."

"Of course you foretold the gale."

"Oh, well, it did not require a shepherd or a skipper
for that."

"Your grand gift will be useful to a yachtsman."

"You like yachting. When I have tried my new
schooner in the Channel, she is at your command for as
long as you and Lady Dunstane please."

"So you acknowledge that birds — things of nature —
have their bad time?"

"They profit ultimately by the deluge and the wreck.
Nothing on earth is 'tucked-up' in perpetuity."

"Except the dead. But why should the schooner be at
our command?"

"I shall be in Ireland."

He could not have said sweeter to her ears or more
touching.

"We shall hardly feel safe without the weatherwise on
board."

"You may count on my man Barnes; I have proved him.
He is up to his work even when he's bilious: only, in that
case, occurring about once a fortnight, you must leave him
to fight it out with the elements."

"I rather like men of action to have a temper."

"I can't say much for a bilious temper."

The weather to-day really seemed of that kind, she remarked. He assented, in the shrug manner — not to dissent: she might say what she would. He helped nowhere to a lead; and so quick are the changes of mood at such moments that she was now far from him under the failure of an effort to come near. But thoughts of Emma pressed.

"The name of the new schooner? Her name is her picture to me."

"I wanted you to christen her."

"Launched without a name?"

"I took a liberty."

Needless to ask, but she did. "With whom?"

"I named her *Diana*."

"May the Goddess of the silver bow and crescent protect her! To me the name is ominous of mischance."

"I would commit my fortunes and life!" . . . He checked his tongue, ejaculating: "Omens!"

She had veered straight away from her romantic aspirations to the blunt extreme of thinking that a widow should be wooed in unornamented matter-of-fact, as she is wedded, with a "wilt thou," and "I will," and no decorative illusions. Downright, for the unpoetic creature, if you please! So she rejected the accompaniment of the silver Goddess and high seas for an introduction of the crisis.

"This would be a thunderer on our coasts. I had a trial of my sailing powers in the Mediterranean."

As she said it, her musings on him then, with the contrast of her position toward him now, fierily brushed her cheeks; and she wished him the man to make one snatch at her poor lost small butterfly bit of freedom, so that she might suddenly feel in haven, at peace with her expectant Emma. He could have seen the inviting consciousness, but he was absurdly watchful lest the flying sprays of border trees should strike her. He mentioned his fear, and it became an excuse for her seeking protection of her veil. "It is our natural guardian," she said.

"Not much against timber," said he.

The worthy creature's anxiety was of the pattern of cavaliers escorting dames — an exaggeration of honest zeal;

a present example of clownish goodness, it might seem; until entering the larch and firwood along the beaten heights, there was a rocking and straining of the shallow-rooted trees in a tremendous gust that quite pardoned him for curving his arm in a hoop about her and holding a shoulder in front. The veil did her positive service.

He was honourably scrupulous not to presume. A right good unimpulsive gentleman: the same that she had always taken him for and liked.

"These firs are not taproots," he observed, by way of apology.

Her dress volumed and her ribands rattled and chirruped on the verge of the slope. "I will take your arm here," she said.

Redworth received the little hand, saying: "Lean to me."

They descended upon great surges of wind piping and driving every light surface-atom as foam; and they blinked and shook; even the man was shaken. But their arms were interlinked and they grappled; the battering enemy made them one. It might mean nothing, or everything: to him it meant the sheer blissful instant.

At the foot of the hill, he said: "It's harder to keep to the terms of yesterday."

"What were they?" said she, and took his breath more than the fury of the storm had done.

"Raise the veil, I beg."

"Widows do not wear it."

The look revealed to him was a fugitive of the wilds, no longer the glittering shooter of arrows.

"Have you? . . ." changed to me, was the signification understood. "Can you? — for life! Do you think you can?"

His poverty in the pleading language melted her. "What I cannot do, my best of friends, is to submit to be seated on a throne, with you petitioning. Yes, as far as concerns this hand of mine, if you hold it worthy of you. We will speak of that. Now tell me the name of the weed trailing along the hedge there."

He knew it well; a common hedgerow weed; but the placid diversion baffled him. It was clematis, he said.

"It drags in the dust when it has no firm arm to cling to. I passed it beside you yesterday with a flaunting mind and not a suspicion of a likeness. How foolish I was! I could volubly sermonize; only it should be a young maid to listen. Forgive me the yesterday."

"You have never to ask. You withdraw your hand — was I rough?"

"No," she smiled demurely; "it must get used to the shackles: but my cottage is in sight. I have a growing love for the place. We will enter it like plain people — if you think of coming in."

As she said it she had a slight shock of cowering under eyes tolerably hawkish in their male glitter; but her coolness was not disturbed, and without any apprehensions she reflected on what has been written of the silly division and war of the sexes: — which two might surely enter on an engagement to live together amiably, unvexed by that barbarous old fowl and falcon interlude. Cool herself, she imagined the same of him, having good grounds for the delusion; so they passed through the cottage-garden and beneath the low porchway, into her little sitting-room, where she was proceeding to speak composedly of her preference for cottages, while untying her bonnet-strings: — "If I had begun my life in a cottage!" — when really a big storm-wave caught her from shore and whirled her to mid-sea, out of every sensibility but the swimming one of her loss of self in the man.

"You would not have been here!" was all he said. She was up at his heart, fast-locked, undergoing a change greater than the sea works; her thoughts one blush, her brain a fire-fount. This was not like being seated on a throne.

"There," said he, loosening his hug, "now you belong to me! I know you from head to foot. After that, my darling, I could leave you for years, and call you wife, and be sure of you. I could swear it for you — my life on it! That's what I think of you. Don't wonder that I took my chance — the first: — I have waited!"

Truer word was never uttered, she owned, coming into some harmony with man's kiss on her mouth: the man violently metamorphozed to a stranger, acting on rights she had given him. And who was she to dream of denying

them? Not an idea in *her* head! Bound verily to be
thankful for such love, on hearing that *it* dated from the
night in Ireland. . . . "So in love with you that, on my
soul, your happiness was my marrow — whatever you
wished; anything you chose. It's reckoned a fool's part.
No, it's love: the love of a woman — the one woman! I
was like the hand of a clock to the springs. I taught this
old watch-dog of a heart to keep guard and bury the bones
you tossed him."

"Ignorantly, admit," said she, and could have bitten her
tongue for the empty words that provoked: "Would you
have flung him nothing?" and caused a lowering of her
eyelids and shamed glimpses of recollections. "I hear you
have again been defending me. I told you, I think, I
wished I had begun my girl's life in a cottage. All that I
have had to endure! . . . or so it seems to me: it may be
my way of excusing myself: — I know my cunning in that
peculiar art. I would take my chance of mixing among
the highest and the brightest."

"Naturally."

"Culpably."

"It brings you to me."

"Through a muddy channel."

"Your husband has full faith in you, my own."

"The faith has to be summoned and is buffeted, as we
were just now on the hill. I wish he had taken me from
a cottage."

"You pushed for the best society, like a fish to its native
sea."

"Pray say, a salmon to the riverheads."

"Better," Redworth laughed joyfully, between admiration of the tongue that always outflew him, and of the face
he reddened.

By degrees her apter and neater terms of speech helped
her to a notion of regaining some steps of her sunken
ascendancy, under the weight of the novel masculine pressure on her throbbing blood; and when he bent to her to
take her lord's farewell of her, after agreeing to go and
delight Emma with a message, her submission and her
personal pride were not so much at variance: perhaps
because her buzzing head had no ideas. "Tell Emma you

have undertaken to wash the blackamoor as white as she can be," she said perversely, in her spite at herself for not coming, as it were, out of the dawn to the man she could consent to wed : and he replied : "I shall tell her my dark girl pleads for a fortnight's grace before she and I set sail for the West coast of Ireland :" conjuring a picture that checked any protest against the shortness of time : — and Emma would surely be his ally.

They talked of the Dublin Ball : painfully to some of her thoughts. But Redworth kissed that distant brilliant night as freshly as if no belabouring years rolled in the chasm : which led her to conceive partly, and wonderingly, the nature of a strong man's passion ; and it subjugated the woman knowing of a contrast. The smart of the blow dealt her by him who had fired the passion in her became a burning regret for the loss of that fair fame she had sacrificed to him, and could not bring to her truer lover : though it was but the outer view of herself — the world's view ; only she was generous and of honest conscience, and but for the sake of the truer lover, she would mentally have allowed the world to lash and abuse her, without a plea of material purity. Could it be named ? The naming of it in her clear mind lessened it to accidental : — By good fortune, she was no worse ! — She said to Redworth, when finally dismissing him : "I bring no real disgrace to you, my friend." — To have had this sharp spiritual battle at such a time, was proof of honest conscience, rarer among women, as the world has fashioned them yet, than the purity demanded of them. — His answer : "You are my wife !" rang in her hearing.

When she sat alone at last, she was incapable, despite her nature's imaginative leap to brightness, of choosing any single period, auspicious or luminous or flattering, since the hour of her first meeting this man, rather than the grey light he cast on her, promising helpfulness, and inspiring a belief in her capacity to help. Not the Salvatore high raptures nor the nights of social applause could appear preferable : she strained her shattered wits to try them. As for her superlunary sphere, it was in fragments ; and she mused on the singularity, considering that she was not deeply enamoured. Was she so at all ? The question drove her to embrace the dignity of being reasonable — under Emma's guidance. For she did not stand firmly alone ; her story confessed it. Marriage might be the archway to the road of good service, even as our passage through the flesh may lead to the better state. She had thoughts of the kind, and had them while encouraging herself to deplore the adieu to her little musk-scented sitting-room, where a modest freedom breathed, and her individuality had seemed pointing to a straighter growth.

She nodded subsequently to the truth of her happy Emma's remark : "You were created for the world, Tony." A woman of blood and imagination in the warring world, without a mate whom she can revere, subscribes to a likeness with those independent minor realms between greedy mighty neighbours, which conspire and undermine when they do not openly threaten to devour. So, then, this union, the return to the wedding yoke, received sanction of grey-toned reason. She was not enamoured : she could say it to herself. She had, however, been surprised, both by the man and her unprotesting submission ; surprised and warmed, unaccountably warmed. Clearness of mind in the woman chaste by nature, however little ignorant it allowed her to be in the general review of herself, could not compass the immediately personal, with its acknowledgement of her subserviency to touch and pressure — and more, stranger, her readiness to kindle. She left it unexplained. Unconsciously the image of Dacier was effaced. Looking backward, her heart was moved to her long-constant lover with most pitying tender wonderment — stormy man, as her threatened senses told her that he was. Looking at him, she had to mask her being abashed and mastered. And looking forward, her soul fell in prayer for this true man's never repenting of his choice. Sure of her now, Mr. Thomas Redworth had returned to the station of the courtier, and her feminine sovereignty was not ruffled to make her feel too feminine. Another revelation was his playful talk when they were more closely intimate. He had his humour as well as his hearty relish of hers.

"If all Englishmen were like him !" she chimed with Emma Dunstane's eulogies, under the influence.

"My dear," the latter replied, " we should simply march

over the Four Quarters and be blessed by the nations! Only, avoid your trick of dashing headlong to the other extreme. He has his faults."

"Tell me of them," Diana cooed for an answer. "Do, I want the flavour. A girl would be satisfied with superhuman excellence. A widow asks for feature."

"To my thinking, the case is, that if it is a widow who sees the superhuman excellence in a man, she may be very well contented to cross the bridge with him," rejoined Emma.

"Suppose the bridge to break, and for her to fall into the water, he rescuing her — then perhaps !"

"But it has been happening !"

"But piecemeal, in extension, so slowly. I go to him a derelict, bearing a story of the sea; empty of ideas. I remember sailing out of harbour passably well freighted for commerce."

"When Tom Redworth has had command of the 'derelict' a week, I should like to see her !"

The mention of that positive captaincy drowned Diana in morning colours. She was dominated, physically and morally, submissively too. What she craved, in the absence of the public whiteness which could have caused her to rejoice in herself as a noble gift, was the spring of enthusiasm. Emma touched a quivering chord of pride with her hint at the good augury, and foreshadowing of the larger Union, in the Irishwoman's bestowal of her hand on the open-minded Englishman she had learned to trust. The aureole glimmered transiently: she could neither think highly of the woman about to be wedded, nor poetically of the man; nor, therefore, rosily of the ceremony, nor other than vacuously of life. And yet, as she avowed to Emma, she had gathered the three rarest good things of life : a faithful friend, a faithful lover, a faithful servant: the two latter exposing an unimagined quality of emotion. Danvers, on the night of the great day for Redworth, had undressed her with trembling fingers, and her mistress was led to the knowledge that the maid had always been all eye; and on reflection to admit that it came of a sympathy she did not share.

But when Celtic brains are reflective on their emotional

vessel they shoot direct as the *arrow of logic*. Diana's glance at the years behind lighted every moving figure to a shrewd transparency, herself among them. She was driven to the conclusion that the granting of any of her heart's wild wishes in those days would have lowered her — or frozen. Dacier was a coldly luminous image; still a toll-ing name; no longer conceivably her mate. Recollection rocked, not she. The politician and citizen was admired: she read the man; — more to her own discredit than to his, but she read him, and if that is done by the one of two lovers who was true to love, it is the God of the passion pronouncing a final release from the shadow of his chains.

Three days antecedent to her marriage, she went down the hill over her cottage chimneys with Redworth, after hearing him praise and cite to Emma Dunstane sentences of a morning's report of a speech delivered by Dacier to his constituents. She alluded to it, that she might air her power of speaking of the man coolly to him, or else for the sake of stirring afresh some sentiment he had roused; and he repeated his high opinion of the orator's political wis-dom: whereby was revived in her memory a certain rep-rehensible view, belonging to her period of mock-girlish naughtiness — too vile! — as to his paternal benevolence, now to clear vision the loftiest manliness. What did she do? She was Irish; therefore intuitively decorous in ama-tory challenges and interchanges. But she was an impul-sive woman, and foliage was thick around, only a few small birds and heaven seeing; and penitence and admiration sprang the impulse. It had to be this or a burst of weep-ing: — she put a kiss upon his arm.

She had omitted to think that she was dealing with a lover a man of smothered fire, who would be electrically alive to it. ... began busily building a nest for it. The impulse of each had wedded; in expression and repression; her sensibility told her of the stronger.

She rose on the morning of her marriage day with his favourite Planxty Kelly at her lips, a natural bubble of the notes. Emma drove down to the cottage to breakfast and superintend her bride's adornment, as to which, Diana had spoken slightingly; as well as of the ceremony, and the institution, and this life itself: — she would be married out of her cottage, a widow, a cottager, a woman under a cloud; yes, a sober person taking at last a right practical step, to please her two best friends. The change was marked. She wished to hide it, wished to confide it. Emma was asked: "How is he this morning?" and at the answer, describing his fresh and spirited looks, and his kind ways with Arthur Rhodes, and his fun with Sir Lukin Smith, and the satisfaction with the bride expectingly informed of the wedding), Diana forgot that she had kissed her, and this time pressed her lips, in a manner to convey the secret bridally.

"He has a lovely day."

"And bride," said Emma.

"If you two think so! I should like to agree with my dear old lord and bless him for the prize he takes, though it feels itself at present rather like a Christmas bon-bon — a piece of sugar in the wrap of a rhymed motto. He is kind to Arthur, you say?"

"Like a cordial elder brother."

"Dear love, I have it at heart that I was harsh upon Mary Paynham for her letter. She meant well — and I fear she suffers. And it may have been a bit my fault. Blind that I was! When you say 'cordial elder brother,' you make him appear beautiful to me. The worst of that is, one becomes aware of the inability to match him."

"Read with his eyes when you meet him this morning, my Tony."

The secret was her... pride in asso... marriage with the man of men had a tinge... menæal brand, exulting over Dacier, and in the compensation coming to her beloved for her first luckless footing on this road.

"How does he go down to the church?" said Diana.

"He walks down. Lukin and his Chief drive. He walks, with your Arthur and Mr. Sullivan Smith. He is on his way now."

Diana looked through the window in the direction of the hill. "That is so like him, to walk to his wedding!"

Emma took the place of Danvers in the office of the robing, for the maid, as her mistress managed to hint, was too steeped "in the colour of the occasion" to be exactly tasteful, and had the art, no doubt through sympathy, of charging permissible common words with explosive meanings : — she was in an amorous palpitation, of the reflected state. After several knockings and enterings of the bed-chamber-door, she came hurriedly to say : "And your pillow, ma'am ? I had almost forgotten it !" A question that caused her mistress to drop the gaze of a moan on Emma, with patience trembling. Diana preferred a hard pillow, and usually carried her own about. "Take it," she had to reply.

The friends embraced before descending to step into the fateful carriage. "And tell me," Emma said, "are not your views of life brighter to-day ?"

"Too dazzled to know ! It may be a lamp close to the eyes or a radiance of sun.. I hope they are."

"You are beginning to think hopefully again ?"

"Who can really *think* and not think hopefully ? You were in my mind last night, and you brought a little boat to sail me past despondency of life and the fear of extinction. When we despair or discolour things, it is our senses in revolt, and they have made the sovereign brain their drudge. I heard you whisper, with your very breath in my ear : '*There is nothing the body suffers that the soul may not profit by.*' That is Emma's history. With that I sail into the dark ; it is my promise of the immortal : teaches me to *see* immortality for us. It comes from you, my Emmy."

If not a great saying, it was in the heart of deep thoughts : proof to Emma that her Tony's mind had resumed its old clear high-aiming activity ; therefore that her nature was working sanely, and that she accepted her happiness, and bore love for a dower to her husband. No blushing confession of the woman's love of the man would have told her so much as the return to mental harmony with the laws of life shown in her darling's pellucid little sentence.

She revolved it long after the day of the wedding. To Emma, constantly on the dark decline of the unillumined

verge, between the two worlds, those words were a radiance
and a nourishment. Had they waned she would have
trimmed them to feed her during her soul-sister's absence.
They shone to her of their vitality. She was lying along
her sofa, facing her South-western window, one afternoon
of late November, expecting Tony from her lengthened
honeymoon trip, while a sunset in the van of frost, not without celestial musical reminders of Tony's husband, began to
deepen; and as her friend was coming, she mused on the
scenes of her friend's departure, and how Tony, issuing from
her cottage porch, had betrayed her feelings in the language
of her sex by stooping to lift above her head and kiss the
smallest of her landlady's children ranged up the garden-
path to bid her farewell over their strewing of flowers; —
and of her murmur to Tony, entering the churchyard,
among the grave-mounds: "Old Ireland won't repent it!"
and Tony's rejoinder, at the sight of the bridegroom advancing, beaming: "A singular transformation of Old England!"
— and how, having numberless ready sources of laughter
and tears down the run of their heart-in-heart intimacy, all
spouting up for a word in the happy tremour of the moment,
they had both bitten their lips and blinked on a moisture of
the eyelids. Now the dear woman was really wedded,
wedded and mated. Her letters breathed, in their own
lively or thoughtful flow, of the perfect mating. Emma
gazed into the depths of the waves of crimson, where
brilliancy of colour came out of central heaven preternaturally near on earth, till one shade less brilliant seemed
an ebbing away to boundless remoteness. Angelical and
mortal mixed, making the glory overhead a sign of the close
union of our human conditions with the ethereal and
psychically divined. Thence it grew that one thought in her
breast became a desire for such extension of days as would
give her the blessedness to clasp in her lap — if those kind
heavens would grant it! — a child of the marriage of the
two noblest of human souls, one the dearest; and so have
proof at heart that her country and our earth are fruitful in
the good, for a glowing future. She was deeply a woman,
dumbly a poet. True poets and true women have the native
sense of the divineness of what the world deems gross
material substance. Emma's exaltation in fervour had not

subsided when she held her beloved in her arms under the dusk of the withdrawing redness.   They sat embraced, with hands locked, in the unlighted room, and Tony spoke of the splendid sky.   " You watched it knowing I was on my way to you ? "

" Praying, dear."

" For me ? "

" That I might live long enough to be a godmother."

There was no reply : there was an involuntary little twitch of Tony's fingers.

THE END.

Butler & Tanner, The Selwood Printing Works, Frome, and London.

THE END.

London: Printed by ...